COLONELS IN BLUE

COLONELS IN BLUE
UNION ARMY COLONELS OF THE CIVIL WAR

New York

ROGER D. HUNT

Schiffer Military History
Atglen, PA

For
Imogene
and
Jennifer

Book design by Robert Biondi.
Union officer shoulder board on front dust jacket from the collection of Robert G. Borrell, Sr.

Copyright © 2003 by Roger D. Hunt.
Library of Congress Catalog Number: 2003101110.

Printed in China.
ISBN: 0-7643-1771-7

We are always looking for people to write books on new and related subjects. If you have an idea for a book, please contact us at the address below.

Published by Schiffer Publishing Ltd.
4880 Lower Valley Road
Atglen, PA 19310
Phone: (610) 593-1777
FAX: (610) 593-2002
E-mail: Info@schifferbooks.com.
Visit our web site at: www.schifferbooks.com
Please write for a free catalog.
This book may be purchased from the publisher.
Please include $3.95 postage.
Try your bookstore first.

In Europe, Schiffer books are distributed by:
Bushwood Books
6 Marksbury Ave.
Kew Gardens
Surrey TW9 4JF
England
Phone: 44 (0)20 8392-8585
FAX: 44 (0)20 8392-9876
E-mail: Bushwd@aol.com.
Free postage in the UK. Europe: air mail at cost.
Try your bookstore first.

Introduction

At the beginning of the Civil War the Regular Army of the United States numbered only 1,098 officers and 15,304 enlisted men. Faced with this shortage of manpower in suppressing the escalating rebellion, President Abraham Lincoln issued a call for 75,000 militia for three months service on April 15, 1861 and then a call for 500,000 volunteers for three years service on July 22, 1861. These calls for troops and others issued later in the war specified that the various state governors would appoint the commanding officers of the regiments raised in their states.

Patriotic fervor throughout the Northern states resulted in spirited competition to complete the organization of regiments to meet the state quotas. In most cases the prospective commanders of these regiments were prominent citizens whose military background (if any) consisted of service in a local militia organization. In general the early war Union army colonels were known more for their patriotic enthusiasm than for their military competence. Many of them were more successful in convincing their fellow townsmen to enlist than they were in actually leading them into battle. Fortunately for the Union cause, the colonels who stayed in the service soon acquired the necessary military skills or were replaced by subordinates who proved their capabilities on the field of battle.

This book is the second in a series of books containing photographs and biographical sketches of that diverse group of motivated citizens who attained the rank of colonel in the Union army, but failed to win promotion to brigadier general or brevet brigadier general. This volume presents the colonels who commanded regiments from the state of New York. Preceding the photographs and biographical sketches is a breakdown by regiment of all the colonels who commanded regiments from New York, with the name of each colonel being followed by the dates of his service. Included in this breakdown are the colonels who were promoted beyond the rank of colonel, with their final rank indicated in bold letters. Those indicated as attaining the rank of brigadier general are covered in the book *Generals in Blue*, by Ezra J. Warner, while those attaining the rank of brevet brigadier general are covered in the book *Brevet Brigadier Generals in Blue*, by Roger D. Hunt and Jack R. Brown.

Some explanatory notes are necessary concerning the content of the biographical sketches:

1.) The date associated with each rank is generally the date when the colonel was commissioned or appointed rather than the date when he was mustered at that rank. However, the date of muster was used whenever the date of commission or appointment was not available. The reader should be aware that these dates were constantly being revised by the War Department, so that any hope of providing totally accurate dates is virtually impossible.

2.) When the word "Colonel" is italicized, this indicates that the colonel was commissioned as colonel but never mustered as such.

3.) The following abbreviations are used in the text:

AAG	Assistant Adjutant General
ADC	Aide-de-Camp
AIG	Assistant Inspector General
AQM	Assistant Quartermaster
Brig.	Brigadier
Bvt.	Brevet
Capt.	Captain
Co.	County or Company
Col.	Colonel
CSA	Confederate States Army

DOW	Died of Wounds
GAR	Grand Army of the Republic
Gen.	General
GSW	Gun Shot Wound
KIA	Killed in Action
Lt.	Lieutenant
MOLLUS	Military Order of the Loyal Legion of the United States
NGSNY	National Guard State of New York
NHDVS	National Home for Disabled Volunteer Soldiers
RQM	Regimental Quartermaster
Twp.	Township
US	United States
USA	United States Army
USAMHI	United States Army Military History Institute
USCT	United States Colored Troops
USMA	United States Military Academy
USV	United States Volunteers
VRC	Veteran Reserve Corps
Vol.	Volume

Acknowledgments

Although I appreciate the contributions of all of the individuals in the following list, I want to mention a few individuals whose contributions to this volume have been especially noteworthy. Henry Deeks, Thomas Harris, Jeff Kowalis, Mike McAfee, Ben Maryniak, Steve Meadow, Steve Rogers, Larry Strayer and Dave Zullo have been especially diligent in locating elusive photographs and providing valued information. Mike Winey and Randy Hackenburg have provided ready access to the unparalleled photo archives of the US Army Military History Institute. Michael Aikey of the New York State Military Museum and Alan Aimone of the US Military Academy Library have been equally hospitable in allowing access to the collections under their supervision. Collectors Michael Albanese, Gil Barrett, Rick Carlile, Mike McAfee, Paul Russinoff, Don Ryberg and Patrick Schroeder have been especially generous in allowing me to use photographs from their collections.

Jill M. Abraham, National Archives, Washington, DC
Michael Aikey, New York State Military Museum, Saratoga Springs, NY
Alan C. Aimone, US Military Academy Library, West Point, NY
Michael Albanese, Kendall, NY
Sal Alberti, New York, NY
Betty Allen, Schaffer Library, Union College, Schenectady, NY
Gil Barrett, Laurel, MD
Richard Baumgartner, Huntington, WV
Elaine H. Bogino, Newburgh, NY
Bruce P. Bonfield, Old Forge, NY
Everitt Bowles, Woodstock, GA
Mike Brackin, Manchester, CT

David L. Callihan, Ithaca, NY
Robert Cammaroto, Alexandria, VA
Brian Caplan, Peekskill, NY
Richard F. Carlile, Dayton, OH
Mr. Chamberlin, Waterford, VA
David W. Charles, Jr., Lancaster, PA
Raymond L. Collins, Alexandria, VA
Henry Deeks, Acton, MA
Bill Dekker, Caldwell, NJ
Charles L. English, Windsor, NY
James Enos, Carlisle, PA
Jacqueline T. Eubanks, Stuart, FL
Jerry Everts, Lambertville, MI
Deborah Ferrell, Wayne County Historian, Lyons, NY
Leslie Fields, The Pierpont Morgan Library, New York, NY
Ellen H. Fladger, Schaffer Library, Union College, Schenectady, NY
Edgar Frutchey, Elk Grove, CA
Borinquen Gallo, The New-York Historical Society, New York, NY
William Gladstone, West Palm Beach, FL
Randy Hackenburg, US Army Military History Institute, Carlisle, PA
Thomas Harris, New York, NY
Scott Hilts, Arcade, NY
Michael A. Hogle, Okemos, MI
Holly Hoods, Healdsburg Museum, Healdsburg, CA
William Howard, Delmar, NY
Lance W. Ingmire, Pittsford, NY
Ed Italo, Chicago, IL
Jon Jensen, Boston, MA
Craig T. Johnson, Towson, MD

Fred Jolly, Muncie, IN

Thomas L. Jones, Palatine, IL

Beverly H. Kallgren, Litchfield, CT

Marybeth Kavanagh, The New-York Historical Society, New York, NY

Dennis Keesee, Westerville, OH

Jeff Kowalis, Orland Park, IL

John W. Kuhl, Pittstown, NJ

Theresa La Bianca, Green-Wood Cemetery, Brooklyn, NY

Mary E. Linne', National Archives, Washington, DC

Daniel Lorello, New York State Archives, Albany, NY

James Lowe, New York, NY

Robert T. Lyon, Muncy, PA

Michael J. McAfee, Newburgh, NY

Robert F. MacAvoy, Clark, NJ

John F. McCormack, Jr., West Chester, PA

Thomas L. MacDonald, Eustis, ME

Edward McGuire, New York State Library, Albany, NY

Robert D. Marcus, Fairfax Station, VA

Benedict R. Maryniak, Lancaster, NY

Steve Meadow, Midland, MI

Marie Melchiori, Vienna, VA

Tom Molocea, North Lima, OH

Philip Murphy, Mechanicsburg, PA

Michael P. Musick, National Archives, Washington, DC

David M. Neville, Export, PA

Howard L. Norton, Little Rock, AR

Olaf, Berkeley, CA

Seward R. Osborne, Olivebridge, NY

Karen D. Osburn, Geneva Historical Society, Geneva, NY

Phillip J. Palen, Gowanda, NY

Ronn Palm, Kittanning, PA

Margaret L. Peirce, Cudahy, WI

Nicholas P. Picerno, Springfield, VT

Brian Pohanka, Alexandria, VA

Patrick E. Purcell, Wayne, PA

James Quinlan, Alexandria, VA

Norman F. Rau, Boothbay, ME

Edmund J. Raus, Jr., Manassas, VA

David M. Reel, West Point Museum, West Point, NY

Stephen B. Rogers, Ithaca, NY

Michael Russert, Cambridge, NY

Paul Russinoff, Washington, DC

Donald K. Ryberg, Westfield, NY

Martin L. Schoenfeld, New Hyde Park, NY

Patrick A. Schroeder, Daleville, VA

Alan J. Sessarego, Gettysburg, PA

Jane Siegel, Columbia University, New York, NY

Leonard L. Smith, Ogden, UT

Dr. Louisa B. Smith, Ogden, UT

Dr. Richard J. Sommers, US Army Military History Institute, Carlisle, PA

Edward Steers, Jr., Berkeley Springs, WV

Eric Stott, New York State Military Museum, Saratoga Springs, NY

Larry Strayer, Dayton, OH

Michael Stretch, Cincinnati, OH

Karl E. Sundstrom, North Riverside, IL

Richard Tibbals, Oak Park, IL

Leo J. Titus, Jr., Ashburn, VA

Robert C. Trownsell, Bensenville, IL

Ken C. Turner, Ellwood City, PA

Michael W. Waskul, Ypsilanti, MI

William Hallam Webber, Gaithersburg, MD

William C. Welch, Allegany, NY

Robert White, Jr., Fancy Gap, VA

Michael J. Winey, US Army Military History Institute, Carlisle, PA

Eric J. Wittenberg, Columbus, OH

Robert J. Younger, Morningside Bookshop, Dayton, OH

Buck Zaidel, Cromwell, CT

Dave Zullo, Olde Soldier Books, Gaithersburg, MD

I am also indebted to the staffs of the following libraries for their capable assistance:

Bangor Public Library, Bangor, MI

British Library (Newspapers), London, England

Broome County Historical Society Library, Binghamton, NY

Civil War Library & Museum, Philadelphia, PA.

Connecticut State Library, Hartford, CT

Corning Public Library, Corning, NY

Daniel A. Reed Library, State University of New York, Fredonia, NY

Dansville Public Library, Dansville, NY

Family History Library, Salt Lake City, UT

Geneva Free Library, Geneva, NY

Geneva Historical Society, Geneva, NY

Goshen Library & Historical Society, Goshen, NY

Grand Rapids Public Library, Grand Rapids, MI

Guernsey Memorial Library, Norwich, NY

Healdsburg Museum and Historical Society, Healdsburg, CA

Hornell Public Library, Hornell, NY

Huntington Library, San Marino, CA

Jervis Public Library, Rome, NY

Library of Congress, Washington, DC

Library of the Society of Genealogists, London, England
Little Falls Public Library, Little Falls, NY
Lockport Public Library, Lockport, NY
Minnesota Historical Society, St. Paul, MN
Naples Library, Naples, NY
National Archives, Washington, DC
National Society Daughters of the American Revolution, Washington, DC
Newburgh Free Library, Newburgh, NY
New England Historic Genealogical Society, Boston, MA
New Jersey State Archives, Trenton, NJ
New York Genealogical and Biographical Society, New York, NY
The New-York Historical Society, New York, NY
New York State Archives, Albany, NY
New York State Historical Association Library, Cooperstown, NY
New York State Library, Albany, NY
New York State Military Museum and Veterans Research Center, Saratgoa Springs, NY
Nyack Library, Nyack, NY
Ogdensburg Public Library, Ogdensburg, NY
Olean Public Library, Olean, NY
Onondaga County Public Library, Syracuse, NY
Orchard Park Public Library, Orchard Park, NY

Oswego City Library, Oswego, NY
Pennsylvania State Library, Harrisburg, PA
Penn Yan Public Library, Penn Yan, NY
The Pierpont Morgan Library, New York, NY
Pulaski Public Library, Pulaski, NY
Rare Book and Manuscript Library, Columbia University, New York, NY
Richmond Memorial Library, Batavia, NY
Riverside Public Library, Riverside, CA
Roswell P. Flowers Memorial Library, Watertown, NY
Schaffer Library, Union College, Schenectady, NY
Schenectady County Public Library, Schenectady, NY
Seneca Falls Historical Society, Seneca Falls, NY
Seymour Library, Auburn, NY
St. Lawrence County Historical Association, Canton, NY
Steele Memorial Library, Elmira, NY
Suffolk County Historical Society Library, Riverhead, NY
Swan Library, Albion, NY
Thrall Library, Middletown, NY
Troy Public Library, Troy, NY
US Army Military History Institute, Carlisle, PA
US Military Academy Library, West Point, NY
Utica Public Library, Utica, NY
West Point Museum, US Military Academy, West Point, NY
White Plains Public Library, White Plains, NY
Yonkers Public Library, Yonkers, NY

COLONELS IN BLUE

Chapter VII

NEW YORK

1st Cavalry

Andrew T. McReynolds	June 15, 1861	Mustered out June 15, 1864
Alonzo W. Adams	June 15, 1864	Mustered out June 27, 1865
		Bvt. Brig. Gen.

2nd Cavalry

J. Mansfield Davies	Aug. 1, 1861	Discharged Dec. 6, 1862
Judson Kilpatrick	Dec. 6, 1862	Promoted **Brig. Gen., USV** June 13, 1863
Henry E. Davies, Jr.	June 16, 1863	Promoted **Brig. Gen., USV** Sept. 16, 1863
Otto Harhaus	Sept. 18, 1863	Mustered out Sept. 10, 1864
Walter C. Hull	Oct. 25, 1864	KIA Nov. 12, 1864
Alanson M. Randol	Nov. 24, 1864	Mustered out June 23, 1865
		Bvt. Brig. Gen.

3rd Cavalry

James H. Van Alen	Aug. 28, 1861	Promoted **Brig. Gen., USV** April 15, 1862
Simon H. Mix	April 8, 1862	DOW June 15, 1864
George W. Lewis	June 15, 1864	Mustered out July 12, 1865

4th Cavalry

Christian F. Dickel	Nov. 1, 1861	Discharged Sept. 10, 1862
Louis P. di Cesnola	Sept. 11, 1862	Discharged Sept. 4, 1864

5th Cavalry

Othneil DeForest	Oct. 1, 1861	Dismissed March 29, 1864
John Hammond	March 29, 1864	Mustered out Sept. 3, 1864
		Bvt. Brig. Gen.
Othneil DeForest	Sept. 3, 1864	Died Dec. 16, 1864
Amos H. White	Nov. 14, 1864	Mustered out July 19, 1865

6th Cavalry

Thomas C. Devin	Nov. 18, 1861	Promoted **Brig. Gen., USV** Oct. 19, 1864
Charles L. Fitzhugh	Dec. 24, 1864	To 2nd NY Provisional Cavalry June 17, 1865
		Bvt. Brig. Gen.

7th Cavalry

Andrew J. Morrison	Nov. 6, 1861	Mustered out March 31, 1862

8th Cavalry

Samuel J. Crooks	Nov. 28, 1861	Resigned Feb. 21, 1862
Benjamin F. Davis	June 6, 1862	KIA June 9, 1863
William L. Markell	June 9, 1863	Resigned Feb. 27, 1864
William H. Benjamin	Feb. 27, 1864	Mustered out Feb. 14, 1865
		Bvt. Brig. Gen.
Edmund M. Pope	Feb. 14, 1865	Mustered out June 27, 1865
		Bvt. Brig. Gen.

9th Cavalry

John Beardsley	Nov. 5, 1861	Resigned March 17, 1863
William Sackett	March 17, 1863	DOW June 14, 1864
		Bvt. Brig. Gen.
George S. Nichols	June 14, 1864	Mustered out July 17, 1865
		Bvt. Brig. Gen.

10th Cavalry

John C. Lemmon	Dec. 12, 1861	Resigned April 3, 1863
William Irvine	June 11, 1863	Mustered out Dec. 6, 1864
		Bvt. Brig. Gen.
Matthew H. Avery	Nov. 24, 1864	To 1st NY Provisional Cavalry June 24, 1865
		Bvt. Brig. Gen.

11th Cavalry

James B. Swain	April 30, 1862	Discharged Feb. 12, 1864
John P. Sherburne	March 1, 1864	Resigned March 15, 1865
Samuel H. Wilkeson	March 15, 1865	Mustered out March 27, 1865

12th Cavalry

James W. Savage	Oct. 4, 1862	Mustered out July 19, 1865

13th Cavalry

Henry S. Gansevoort	June 1, 1863	Mustered out Aug. 17, 1865
		Bvt. Brig. Gen.

14th Cavalry

Thaddeus P. Mott	July 10, 1863	Discharged Jan. 18, 1864
Abraham Bassford	Aug. 10, 1864	Mustered out June 12, 1865

15th Cavalry

Robert M. Richardson	May 29, 1863	Resigned Jan. 17, 1865
John J. Coppinger	Jan. 19, 1865	Mustered out June 29, 1865

16th Cavalry

Henry M. Lazelle	Sept. 3, 1863	Resigned Oct. 18, 1864
Nelson B. Sweitzer	Oct. 25, 1864	To 3rd NY Provisional Cavalry Aug. 17, 1865 **Bvt. Brig. Gen.**

17th Cavalry (Organization failed)

Henry D. Townsend	June 30, 1863	Authority revoked

18th Cavalry

James J. Byrne	May 11, 1863	Mustered out May 31, 1866 **Bvt. Brig. Gen.**

19th Cavalry (see 1st Dragoons)

20th Cavalry

Newton B. Lord	June 19, 1863	Resigned March 23, 1865
David M. Evans	April 1, 1865	Mustered out July 31, 1865

21st Cavalry

William B. Tibbits	June 17, 1863	Promoted **Brig. Gen., USV** Oct. 18, 1865
Charles Fitzsimons	Sept. 9, 1865	Mustered out June 25, 1866 **Bvt. Brig. Gen.**

22nd Cavalry

Samuel J. Crooks	Sept. 24, 1863	Discharged March 21, 1865
George C. Cram	Aug. 13, 1864	Not mustered
Horatio B. Reed	Jan. 24, 1865	Mustered out Aug. 1, 1865

23rd Cavalry (Organization failed)

Simon H. Mix	Oct. 27, 1862	Not mustered

24th Cavalry

William C. Raulston	Aug. 25, 1863	DOW Dec. 15, 1864
Walter C. Newberry	Dec. 15, 1864	Mustered out June 24, 1865 **Bvt. Brig. Gen.**

25th Cavalry

Henry F. Liebenau	Sept. 14, 1863	Not mustered
Gurden Chapin	Oct. 31, 1864	Resigned Feb. 10, 1865

26th Cavalry

Burr B. Porter	Jan. 26, 1865	Mustered out June 14, 1865
Ferris Jacobs, Jr.	June 14, 1865	Mustered out July 1, 1865 **Bvt. Brig. Gen.**

1st Mounted Rifles

Charles C. Dodge	Aug. 13, 1862	Promoted **Brig. Gen., USV** April 29, 1863
Benjamin F. Onderdonk	April 29, 1863	Dismissed July 19, 1864
Edwin V. Sumner, Jr.	Aug. 13, 1864	To 4th NY Provisional Cavalry Sept. 6, 1865 **Bvt. Brig. Gen.**

2nd Mounted Rifles

John Fisk	July 2, 1863	Discharged Dec. 5, 1864
Louis P. Siebert	Dec. 31, 1864	Not mustered
John Fisk	March 9, 1865	Discharged May 18, 1865

1st Dragoons

William S. Fullerton	July 25, 1862	Resigned Sept. 3, 1862
Alfred Gibbs	Sept. 6, 1862	Promoted **Brig. Gen., USV** Oct. 19, 1864

Thomas J. Thorp	Dec. 17, 1864	Mustered out June 30, 1865 **Bvt. Brig. Gen.**

1st Veteran Cavalry

Robert F. Taylor	July 20, 1863	Discharged Nov. 17, 1864
John S. Platner	Dec. 3, 1864	Mustered out July 20, 1865 **Bvt. Brig. Gen.**

2nd Veteran Cavalry

Morgan H. Chrysler	Dec. 5, 1863	Promoted **Brig. Gen., USV** Nov. 11, 1865

1st Provisional Cavalry

Matthew H. Avery	June 24, 1865	Mustered out July 19, 1865 **Bvt. Brig. Gen.**

2nd Provisional Cavalry

Charles L. Fitzhugh	June 17, 1865	Mustered out Aug. 9, 1865 **Bvt. Brig. Gen.**

3rd Provisional Cavalry

Nelson B. Sweitzer	Aug. 17, 1865	Mustered out Sept. 21, 1865 **Bvt. Brig. Gen.**

4th Provisional Cavalry

Edwin V. Sumner, Jr.	Sept. 6, 1865	Mustered out Nov. 29, 1865 **Bvt. Brig. Gen.**

1st Light Artillery

Guilford D. Bailey	Sept. 25, 1861	KIA May 31, 1862
Charles S. Wainwright	June 1, 1862	Mustered out June 21, 1865 **Bvt. Brig. Gen.**

2nd Heavy Artillery

Jeremiah Palmer	Oct. 17, 1861	Discharged Feb. 20, 1862
Gustave Waagner	March 14, 1862	Dismissed Aug. 26, 1862
Milton Cogswell	Sept. 29, 1862	Resigned April 7, 1863 **Bvt. Brig. Gen.**
Joseph N.G. Whistler	April 14, 1863	Mustered out Sept. 29, 1865 **Bvt. Brig. Gen.**

3rd Light Artillery

James H. Ledlie	Nov. 18, 1861	Promoted to **Brig. Gen., USV** Dec. 24, 1862
Charles H. Stewart	Jan. 1, 1863	Mustered out July 15, 1865

4th Heavy Artillery

Thomas D. Doubleday	Nov. 1, 1861	Discharged March 17, 1863
Gustavus A. DeRussy	March 17, 1863	Promoted **Brig. Gen., USV** May 23, 1863
Henry H. Hall	May 23, 1863	Discharged Aug. 5, 1863
John C. Tidball	Aug. 25, 1863	Mustered out Sept. 26, 1865 **Bvt. Brig. Gen.**

4th Heavy Artillery Militia

Daniel W. Teller	June 20, 1863	Mustered out July 24, 1863

5th Heavy Artillery

Samuel Graham	March 6, 1862	Dismissed Dec. 29, 1862
Edward Murray	Dec. 29, 1862	Revoked March 6, 1863 **Bvt. Brig. Gen.**
Samuel Graham	March 6, 1863	Mustered out July 19, 1865 **Bvt. Brig. Gen.**

6th Heavy Artillery

Lewis G. Morris	Aug. 14, 1862	Succeeded by William H. Morris
William H. Morris	Sept. 2, 1862	Promoted to **Brig. Gen., USV** April 2, 1863
J. Howard Kitching	April 1, 1863	DOW Jan. 10, 1865 **Bvt. Brig. Gen.**
George C. Kibbe	Jan. 10, 1865	Mustered out June 28, 1865
Stephen Baker	June 27, 1865	Mustered out Aug. 24, 1865

7th Heavy Artillery

Lewis O. Morris	Aug. 1, 1862	KIA June 4, 1864
Joseph S. Conrad	June 13, 1864	Not mustered, declined
Edward A. Springsteed	July 26, 1864	KIA Aug. 25, 1864
Richard C. Duryea	Dec. 28, 1864	Mustered out July 3, 1865

8th Heavy Artillery

Peter A. Porter	July 7, 1862	KIA June 3, 1864
Willard W. Bates	June 3, 1864	DOW June 25, 1864
James M. Willett	July 1, 1864	Discharged Jan. 14, 1865
Joel B. Baker	Jan. 14, 1865	To 10th NY Infantry June 5, 1865

9th Heavy Artillery

Joseph Welling	Aug. 12, 1862	Discharged May 21, 1864
William H. Seward, Jr.	May 21, 1864	Promoted **Brig. Gen., USV** Sept. 13, 1864
Edward P. Taft	Sept. 15, 1864	Discharged Nov. 28, 1864
James W. Snyder	Nov. 28, 1864	Mustered out July 6, 1865
Edward P. Taft	Jan. 5, 1865	Mustered out July 6, 1865

10th Heavy Artillery

Alexander Piper	Dec. 31, 1862	Mustered out July 6, 1865

11th Heavy Artillery

William B. Barnes	Feb. 7, 1863	Dismissed Sept. 30, 1863

12th Heavy Artillery

Robert P. Gibson	March 31, 1863	Revoked June 22, 1863

13th Heavy Artillery

William A. Howard	May 11, 1863	Mustered out July 4, 1865

14th Heavy Artillery

Elisha G. Marshall	May 23, 1863	Mustered out Aug. 26, 1865 **Bvt. Brig. Gen.**

15th Heavy Artillery

Louis Schirmer	Oct. 6, 1863	Discharged Aug. 3, 1865
Michael Wiedrich	Aug. 12, 1865	Not mustered

16th Heavy Artillery

Joseph J. Morrison	July 31, 1863	Mustered out Aug. 21, 1865 **Bvt. Brig. Gen.**

1st Marine Artillery

William A. Howard	Sept. 1, 1861	Discharged March 28, 1863

1st Engineers

Edward W. Serrell	Feb. 14, 1862	Mustered out Feb. 13, 1865 **Bvt. Brig. Gen.**
James F. Hall	Feb. 16, 1865	Mustered out June 30, 1865 **Bvt. Brig. Gen.**

2nd Engineers

James A. Magruder	July 22, 1863	Mustered out Oct. 9, 1863

15th Engineers

J. McLeod Murphy	May 11, 1861	Resigned Dec. 12, 1862
Clinton G. Colgate	Dec. 12, 1862	Mustered out June 25, 1863
Wesley Brainerd	Oct. 15, 1864	Mustered out June 14, 1865

50th Engineers

Charles B. Stuart	Aug. 15, 1861	Resigned June 3, 1863
William H. Pettes	June 3, 1863	Mustered out July 5, 1865

1st Infantry

William H. Allen	May 7, 1861	Dismissed Sept. 10, 1861
Garret W. Dyckman	Sept. 10, 1861	Discharged Oct. 9, 1862
J. Fred Pierson	Oct. 9, 1862	Mustered out May 25, 1863 **Bvt. Brig. Gen.**

2nd Infantry

George L. Willard	April 24, 1861	Not mustered, declined
Joseph B. Carr	May 10, 1861	Promoted **Brig. Gen., USV** Sept. 12, 1862
Sidney W. Park	Sept. 18, 1862	Mustered out May 26, 1863 **Bvt. Brig. Gen.**

2nd State Militia (see also 82nd Infantry)

George W. B. Tompkins	May 21, 1861	To 82nd Infantry Dec. 7, 1861

3rd Infantry

Frederick Townsend	April 25, 1861	Resigned June 26, 1861 **Bvt. Brig. Gen.**
Samuel M. Alford	July 2, 1861	Discharged June 14, 1864
Elbridge G. Floyd	June 14, 1864	Discharged Dec. 7, 1864
John H. Edson	Dec. 31, 1864	Not mustered
John E. Mulford	Dec. 20, 1864	Discharged June 30, 1866 **Bvt. Brig. Gen.**

4th Infantry

Edward McK. Hudson	April 25, 1861	Not mustered, declined
Alfred W. Taylor	May 15, 1861	Resigned July 7, 1862
John D. MacGregor	July 7, 1862	Mustered out May 25, 1863 **Bvt. Brig. Gen.**

5th Infantry

Abram Duryee	May 10, 1861	Promoted **Brig. Gen., USV** Sept. 10, 1861
Gouverneur K. Warren	Sept. 3, 1861	Promoted **Brig. Gen., USV** Sept. 26, 1862
Hiram Duryea	Sept. 17, 1862	Resigned Nov. 30, 1862 **Bvt. Brig. Gen.**
Cleveland Winslow	Dec. 4, 1862	Mustered out May 14, 1863

5th Veteran Infantry

Cleveland Winslow	May 25, 1863	DOW July 7, 1864
Henry W. Ryder	July 4, 1864	Not mustered, declined
Frederick Winthrop	Aug. 2, 1864	KIA April 1, 1865 **Bvt. Brig. Gen.**
William F. Drum	April 1, 1865	Mustered out Aug. 21, 1865

5th State Militia

Christian Schwarzwaelder	May 1, 1861	Mustered out Aug. 7, 1861
Louis Burger	June 19, 1863	Mustered out July 22, 1863

6th Infantry
William Wilson | April 19, 1861 | Mustered out June 25, 1863
Bvt. Brig. Gen.

6th State Militia
Joseph C. Pinckney | May 14, 1861 | Mustered out July 31, 1861
Bvt. Brig. Gen.

Joel W. Mason | June 22, 1863 | Mustered out July 22, 1863

7th Infantry
John E. Bendix | April 23, 1861 | Resigned Aug. 6, 1861
Bvt. Brig. Gen.

Edward Kapff | July 3, 1861 | Resigned Feb. 8, 1862
George W. Von Schack | Feb. 8, 1862 | Mustered out May 8, 1863
Bvt. Brig. Gen.

7th Veteran Infantry
George W. Von Schack | Oct. 22, 1864 | Mustered out Aug. 4, 1865
Bvt. Brig. Gen.

7th State Militia
Marshall Lefferts | April 26, 1861 | Mustered out June 3, 1861
Marshall Lefferts | May 25, 1862 | Mustered out Sept. 5, 1862
Marshall Lefferts | June 16, 1863 | Mustered out July 20, 1863

8th Infantry
Louis Blenker | April 23, 1861 | Promoted **Brig. Gen., USV** Aug. 10, 1861

Julius Stahel | Aug. 10, 1861 | Promoted **Brig. Gen., USV** Nov. 15, 1861

Francis Wutschel | Nov. 12, 1861 | Dismissed Aug. 23, 1862
Felix Prince Salm | Oct. 22, 1862 | Mustered out April 23, 1863
Bvt. Brig. Gen.

8th State Militia
George Lyons | April 25, 1861 | Mustered out Aug. 2, 1861
Joshua M. Varian | May 29, 1862 | Mustered out Sept. 10, 1862
Joshua M. Varian | June 17, 1863 | Mustered out July 23, 1863

9th Infantry
Rush C. Hawkins | May 4, 1861 | Mustered out May 20, 1863
Bvt. Brig. Gen.

9th State Militia (see also 83rd Infantry)
John W. Stiles | May 16, 1861 | To 83rd Infantry Dec. 7, 1861

10th Infantry
Waters W. McChesney | May 2, 1861 | Discharged Sept. 1, 1861
John E. Bendix | Sept. 2, 1861 | Mustered out May 7, 1863
Bvt. Brig. Gen.

Joseph Yeamans | Dec. 9, 1863 | Not mustered
George F. Hopper | Jan. 5, 1865 | Mustered out June 30, 1865
Joel B. Baker | June 5, 1865 | Mustered out June 30, 1865

11th Infantry
E. Elmer Ellsworth | May 7, 1861 | KIA May 24, 1861
Noah L. Farnham | June 4, 1861 | DOW Aug. 14, 1861
Charles McK. Leoser | Aug. 15, 1861 | Resigned April 17, 1862

11th Infantry (Reorganizing)
James C. Burke | May 18, 1863 | Not mustered
Henry F. O'Brien | June 27, 1863 | KIA July 14, 1863
Augustus B. Sage | July 27, 1863 | Not mustered

11th State Militia
Joachim Maidhof | May 28, 1862 | Mustered out Sept. 16, 1862
Joachim Maidhof | June 16, 1863 | Mustered out July 20, 1863

12th Infantry
Ezra L. Walrath | May 7, 1861 | Resigned Sept. 25, 1861
George W. Snyder | Sept. 25, 1861 | Not mustered, declined
Henry A. Weeks | Jan. 24, 1862 | Mustered out May 17, 1863
Benjamin A. Willis | Jan. 23, 1864 | Not mustered

12th State Militia
Daniel Butterfield | May 2, 1861 | Mustered out Aug. 5, 1861
Later Brig. Gen., USV

William G. Ward | May 31, 1862 | Mustered out Oct. 8, 1862
William G. Ward | June 19, 1863 | Mustered out July 20, 1863

13th Infantry
Isaac F. Quinby | May 1, 1861 | Resigned Aug. 5, 1861
Later Brig. Gen., USV

John Pickell | Aug. 17, 1861 | Discharged March 31, 1862
Elisha G. Marshall | April 1, 1862 | Mustered out May 13, 1863
Bvt. Brig. Gen.

13th State Militia
Abel Smith | May 17, 1861 | Mustered out Aug. 6, 1861
Robert B. Clark | May 28, 1862 | Mustered out Sept. 12, 1862
John B. Woodward | June 20, 1863 | Mustered out July 21, 1863

14th Infantry
James McQuade | May 10, 1861 | Mustered out May 24, 1863
Bvt. Brig. Gen.

14th State Militia (see also 84th Infantry)
Alfred M. Wood | May 23, 1861 | To 84th Infantry Dec. 7, 1861

15th Infantry (see 15th Engineers)

15th State Militia
Charles H. Burtis | June 6, 1864 | Mustered out July 7, 1864

16th Infantry
Thomas A. Davies | May 10, 1861 | Promoted **Brig. Gen., USV** March 7, 1862

Joseph Howland | March 7, 1862 | Resigned Sept. 28, 1862
Bvt. Brig. Gen.

Joel J. Seaver | Sept. 29, 1862 | Mustered out May 22, 1863
Bvt. Brig. Gen.

16th State Militia
Alfred Wagstaff, Jr. | June 19, 1863 | Date of discharge unknown

17th Infantry
Henry S. Lansing | May 18, 1861 | Mustered out June 2, 1863
Bvt. Brig. Gen.

17th Veteran Infantry

William T.C. Grower	June 3, 1863	DOW Sept. 3, 1864
Joel O. Martin	Sept. 3, 1864	Discharged Jan. 4, 1865
James Lake	Jan. 3, 1865	Mustered out July 13, 1865

18th Infantry

William A. Jackson	May 13, 1861	Died Nov. 10, 1861
William H. Young	Nov. 11, 1861	Resigned Aug. 14, 1862
George R. Myers	Aug. 14, 1862	Mustered out May 28, 1863 **Bvt. Brig. Gen.**

18th State Militia

James Ryder	July 8, 1863	Mustered out Aug. 15, 1863

19th Infantry

John S. Clark	May 17, 1861	Resigned Nov. 18, 1861 **Bvt. Brig. Gen.**

19th State Militia

William R. Brown	May 26, 1862	Mustered out Sept. 6, 1862

20th Infantry

Max Weber	May 9, 1861	Promoted **Brig. Gen., USV** April 28, 1862
Francis Weiss	April 28, 1862	Resigned July 4, 1862
Ernest Von Vegesack	July 19, 1862	Mustered out June 1, 1863 **Bvt. Brig. Gen.**

20th Infantry (Reorganizing)

Engelbert Schnepf	July 20, 1863	Not mustered

20th State Militia (see also 80th Infantry)

George W. Pratt	April 23, 1861	Mustered out Aug. 2, 1861
George W. Pratt	Oct. 3, 1861	To 80th Infantry Dec. 7, 1861

21st Infantry

William F. Rogers	May 15, 1861	Mustered out May 18, 1863 **Bvt. Brig. Gen.**

21st Infantry (Reorganizing)

Chester W. Sternberg	May 21, 1863	Not mustered

21st State Militia

Joseph Wright	June 27, 1863	Mustered out Aug. 6, 1863

22nd Infantry

Walter Phelps, Jr.	May 16, 1861	Mustered out June 19, 1863 **Bvt. Brig. Gen.**

22nd State Militia

James Monroe, Jr.	May 28, 1862	Died July 31, 1862
Lloyd Aspinwall	June 18, 1863	Mustered out July 24, 1863

23rd Infantry

Henry C. Hoffman	May 16, 1861	Mustered out May 22, 1863 **Bvt. Brig. Gen.**

23rd State Militia

William Everdell, Jr.	June 18, 1863	Mustered out July 22, 1863

24th Infantry

Timothy Sullivan	May 16, 1861	Resigned Jan. 14, 1863
Samuel R. Beardsley	Jan. 16, 1863	Mustered out May 29, 1863

25th Infantry

James E. Kerrigan	May 21, 1861	Dismissed March 6, 1862
Charles A. Johnson	Feb. 21, 1862	Mustered out July 10, 1863 **Bvt. Brig. Gen.**

25th State Militia

Michael K. Bryan	May 4, 1861	Mustered out Aug. 4, 1861
Michael K. Bryan	May 31, 1862	Mustered out Sept. 8, 1862

26th Infantry

William H. Christian	May 17, 1861	Resigned Sept. 19, 1862 **Bvt. Brig. Gen.**
Richard H. Richardson	Sept. 19, 1862	Mustered out May 28, 1863

27th Infantry

Henry W. Slocum	May 21, 1861	Promoted **Brig. Gen., USV** Aug. 9, 1861
Joseph J. Bartlett	Aug. 9, 1861	Promoted **Brig. Gen., USV** Oct. 4, 1862
Alexander D. Adams	Oct. 4, 1862	Mustered out May 31, 1863

28th Infantry

Dudley Donnelly	May 18, 1861	DOW Aug. 15, 1862
Edwin F. Brown	Aug. 15, 1862	Mustered out June 2, 1863

28th State Militia

Michael Bennett	May 5, 1861	Mustered out Aug. 5, 1861
Michael Bennett	June 16, 1863	Mustered out July 22, 1863
David A. Bokee	Sept. 1, 1864	Mustered out Nov. 13, 1864

29th Infantry

Adolph Von Steinwehr	May 23, 1861	Promoted **Brig. Gen., USV** July 2, 1862
Clemens Soest	June 9, 1862	Resigned April 13, 1863
Louis Hartmann	April 14, 1863	Mustered out June 20, 1863

29th Infantry (Reorganizing)

John Gittermann	July 25, 1863	Not mustered
Peter Degive	Sept. 10, 1863	Not mustered

30th Infantry

Edward Frisby	May 21, 1861	KIA Aug. 30, 1862
William M. Searing	Aug. 30, 1862	Mustered out June 18, 1863

31st Infantry

Calvin E. Pratt	May 21, 1861	Promoted **Brig. Gen., USV** Sept. 10, 1862
Francis E. Pinto	Sept. 13, 1862	Not mustered, declined **Bvt. Brig. Gen.**
Frank Jones	Sept. 13, 1862	Mustered out June 4, 1863

32nd Infantry

Roderick Matheson	May 22, 1861	DOW Oct. 2, 1862
Francis E. Pinto	Oct. 2, 1862	Mustered out June 9, 1863 **Bvt. Brig. Gen.**

33rd Infantry

Robert F. Taylor	May 22, 1861	Mustered out June 2, 1863

34th Infantry

William Ladew	May 30, 1861	Resigned March 20, 1862
James A. Suiter	March 20, 1862	Resigned Jan. 22, 1863
Byron Laflin	Jan. 22, 1863	Mustered out June 30, 1863
		Bvt. Brig. Gen.

35th Infantry

William C. Browne	June 3, 1861	Discharged Aug. 2, 1861
Newton B. Lord	Aug. 10, 1861	Discharged Feb. 9, 1863
John G. Todd	Feb. 9, 1863	Mustered out June 5, 1863

36th Infantry

Charles H. Innes	June 11, 1861	Discharged July 6, 1862
William H. Browne	July 6, 1862	Mustered out July 15, 1863
		Bvt. Brig. Gen.

37th Infantry

John H. McCunn	May 28, 1861	Discharged Aug. 31, 1861
Samuel B. Hayman	Sept. 28, 1861	Mustered out June 22, 1863
		Bvt. Brig. Gen.

37th Infantry (Reorganizing)

William DeLacy	June 26, 1863	Not mustered
		Bvt. Brig. Gen.

37th State Militia

Charles Roome	May 29, 1862	Mustered out Sept. 2, 1862
Charles Roome	June 24, 1863	Mustered out July 22, 1863
		Bvt. Brig. Gen.
Ossian D. Ashley	May 6, 1864	Mustered out June 6, 1864

38th Infantry

John H.H. Ward	May 30, 1861	Promoted **Brig. Gen., USV** Oct. 4, 1862
James C. Strong	Oct. 10, 1862	Mustered out June 22, 1863 **Bvt. Brig. Gen.**
Philip R. DeTrobriand	Dec. 21, 1862	Mustered out Nov. 21, 1863 Later **Brig. Gen., USV**

38th Infantry (Reorganizing)

Augustus Funk	June 23, 1863	Not mustered

39th Infantry

George F. d'Utassy	May 28, 1861	Dismissed May 29, 1863
Augustus Funk	Nov. 13, 1863	Mustered out July 1, 1865

40th Infantry

John S. Cocks	June 14, 1861	Discharged June 29, 1861
Edward J. Riley	June 14, 1861	Discharged June 5, 1862
Thomas W. Egan	June 5, 1862	Promoted **Brig. Gen., USV** Sept. 3, 1864
Madison M. Cannon	Sept. 16, 1864	Mustered out June 27, 1865

41st Infantry

Leopold Von Gilsa	June 6, 1861	Mustered out June 27, 1864

42nd Infantry

William D. Kennedy	June 22, 1861	Died July 22, 1861
Milton Cogswell	July 21, 1861	To 2nd NY Heavy Artillery Sept. 29, 1862 **Bvt. Brig. Gen.**
Edmund C. Charles	Dec. 18, 1861	Discharged March 17, 1863

James E. Mallon	March 17, 1863	KIA Oct. 14, 1863
William A. Lynch	Oct. 14, 1863	Mustered out July 13, 1864

43rd Infantry

Francis L. Vinton	Aug. 3, 1861	Promoted **Brig. Gen., USV** Sept. 19, 1862
Benjamin F. Baker	Sept. 24, 1862	Discharged Feb. 1, 1864 **Bvt. Brig. Gen.**
John Wilson	Feb. 1, 1864	DOW May 7, 1864
Charles A. Milliken	May 7, 1865	Mustered out June 27, 1865

44th Infantry

Stephen W. Stryker	Aug. 30, 1861	Discharged July 4, 1862
James C. Rice	July 4, 1862	Promoted **Brig. Gen., USV** Aug. 16, 1863
Freeman Conner	Aug. 27, 1863	Mustered out Oct. 11, 1864

45th Infantry

George Von Amsberg	Oct. 7, 1861	Discharged Jan. 22, 1864
Adolphus Dobke	Jan. 22, 1864	To 58th NY Infantry June 30, 1865

46th Infantry

Rudolph Rosa	Sept. 16, 1861	Discharged Dec. 17, 1862
Joseph Gerhardt	Dec. 17, 1862	Discharged Nov. 8, 1863 **Bvt. Brig. Gen.**
George W. Travers	Nov. 8, 1863	Mustered out Oct. 15, 1864

47th Infantry

Henry Moore	Sept. 14, 1861	Discharged Aug. 5, 1862
James L. Fraser	Aug. 5, 1862	Discharged March 17, 1863
Henry Moore	March 17, 1863	Mustered out Oct. 27, 1864
Christopher R. McDonald	Oct. 27, 1864	Mustered out Aug. 30, 1865

47th State Militia

Jeremiah V. Meserole	May 27, 1862	Mustered out Sept. 1, 1862
Jeremiah V. Meserole	June 17, 1863	Mustered out July 23, 1863

48th Infantry

James H. Perry	Oct. 26, 1861	Died June 18, 1862
William B. Barton	June 18, 1862	Mustered out Dec. 3, 1864 **Bvt. Brig. Gen.**
William B. Coan	Dec. 3, 1864	Mustered out Sept. 1, 1865

49th Infantry

Daniel D. Bidwell	Sept. 18, 1861	Promoted **Brig. Gen., USV** Aug. 18, 1864
Erastus D. Holt	Aug. 20, 1864	DOW April 7, 1865
George H. Selkirk	April 3, 1865	Mustered out June 27, 1865

50th Infantry (see 50th Engineers)

51st Infantry

Edward Ferrero	Oct. 4, 1861	Promoted **Brig. Gen., USV** Sept. 10, 1862
Robert B. Potter	Sept. 10, 1862	Promoted **Brig. Gen., USV** March 14, 1863
Charles W. LeGendre	March 14, 1863	Discharged Oct. 4, 1864 **Bvt. Brig. Gen.**
Gilbert H. McKibbin	Dec. 9, 1864	Not mustered, declined **Bvt. Brig. Gen.**
John G. Wright	April 29, 1865	Mustered out July 25, 1865 **Bvt. Brig. Gen.**

52nd Infantry

Emil E. Von Schoening	Oct. 2, 1861	Mustered out Feb. 20, 1862
Paul Frank	Oct. 29, 1861	Mustered out Nov. 9, 1864 **Bvt. Brig. Gen.**
Henry M. Karples	Nov. 9, 1864	Mustered out July 1, 1865

52nd State Militia

Matthias W. Cole	June 19, 1863	Mustered out July 25, 1863

53rd Infantry (First Organization)

Lionel J. d'Epineuil	Oct. 16, 1861	Mustered out March 11, 1862

53rd Infantry (Second Organization)

George A. Buckingham	Aug. 8, 1862	Not mustered

54th Infantry

Eugene A. Kozlay	Nov. 20, 1861	Mustered out April 14, 1866 **Bvt. Brig. Gen.**

54th State Militia

Charles H. Clark	July 26, 1864	Mustered out Nov. 10, 1864

55th Infantry

Philip R. DeTrobriand	Aug. 28, 1861	To 38th NY Infantry Later **Brig. Gen., USV**

55th State Militia

Eugene LeGal	June 24, 1863	Mustered out July 27, 1863

56th Infantry

Charles H. Van Wyck	Sept. 4, 1861	Promoted **Brig. Gen., USV** Sept. 27, 1865
Rockwell Tyler	Sept. 27, 1865	Mustered out March 5, 1866

56th State Militia

John Q. Adams	June 18, 1863	Mustered out July 24, 1863
John Q. Adams	Aug. 2, 1864	Mustered out Nov. 6, 1864

57th Infantry

Samuel K. Zook	Oct. 19, 1861	Promoted **Brig. Gen., USV** April 23, 1863
Alford B. Chapman	April 24, 1863	KIA May 5, 1864
James W. Britt	May 5, 1864	Mustered out Jan. 5, 1865 **Bvt. Brig. Gen.**

58th Infantry

Wladimir Krzyzanowski	Oct. 22, 1861	Mustered out Oct. 1, 1865 **Brig. Gen., USV**

58th State Militia

Reuben P. Wisner	Sept. 2, 1864	Mustered out Dec. 2, 1864

59th Infantry

William L. Tidball	Oct. 23, 1861	Discharged Jan. 8, 1863
William Northedge	Jan. 8, 1863	Dismissed June 27, 1863
William L. Tidball	Aug. 1, 1863	Discharged Nov. 19, 1863
Henry W. Hudson	July 18, 1864	Not mustered
William A. Olmsted	Sept. 26, 1864	Mustered out June 30, 1865 **Bvt. Brig. Gen.**

60th Infantry

William B. Hayward	Oct. 25, 1861	Discharged Jan. 8, 1862
George S. Greene	Jan. 18, 1862	Promoted **Brig. Gen., USV** April 28, 1862
William B. Goodrich	May 1, 1862	KIA Sept. 17, 1862
Abel Godard	Dec. 30, 1862	Discharged Sept. 13, 1864
Winslow M. Thomas	Sept. 13, 1864	Discharged April 3, 1865
Lester S. Willson	May 1, 1865	Mustered out July 17, 1865 **Bvt. Brig. Gen.**

61st Infantry

Spencer W. Cone	Oct. 26, 1861	Discharged April 14, 1862
Francis C. Barlow	April 14, 1862	Promoted **Brig. Gen., USV** Sept. 19, 1862
Nelson A. Miles	Sept. 30, 1862	Promoted **Brig. Gen., USV** May 12, 1864
Knut O. Broady	May 12, 1864	Mustered out Oct. 29, 1864
George W. Scott	Oct. 31, 1864	Mustered out July 14, 1865 **Bvt. Brig. Gen.**

62nd Infantry

John L. Riker	July 3, 1861	KIA May 31, 1862
David J. Nevin	May 31, 1862	Mustered out June 29, 1864
Theodore B. Hamilton	June 30, 1864	Mustered out Aug. 30, 1865

63rd Infantry

Richard C. Enright	Nov. 2, 1861	Discharged Feb. 5, 1862
John Burke	Jan. 21, 1862	Discharged Oct. 20, 1862
Henry Fowler	Oct. 25, 1862	Discharged July 4, 1863
Richard C. Bentley	Sept. 5, 1863	Discharged Sept. 18, 1864 **Bvt. Brig. Gen.**
John H. Gleason	Sept. 19, 1864	Mustered out May 18, 1865 **Bvt. Brig. Gen.**
James D. Brady	May 18, 1865	Mustered out June 30, 1865

64th Infantry

Thomas J. Parker	Nov. 13, 1861	Discharged July 12, 1862
Daniel G. Bingham	July 12, 1862	Discharged Feb. 10, 1864
Leman W. Bradley	July 4, 1864	Mustered out Oct. 5, 1864
William Glenny	Oct. 6, 1864	Mustered out July 14, 1865 **Bvt. Brig. Gen.**

65th Infantry

John Cochrane	June 11, 1861	Promoted **Brig. Gen., USV** July 17, 1862
Alexander Shaler	July 17, 1862	Promoted **Brig. Gen., USV** May 26, 1863
Joseph E. Hamblin	May 26, 1863	Promoted **Brig. Gen., USV** May 19, 1865
Henry C. Fisk	May 31, 1865	Mustered out July 17, 1865 **Bvt. Brig. Gen.**

65th State Militia

Jacob Krettner	June 18, 1863	Discharged June 22, 1863

66th Infantry

Joseph C. Pinckney	Oct. 29, 1861	Discharged Dec. 3, 1862 **Bvt. Brig. Gen.**
Orlando H. Morris	Dec. 3, 1862	KIA June 3, 1864
John S. Hammell	June 4, 1864	Mustered out Aug. 30, 1865 **Bvt. Brig. Gen.**

67th Infantry

Julius W. Adams	June 24, 1861	Discharged Oct. 19, 1862
Nelson Cross	Oct. 19, 1862	Mustered out July 4, 1864
		Bvt. Brig. Gen.

67th State Militia

Chauncey Abbott	June 25, 1863	Mustered out Aug. 3, 1863

68th Infantry

Robert J. Betge	Aug. 1, 1861	Discharged Aug. 6, 1862
Gotthilf Bourry DeIvernois	Aug. 6, 1862	Cashiered Oct. 25, 1863
Felix Prince Salm	Oct. 25, 1863	Mustered out Nov. 30, 1865
		Bvt. Brig. Gen.

68th State Militia

David S. Forbes	June 25, 1863	Mustered out July 29, 1863

69th Infantry

Robert Nugent	Nov. 1, 1861	Mustered out Nov. 28, 1863
		Bvt. Brig. Gen.
William Wilson	April 12, 1864	Not mustered
		Bvt. Brig. Gen.
Robert Nugent	Oct. 30, 1864	Mustered out June 30, 1865
		Bvt. Brig. Gen.

69th State Militia

Michael Corcoran	April 20, 1861	Promoted **Brig. Gen., USV** July 21, 1861
James Bagley	May 26, 1862	Mustered out Sept. 3, 1862
James Bagley	June 22, 1863	Mustered out July 27, 1863
James Bagley	July 6, 1864	Mustered out Oct. 6, 1864

70th Infantry

Daniel E. Sickles	June 29, 1861	Promoted **Brig. Gen., USV** Sept. 3, 1861
William Dwight, Jr.	July 1, 1861	Promoted **Brig. Gen., USV** Nov. 29, 1862
J. Egbert Farnum	Dec. 1, 1862	Mustered out July 1, 1864
		Bvt. Brig. Gen.

70th State Militia

William J. Cropsey	Feb. 23, 1863	Date of discharge unknown

71st Infantry

George B. Hall	July 18, 1861	Discharged April 28, 1863
Henry L. Potter	May 1, 1863	Mustered out Dec. 31, 1864

71st State Militia

Abram S. Vosburgh	May 3, 1861	Died May 20, 1861
Henry P. Martin	June 3, 1861	Mustered out July 31, 1861
Henry P. Martin	May 28, 1862	Mustered out Sept. 2, 1862
Benjamin L. Trafford	June 30, 1863	Mustered out July 22, 1863

72nd Infantry

Nelson Taylor	July 23, 1861	Promoted **Brig. Gen., USV** Sept. 7, 1862
William O. Stevens	Sept. 8, 1862	KIA May 3, 1863
John S. Austin	May 4, 1863	Discharged June 27, 1864

73rd Infantry

James Fairman	Aug. 16, 1861	Not mustered
William R. Brewster	Sept. 12, 1861	Mustered out Oct. 24, 1864
		Bvt. Brig. Gen.
Michael W. Burns	Oct. 27, 1864	Mustered out June 29, 1865

74th Infantry

Charles K. Graham	Oct. 15, 1861	Discharged April 10, 1862
		Later **Brig. Gen., USV**
Charles H. Burtis	April 11, 1862	Not mustered
Charles K. Graham	May 26, 1862	Promoted **Brig. Gen., USV** March 15, 1863
Thomas Holt	May 16, 1863	To 70th NY Infantry Nov. 30, 1863
		Bvt. Brig. Gen.

74th State Militia

Watson A. Fox	June 19, 1863	Mustered out Aug. 3, 1863
Watson A. Fox	Nov. 20, 1863	Mustered out Dec. 16, 1863

75th Infantry

John A. Dodge	Nov. 14, 1861	Discharged July 21, 1862
Robert B. Merritt	July 21, 1862	Discharged Sept. 20, 1864
Robert P. York	Jan. 1, 1865	Mustered out Aug. 31, 1865

76th Infantry

Nelson W. Green	Oct. 29, 1861	Discharged June 3, 1862
William P. Wainwright	June 3, 1862	Discharged June 25, 1863
		Bvt. Brig. Gen.
Charles E. Livingston	June 25, 1863	Discharged Dec. 1, 1864

77th Infantry

James B. McKean	Oct. 14, 1861	Discharged July 27, 1863
Winsor B. French	July 27, 1863	Mustered out Dec. 13, 1864
		Bvt. Brig. Gen.
David J. Caw	Jan. 1, 1865	Mustered out June 27, 1865

77th State Militia

Thomas Lynch	Aug. 2, 1864	Mustered out Nov. 9, 1864

78th Infantry

Daniel Ullmann	April 28, 1862	Promoted **Brig. Gen., USV** Jan. 13, 1863
Herbert Von Hammerstein	July 30, 1863	To 102nd NY Infantry July 12, 1864

79th Infantry

James Cameron	May 29, 1861	KIA July 21, 1861
Isaac I. Stevens	July 30, 1861	Promoted **Brig. Gen., USV** Sept. 28, 1861
Addison Farnsworth	Dec. 17, 1861	Discharged Feb. 17, 1863
		Bvt. Brig. Gen.
David Morrison	Feb. 17, 1863	Mustered out May 31, 1864
		Bvt. Brig. Gen.

80th Infantry (see also 20th State Militia)

George W. Pratt	Dec. 7, 1861	DOW Sept. 11, 1862
Theodore B. Gates	Sept. 11, 1862	Discharged Nov. 22, 1864
		Bvt. Brig. Gen.
Jacob B. Hardenbergh	Nov. 22, 1864	Mustered out Jan. 29, 1866
		Bvt. Brig. Gen.

81st Infantry

Oliver B. Peirce	————	Not mustered
Edwin Rose	Sept. 25, 1861	Discharged July 7, 1862
Jacob J. DeForest	July 7, 1862	Discharged Sept. 1, 1864
John B. Raulston	Sept. 1, 1864	Mustered out Jan. 15, 1865
David B. White	March 1, 1865	Mustered out Aug. 31, 1865
		Bvt. Brig. Gen.

82nd Infantry (see also 2nd State Militia)

George W. B. Tompkins	Dec. 7, 1861	Discharged May 26, 1862
Henry W. Hudson	May 26, 1862	Dismissed May 20, 1863
James F. X. Huston	May 20, 1863	KIA July 2, 1863
Henry W. Hudson	July 2, 1863	Mustered out June 25, 1864

83rd Infantry (see also 9th State Militia)

John W. Stiles	Dec. 7, 1861	Discharged Jan. 18, 1863
John Hendrickson	Jan. 18, 1863	Discharged Aug. 3, 1863
		Bvt. Brig. Gen.
Joseph A. Moesch	Oct. 13, 1863	KIA May 6, 1864

84th Infantry (see also 14th State Militia)

Alfred M. Wood	Dec. 7, 1861	Discharged Oct. 18, 1862
Edward B. Fowler	Oct. 24, 1862	Mustered out June 6, 1864
		Bvt. Brig. Gen.

84th State Militia

Frederick A. Conkling	July 3, 1863	Mustered out Aug. 4, 1863
Frederick A. Conkling	July 13, 1864	Mustered out Oct. 29, 1864

85th Infantry

Uriah L. Davis	Nov. 7, 1861	Discharged Feb. 8, 1862
Robert B. Van Valkenburgh	Feb. 8, 1862	Not mustered, declined
Jonathan S. Belknap	Feb. 8, 1862	Discharged June 13, 1863
Enrico Fardella	June 26, 1863	Discharged May 15, 1865
		Bvt. Brig. Gen.
William W. Clarke	May 15, 1865	Mustered out June 27, 1865

86th Infantry

Benajah P. Bailey	Nov. 12, 1861	Discharged June 12, 1863
Benjamin L. Higgins	June 12, 1863	Discharged June 25, 1864
Jacob H. Lansing	June 25, 1864	Mustered out Nov. 14, 1864
Nathan H. Vincent	Nov. 13, 1864	Mustered out June 27, 1865

87th Infantry

Stephen A. Dodge	Nov. 19, 1861	Mustered out Sept. 6, 1862

88th Infantry

Henry M. Baker	Sept. 28, 1861	Discharged Sept. 30, 1862
Patrick Kelly	Sept. 22, 1862	KIA June 16, 1864
Denis F. Burke	Nov. 15, 1864	Mustered out June 30, 1865

89th Infantry

Harrison S. Fairchild	Dec. 4, 1861	Mustered out Aug. 3, 1865
		Bvt. Brig. Gen.

90th Infantry

Joseph S. Morgan	Nov. 27, 1861	Dismissed April 19, 1864
Nelson Shaurman	May 20, 1864	Mustered out Feb. 9, 1866
		Bvt. Brig. Gen.

91st Infantry

Jacob Van Zandt	Dec. 16, 1861	Dismissed Feb. 2, 1865
Jonathan Tarbell	Feb. 2, 1865	Mustered out July 3, 1865
		Bvt. Brig. Gen.

92nd Infantry

Jonah Sanford	Dec. 9, 1861	Discharged May 15, 1862
Lewis C. Hunt	May 10, 1862	Promoted **Brig. Gen., USV** Dec. 24, 1862
Thomas S. Hall	Dec. 27, 1862	Mustered out June 10, 1863

93rd Infantry

John S. Crocker	Jan. 1, 1862	Discharged Sept. 7, 1864
		Bvt. Brig. Gen.
Thomas F. Morris	May 10, 1862	Not mustered
Samuel McConihe	Sept. 7, 1864	Discharged Feb. 15, 1865
		Bvt. Brig. Gen.
Haviland Gifford	March 1, 1865	Mustered out June 29, 1865

93rd State Militia

William R. W. Chambers	July 20, 1864	Mustered out Nov. 1, 1864

94th Infantry

Walter B. Camp	Oct. 1861	Not mustered
John J. Viele	Nov. 4, 1861	Not mustered
Henry K. Viele	Jan. 6, 1862	Discharged May 2, 1862
Adrian R. Root	May 2, 1862	Mustered out July 18, 1865
		Bvt. Brig. Gen.

95th Infantry

George H. Biddle	March 6, 1862	Discharged Oct. 9, 1863
Edward Pye	Oct. 9, 1863	DOW June 12, 1864
James Creney	June 3, 1864	Mustered out July 16, 1865

96th Infantry

James Fairman	March 5, 1862	Discharged Sept. 25, 1862
Charles O. Gray	Sept. 25, 1862	KIA Dec. 14, 1862
Edgar M. Cullen	Dec. 26, 1862	Discharged March 21, 1865
Stephen Moffitt	April 22, 1865	Mustered out Feb. 6, 1866
		Bvt. Brig. Gen.

97th Infantry

Charles Wheelock	Jan. 16, 1862	Died Jan. 21, 1865
		Bvt. Brig. Gen.
John P. Spofford	Jan. 21, 1865	Mustered out July 18, 1865
		Bvt. Brig. Gen.

98th Infantry

William Dutton	Jan. 23, 1862	Died July 4, 1862
Charles Durkee	July 4, 1862	Discharged Feb. 25, 1863
Frederick F. Wead	Feb. 25, 1863	KIA June 3, 1864
William Kreutzer	June 3, 1864	Mustered out Aug. 31, 1865

98th State Militia

George Abbott	Aug. 10, 1864	Mustered out Dec. 22, 1864

99th Infantry

Washington A. Bartlett	May 22, 1861	Not mustered
David W. Wardrop	Aug. 21, 1861	Discharged Dec. 10, 1864

99th State Militia

John O'Mahony	Aug. 2, 1864	Mustered out Nov. 9, 1864

100th Infantry

James M. Brown	Jan. 10, 1862	KIA May 31, 1862
George B. Dandy	Aug. 28, 1862	Mustered out Aug. 28, 1865
		Bvt. Brig. Gen.

101st Infantry

Enrico Fardella	March 7, 1862	Discharged July 8, 1862
		Bvt. Brig. Gen.
George F. Chester	July 25, 1862	Mustered out Dec. 24, 1862

102nd Infantry

Thomas B. Van Buren	Feb. 8, 1862	Discharged Dec. 13, 1862 **Bvt. Brig. Gen.**
James C. Lane	Dec. 13, 1862	Mustered out July 12, 1864
Herbert Von Hammerstein	July 12, 1864	Discharged Jan. 7, 1865
Harvey S. Chatfield	Jan. 7, 1865	Mustered out July 21, 1865

102nd State Militia

John N. Wilsey	Aug. 25, 1864	Mustered out Nov. 13, 1864

103rd Infantry

Frederick W. Von Egloffstein	Feb. 20, 1862	Discharged Nov. 1, 1862 **Bvt. Brig. Gen.**
Benjamin Ringold	Sept. 15, 1862	DOW May 3, 1863
William Heine	May 15, 1863	Mustered out March 17, 1865 **Bvt. Brig. Gen.**

104th Infantry

John Rorbach	March 15, 1862	Discharged Oct. 21, 1862
Lewis C. Skinner	Oct. 21, 1862	Not mustered, declined
Gilbert G. Prey	Oct. 21, 1862	Discharged March 3, 1865
John R. Strang	March 3, 1865	Mustered out July 17, 1865

105th Infantry

James M. Fuller	March 26, 1862	Discharged Aug. 2, 1862
Howard Carroll	Aug. 2, 1862	DOW Sept. 29, 1862
John W. Shedd	Oct. 6, 1862	Mustered out March 19, 1863

106th Infantry

Schuyler F. Judd	June 30, 1862	Resigned Sept. 30, 1862
Edward C. James	Sept. 30, 1862	Discharged Aug. 4, 1863
Frederic E. Embick	Aug. 4, 1863	Dismissed Sept. 23, 1863
Frederic E. Embick	Dec. 15, 1863	Not mustered
Lewis T. Barney	Aug. 2, 1864	Not mustered, declined **Bvt. Brig. Gen.**
Andrew N. McDonald	Dec. 20, 1864	Mustered out June 22, 1865

107th Infantry

Robert B. Van Valkenburgh	July 18, 1862	Discharged Oct. 9, 1862
Alexander S. Diven	Oct. 21, 1862	Discharged May 11, 1863 **Bvt. Brig. Gen.**
Nirom M. Crane	May 19, 1863	Mustered out June 5, 1865 **Bvt. Brig. Gen.**

108th Infantry

John Williams	July 10, 1862	Resigned July 28, 1862
Oliver H. Palmer	July 28, 1862	Discharged March 2, 1863 **Bvt. Brig. Gen.**
Charles J. Powers	March 2, 1863	Discharged May 28, 1865 **Bvt. Brig. Gen.**

109th Infantry

Benjamin F. Tracy	July 22, 1862	Discharged May 17, 1864 **Bvt. Brig. Gen.**
Isaac S. Catlin	May 17, 1864	Mustered out June 4, 1865 **Bvt. Brig. Gen.**

110th Infantry

Cheney Ames	May 23, 1862	Resigned July 29, 1862
DeWitt C. Littlejohn	July 29, 1862	Discharged Feb. 3, 1863 **Bvt. Brig. Gen.**
Clinton H. Sage	Feb. 4, 1863	Discharged Dec. 10, 1863
Charles Hamilton	Dec. 10, 1863	Mustered out Aug. 28, 1865

111th Infantry

Jesse Segoine	July 19, 1862	Discharged Jan. 3, 1863
Clinton D. MacDougall	Jan. 3, 1863	Mustered out June 4, 1865 **Bvt. Brig. Gen.**
Lewis W. Husk	Feb. 25, 1865	Mustered out June 4, 1865

112th Infantry

Augustus F. Allen	July 21, 1862	Not mustered
Jeremiah C. Drake	Sept. 2, 1862	DOW June 2, 1864
John F. Smith	June 1, 1864	DOW Jan. 18, 1865
Ephraim A. Ludwick	Jan. 18, 1865	Mustered out June 13, 1865

113th Infantry (see 7th Heavy Artillery)

114th Infantry

Elisha B. Smith	July 21, 1862	DOW June 19, 1863
Samuel R. PerLee	June 19, 1863	Mustered out June 8, 1865 **Bvt. Brig. Gen.**

115th Infantry

Simeon Sammons	July 19, 1862	Discharged Nov. 19, 1864
Nathan J. Johnson	April 29, 1865	Mustered out June 17, 1865

116th Infantry

Edward P. Chapin	July 14, 1862	KIA May 27, 1863 **Brig. Gen., USV**
George M. Love	May 27, 1863	Mustered out June 8, 1865 **Bvt. Brig. Gen.**

117th Infantry

William R. Pease	July 19, 1862	Discharged Aug. 26, 1863 **Bvt. Brig. Gen.**
Alvin White	Aug. 26, 1863	Discharged July 18, 1864
Rufus Daggett	July 18, 1864	Mustered out June 8, 1865 **Bvt. Brig. Gen.**

118th Infantry

Samuel T. Richards	July 7, 1862	Discharged July 8, 1863
Oliver Keese, Jr.	July 8, 1863	Discharged Sept. 16, 1864
George F. Nichols	Sept. 16, 1864	Mustered out June 13, 1865 **Bvt. Brig. Gen.**

119th Infantry

Elias Peissner	Sept. 1, 1862	KIA May 2, 1863
John T. Lockman	May 2, 1863	Mustered out June 7, 1865 **Bvt. Brig. Gen.**

120th Infantry

George H. Sharpe	July 14, 1862	Mustered out June 3, 1865 **Bvt. Brig. Gen.**

121st Infantry

Richard Franchot	July 19, 1862	Discharged Sept. 25, 1862 **Bvt. Brig. Gen.**
Emory Upton	Sept. 25, 1862	Promoted **Brig. Gen., USV** May 12, 1864
Egbert Olcott	July 4, 1864	Mustered out June 25, 1865

122nd Infantry

Silas Titus	July 22, 1862	Discharged Jan. 23, 1865
Augustus W. Dwight	Jan. 27, 1865	KIA March 25, 1865
Horace H. Walpole	March 25, 1865	Mustered out June 23, 1865

123rd Infantry

Archibald L. McDougall	July 23, 1862	DOW June 23, 1864
Ambrose Stevens	July 1, 1864	To 176th NY Infantry Nov. 19, 1864
James C. Rogers	Nov. 19, 1864	Mustered out June 8, 1865 **Bvt. Brig. Gen.**

124th Infantry

Augustus Van Horne Ellis	July 11, 1862	KIA July 2, 1863 **Bvt. Brig. Gen.**
Francis M. Cummins	July 2, 1863	Discharged Sept. 19, 1864
Charles H. Weygant	Sept. 19, 1864	Mustered out June 3, 1865

125th Infantry

John A. Griswold	July 28, 1862	Resigned Aug. 22, 1862
George L. Willard	Aug. 15, 1862	KIA July 2, 1863
Levin Crandell	July 3, 1863	Discharged Dec. 14, 1864
Ambrose S. Cassidy	Dec. 2, 1864	Not mustered, declined **Bvt. Brig. Gen.**
Joseph Hyde	Jan. 20, 1865	Mustered out June 5, 1865

126th Infantry

Eliakim Sherrill	July 15, 1862	KIA July 3, 1863
James M. Bull	July 3, 1863	Discharged April 18, 1864
William H. Baird	April 18, 1864	KIA June 16, 1864
John Smith Brown	June 17, 1864	Mustered out June 3, 1865

127th Infantry

William Gurney	July 10, 1862	Mustered out June 30, 1865 **Bvt. Brig. Gen.**

128th Infantry

David S. Cowles	July 19, 1862	KIA May 27, 1863
James Smith	May 27, 1863	Discharged Dec. 18, 1863 **Bvt. Brig. Gen.**
James P. Foster	Dec. 18, 1863	Dismissed Nov. 28, 1864

129th Infantry (see 8th Heavy Artillery)

130th Infantry (see 1st Dragoons)

131st Infantry

Charles S. Turnbull	Aug. 15, 1862	Discharged Jan. 15, 1863
Nicholas W. Day	Jan. 14, 1863	Mustered out July 26, 1865 **Bvt. Brig. Gen.**

132nd Infantry

Peter J. Claassen	July 23, 1862	Mustered out June 29, 1865

133rd Infantry

Leonard D. H. Currie	Sept. 24, 1862	Mustered out June 6, 1865

134th Infantry

George E. Danforth	July 9, 1862	Not mustered
Charles R. Coster	Oct. 8, 1862	Discharged Nov. 4, 1863
Allan H. Jackson	Nov. 4, 1863	Mustered out June 10, 1865

135th Infantry (see 6th Heavy Artillery)

136th Infantry

James Wood, Jr.	Aug. 8, 1862	Mustered June 13, 1865 **Bvt. Brig. Gen.**

137th Infantry

David Ireland	Aug. 31, 1862	Died Sept. 10, 1864
Koert S. Van Voorhees	Oct. 14, 1864	Mustered out June 9, 1865

138th Infantry (see 9th Heavy Artillery)

139th Infantry

Anthony Conk	July 28, 1862	Discharged July 29, 1863
Samuel H. Roberts	July 29, 1863	Mustered out June 19, 1865 **Bvt. Brig. Gen.**

140th Infantry

Hiram Smith	Aug. 8, 1862	Not mustered
Patrick H. O'Rorke	Sept. 8, 1862	KIA July 2, 1863
George Ryan	July 17, 1863	KIA May 8, 1864
Elwell S. Otis	Aug. 8, 1864	Discharged Jan. 24, 1865 **Bvt. Brig. Gen.**
William S. Grantsynn	Jan. 24, 1865	Mustered out June 3, 1865

141st Infantry

Samuel G. Hatheway, Jr.	Aug. 9, 1862	Discharged Feb. 11, 1863
John W. Dininny	Feb. 11, 1863	Discharged June 1, 1863
William K. Logie	June 1, 1863	KIA July 20, 1864
Andrew J. McNett	July 20, 1864	Mustered out June 8, 1865 **Bvt. Brig. Gen.**

142nd Infantry

Roscius W. Judson	Aug. 19, 1862	Discharged Jan. 21, 1863 **Bvt. Brig. Gen.**
Newton M. Curtis	Jan. 21, 1863	Promoted **Brig. Gen., USV** Jan. 15, 1865
Albert M. Barney	Jan. 14, 1865	Mustered out June 7, 1865 **Bvt. Brig. Gen.**

143rd Infantry

John C. Holley	Aug. 14, 1862	Not mustered, declined
David P. DeWitt	Sept. 25, 1862	Discharged April 29, 1863 **Bvt. Brig. Gen.**
Horace Boughton	April 29, 1863	Mustered out July 20, 1865 **Bvt. Brig. Gen.**

144th Infantry

Robert S. Hughston	Aug. 17, 1862	Discharged May 24, 1863
David E. Gregory	May 24, 1863	Discharged Oct. 24, 1863
William J. Slidell	Dec. 29, 1863	Discharged Sept. 25, 1864
James Lewis	Sept. 25, 1864	Mustered out June 25, 1865

145th Infantry

William H. Allen	Sept. 11, 1862	Not mustered
Edward L. Price	Dec. 17, 1862	Dismissed Dec. 9, 1863

146th Infantry

DeLancey Floyd-Jones	Sept. 6, 1862	Not mustered, declined **Bvt. Brig. Gen.**
Kenner Garrard	Sept. 23, 1862	Promoted **Brig. Gen., USV** July 23, 1863
David T. Jenkins	July 23, 1863	KIA May 5, 1864
J. Neilson Potter	Dec. 31, 1864	Commission revoked
James G. Grindlay	Feb. 1, 1865	Mustered out July 16, 1865 **Bvt. Brig. Gen.**

147th Infantry

Andrew S. Warner	Aug. 25, 1862	Discharged Feb. 4, 1863
John G. Butler	Feb. 4, 1863	Discharged Nov. 5, 1863
Francis C. Miller	Nov. 5, 1863	Mustered out June 7, 1865

148th Infantry

William Johnson	Aug. 20, 1862	Discharged Oct. 26, 1863
George M. Guion	Oct. 26, 1863	Discharged Oct. 16, 1864
John B. Murray	Oct. 16, 1864	Mustered out June 22, 1865 **Bvt. Brig. Gen.**

149th Infantry

Henry A. Barnum	Aug. 28, 1862	Promoted **Brig. Gen., USV** May 31, 1865
Nicholas Grumbach	June 7, 1865	Mustered out June 12, 1865

150th Infantry

John H. Ketcham	Aug. 27, 1862	Promoted **Brig. Gen., USV** April 1, 1865
Alfred B. Smith	April 24, 1865	Mustered out June 8, 1865 **Bvt. Brig. Gen.**

151st Infantry

Franklin Spalding	Aug. 20, 1862	Not mustered
William Emerson	Sept. 3, 1862	Discharged Dec. 21, 1864

152nd Infantry

Leonard Boyer	Aug. 23, 1862	Discharged Jan. 10, 1863
Alonzo Ferguson	Jan. 10, 1863	Discharged Nov. 23, 1863
George W. Thompson	Nov. 15, 1863	Mustered out June 24, 1865
James E. Curtiss	June 1, 1865	Mustered out July 13, 1865 **Bvt. Brig. Gen.**

153rd Infantry

Timothy W. Miller	Aug. 23, 1862	Not mustered
Duncan McMartin	Sept. 5, 1862	Discharged April 21, 1863
Edwin P. Davis	April 21, 1863	Mustered out Oct. 2, 1865 **Bvt. Brig. Gen.**

154th Infantry

Addison G. Rice	Aug. 19, 1862	Not mustered
Patrick H. Jones	Oct. 8, 1862	Promoted **Brig. Gen., USV** April 18, 1865
Lewis D. Warner	Feb. 20, 1865	Mustered out June 11, 1865

155th Infantry

William McEvily	Oct. 10, 1862	Discharged Nov. 3, 1863
Hugh C. Flood	Nov. 3, 1863	Discharged Oct. 13, 1864
John Byrne	Jan. 1, 1865	Mustered out July 15, 1865

156th Infantry

Erastus Cooke	Aug. 23, 1862	Discharged March 28, 1863
Jacob Sharpe	March 28, 1863	Mustered out Oct. 23, 1865 **Bvt. Brig. Gen.**

157th Infantry

Philip P. Brown, Jr.	Aug. 13, 1862	Mustered out June 12, 1865 **Bvt. Brig. Gen.**
James C. Carmichael	June 8, 1865	Mustered out July 10, 1865

158th Infantry

Francis B. Spinola	July 23, 1862	Not mustered Later **Brig. Gen., USV**
James Jourdan	Aug. 13, 1862	Discharged March 17, 1865 **Bvt. Brig. Gen.**
William H. McNary	March 17, 1865	Mustered out June 30, 1865 **Bvt. Brig. Gen.**

159th Infantry

Homer A. Nelson	Oct. 31, 1862	Discharged Nov. 25, 1862
Edward L. Molineux	Nov. 25, 1862	Discharged Aug. 4, 1865 **Bvt. Brig. Gen.**
William Waltermire	Aug. 4, 1865	Mustered out Oct. 12, 1865

160th Infantry

Charles C. Dwight	Sept. 6, 1862	Discharged May 25, 1865
Henry P. Underhill	May 30, 1865	Mustered out Nov. 1, 1865

161st Infantry

Gabriel T. Harrower	Sept. 6, 1862	Discharged Nov. 25, 1863
Henry G. Harrower	March 3, 1864	Not mustered

162nd Infantry

Lewis Benedict	Sept. 9, 1862	KIA April 9, 1864 **Bvt. Brig. Gen.**
Justus W. Blanchard	April 9, 1864	Mustered out Oct. 12, 1865 **Bvt. Brig. Gen.**

163rd Infantry (consolidated into six companies)

Hale Kingsley	July 11, 1862	Not mustered, declined
Marriott N. Croft	————	Not mustered
Francis H. Braulik	————	Not mustered

164th Infantry

John E. McMahon	Aug. 8, 1862	Died March 3, 1863
James P. McMahon	March 23, 1863	KIA June 3, 1864
William DeLacy	June 13, 1864	Mustered out July 15, 1865 **Bvt. Brig. Gen.**

165th Infantry (six companies only)

Harmon D. Hull	Sept. 4, 1862	Not mustered

166th Infantry (consolidated with 176th Infantry)

Isaac Wood, Jr.	Sept. 6, 1862	Not mustered

167th Infantry

Homer A. Nelson	Sept. 3, 1862	To 159th NY Infantry Oct. 28, 1862

168th Infantry

William R. Brown	Feb. 11, 1863	Mustered out Oct. 31, 1863

169th Infantry

Clarence Buel	Sept. 24, 1862	Discharged Feb. 13, 1864
John McConihe	Feb. 13, 1864	KIA June 1, 1864 **Bvt. Brig. Gen.**
Alonzo Alden	June 1, 1864	Mustered out July 19, 1865 **Bvt. Brig. Gen.**

170th Infantry

Peter McDermott	July 17, 1862	Discharged Jan. 4, 1863
James P. MacIvor	Jan. 4, 1863	Mustered out July 15, 1865 **Bvt. Brig. Gen.**

171st Infantry
William Mayer — Sept. 2, 1862 — Not mustered

172nd Infantry
Chauncey M. Depew — —————— — Not mustered
John P. Jenkins — Sept. 10, 1862 — Not mustered

173rd Infantry
Charles B. Morton — Sept. 22, 1862 — Discharged March 15, 1863
Lewis M. Peck — March 15, 1863 — Mustered out Oct. 18, 1865
Bvt. Brig. Gen.

174th Infantry
Theodore W. Parmele — Oct. 3, 1862 — Discharged Oct. 17, 1863
Benjamin F. Gott — Oct. 17, 1863 — Discharged Feb. 9, 1864

175th Infantry
Michael K. Bryan — Sept. 24, 1862 — KIA June 14, 1863
John A. Foster — June 14, 1863 — Discharged Aug. 5, 1865
Bvt. Brig. Gen.

176th Infantry
Charles Gould — Sept. 4, 1862 — Not mustered
Mark Hoyt — Oct. 2, 1862 — Not mustered
Charles C. Nott — Dec. 31, 1862 — Mustered out Aug. 8, 1864
Ambrose Stevens — Nov. 19, 1864 — Mustered out Sept. 12, 1865
Charles Lewis — Oct. 18, 1865 — Mustered out April 27, 1866

177th Infantry
Ira W. Ainsworth — Nov. 5, 1862 — Mustered out Sept. 10, 1863

178th Infantry
Edward Wehler — June 20, 1863 — Mustered out Jan. 21, 1865

179th Infantry
William M. Gregg — Sept. 5, 1864 — Mustered out June 8, 1865
Bvt. Brig. Gen.

180th Infantry
Lewis T. Barney — May 24, 1864 — Authority revoked
Bvt. Brig. Gen.

181st Infantry
John H. Coster — March 24, 1864 — Authority revoked

182nd Infantry
Mathew Murphy — Nov. 8, 1862 — DOW April 16, 1865
John Coonan — April 19, 1865 — Mustered out July 15, 1865

183rd Infantry
George A. Buckingham — March 26, 1864 — Authority revoked

184th Infantry
Wardwell G. Robinson — Sept. 16, 1864 — Mustered out June 29, 1865

185th Infantry
Edwin S. Jenney — Aug. 26, 1864 — Discharged Feb. 3, 1865
Gustavus Sniper — Feb. 3, 1865 — Mustered out May 30, 1865
Bvt. Brig. Gen.

186th Infantry
Bradley Winslow — Sept. 21, 1864 — Discharged June 2, 1865
Bvt. Brig. Gen.

187th Infantry
William F. Berens — Sept. 1, 1864 — Not mustered

188th Infantry
James R. Chamberlin — Sept. 14, 1864 — Not mustered
John McMahon — Oct. 10, 1864 — Mustered out July 1, 1865
Bvt. Brig. Gen.

189th Infantry
William W. Hayt — Oct. 1, 1864 — Died Nov. 8, 1864
John J. Coppinger — Dec. 31, 1864 — Revoked
Allen L. Burr — Dec. 29, 1864 — Mustered out June 1, 1865

190th Infantry
Paul Frank — Jan. 12, 1865 — Not mustered
Bvt. Brig. Gen.

191st Infantry
Leopold Von Gilsa — Jan. 12, 1865 — Not mustered

192nd Infantry
Nathan G. Axtell — Jan. 14, 1865 — Discharged Dec. 11, 1865

193rd Infantry
John B. Van Petten — Jan. 21, 1865 — Mustered out Jan. 18, 1866
Bvt. Brig. Gen.

194th Infantry
Joseph W. Corning — Jan. 27, 1865 — Not mustered

Independent Corps, Light Infantry (Enfants Perdus)
Felix Confort — Nov. 22, 1861 — Resigned May 9, 1863

Chauncey Abbott

Colonel, 67 NY National Guard, June 25, 1863. Honorably
mustered out, Aug. 3, 1863.

Born: Sept. 22, 1816 East Hamburg, Erie Co., NY
Died: Dec. 18, 1890 Orchard Park, NY
Occupation: Merchant and farmer
Miscellaneous: Resided Buffalo, NY; and Orchard Park, Erie
  Co., NY
Buried: Woodlawn Cemetery, Orchard Park, NY
References: Lemuel A. Abbott. *Descendants of George Abbott
  of Rowley, MA.* Boston, MA, 1906. Death notice, *Buffalo
  Courier,* Dec. 19, 1890.

George Abbott

Surgeon, 67 NY National Guard, June 25, 1863. Honorably
mustered out, Aug. 3, 1863. Colonel, 98 NY National
Guard, Aug. 10, 1864. Honorably mustered out, Dec. 22,
1864.

Born: Nov. 2, 1826 Palmyra, NY
Died: March 26, 1911 Hamburg, NY
Education: Attended Geneva (NY) Medical College. M. D.,
  University of Buffalo Medical College, 1852.
Occupation: Physician
Miscellaneous: Resided Hamburg, Erie Co., NY
Buried: Prospect Lawn Cemetery, Hamburg, NY
References: Lemuel A. Abbott. *Descendants of George Abbott
  of Rowley, MA.* Boston, MA, 1906. Pension File, National
  Archives. Obituary, *Buffalo Morning Express,* March 28,
  1911.

Alexander Duncan Adams

Captain, Co. B, 27 NY Infantry, May 2, 1861. Lieutenant Colonel, 27 NY Infantry, Sept. 1, 1861. Colonel, 27 NY Infantry, Oct. 4, 1862. Honorably mustered out, May 31, 1863.

Born: Dec. 25, 1832 Lyons, NY
Died: Oct. 28, 1872 Lyons, NY
Education: Attended Hobart College, Geneva, NY (Class of
  1854)
Occupation: Civil engineer and school principal

Above Right: George Abbott (postwar)
Descendants of George Abbott of Rowley, MA.
Right: Alexander Duncan Adams
Frederick H. Meserve. Historical Portraits. Courtesy of New York State Li-
brary.

Offices/Honors: Principal, Lyons (NY) Union School, 1866-71

Miscellaneous: Resided Lyons, Wayne Co., NY

Buried: South Cemetery, Lyons, NY

References: Pension File, National Archives. *History of Wayne County, NY.* Philadelphia, PA, 1877. *Catalogue of the Sigma Phi.* N.p., 1915. Obituary, *Wayne Democratic Press*, Oct. 30, 1872. Charles B. Fairchild. *History of the 27th Regiment New York Volunteers.* Binghamton, NY, 1888.

John Quincy Adams

Colonel, 56 NY National Guard, June 18, 1863. Honorably mustered out, July 24, 1863. Colonel, 56 NY National Guard, Aug. 2, 1864. Honorably mustered out, Nov. 6, 1864.

Born: March 22, 1826 Ashford (now Eastford), CT

Died: Dec. 6, 1870 Brooklyn, NY

Occupation: Lawyer

Miscellaneous: Resided Brooklyn, NY

Buried: Green-Wood Cemetery, Brooklyn, NY (Section 61, Lot 12774)

References: Obituary, *Brooklyn Daily Eagle,* Dec. 12, 1870. Andrew N. Adams. *A Genealogical History of Robert Adams of Newbury, MA, and his Descendants.* Rutland, VT, 1900.

Alexander Duncan Adams
Massachusetts MOLLUS Collection, USAMHI.

Julius Walker Adams

Colonel, 67 NY Infantry, June 24, 1861. Commanded 2 Brigade, 1 Division, 4 Army Corps, Army of the Potomac, April-May 1862. Discharged for disability, Oct. 19, 1862, due to "continued ill health brought on by fatigue and exposure in the Peninsula." *Colonel*, 2 Regiment, Hawkins' Zouaves, Nov. 12, 1862. Transferred to Blair Rifles, April 21, 1863. Out of service by consolidation, June 22, 1863.

Born: Oct. 18, 1812 Boston, MA

Died: Dec. 13, 1899 Brooklyn, NY

Education: Attended US Military Academy, West Point, NY (Class of 1834)

Occupation: Civil engineer, engaged early in life in railroad construction. Later employed primarily on harbor and public works projects. Chief Engineer of the New Haven (CT) Water Works at the start of the war.

Offices/Honors: One of the founders of the American Society of Civil Engineers

Miscellaneous: Resided Brooklyn, NY

Buried: Green-Wood Cemetery, Brooklyn, NY (Sections 93/94, Lots 2018/3490)

Alexander Duncan Adams
Roger D. Hunt Collection, USAMHI.

Julius Walker Adams
Massachusetts MOLLUS Collection, USAMHI.

Julius Walker Adams
West Point Museum Collection, US Military Academy.

References: Obituary, *Brooklyn Daily Eagle*, Dec. 14, 1899. Henry I. Hazelton. *The Boroughs of Brooklyn and Queens.* New York and Chicago, 1925. Andrew N. Adams. *A Genealogical History of Henry Adams of Braintree, MA, and His Descendants.* Rutland, VT, 1898.

Field Officers of the 67th New York (1st Long Island) Infantry (Major P. Mark DeZeng, left; Colonel Julius W. Adams, center; Lt. Col. Nelson Cross, right)
Roger D. Hunt Collection, USAMHI.

Ira Washington Ainsworth

Colonel, 177 NY Infantry, Nov. 5, 1862. Honorably mustered out, Sept. 10, 1863.

Born: April 3, 1814 Barre, VT
Died: July 10, 1876 Albany, NY
Occupation: Wholesale grocer
Miscellaneous: Resided Albany, NY
Buried: Rural Cemetery, Albany, NY (Section 8, Lot 12)
References: Francis J. Parker. *Genealogy of the Ainsworth Families in America*. Boston, MA, 1894. Obituary, *Albany Evening Journal*, July 10, 1876.

Samuel M. Alford

Lieutenant Colonel, 3 NY Infantry, April 25, 1861. Colonel, 3 NY Infantry, July 2, 1861. Commanded 1 Brigade, 2 Division, 7 Army Corps, Department of Virginia, June 17, 1863-Aug. 1863. Commanded 1 Brigade, 2 Division, 18 Army Corps, Department of the South, Sept.-Oct. 1863. Commanded 2 Brigade, US Forces, North End, Folly Island, SC, Nov. 1863-March 1864. Commanded 1 Brigade, 2 Division, 10 Army Corps, Army of the James, April 1864-May 30, 1864. Dismissed June 14, 1864, for "having tendered his resignation in the face of the enemy and on

Above: *Ira Washington Ainsworth Courtesy of Henry Deeks. S. J. Thompson & Co., Photographers, No. 478 Broadway, Albany, NY.*

Ira Washington Ainsworth (seated center, with officers of the 177th New York) Michael J. McAfee Collection. S. J. Thompson & Co., Photographers, No. 478 Broadway, Albany, NY.

grounds deemed unworthy of consideration." His dismissal was revoked Aug. 30, 1864, "on account of previous good conduct and meritorious services," and he was honorably discharged to date, June 14, 1864.

Born: July 4, 1823 Windsor, CT
Died: Dec. 11, 1879 Edenburg (now Knox), Clarion Co., PA
Occupation: Hardware merchant before war. Grocer after war.
Miscellaneous: Resided New York City, NY; Albany, NY; Pithole, Venango Co., PA; and Edenburg (now Knox), Clarion Co., PA
Buried: Knox Union Cemetery, Knox, PA (Section C, Lot 8)
References: Obituary, *New York Herald*, Dec. 18, 1879. Military Service File, National Archives. Letters Received, Commission Branch, Adjutant General's Office, File A272(CB)1863, National Archives. William C. Darrah. *Pithole, The Vanished City*. N.p., 1972. Henry R. Stiles. *History of Ancient Windsor*. Hartford, CT, 1891.

Augustus Franklin Allen

Colonel, 112 NY Infantry, July 21, 1862. Succeeded by Colonel Jeremiah C. Drake, Sept. 2, 1862.

Born: Sept. 13, 1813 Wardsboro, VT
Died: Jan. 20, 1875 Jamestown, NY
Occupation: Early in life engaged in mercantile and lumber business. Later involved in woolen manufacturing.
Offices/Honors: Elected to US House of Representatives, 1874, but died before taking office
Miscellaneous: Resided Jamestown, Chautauqua Co., NY
Buried: Lakeview Cemetery, Jamestown, NY (Wildwood Section, Lots 23-25)
References: Andrew W. Young. *History of Chautauqua County, NY*. Buffalo, NY, 1875. John P. Downs, editor. *History of Chautauqua County and Its People*. Boston, MA, 1921. William R. Cutter. *Genealogical and Family History of Western New York*. New York City, NY, 1912.

William H. Allen

Colonel, 1 NY Infantry, May 7, 1861. Cashiered Sept. 10, 1861, on charges of "disobedience of orders, maliciously causing private property to be destroyed, conduct unbecoming an officer and a gentleman, and breach of arrest," all related to an incident occurring June 27, 1861, in which he sent a portion of his command, in violation of orders, to

Augustus Franklin Allen (1867)
Courtesy of the author. Jeffers & McDonnald, No. 519 Broadway, Albany, NY.

William H. Allen
Massachusetts MOLLUS Collection, USAMHI. Brady's National Photographic Portrait Gallery, Broadway & Tenth Street, New York.

burn 25 acres of wheat on a nearby farm. *Colonel*, 145 NY Infantry, Sept. 11, 1862. Commission canceled since regiment was under minimum strength.

Born: 1821?
Died: June 5, 1867 Washington, DC
Occupation: Civil engineer engaged in bridge construction before war. Pension claim agent after war.
Miscellaneous: Resided New York City, NY; and Washington, DC
Buried: Green-Wood Cemetery, Brooklyn, NY (Section 94, Lot 10875, under a stone inscribed "Wm. H. Gallagher")
References: Letters of Application and Recommendation During the Administrations of Abraham Lincoln and Andrew Johnson, National Archives. Emmons Clark. *History of the 7th Regiment of New York*. New York City, NY, 1890. Obituary, *Washington Daily Morning Chronicle*, June 6, 1867. Military Service File, National Archives. Thomas P.

Lowry. *Tarnished Eagles: The Courts-Martial of Fifty Union Colonels and Lieutenant Colonels*. Mechanicsburg, PA, 1997. Letters Received, Volunteer Service Branch, Adjutant General's Office, File A570(VS)1862, National Archives.

Cheney Ames

Colonel, 110 NY Infantry, May 23, 1862. Succeeded by Colonel DeWitt C. Littlejohn, July 29, 1862.

Born: June 19, 1808 Mexico, NY
Died: Sept. 14, 1892 Chicago, IL
Occupation: Capitalist identified with many manufacturing enterprises, including a knitting mill, a flour mill and a grain elevator
Offices/Honors: NY State Senate, 1858-59 and 1864-65
Miscellaneous: Resided Oswego, NY; and Chicago, IL

William H. Allen
Massachusetts MOLLUS Collection, USAMHI. Brady's National Photographic Portrait Gallery, Broadway & Tenth Street, New York.

William H. Allen
Massachusetts MOLLUS Collection, USAMHI.

Buried: Riverside Cemetery, Oswego, NY (Section N, Lot 20)

References: Crisfield Johnson. *History of Oswego County, NY.* Philadelphia, PA, 1877. *Encyclopedia of Contemporary Biography of New York.* New York City, NY, 1884. Obituary, *Oswego Daily Palladium*, Sept. 15, 1892.

Ossian Doolittle Ashley

Lieutenant Colonel, 37 NY National Guard, May 29, 1862. Honorably mustered out, Sept. 2, 1862. Colonel, 37 NY National Guard, May 6, 1864. Honorably mustered out, June 6, 1864.

Born: April 9, 1821 Townshend, VT

Died: Dec. 16, 1904 New York City, NY

Occupation: Banker, stock broker and railroad president

Miscellaneous: Resided Boston, MA; and New York City, NY

Buried: Woodlawn Cemetery, New York City, NY (Section 70, Lawn Plot, Lot 10595)

References: *National Cyclopedia of American Biography.* Obituary, *New York Times*, Dec. 17, 1904. Henry Whittemore. *History of the 71st Regiment N. G. S. N. Y.* New York City, NY, 1886.

Lloyd Aspinwall

Lieutenant Colonel, 22 NY National Guard, May 28, 1862. Honorably mustered out, Sept. 5, 1862. Colonel, 22 NY National Guard, June 18, 1863. Honorably mustered out, July 24, 1863.

Born: Dec. 12, 1834 New York City, NY

Died: Sept. 4, 1886 Bristol, RI

Occupation: Head of the shipping firm of Howland & Aspinwall

Cheney Ames (postwar)
History of Oswego County, NY.

Ossian Doolittle Ashley (postwar)
National Cyclopedia of American Biography.

Left: *Lloyd Aspinwall*
Massachusetts MOLLUS Collection, USAMHI.
Below Left: *Lloyd Aspinwall (postwar)*
Courtesy of the author. Naegeli, 46 East 14th Street, Union Square, New York.

Offices/Honors: Brig. Gen., NY National Guard, 1865-69

Miscellaneous: Resided New York City, NY

Buried: Green-Wood Cemetery, Brooklyn, NY (Section 21, Lots 2076-2078)

References: Obituary circular, Whole No. 260, New York MOLLUS. Algernon A. Aspinwall. *Aspinwall Genealogy.* Rutland, VT, 1901. Obituary, *New York Times*, Sept. 5, 1886. Obituary, *New York Tribune*, Sept. 5, 1886. George W. Wingate. *History of the 22nd Regiment of the National Guard of the State of New York*. New York City, NY, 1896.

Lloyd Aspinwall
Massachusetts MOLLUS Collection, USAMHI. Brady's National Photographic Portrait Gallery, Broadway & Tenth Street, New York.

John S. Austin

Captain, Co. K, 72 NY Infantry, June 21, 1861. Acting Brigade Quartermaster, Staff of Brig. Gen. Daniel E. Sickles, Dec. 18, 1861-June 1862. Colonel, 72 NY Infantry, May 4, 1863. Shell wound right wrist, hand and lower part of forearm, Gettysburg, PA, July 2, 1863. Discharged for disability, June 27, 1864, due to "nephritis and enlarged prostate with general debility."

Born: June 1812 NY
Died: May 8, 1865
Occupation: Clerk, Washington Market, New York City, NY
Miscellaneous: Resided New York City, NY
Buried: Green-Wood Cemetery, Brooklyn, NY (Section 45, Lot 6218, unmarked)

References: Military Service File, National Archives. Death and funeral notice, *New York Herald*, May 13, 1865. Obituary, *New York Herald*, May 15, 1865. Research files of Edmund J. Raus, Jr. Henri L. Brown. *History of the Third Regiment Excelsior Brigade, 72nd New York Volunteer Infantry.* Jamestown, NY, 1902.

Nathan Gibbs Axtell

Chaplain, 30 NY Infantry, June 1, 1861. Major, 142 NY Infantry, Oct. 8, 1862. GSW back of neck and right thigh, Ware Bottom Church, VA, May 20, 1864. Resigned Oct. 22, 1864, "feeling after three and a half years of service that claims of family are paramount." Colonel, 192 NY Infantry, April 10, 1865. Honorably mustered out, Dec. 11, 1865.

John S. Austin
History of the Third Regiment, Excelsior Brigade, 72d New York Volunteeer Infantry.

John S. Austin (standing right, with Brig. Gen. John H. H. Ward, seated)
Massachusetts MOLLUS Collection, USAMHI.

Born: Jan. 7, 1827 Pierrepont, NY
Died: Jan. 11, 1903 Evanston, IL
Education: Attended Victoria College, Canada
Occupation: Methodist clergyman and farmer
Offices/Honors: NY Constitutional Convention, 1867
Miscellaneous: Resided Oswego, NY; Peru, Clinton Co., NY; Albany, NY; and Evanston, Cook Co., IL
Buried: Rosehill Cemetery, Chicago, IL (Section 106, Lot 48)
References: Pension File, National Archives. Carson A. Axtell, compiler. *Axtell Genealogy*. New Bedford, MA, 1945. Obituary, *Chicago Record-Herald*, Jan. 12, 1903. Letters Received, Volunteer Service Branch, Adjutant General's Office, File A233(VS)1862, National Archives.

Left: *Nathan Gibbs Axtell (1867)*
Courtesy of the author. Jeffers & McDonnald, No. 519 Broadway, Albany, NY.

Nathan Gibbs Axtell
Courtesy of Henry Deeks. Schoonmaker's Palace of Art, 282 River St., Troy, NY.

Nathan Gibbs Axtell
Courtesy of Dave Zullo. Schoonmaker's Palace of Art, 282 River St., Troy, NY.

James Bagley

Major, 69 NY State Militia, April 20, 1861. Honorably mustered out, Aug. 3, 1861. Colonel, 69 NY National Guard, May 26, 1862. Honorably mustered out, Sept. 3, 1862. Colonel, 69 NY National Guard, June 22, 1863. Honorably mustered out, July 27, 1863. Colonel, 69 NY National Guard, July 6, 1864. Honorably mustered out, Oct. 6, 1864.

Born: Jan. 11, 1821 NY
Died: Dec. 21, 1876 New York City, NY
Occupation: Coal merchant
Offices/Honors: New York City alderman, 1859-61
Miscellaneous: Resided New York City, NY. A Sachem of the Tammany Society.
Buried: Calvary Cemetery, Long Island City, NY (Section 7, Range 11, Plot AA, unmarked)
References: Obituary, *New York Times*, Dec. 25, 1876. Obituary, *New York Herald*, Dec. 24, 1876.

Benajah P. Bailey

Colonel, 86 NY Infantry, Nov. 12, 1861. Commanded 1 Brigade, 3 Division, 3 Army Corps, Army of the Potomac, Dec. 17, 1862-Jan. 1863 and Feb. 1863-April 1863. Discharged for disability, June 12, 1863, due to chronic diarrhea.

Born: Nov. 26, 1799 Norwich, CT
Died: May 12, 1866 Corydon, Warren Co., PA
Occupation: Lumber manufacturer
Offices/Honors: NY State Assembly, 1852 and 1854
Miscellaneous: Resided Dundaff, Susquehanna Co., PA; Corning, Steuben Co., NY; and Corydon, Warren Co., PA
Buried: Hope Cemetery, Corning, NY
References: William S. Bailey, editor. *Milton Bailey: An Autobiography*. Jamestown, NY, 1911. Pension File and Military Service File, National Archives. Obituary, *Corning Journal*, May 17, 1866.

James Bagley
Frederick H. Meserve. Historical Portraits. Courtesy of New York State Library.

James Bagley (standing)
USAMHI.

Left: *Benajah P. Bailey*
Massachusetts MOLLUS Collection, USAMHI.
Below Left: *Benajah P. Bailey*
Milton Bailey: An Autobiography.

Guilford Dudley Bailey

1 Lieutenant, 2 US Artillery, May 14, 1861. Captain, Commissary of Subsistence, Aug. 3, 1861. Colonel, 1 NY Light Artillery, Sept. 25, 1861. GSW head, Fair Oaks, VA, May 31, 1862.

Born: June 4, 1834 Martinsburg, Lewis Co., NY
Died: May 31, 1862 KIA Fair Oaks, VA
Education: Graduated US Military Academy, West Point, NY, 1856
Occupation: Regular Army (1 Lieutenant, 2 US Artillery)
Miscellaneous: Resided Oswego, NY; and Poughkeepsie, Dutchess Co., NY
Buried: Poughkeepsie Rural Cemetery, Poughkeepsie, NY (Section C, Lots 11-12)
References: *National Cyclopedia of American Biography.* George W. Cullum. *Biographical Register of the Officers and Graduates of the US Military Academy.* Third Edition. Boston and New York, 1891. Obituary, *New York Daily Tribune*, June 5, 1862.

Guilford Dudley Bailey
Roger D. Hunt Collection, USAMHI. Moulton & Larkin, Photographers, 114, 116 & 118 Water Street, Elmira, NY.

Guilford Dudley Bailey
Courtesy of Steve Meadow. W. J. Moulton, Photographer, 116 & 118 Water Street, Elmira, NY.

Guilford Dudley Bailey
Michael J. McAfee Collection. Brady's National Photographic Portrait Gallery, Broadway & Tenth Street, New York.

Guilford Dudley Bailey (seated, with Officers of the 1st NY Light Artillery)
Massachusetts MOLLUS Collection, USAMHI.

William Henderson Baird

Captain, Co. H, 38 NY Infantry, June 3, 1861. Major, 38 NY
Infantry, Jan. 11, 1862. Major, 126 NY Infantry, Aug. 9,
1862. Captured Harper's Ferry, WV, Sept. 15, 1862. Paroled Sept. 16, 1862. Dismissed Nov. 8, 1862, for "bad
conduct" at Harper's Ferry. Disability resulting from dismissal removed June 26, 1863. Lieutenant Colonel, 126
NY Infantry, Nov. 5, 1863. *Colonel*, 126 NY Infantry, April
18, 1864. GSW right side, passing through both lungs,
Petersburg, VA, June 16, 1864.

Born: Aug. 19, 1831 Auburn, NY
Died: June 16, 1864 KIA Petersburg, VA
Occupation: Carriage maker
Miscellaneous: Resided Janesville, Rock Co., WI; and Geneva,
Ontario Co., NY
Buried: Mound Cemetery, Moravia, NY (Section 3, Lots 16-
17)
References: Arabella M. Willson. *Disaster, Struggle, Triumph:
The Adventures of 1000 "Boys in Blue."* Albany, NY, 1870.
Wayne Mahood. *"Written in Blood," A History of the 126th
New York Infantry in the Civil War.* Hightstown, NJ, 1997.
Pension File and Military Service File, National Archives.
William H. Baird Papers, Geneva (NY) Historical Soci-
ety. Letters Received, Volunteer Service Branch, Adjutant
General's Office, File B213(VS)1863, National Archives.

William Henderson Baird
Roger D. Hunt Collection, USAMHI.

William Henderson Baird
The Gilder Lehrman Collection on deposit at the Pierpont Mor-
gan Library, New York. Avery & Parker, Moravia, NY.

William Henderson Baird
Meade Album, Civil War Library & Museum, Philadelphia, PA.

Henry Michael Baker

Colonel, 2 NJ Militia, May 1, 1861. Honorably mustered out, July 31, 1861. Colonel, 88 NY Infantry, Sept. 28, 1861. Dismissed Sept. 22, 1862 for "absence from his command without authority" and for "cowardice in the face of the enemy" at Fair Oaks, VA, June 28, 1862. Dismissal revoked July 1, 1871, and he was honorably discharged, upon tender of resignation, to date Sept. 30, 1862.

Born: 1820? Dublin, Ireland
Died: Nov. 8, 1872 Jersey City, NJ
Occupation: Proprietor of a clothing store
Miscellaneous: Resided Jersey City, Hudson Co., NJ
Buried: St. Peters Catholic Cemetery, Jersey City, NJ (South Division, Lot 88)
References: Pension File, National Archives. Obituary, *Jersey City Times*, Nov. 8, 9 and 11, 1872. Letters Received, Volunteer Service Branch, Adjutant General's Office, Files B1834(VS)1862 and M1226(VS)1862, National Archives. David P. Conyngham. *The Irish Brigade and Its Campaigns*. Boston, MA, 1869.

Joel Brigham Goodell Baker

Captain, Co. B, 8 NY Heavy Artillery, Aug. 5, 1862. Major, 8 NY Heavy Artillery, June 3, 1864. Lieutenant Colonel, 8 NY Heavy Artillery, Jan. 1, 1865. Colonel, 8 NY Heavy Artillery, Jan. 14, 1865. Commanded 2 Brigade, 2 Division, 2 Army Corps, Army of the Potomac, May 28, 1865-June 29, 1865. Colonel, 10 NY Infantry, June 5, 1865. Honorably mustered out, June 30, 1865.

Born: Aug. 9, 1833 Ancaster, Ontario, Canada
Died: June 1, 1876 Hartford, CT
Education: Attended Wilson (NY) Collegiate Institute
Occupation: School teacher
Miscellaneous: Resided Warren's Corners, Niagara Co., NY; Troy, Rensselaer Co., NY; East Orange, NJ; and Hartford, CT
Buried: Budd Cemetery, near Warren's Corners, Niagara Co., NY
References: Edward T. Williams. *Niagara County, NY, 1821-1921*. Chicago, IL, 1921. Obituary, *Hartford Courant*, June 2, 1876. Pension File, National Archives. Naomi B. Baker, compiler. *Letters Home: Joel B. Baker*. N.p., N.d.

Henry Michael Baker
Collection of The New-York Historical Society. Bailey, Photographer, Monticello Avenue, Jersey City, NJ.

Joel Brigham Goodell Baker
Donald K. Ryberg Collection.

Stephen Baker

1 Lieutenant, Co. G, 6 NY Heavy Artillery, Aug. 27, 1862. Captain, Co. L, 6 NY Heavy Artillery, June 1, 1863. Major, 6 NY Heavy Artillery, Nov. 1, 1864. Lieutenant Colonel, 6 NY Heavy Artillery, Jan. 10, 1865. Colonel, 6 NY Heavy Artillery, June 27, 1865. Honorably mustered out, Aug. 24, 1865.

Born: Dec. 24, 1835 Southeast, Putnam Co., NY
Died: Dec. 5, 1898 Brooklyn, NY
Occupation: Early life in Kansas, Nebraska and Colorado, where he engaged in freighting and gold prospecting. Lumber and feed merchant, hat manufacturer, and clerk in US Customs service after war.
Offices/Honors: NY State Assembly, 1866-67
Miscellaneous: Resided Southeast, Putnam Co., NY; and Brooklyn, NY.
Buried: Cypress Hills Cemetery, Brooklyn, NY (Section 14, Lot 851)

References: William S. Pelletreau. *History of Putnam County, NY*. Philadelphia, PA, 1886. Pension File, National Archives. S. R. Harlow and H. H. Boone. *Life Sketches of the State Officers, Senators, and Members of the Assembly of the State of New York in 1867*. Albany, NY, 1867.

William Benson Barnes

Captain, Co. C, 4 NY Heavy Artillery, Jan. 2, 1862. Appointed Colonel, 11 NY Heavy Artillery, Feb. 7, 1863. Mustered as Major, 11 NY Heavy Artillery, June 21, 1863. Dismissed Sept. 30, 1863, for "fraudulent conduct in connection with the recruitment of the force." Dismissal revoked, March 7, 1864. By Act of Congress, Feb. 21, 1905, he was honorably discharged to date Sept. 30, 1863.

Born: 1838? NY
Died: Nov. 9, 1872 St. Joseph, MI
Occupation: Clerk
Miscellaneous: Resided Rochester, NY; and St. Joseph, Berrien Co., MI

Joel Brigham Goodell Baker (postwar)
Niagara County, NY, 1821-1921.

Stephen Baker (1866)
Roger D. Hunt Collection, USAMHI. Haines & Wickes, Photographers, 478 Broadway, Albany, NY.

William Benson Barnes (Top center)
Heavy Guns and Light: A History of the 4th New York Heavy Artillery.

Buried: Lakeview City Cemetery, St. Joseph, MI
References: Pension File and Military Service File, National Archives. Hyland C. Kirk. *Heavy Guns and Light: A History of the 4th New York Heavy Artillery.* New York City, NY, 1890. Letters Received, Volunteer Service Branch, Adjutant General's Office, File B151(VS)1863, National Archives.

Washington Allen Bartlett

Colonel, Naval Brigade, May 22, 1861. Regiment not being accepted for US service, it was reorganized as 99 NY Infantry, Aug. 21, 1861, with Colonel David W. Wardrop as colonel.

Born: 1816? ME
Died: Feb. 6, 1865 New York City, NY
Other Wars: Mexican War (Lieutenant, US Navy)
Occupation: US Navy (Lieutenant, dropped Sept. 28, 1855). Newspaper editor.
Offices/Honors: As Alcade of Yerba Buena, CA, 1846-47, he served as the first chief magistrate of the city of San Francisco
Miscellaneous: Resided San Francisco, CA; and New York City, NY
Buried: Green-Wood Cemetery, Brooklyn, NY (Section 90, Lots 772/775, unmarked)
References: *National Cyclopedia of American Biography.* Death Notice, *New York Times,* Feb. 10, 1865. Obituary,

New York World, Feb. 28, 1865. Letters Received, Volunteer Service Branch, Adjutant General's Office, File W183(VS)1861, National Archives. "Col. Washington A. Bartlett and the Naval Brigade," *New York Times,* June 26, 1861.

Abraham Bassford

Private, Co. F, 8 NY State Militia, April 25, 1861. Honorably mustered out, Aug. 2, 1861. 1 Lieutenant, Co. A, 14 NY Cavalry, Oct. 18, 1862. 1 Lieutenant, Adjutant, 14 NY Cavalry, Dec. 19, 1862. Major, 14 NY Cavalry, July 10, 1863. Colonel, 14 NY Cavalry, Aug. 10, 1864. Commanded 2 Separate Cavalry Brigade, Department of the Gulf, Nov. 23, 1864-Dec. 17, 1864. GSW right thigh, Morganza, LA, March 12, 1865. Honorably mustered out, June 12, 1865.

Born: Dec. 13, 1837 New York City, NY
Died: Sept. 30, 1922 Long Branch, NJ
Occupation: Jeweller. Regular Army (Captain, 8 US Cavalry, resigned Nov. 9, 1869). Real estate agent.
Miscellaneous: Resided Fordham, Westchester Co., NY; New York City, NY; and Hartsdale, Westchester Co., NY
Buried: Rural Cemetery, White Plains, NY
References: Pension File, National Archives. Circular, Whole No. 394, New York MOLLUS.

Washington Allen Bartlett
National Cyclopedia of American Biography.

Willard W. Bates

Sergeant, Co. F, 13 NY Infantry, May 14, 1861. 1 Lieutenant, Co. C, 25 NY Infantry, Nov. 7, 1861. Captain, Co. I, 25 NY Infantry, Jan. 20, 1862. GSW Chickahominy, VA, June 27, 1862. Lieutenant Colonel, 8 NY Heavy Artillery, Aug. 11, 1862. Colonel, 8 NY Heavy Artillery, June 3, 1864. GSW abdomen, Petersburg, VA, June 22, 1864.

Born: May 19, 1835 Kendall, Orleans Co., NY
Died: June 24, 1864 DOW City Point, VA
Occupation: Farmer
Miscellaneous: Resided Kendall, Orleans Co., NY
Buried: Union Cemetery, Morton, Orleans Co., NY
References: Isaac S. Signor, editor. *Landmarks of Orleans County, NY.* Syracuse, NY, 1894. Obituary, *Orleans Republican*, July 6, 1864. James M. Hudnut. *Casualties by Battles and by Names in the 8th New York Heavy Artillery, August 22, 1862-June 5, 1865, Together With a Review of the Service of the Regiment Fifty Years After Muster-in.* New York City, NY, 1913.

Willard W. Bates
Donald K. Ryberg Collection. J. H. Young, Photographer, 231 Baltimore Street, Corner of Charles, Baltimore, MD.

Willard W. Bates
New York State Military Museum and Veterans Research Center.

cowardice, and conduct unbecoming an officer and a gentleman," he resigned April 18, 1863, citing "important individual interests" at home and the fact that "another officer whom I rank ... is preferred to command the brigade to which my regiment is attached."

Born: Oct. 12, 1816 Fairfield, Herkimer Co., NY

Died: Feb. 18, 1906 Athens, NY

Education: Graduated US Military Academy, West Point, NY, 1841

Other Wars: Mexican War (Bvt. Captain, 8 US Infantry) (GSW right leg, Molino del Ray, Mexico, Sept. 8, 1847)

Occupation: Regular Army (Captain, 8 US Infantry, resigned Dec. 31, 1853), farmer, and trust agent

Miscellaneous: Resided Athens, Greene Co., NY

Buried: Athens Rural Cemetery, Athens, NY

References: Pension File and Military Service File, National Archives. *Annual Reunion*, Association of the Graduates of the US Military Academy, 1906.

Officers of the 8th New York Heavy Artillery (Surgeon James M. Leet, left; Lt. Col. Willard W. Bates, right; at Headquarters, Fort Federal Hill, Baltimore, MD, 1862)
Casualties by Battles and by Names in the 8th New York Heavy Artillery.

John Beardsley

Colonel, 9 NY Cavalry, Nov. 5, 1861. Commanded Cavalry Brigade, 1 Army Corps, Army of Virginia, Aug.-Sept. 1862. Commanded 3 Brigade, Bayard's Cavalry Division, 11 Army Corps, Army of the Potomac, Oct.-Nov. 1862. Facing court martial on charges of "uttering disloyal sentiments and language tending to demoralize his command,

John Beardsley
Undated article from a Jamestown (NY) newspaper, courtesy of Eric J. Wittenberg.

John Beardsley
Courtesy of the author.

John Beardsley (postwar)
Annual Reunion, Association of the Graduates of the US Military Academy,
1906.

Samuel Raymond Beardsley

Lieutenant Colonel, 24 NY Infantry, May 16, 1861. GSW
    Groveton, VA, Aug. 29, 1862. Colonel, 24 NY Infantry,
    Jan. 16, 1863. Honorably mustered out, May 29, 1863.
    Captain, AAG, USV, Sept. 28, 1863. Captain, AAG, 3
    Brigade, 1 Division, 2 Army Corps, Army of the Potomac,
    Sept.-Dec. 1863.

Born: Dec. 31, 1814 Cherry Valley, NY
Died: Dec. 28, 1863 Stevensburg, VA (apoplexy)
Education: Graduated Union College, Schenectady, NY, 1836
Occupation: Merchant and flour miller
Offices/Honors: Mayor, Oswego, NY, 1851. Postmaster, Os-
    wego, NY, 1853-58.
Miscellaneous: Resided Oswego, NY
Buried: Riverside Cemetery, Oswego, NY (Section T, Lot 2)
References: Nellie B. and Charles E. Holt, compilers. *The
    Family of William Beardsley*. West Hartford, CT, 1951.
    Pension File, National Archives. Obituary, *Oswego Daily
    Palladium*, Jan. 2, 1864. Henry C. Johnson, editor. *Tenth
    General Catalogue of the Psi Upsilon Fraternity*.
    Bethlehem, PA, 1888. Class questionaire, Special Collec-
    tions, Schaffer Library, Union College.

Jonathan S. Belknap

Lieutenant Colonel, 85 NY Infantry, Nov. 7, 1861. Colonel, 85
    NY Infantry, Feb. 8, 1862. Commanded 1 Brigade, 4 Di-
    vision, 18 Army Corps, Department of North Carolina,
    March 12, 1863-April 13, 1863. Discharged for disability,
    June 13, 1863, due to bilious remittent fever contracted in
    the Peninsula Campaign.

Born: April 22, 1819 Trumansburg, NY
Died: Jan. 27, 1904 Westons Mills, NY
Occupation: Lumberman, oil speculator and grocer
Miscellaneous: Resided Pithole, Venango Co., PA; Big Foot,
    McHenry Co., IL; and Westons Mills, Cattaraugus Co.,
    NY
Buried: Allegany Protestant Cemetery, Allegany, NY
References: H. H. Hardesty. *Presidents, Soldiers, Statesmen*.
    Western New York Edition. New York, Toledo and Chi-
    cago, 1895. Obituary, *Olean Morning Times*, Jan. 29, 1904.
    Pension File and Military Service File, National Archives.
    Letters Received, Volunteer Service Branch, Adjutant
    General's Office, File B467(VS)1863, National Archives.
    Wayne Mahood. *The Plymouth Pilgrims: A History of the
    85th New York Infantry in the Civil War*. Hightstown, NJ,
    1989.

Michael Bennett

Colonel, 28 NY State Militia, May 5, 1861. Honorably mustered out, Aug. 5, 1861. Colonel, 28 NY National Guard, June 16, 1863. Honorably mustered out, July 22, 1863.

Born: July 28, 1826 Edenderry, Kings County, Ireland
Died: Sept. 8, 1901 Brooklyn, NY
Occupation: Hotelkeeper, real estate agent and merchant
Miscellaneous: Resided Brooklyn, NY
Buried: Holy Cross Cemetery, Brooklyn, NY (St. Mark's Section, Range B, Plot 5, unmarked)
References: Obituary, *Brooklyn Daily Eagle*, Sept. 9, 1901. Pension File, National Archives. Henry I. Hazelton. *The Boroughs of Brooklyn and Queens*. New York and Chicago, 1925. William Harper Bennett. "Some Pre-Civil War Irish Militiamen of Brooklyn, New York," *Journal of the American Irish Historical Society*, Vol. 21 (1922).

William F. Berens

Captain, Co. C, 5 WI Infantry, June 18, 1861. Major, 5 WI Infantry, July 26, 1862. Resigned Dec. 26, 1862, suffering from "oedema of the legs resulting from varicose veins." Lieutenant Colonel, 65 NY National Guard, June 19, 1863. Honorably mustered out, July 30, 1863. *Colonel*, 187 NY Infantry, Sept. 1, 1864. Not mustered, regiment never reaching full strength.

Born: 1826? Hanover, Germany
Died: Dec. 31, 1870
Occupation: Butcher
Miscellaneous: Resided Buffalo, NY; and Evans, Erie Co., NY
Buried: Evans (now Jerusalem Corners) Cemetery, Jerusalem Corners, Erie Co., NY (unmarked)
References: Pension File and Military Service File, National Archives.

Robert J. Betge

Colonel, 68 NY Infantry, Aug. 1, 1861. Discharged for disability, Aug. 6, 1862, due to "rheumatism, great nervousness, and physical debility."

Born: 1824? Germany
Died: Sept. 9, 1877 Goppingen, Wurttemberg, Germany
Occupation: Stationer before war. Importing stationer and bookseller after war.
Offices/Honors: California State Senate, 1869-72
Miscellaneous: Resided New York City, NY; San Francisco, CA; and Goppingen, Wurttemberg, Germany

Jonathan S. Belknap
Massachusetts MOLLUS Collection, USAMHI.

Robert J. Betge
Massachusetts MOLLUS Collection, USAMHI. Brady's National Photographic Portrait Gallery, 352 Pennsylvania Avenue, Washington, DC.

Right: *Robert J. Betge*
Massachusetts MOLLUS Collection, USAMHI.

Buried: Goppingen, Germany?

References: Pension File and Military Service File, National Archives. Letters Received, Volunteer Service Branch, Adjutant General's Office, File B1287(VS)1862, National Archives.

George H. Biddle

Lieutenant Colonel, 95 NY Infantry, Dec. 20, 1861. Colonel, 95 NY Infantry, March 6, 1862. Commanded 2 Brigade, 1 Division, 1 Army Corps, Army of the Potomac, Dec. 28, 1862-Jan. 4, 1863 and Aug. 16, 1863-Sept. 23, 1863. GSW right breast, Gettysburg, PA, July 1, 1863. Resigned Oct. 9, 1863, "for the reason that unmerited attempts have been made and are again set on foot to have me arrested, thereby

casting reproach upon a man who has known of no fault excepting to deal mercy with justice, serve his country faithfully and his God."

Born: Oct. 1, 1802 New York City, NY
Died: June 11, 1884 New York City, NY
Other Wars: Mexican War (Volunteer staff officer)
Occupation: Merchant (auction and commission business) and appraiser before war. Clerk and superintendent after war.
Miscellaneous: Resided New York City, NY
Buried: Green-Wood Cemetery, Brooklyn, NY (Sections 106/107, Lot 10499)
References: Pension File, National Archives. Obituary, *New York Times*, June 12, 1884. Letters Received, Volunteer Service Branch, Adjutant General's Office, File B1696(VS)1863, National Archives.

George H. Biddle
Massachusetts MOLLUS Collection, USAMHI. Published by E. & H. T. Anthony, 501 Broadway, New York, from Photographic Negative in Brady's National Portrait Gallery.

George H. Biddle
National Archives.

Daniel Galusha Bingham
Massachusetts MOLLUS Collection, USAMHI.

Daniel Galusha Bingham

Lieutenant Colonel, 64 NY Infantry, Nov. 13, 1861. GSW left thigh, Fair Oaks, VA, June 1, 1862. Colonel, 64 NY Infantry, July 12, 1862. GSW slight, Chancellorsville, VA, May 3, 1863. Contused GSW hip, Gettysburg, PA, July 2, 1863. Discharged for disability, Feb. 10, 1864, due to wounds received, chronic bronchitis, tuberculosis of the right lung, and also valvular disease of the heart.

Born: Jan. 30, 1827 Riga, Monroe Co., NY
Died: July 21, 1864 Le Roy, NY
Occupation: Lawyer and civil engineer
Miscellaneous: Resided Ellicottville, Cattaraugus Co., NY; and Le Roy, Genesee Co., NY
Buried: Riga Cemetery, Riga, NY
References: Franklin Ellis. *History of Cattaraugus County, NY*. Philadelphia, PA, 1879. Donna Bingham Munger. *The Bingham Family in the United States: The Descendants of Thomas Bingham of Connecticut*. New York City, NY, 1996. Letters Received, Volunteer Service Branch, Adjutant General's Office, File B1137(VS)1862, National Archives.

Daniel Galusha Bingham
New York State Military Museum and Veterans Research Center. Brady's National Photographic Portrait Gallery, Broadway & Tenth Street, New York.

David Alexander Bokee
Roger D. Hunt Collection, USAMHI. J. E. Swanton, Photographer, 364 Fulton Street, Opposite City Hall, Brooklyn, NY.

David Alexander Bokee

1 Lieutenant, Adjutant, 28 NY State Militia, May 11, 1861. Honorably mustered out, Aug. 5, 1861. 1 Lieutenant, Adjutant, 132 NY Infantry, July 14, 1862. Resigned, Dec. 20, 1862, "having been sick and unfit for duty for over sixty days." Lieutenant Colonel, 28 NY National Guard, June 16, 1863. Honorably mustered out, July 22, 1863. Colonel, 28 NY National Guard, Sept. 1, 1864. Honorably mustered out, Nov. 13, 1864.

Born: Dec. 31, 1840 Brooklyn, NY
Died: Feb. 23, 1884 Brooklyn, NY
Occupation: Clerk
Miscellaneous: Resided Brooklyn, NY
Buried: Green-Wood Cemetery, Brooklyn, NY (Section 119, Lot 133, unmarked)
References: Death notice, *New York Herald*, Feb. 25, 1884. Military Service File, National Archives.

Leonard Boyer

Colonel, 152 NY Infantry, Aug. 23, 1862. Resigned Jan. 10, 1863, so that "a man of military experience might be appointed in my place."

Born: July 4, 1819 Theresa, Jefferson Co., NY
Died: March 9, 1892 Little Falls, NY
Occupation: Building contractor
Miscellaneous: Resided Little Falls, Herkimer Co., NY
Buried: Church Street Cemetery, Little Falls, NY (Lot 124)
References: Pension File and Military Service File, National Archives. Obituary, *Little Falls Journal and Courier*, March 15, 1892. Henry Roback. *The Veteran Volunteers of Herkimer and Otsego Counties in the War of the Rebellion, Being a History of the 152nd New York Volunteers*. Little Falls, NY, 1888.

Leman W. Bradley

1 Lieutenant, Co. K, 14 NY Infantry, May 17, 1861. Honorably discharged, Sept. 24, 1861, "for reasons (physical disability) assigned by his regimental commander." 1 Lieutenant, Co. H, 64 NY Infantry, Dec. 23, 1861. Captain, Co. H, 64 NY Infantry, April 20, 1862. GSW left arm, Fair Oaks, VA, June 1, 1862. Major, 64 NY Infantry, July 12, 1862. Commanded 4 Brigade, 1 Division, 2 Army Corps, Army of the Potomac, Jan. 10, 1864-Feb. 12, 1864. Lieutenant Colonel, 64 NY Infantry, May 4, 1864. GSW right

Leman W. Bradley
Roger D. Hunt Collection, USAMHI. F. Forshew, Photographer, Hudson, NY.

James Dennis Brady (postwar)
Civil War Library & Museum, Philadelphia, PA.

James Dennis Brady

Private, Co. A, 37 NY Infantry, June 6, 1861. 1 Lieutenant, Co. B, 63 NY Infantry, Dec. 6, 1861. 1 Lieutenant, Adjutant, 63 NY Infantry, Feb. 6, 1862. GSW head, Fredericksburg, VA, Dec. 13, 1862. Captain, Co. D, 63 NY Infantry, Feb. 11, 1863. Acting AIG, 3 Brigade, 1 Division, 2 Army Corps, Army of the Potomac, April 1863-April 1864. Captain, Co. B, 63 NY Infantry, June 12, 1863. Acting AIG, 4 Brigade, 1 Division, 2 Army Corps, April-June 1864 and Nov. 1864-April 1865. GSW left breast and left arm, Cold Harbor, VA, June 3, 1864 (same ball mortally wounded Colonel Richard Byrnes). Major, 63 NY Infantry, Sept. 18, 1864. Lieutenant Colonel, 63 NY Infantry, Oct. 15, 1864. Acting AIG, 3 Division, 2 Army Corps, April-June 1865. *Colonel*, 63 NY Infantry, May 18, 1865. Honorably mustered out, June 30, 1865.

Born: April 3, 1843 Portsmouth, VA
Died: Nov. 30, 1900 Petersburg, VA
Occupation: Merchant, accountant and lawyer
Offices/Honors: US Collector of Internal Revenue. US House of Representatives, 1885-87.
Miscellaneous: Resided New York City, NY; Portsmouth, Norfolk Co., VA; and Petersburg, Dinwiddie Co., VA
Buried: St. Joseph's Catholic Cemetery, Petersburg, VA
References: Pension File and Military Service File, National Archives. *Biographical Directory of the American Congress.* Joseph P. Brady. "A Brief Sketch of the Life of Colonel James D. Brady," *Journal of the American Irish Historical Society,* Vol. 9 (1910). David P. Conyngham. *The Irish Brigade and Its Campaigns.* Boston, MA, 1869. Letters Received, Volunteer Service Branch, Adjutant General's Office, File I343(VS)1863, National Archives.

Wesley Brainerd

Captain, Co. C, 50 NY Engineers, Sept. 17, 1861. Major, 50 NY Engineers, Nov. 28, 1862. GSW left arm, Fredericksburg, VA, Dec. 11, 1862. Colonel, 15 NY Engineers, Dec. 13, 1864. Honorably mustered out, June 14, 1865.

Born: Sept. 27, 1832 Rome, NY
Died: Aug. 19, 1910 Point Loma, CA
Occupation: Civil engineer engaged in railroad construction before war. Engaged in lumber manufacture and mining enterprises after war.

arm, Spotsylvania, VA, May 12, 1864. *Colonel,* 64 NY Infantry, July 4, 1864. Honorably mustered out, Oct. 5, 1864.

Born: March 6, 1820 Sharon, CT
Died: Aug. 13, 1912 Hudson, NY
Occupation: Engaged in the iron business and later the cutlery business
Miscellaneous: Resided Hudson, Columbia Co., NY
Buried: City Cemetery, Hudson, NY
References: Pension File, National Archives. Obituary, *Hudson Republican,* Aug. 14, 1912. Obituary, *Hudson Evening Register,* Aug. 14, 1912. Edmund J. Raus, Jr. *A Generation on the March: The Union Army at Gettysburg.* Gettysburg, PA, 1996. Letters Received, Volunteer Service Branch, Adjutant General's Office, File I219(VS)1863, National Archives.

Wesley Brainerd
Michael J. McAfee Collection.

Wesley Brainerd
Massachusetts MOLLUS Collection, USAMHI. Brady's National Photographic Portrait Gallery, 352 Pennsylvania Avenue, Washington, DC.

Miscellaneous: Resided Rome, Oneida Co., NY; Chicago, IL, 1865-76; Colorado (Boulder) and Nebraska, 1876-1905; and Point Loma, San Diego Co., CA, 1905-10

Buried: Rosehill Cemetery, Chicago, IL (Section N, Lot 91)

References: *Portrait and Biographical Record of the State of Colorado*. Chicago, IL, 1899. Pension File, National Archives. Obituary Circular, Whole No. 206, Colorado MOLLUS. Ed Malles, editor. *Bridge Building in Wartime: Colonel Wesley Brainerd's Memoir of the 50th New York Volunteer Engineers*. Knoxville, TN, 1997.

Francis H. Braulik

1 Lieutenant, RQM, 41 NY Infantry, June 6, 1861. Resigned Aug. 2, 1861. *Colonel*, 163 NY Infantry, Oct. 1862. Regiment never reaching full strength, it was consolidated with the 73 NY Infantry, Jan. 20, 1863. *Colonel*, Defenders, Feb. 11, 1863. Out of service, June 20, 1863, by consolidation with several other units to form the 178 NY Infantry.

Wesley Brainerd
Donald K. Ryberg Collection.

Born: 1831?
Died: ?
Buried: ?
References: Frederick Phisterer, compiler. *New York in the War of the Rebellion, 1861 to 1865*. Third Edition. Albany, NY, 1912. Letters Received, Volunteer Service Branch, Adjutant General's Office, File O133(VS)1863, National Archives. Military Service File, National Archives.

Knut Oscar Broady

Captain, Co. C, 61 NY Infantry, Sept. 19, 1861. Lieutenant Colonel, 61 NY Infantry, Sept. 30, 1862. *Colonel*, 61 NY Infantry, May 12, 1864. Commanded 1 Brigade, 1 Division, 2 Army Corps, Army of the Potomac, March 14-25, 1864 and Oct. 27-29, 1864. Commanded 4 Brigade, 1 Division, 2 Army Corps, July 25, 1864-Aug. 25, 1864. GSW right shoulder, Reams' Station, VA, Aug. 25, 1864. Honorably mustered out, Oct. 29, 1864. Bvt. Colonel, USV, Aug. 25, 1864, for good conduct throughout the campaign, and particularly for distinguished service at Reams' Station, VA.

Born: May 28, 1832 Upsala, Sweden
Died: March 13, 1922 Stockholm, Sweden
Education: Graduated Madison (now Colgate) University, Hamilton, NY, 1861
Occupation: Missionary of the American Baptist Foreign Missionary Society
Miscellaneous: Resided Mohawk, Herkimer Co., NY, to 1866; and Stockholm, Sweden, after 1866.
Buried: Norra Begrafningsplats, Stockholm, Sweden (Grave 6620)
References: Nels Hokanson. *Swedish Immigrants in Lincoln's Time*. New York and London, 1942. Pension File, National Archives. *The First Half Century of Madison University, 1819-1869*. New York and Boston, 1872. Letters Received, Volunteer Service Branch, Adjutant General's Office, File B579(VS)1862, National Archives.

Knut Oscar Broady
National Archives.

Knut Oscar Broady
New York State Military Museum and Veterans Research Center. J. B. Smith, Marble Block, Utica, NY.

Edwin Franklin Brown

Lieutenant Colonel, 28 NY Infantry, May 22, 1861. GSW left
arm (amputated), Cedar Mountain, VA, Aug. 9, 1862. Captured Culpeper, VA, Aug. 19, 1862. Confined Libby Prison,
Richmond, VA. Paroled Oct. 6, 1862. Colonel, 28 NY Infantry, Nov. 1, 1862. Honorably mustered out, June 2, 1863.

Born: April 23, 1823 Ridgeway, Orleans Co., NY
Died: Jan. 10, 1903 New York City, NY
Occupation: Farmer and grain merchant before war. Merchant
after war.
Offices/Honors: Governor, Central Branch, NHDVS, Dayton,
OH, 1869-80. Inspector General, NHDVS, 1880-1903.
Miscellaneous: Resided Medina, Orleans Co., NY;
Leavenworth, KS; and New York City, NY
Buried: Boxwood Cemetery, Medina, NY
References: Pension File, National Archives. Obituary Circu-
lar, Whole No. 545, Ohio MOLLUS. Obituary, *Orleans
Republican*, Jan. 14, 1903. Obituary, *New York Times*, Jan.
11, 1903. Charles W. Boyce. *A Brief History of the 28th
Regiment New York State Volunteers*. Buffalo, NY, 1896.

Edwin Franklin Brown
*Massachusetts MOLLUS Collection, USAMHI. Brady's National Photographic
Portrait Gallery, 352 Pennsylvania Avenue, Washington, DC.*

Edwin Franklin Brown
*Civil War Times Illustrated Collection, USAMHI. George P. Hopkins, Albion,
NY.*

Edwin Franklin Brown
A Brief History of the 28th Regiment New York State Volunteers.

Edwin Franklin Brown
Courtesy of Tom Molocea. George P. Hopkins, Albion, NY.

Edwin Franklin Brown (postwar)
A Brief History of the 28th Regiment New York State Volunteers.

James Malcolm Brown

Captain, Co. B, 72 NY Infantry, June 20, 1861. Honorably discharged, Nov. 5, 1861. Colonel, 100 NY Infantry, Jan. 10, 1862. GSW Fair Oaks, VA, May 31, 1862.

Born: Nov. 24, 1825 Dundee, Scotland
Died: May 31, 1862 KIA Fair Oaks, VA
Other Wars: Mexican War (Assistant Surgeon)
Occupation: Physician and lawyer
Miscellaneous: Resided Jamestown, Chautauqua Co., NY
Buried: Fair Oaks, VA (body never recovered)
References: William R. Cutter. *Genealogical and Family History of Western New York*. New York City, NY, 1912. George H. Stowits. *History of the 100th Regiment of New York State Volunteers*. Buffalo, NY, 1870. Obituary, *New York Daily Tribune*, June 5, 1862.

John Smith Brown

Private, Co. B, 1 US Sharpshooters, July 11, 1861. Sergeant Major, 1 US Sharpshooters, Aug. 2, 1861. 2 Lieutenant, Co. A, 1 US Sharpshooters, March 1, 1862. Resigned, Oct. 3, 1862, due to ill health from the effects of consumption. 1 Lieutenant, Adjutant, 126 NY Infantry, Sept. 2, 1862. Joined regiment, Nov. 17, 1862. Major, 126 NY Infantry, Nov. 13, 1863. Detached April 2, 1864 as Inspector General, State of Wisconsin. Lieutenant Colonel, 126 NY Infantry, April 18, 1864. *Colonel*, 126 NY Infantry, June 17, 1864. Returned to 126 NY Infantry, May 11, 1865. Honorably mustered out, June 3, 1865.

James Malcolm Brown
Roger D. Hunt Collection, USAMHI.

James Malcolm Brown
Roger D. Hunt Collection, USAMHI.

James Malcolm Brown
Roger D. Hunt Collection, USAMHI.

Born: July 16, 1835 Hammondsport, NY
Died: April 27, 1866 Jerusalem, Yates Co., NY
Education: Attended Yale University, New Haven, CT
Occupation: School teacher and law student
Miscellaneous: Resided Penn Yan, Yates Co., NY; and St. Louis, MO
Buried: Lakeview Cemetery, Penn Yan, NY
References: Obituary, *Yates County Chronicle*, May 3, 1866. Arabella M. Willson. *Disaster, Struggle, Triumph: The Adventures of 1000 "Boys in Blue."* Albany, NY, 1870. Wayne Mahood. *"Written in Blood," A History of the 126th New York Infantry in the Civil War.* Hightstown, NJ, 1997. Pension File and Military Service File, National Archives. Robert H. Graham, compiler. *Yates County's "Boys in Blue" 1861-1865, Who They Were-What They Did.* Penn Yan, NY, 1926.

William Rufus Brown

Colonel, 19 NY National Guard, May 26, 1862. Honorably mustered out, Sept. 6, 1862. Colonel, 168 NY Infantry, Feb. 11, 1863. Honorably mustered out, Oct. 31, 1863.

Born: June 24, 1819 Newburgh, NY
Died: Nov. 18, 1878 Newburgh, NY
Occupation: Engaged in the manufacture of lime
Offices/Honors: Brig. Gen., NY National Guard
Miscellaneous: Resided Newburgh, Orange Co., NY
Buried: Woodlawn Cemetery, New Windsor, NY (Section H, Lot 11)
References: Obituary, *Newburgh Daily Journal*, Nov. 18, 1878. *Portrait and Biographical Record of Orange County, NY.* New York and Chicago, 1895.

John Smith Brown
Courtesy of Henry Deeks.

Right: *William Rufus Brown (postwar)*
Courtesy of the author. Remillard's Gallery of Art, No. 82 Water Street, Newburgh, NY.

William Rufus Brown
Roger D. Hunt Collection, USAMHI. Kertson & Barker, 142 Chatham Street, New York.

William Cresap Browne

Colonel, 35 NY Infantry, June 3, 1861. Resigned Aug. 2, 1861.

Born: 1805? MD
Died: July 21, 1883 St. James, Suffolk Co., NY
Occupation: 2 Lieutenant, 8 US Infantry, July 7, 1838. 1 Lieutenant, 8 US Infantry, Oct. 1, 1840. Resigned Dec. 31, 1845. Later practiced law.
Miscellaneous: Resided Watertown, Jefferson Co., NY; and St. James, Suffolk Co., NY
Buried: Brookside Cemetery, Watertown, NY (Section E, Lot 22)
References: Military Service File, National Archives. Obituary, *Watertown Daily Times*, July 23, 1883. Joseph O. and Bernarr Cresap. *History of the Cresaps*. Gallatin, TN, 1987. John A. Haddock, compiler. *The Growth of a Century: As Illustrated in the History of Jefferson County*. Albany, NY, 1894.

Michael Kirk Bryan

Michael Kirk Bryan
Michael J. McAfee Collection.

Left: *William Rufus Brown*
Michael J. McAfee Collection. Remillard, No. 82 Water Street, Newburgh, NY.

Colonel, 25 NY State Militia, May 4, 1861. Honorably mustered out, Aug. 4, 1861. Colonel, 25 NY National Guard, May 31, 1862. Honorably mustered out, Sept. 8, 1862. Colonel, 175 NY Infantry, Sept. 24, 1862. Shell wounds both legs, Port Hudson, LA, June 14, 1863.

Born: Sept. 22, 1822 County Cork, Ireland
Died: June 14, 1863 KIA Port Hudson, LA
Occupation: Hotel and restaurant proprietor
Miscellaneous: Resided Albany, NY
Buried: Rural Cemetery, Albany, NY (Section 43, Lot 4)
References: Rufus W. Clark. *The Heroes of Albany*. Albany, NY, 1867. Obituary, *New York Times*, July 2, 1863. Pension File, National Archives.

Michael Kirk Bryan
Courtesy of Henry Deeks. S. J. Thompson & Co., Photographers, No. 478 Broadway, Albany, NY.

George Andrew Buckingham

Major, 71 NY State Militia, May 3, 1861. Honorably mustered out, July 31, 1861. Lieutenant Colonel, 53 NY Infantry, June 23, 1862. *Colonel*, 53 NY Infantry, Aug. 8, 1862. Organization discontinued and he was mustered out, Dec. 23, 1862. *Colonel*, 183 NY Infantry, March 26, 1864. Organization not completed and authority revoked, Aug. 3, 1864.

Born: Oct. 2, 1817 Hartford, CT
Died: Jan. 9, 1882 New York City, NY
Occupation: Dry goods merchant and auctioneer before war. Broker in foreign exchanges and gold after war.
Miscellaneous: Resided New York City, NY
Buried: Green-Wood Cemetery, Brooklyn, NY (Section 73, Lot 1171)
References: Obituary, *New York Times*, Jan. 11, 1882. F. W. Chapman. *The Buckingham Family*. Hartford, CT, 1872. Military Service File, National Archives.

George Andrew Buckingham
Roger D. Hunt Collection, USAMHI. J. Gurney & Son, Photographic Artists, 707 Broadway, New York.

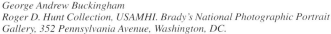

George Andrew Buckingham
Roger D. Hunt Collection, USAMHI. Brady's National Photographic Portrait Gallery, 352 Pennsylvania Avenue, Washington, DC.

Clarence Buel
Massachusetts MOLLUS Collection, USAMHI. Brady's National Photographic Portrait Gallery, Broadway & Tenth Street, New York.

Clarence Buel

Captain, Co. E, 2 NY Cavalry, Aug. 14, 1861. Colonel, 169 NY Infantry, Oct. 8, 1862. Commanded Provisional Brigade, Abercrombie's Division, Military District of Washington, Oct. 1862-Feb. 1863. Shell wound left hand, Suffolk, VA, April 24, 1863. Discharged for disability, Feb. 13, 1864, due to malarial and typhoid fever and the debilitating effects of his wound.

Born: Oct. 5, 1830 Troy, NY
Died: July 24, 1915 Williamstown, MA

Education: Attended Williams College, Williamstown, MA. Graduated Union College, Schenectady, NY, 1849.
Occupation: Lawyer before war. Episcopal clergyman after war.
Miscellaneous: Resided Troy, Rensselaer Co., NY; New York City, NY; Ossining, Westchester Co., NY; Cumberland, Allegany Co., MD; and Detroit, MI
Buried: Oakwood Cemetery, Troy, NY (Section I-1, Lot 78)
References: Albert Welles. *History of the Buell Family in England and in America*. New York City, NY, 1881. Pension File and Military Service File, National Archives. Obituary, *Troy Daily Times*, July 26, 1915. Obituary, *Union Alumni Monthly*, Vol. 5, No. 4 (Feb. 1916).

James Marsh Bull

Lieutenant Colonel, 126 NY Infantry, Aug. 15, 1862. Colonel, 126 NY Infantry, July 3, 1863. Commanded 3 Brigade, 3 Division, 2 Army Corps, Army of the Potomac, July 3, 1863-July 17, 1863. Discharged for disability, April 18, 1864, due to "lumbago, accompanied with general nervous irritability."

Born: 1825 Canandaigua, NY
Died: July 25, 1867 Canandaigua, NY
Occupation: Lawyer
Miscellaneous: Resided Canandaigua, Ontario Co., NY
Buried: Pioneer Cemetery, Canandaigua, NY
References: Arabella M. Willson. *Disaster, Struggle, Triumph: The Adventures of 1000 "Boys in Blue."* Albany, NY, 1870. Wayne Mahood. *"Written in Blood," A History of the 126th New York Infantry in the Civil War.* Hightstown, NJ, 1997. *Dedication of the New York Auxiliary State Monument on the Battlefield of Gettysburg.* Albany, NY, 1926. Military Service File, National Archives. Obituary, *Ontario Repository and Messenger*, July 31, 1867.

James Marsh Bull
Courtesy of Henry Deeks. R. W. Addis, Photographer, 308 Penna. Ave., Washington, DC.

Louis Burger

Lieutenant Colonel, 5 NY State Militia, May 1, 1861. Honorably mustered out, Aug. 7, 1861. Colonel, 5 NY National Guard, June 19, 1863. Honorably mustered out, July 22, 1863.

Born: Feb. 6, 1821 Kaiserlautern, Germany
Died: May 25, 1871 Brooklyn, NY
Occupation: Architect and builder
Offices/Honors: Brig. Gen., NY National Guard, 1866-71
Miscellaneous: Resided Brooklyn, NY. His full christian name was George Louis Burger.
Buried: Green-Wood Cemetery, Brooklyn, NY (Section F, Lots 21022-21023)
References: Obituary, *New York Times*, May 27, 1871. Obituary, *Brooklyn Daily Eagle*, May 29, 1871. Pension File, Department of Veterans Affairs.

Louis Burger
Michael J. McAfee Collection. Charles D. Fredricks & Co., "Specialite," 587 Broadway, New York.

Louis Burger
Michael J. McAfee Collection. Semsey & Co., 142 Bowery, New York.

Denis Francis Burke
Massachusetts MOLLUS Collection, USAMHI.

Denis Francis Burke

2 Lieutenant, Co. C, 88 NY Infantry, Sept. 30, 1861. 1 Lieutenant, Co. C, 88 NY Infantry, July 3, 1862. Captain, Co. C, 88 NY Infantry, Sept. 17, 1862. GSW left arm, Fredericksburg, VA, Dec. 13, 1862. Shell wound head, Chancellorsville, VA, May 3, 1863. Captain, Co. A, 88 NY Infantry, June 12, 1863. Lieutenant Colonel, 88 NY Infantry, July 13, 1864. GSW right knee, Fort Mahone, VA, Oct. 31, 1864. Commanded 2 Brigade, 1 Division, 2 Army Corps, Army of the Potomac, Nov. 2-5, 1864. *Colonel*, 88 NY Infantry, Nov. 15, 1864. Honorably mustered out, June 30, 1865. Bvt. Colonel, USV, April 9, 1865, for conspicuous gallantry in the engagement near Boydton Plank Road, VA, for efficient services on all subsequent occasions, and for particularly meritorious services during the campaign terminating with the surrender of the insurgent army under General Robert E. Lee.

Born: April 19, 1841 County Cork, Ireland
Died: Oct. 19, 1893 New York City, NY
Occupation: Dry goods merchant before war. Publisher and US Customs appraiser after war.
Miscellaneous: Resided New York City, NY
Buried: Woodlawn Cemetery, New York City, NY (Section 87, Locust Plot, Lot 8781)
References: Pension File, National Archives. Obituary, *New York Times*, Oct. 20, 1893. David P. Conyngham. *The Irish Brigade and Its Campaigns*. Boston, MA, 1869. William H. Powell, editor. *Officers of the Army and Navy (Volunteer) Who Served in the Civil War*. Philadelphia, PA, 1893.

James C. Burke

Private, Co. B, 13 NY State Militia, April 23, 1861. Honorably discharged, June 1, 1861. Captain, Co. I, 40 NY Infantry, June 26, 1861. Discharged for incompetency, Nov. 4, 1861. Appointed *Colonel*, 4 Regiment Empire Brigade, July 23, 1862. This regiment was assigned to the Corcoran Brigade and consolidated with other organizations to form the 164 NY Infantry. Lieutenant Colonel, 164 NY Infantry, Sept. 6, 1862. *Colonel*, 11 NY Infantry (reorganizing), May 18, 1863. Succeeded as colonel by Henry F. O'Brien, June 27, 1863. Dismissed July 21, 1863, for "forging the name of a special contractor to a subsistence bill" and "securing authority to remain away from his regiment" in order to avoid standing trial for "certain grave charges pending against him."

Born: 1829?

Died: ?
Occupation: Dry goods merchant
Miscellaneous: Resided Brooklyn, NY
Buried: ?
References: Military Service File, National Archives. Letters Received, Volunteer Service Branch, Adjutant General's Office, File O409(VS) 1863, National Archives.

John Burke

Captain, Co. A, 37 NY Infantry, May 14, 1861. Lieutenant Colonel, 37 NY Infantry, May 28, 1861. Colonel, 63 NY Infantry, Jan. 21, 1862. GSW left knee, Malvern Hill, VA, July 1, 1862. Commanded 2 Brigade, 1 Division, 2 Army Corps, Army of the Potomac, Sept. 17-18, 1862. Dismissed Oct. 20, 1862, for "misbehavior before the enemy" in "deserting his post ... while his regiment was engaged with the enemy" at Antietam, Sept. 17, 1862. Disability resulting from dismissal removed, Feb. 27, 1869.

Born: 1830? Ireland
Died: ?
Buried: ?
References: Military Service File, National Archives. Letters Received, Volunteer Service Branch, Adjutant General's Office, File J859(VS)1863, National Archives. A. Milburn Petty. "History of the 37th Regiment, New York Volunteers," *Journal of the American Irish Historical Society*, Vol. 31 (1937). David P. Conyngham. *The Irish Brigade and Its Campaigns*. Boston, MA, 1869.

Michael William Burns

Captain, Co. A, 73 NY Infantry, Aug. 14, 1861. Captured Gaines' Mill, VA, June 27, 1862. Confined Libby Prison, Richmond, VA. Exchanged Aug. 12, 1862. GSW left breast, Bristoe Station, VA, Aug. 27, 1862. Major, 73 NY Infantry, Nov. 1, 1862. Lieutenant Colonel, 73 NY Infantry, Jan. 16, 1863. *Colonel*, 73 NY Infantry, Oct. 27, 1864. Honorably mustered out, June 29, 1865. Bvt. Colonel, USV, April 6, 1865, for gallant services before Petersburg and at the battle of Little Sailor's Creek, VA.

Born: 1834 Ireland
Died: Dec. 7, 1883 New York City, NY
Occupation: City inspector and fireman before war. Weigher in New York Custom House and harbor master after war.
Miscellaneous: Resided New York City, NY
Buried: Calvary Cemetery, Long Island City, NY (Section 6, Range 20, Plot T)

References: Pension File and Military Service File, National Archives. Edmund J. Raus, Jr. *A Generation on the March: The Union Army at Gettysburg*. Gettysburg, Pa, 1996. "Col. M. W. Burns Dying," *New York Times,* Dec. 4, 1883.

Allen Lysander Burr

Captain, Co. I, 160 NY Infantry, Nov. 15, 1862. Discharged for disability, May 3, 1863. Lieutenant Colonel, 189 NY Infantry, Oct. 1, 1864. Colonel, 189 NY Infantry, Dec. 29, 1864. Commanded 2 Brigade, 1 Division, 5 Army Corps, Army of the Potomac, Jan. 22, 1865-Feb. 25, 1865. Honorably mustered out, June 1, 1865.

Born: Dec. 12, 1821 Camden, Allegany Co., NY
Died: Dec. 20, 1878 Caneadea, NY
Occupation: Canal contractor and farmer. Inspector in New York Custom House, 1871-76.
Miscellaneous: Resided Caneadea, Allegany Co., NY; and New York City, NY.
Buried: Caneadea Cemetery, Caneadea, NY
References: Obituary, *Allegany County Reporter*, Dec. 26, 1878. Pension File, National Archives. Mrs. Georgia D. Merrill, editor. *Allegany County and Its People: A Centennial Memorial History of Allegany County*. Alfred, NY, 1896. William H. Rogers. *History of the 189th Regiment of New York Volunteers*. New York City, NY, 1865.

Allen Lysander Burr
Courtesy of Alan J. Sessarego. Masterson & Wood, Arcade Gallery, Rochester, NY.

Charles H. Burtis
Strong's Pictorial and Biographical Record of the Great Rebellion.

Charles H. Burtis

Lieutenant Colonel, 74 NY Infantry, Sept. 2, 1861. *Colonel*, 74 NY Infantry, April 11, 1862. Discharged for disability, Sept. 18, 1862, on account of "exposure, fatigue, and fever contracted during the Peninsula Campaign." Colonel, 15 NY State Militia, June 6, 1864. Honorably mustered out, July 7, 1864.

Born: 1832? Oyster Bay, Long Island, NY
Died: June 2, 1893 Brooklyn, NY
Occupation: Engaged in placing railroad bonds and was connected with several corporations
Miscellaneous: Resided Brooklyn, NY
Buried: Green-Wood Cemetery, Brooklyn, NY (Sections 100/118, Lot 4295, family mausoleum)
References: Obituary, *New York Tribune*, June 3, 1893. Obituary, *Brooklyn Daily Eagle*, June 3, 1893. Julian K. Larke, editor. *Strong's Pictorial and Biographical Record of the Great Rebellion*. New York City, 1866?. Letters Received, Volunteer Service Branch, Adjutant General's Office, File P330(VS)1862, National Archives. Military Service File, National Archives.

John Germond Butler

Captain, Co. D, 3 NY Infantry, April 21, 1861. Lieutenant Colonel, 147 NY Infantry, Sept. 13, 1862. Colonel, 147 NY Infantry, Feb. 4, 1863. Discharged for disability, Nov. 5, 1863, due to chronic diarrhea.

Born: March 16, 1834 Utica, NY
Died: Oct. 4, 1917 Syracuse, NY
Other Wars: Spanish American War (Captain, Co. C, 3 NY Infantry)
Occupation: Bank teller before war. Cashier and accountant at Syracuse Water Works during last 27 years of his life.
Miscellaneous: Resided Glens Falls, NY; Annapolis, Anne Arundel Co., MD; and Syracuse, Onondaga Co., NY
Buried: St. Agnes Cemetery, Syracuse, NY (Section 25, Lot 274)
References: Obituary, *Syracuse Post-Standard*, Oct. 5, 1917. William M. Beauchamp. *Past and Present of Syracuse and Onondaga County, NY*. New York and Chicago, 1908. *The Union Army*. New York Edition. Madison, WI, 1908. Pension File, National Archives.

John Germond Butler
Roger D. Hunt Collection, USAMHI. Anson's, 589 Broadway, Opposite Metropolitan Hotel, New York.

John Byrne

Captain, Co. I, 155 NY Infantry, Sept. 6, 1862. Major, 155 NY
 Infantry, March 27, 1863. Lieutenant Colonel, 155 NY
 Infantry, Dec. 1, 1863. GSW left side of face, Spotsylvania,
 VA, May 18, 1864. Captured Reams' Station, VA, Aug.
 25, 1864. Confined at Richmond, VA, and Salisbury, NC.
 Paroled Feb. 22, 1865. *Colonel*, 155 NY Infantry, Jan. 1,
 1865. Honorably mustered out, July 15, 1865.

Born: June 24, 1840 County Wicklow, Ireland
Died: Dec. 30, 1909 Buffalo, NY
Occupation: Police detective and special agent. Chief of de-
 tectives for the American and United States Express Com-
 panies.
Offices/Honors: Chief of Buffalo Police Department, 1872-
 79
Miscellaneous: Resided Buffalo, NY
Buried: Post Cemetery, West Point, NY (Section 8, Row D,
 Grave 224)
References: Pension File, National Archives. Obituary Circu-
 lar, Whole No. 1017, New York MOLLUS. Obituary, *Buf-
 falo Morning Express*, Dec. 31, 1909.

John Byrne
Martin L. Schoenfeld Collection, USAMHI.

James Cameron

Colonel, 79 NY Infantry, May 29, 1861. GSW breast, 1st Bull
 Run, VA, July 21, 1861.

Born: March 1, 1800 Maytown, Lancaster Co., PA
Died: July 21, 1861 KIA 1st Bull Run, VA
Occupation: Newspaper editor and lawyer
Miscellaneous: Resided Lewisburg, Union Co., PA. Brother
 of Secretary of War Simon Cameron.
Buried: Lewisburg Cemetery, Lewisburg, PA
References: William J. Tenney. *Military and Naval History of
 the Rebellion in the United States*. New York City, NY,
 1865. William Todd. *The 79th Highlanders, New York
 Volunteers in the War of the Rebellion*. Albany, NY, 1886.
 Pension File, National Archives.

John Byrne
*USAMHI. Brady's National Photographic Portrait Gallery, 352 Pennsylvania
Avenue, Washington, DC.*

WE HOPE THAT YOU ENJOY THIS BOOK...and that it will occupy a proud place in your library. We would like to keep you informed about other publications from Schiffer Books. Please return this card with your requests and comments. **(Please print clearly in ink.)**
Note: We don't share our mailing list with anyone.

Title of Book Purchased _____

☐ Purchased at: _____ ☐ received as a gift

Comments or ideas for books you would like to see us publish: _____

_____

_____

Your Name: _____

Address _____

City _____ State _____ Zip _____ Country _____

E-mail Address _____
Please provide your email address to receive announcements of new releases

☐ Please send me a **free** Schiffer Antiques, Collectibles, & the Arts
☐ Please send me a **free** Schiffer Woodcarving, Woodworking, and Crafts Catalog
☐ Please send me a **free** Schiffer Military, Aviation, and Automotive History Catalog
☐ Please send me a **free** Schiffer Lifestyle, Design, and Body, Mind, & Spirit Catalog

See our most current books on the web at **www.schifferbooks.com**
Contact us at: Phone: 610-593-1777; Fax: 610-593-2002; or E-mail: info@schifferbooks.com
SCHIFFER BOOKS ARE CURRENTLY AVAILABLE FROM YOUR BOOKSELLER

Printed in China

K:\user\dtp\wp\basic\bounceback

For the latest releases and
thousands of books in print,
fill out the back of this card
and return it today!

SCHIFFER PUBLISHING LTD
4880 LOWER VALLEY ROAD
ATGLEN, PA 19310-9917 USA

James Cameron
Massachusetts MOLLUS Collection, USAMHI.

James Cameron
Massachusetts MOLLUS Collection, USAMHI. Brady's National Photographic
Portrait Gallery, 352 Pennsylvania Avenue, Washington, DC.

Walter Bicker Camp

Colonel, 94 NY Infantry, Oct. 1861. Succeeded by Colonel
John J. Viele, Nov. 4, 1861.

Born: Oct. 1, 1822 Sackets Harbor, NY
Died: Jan. 28, 1916 Sackets Harbor, NY
Occupation: Druggist before war. Engaged in railroad enter-
prises after war.
Miscellaneous: Resided Sackets Harbor, Jefferson Co., NY
Buried: Sackets Harbor Cemetery, Sackets Harbor, NY
References: Obituary, *Watertown Daily Times*, Jan. 28, 1916.
John W. Leonard, editor. *Who's Who in New York City and
State*. New York City, NY, 1907. W. H. Horton, editor.
*Geographical Gazetteer of Jefferson County, NY, 1684-
1890*. Syracuse, NY, 1890.

Walter Bicker Camp
Geographical Gazetteer of Jefferson County, NY, 1684-1890.

James Cameron
Roger D. Hunt Collection, USAMHI.

James Cameron
USAMHI.

Madison Mott Cannon

Corporal, Co. I, 1 NJ Infantry, June 4, 1861. 2 Lieutenant, Co. G, 40 NY Infantry, Aug. 11, 1862. 1 Lieutenant, Adjutant, 40 NY Infantry, Oct. 13, 1862. Captain, Co. E, 40 NY Infantry, Feb. 23, 1863. GSW left side, Gettysburg, PA, July 2, 1863. Major, 40 NY Infantry, July 6, 1864. Lieutenant Colonel, 40 NY Infantry, Sept. 15, 1864. *Colonel*, 40 NY Infantry, Sept. 16, 1864. Honorably mustered out, June 27, 1865.

Madison Mott Cannon
Courtesy of Jacqueline T. Eubanks. Anson's, 589 Broadway, Opposite Metropolitan Hotel, New York.

Born: Feb. 17, 1840 Salisbury Mills, Orange Co., NY

Died: Feb. 11, 1892 Englewood, NJ

Education: Attended New York Free Academy, New York City, NY

Occupation: Printer before war. Printer and US Customs clerk after war.

Miscellaneous: Resided Hoboken, NJ; Brooklyn, NY; and Pigeon Cove, Essex Co., MA

Buried: Locust Grove Cemetery, Pigeon Cove, MA

References: Pension File, National Archives. Obituary circular, Whole No. 366, New York MOLLUS. Fred C. Floyd. *History of the 40th (Mozart) Regiment New York Volunteers*. Boston, MA, 1909.

Madison Mott Cannon
Paul Russinoff Collection. M. H. Kimball, Photographer, 477 Broadway, New York.

Madison Mott Cannon
Shelby County Historical Society Collection, USAMHI.

Madison Mott Cannon (postwar)
History of the 40th (Mozart) Regiment New York Volunteers.

James Campbell Carmichael

Major, 157 NY Infantry, Aug. 23, 1862. Assistant Commissary of Musters, Staff of Major Gen. Carl Schurz, June-Aug. 1863. Lieutenant Colonel, 157 NY Infantry, July 2, 1863. Commanded Fort Pulaski, GA, Oct. 27-Nov. 28, 1864. Commanded Post of Georgetown, SC, March-April 1865. *Colonel*, 157 NY Infantry, June 8, 1865. Honorably mustered out, July 10, 1865.

Born: Aug. 30, 1829 Mayfield, Fulton Co., NY

Died: Oct. 2, 1889 Cortland, NY

Occupation: Furniture dealer and agricultural implement manufacturer

Miscellaneous: Resided Cortland, Cortland Co., NY; and Phelps, Ontario Co., NY

Buried: Cortland Rural Cemetery, Cortland, NY (Section L, Lot 9)

References: *Souvenir Memorial, Col. James C. Carmichael, 157th Regiment N. Y. S. V.* N.p., 1891. Pension File and Military Service File, National Archives. Letters Received, Volunteer Service Branch, Adjutant General's Office, File G623(VS)1863, National Archives. Isabel Bracy. *157th New York Volunteer (Infantry) Regiment*. Interlaken, NY, 1991.

James Campbell Carmichael
Courtesy of the author.

James Campbell Carmichael
Roger D. Hunt Collection, USAMHI.

James Campbell Carmichael (postwar)
Souvenir Memorial, Col. James C. Carmichael, 157th Regiment N. Y. S. V.

Howard Carroll
Meade Album, Civil War Library & Museum, Philadelphia, PA.

David J. Caw
Report of the 43rd Annual Reunion of the Survivors Association of the 77th Regiment New York State Infantry Volunteers of 1861-65.

Howard Carroll

Quartermaster, 2 Battalion, NY Light Artillery, Oct. 17, 1861. Lieutenant Colonel, 105 NY Infantry, March 27, 1862. *Colonel*, 105 NY Infantry, Aug. 2, 1862. GSW left leg, Antietam, MD, Sept. 17, 1862.

Born: 1827? Dublin, Ireland
Died: Sept. 29, 1862 DOW Washington, DC
Education: Graduated Trinity College, University of Dublin, Ireland, 1846
Occupation: Civil engineer connected with the New York Central Railroad
Miscellaneous: Resided Albany, NY
Buried: Rural Cemetery, Albany, NY (Section 33, Lot 2)
References: Rufus W. Clark. *The Heroes of Albany*. Albany, NY, 1867. Franklin B. Hough. *History of Duryee's Brigade*. Albany, NY, 1864. Pension File, National Archives.

David J. Caw

1 Sergeant, Co. H, 77 NY Infantry, Oct. 1, 1861. 2 Lieutenant, Co. H, 77 NY Infantry, Jan. 30, 1862. 1 Lieutenant, Co. H, 77 NY Infantry, May 31, 1862. Captain, Co. E, 77 NY Infantry, Oct. 4, 1862. Captain, Co. H, 77 NY Infantry, Dec. 28, 1862. Major, 77 NY Infantry, Nov. 19, 1864. Lieutenant Colonel, 77 NY Infantry, Dec. 13, 1864. *Colonel*, 77 NY Infantry, Jan. 1, 1865. GSW left arm, Petersburg, VA, April 2, 1865. Honorably mustered out, June 27, 1865. Bvt. Colonel, USV, April 2, 1865, for gallant and meritorious services before Petersburg, VA.

Born: Sept. 2, 1835 Scotia, Schenectady Co., NY
Died: May 18, 1882 Brooklyn, NY
Occupation: School teacher before war. Returning to Schenectady after the war, he served several years as Chief of Police, after which he moved to New York City, where he was Superintendent of the Wagner Coach Co. at Grand Central Depot and later foreman in the Weigher's Department of the New York Custom House.
Miscellaneous: Resided Schenectady, NY; and New York City, NY
Buried: 1st Reformed Dutch Churchyard, Scotia, NY
References: Obituary, *New York Times*, May 19, 1882. Obituary, *Brooklyn Daily Eagle*, May 19, 1882. Military Service File, National Archives. *Report of the 43rd Annual Reunion of the Survivors Association of the 77th Regiment New York State Infantry Volunteers of 1861-65*. N.p., 1915.

James Roswell Chamberlin

1 Sergeant, Co. H, 3 NY Cavalry, Aug. 31, 1861. 2 Lieutenant, Co. C, 3 NY Cavalry, Sept. 7, 1861. 1 Lieutenant, Co. F, 3 NY Cavalry, Dec. 30, 1862. Captain, Co. A, 3 NY Cavalry, March 3, 1863. GSW left hip, Petersburg, VA, June 15, 1864. Honorably mustered out, Aug. 13, 1864. *Colonel*, 188 NY Infantry, Sept. 14, 1864. Succeeded by Colonel John McMahon, Oct. 12, 1864.

Born: 1825? Troy, NY
Died: Jan. 29, 1910 Rochester, NY
Education: Attended Rensselaer Polytechnic Institute, Troy, NY (Class of 1847)
Occupation: Lumber merchant
Miscellaneous: Resided Rochester, NY
Buried: Pittsford Cemetery, Pittsford, NY (Section C, Lot 44)
References: Obituary, *Rochester Democrat and Chronicle*, Jan. 30, 1910. Pension File, National Archives.

William Richard Washington Chambers

1 Lieutenant, Co. E, 11 NY Infantry, April 20, 1861. Resigned Sept. 30, 1861. Colonel, 93 NY National Guard, July 20, 1864. Honorably mustered out, Nov. 1, 1864.

Born: Aug. 11, 1830 New York City, NY
Died: March 13, 1894 New York City, NY
Occupation: Chief clerk in the New York City Register's Office before war. Resumed clerkship after war and later became Recording Clerk in the County Clerk's office.
Miscellaneous: Resided New York City, NY
Buried: Evergreens Cemetery, Brooklyn, NY (Whispering Grove Section, Lot 247)
References: Pension File, National Archives. Obituary, *New York Herald*, March 14, 1894.

Gurden Chapin

Captain, 7 US Infantry, April 22, 1861. Major, 14 US Infantry, May 18, 1864. *Colonel*, 25 NY Cavalry, Oct. 31, 1864. Resigned volunteer commission, Feb. 10, 1865.

Born: Feb. 17, 1831 Lexington, VA
Died: Aug. 22, 1875 Culpeper, VA
Education: Graduated US Military Academy, West Point, NY, 1851
Occupation: Regular Army (Major, 32 US Infantry, retired Jan. 27, 1869)

Gurden Chapin
The Gilder Lehrman Collection on deposit at the Pierpont Morgan Library, New York. Gentile, Portrait and Landscape Photographer, S. E. Corner State & Washington St., Chicago, IL.

Miscellaneous: Resided Culpeper, VA. Son-in-law of Brig. Gen. Gabriel R. Paul.
Buried: Culpeper National Cemetery, Culpeper, VA (Plot 1359)
References: Gilbert W. Chapin, compiler. *The Chapin Book of Genealogical Data*. Hartford, CT, 1924. Constance Wynn Altshuler. *Cavalry Yellow & Infantry Blue*. Tucson, AZ, 1991. Pension File, National Archives. *Annual Reunion*, Association of the Graduates of the US Military Academy, 1876.

Alford B. Chapman

Private, Co. D, 7 NY State Militia, April 26, 1861. Honorably mustered out, June 3, 1861. Captain, Co. A, 57 NY Infantry, Sept. 12, 1861. Major, 57 NY Infantry, Feb. 3, 1862. Lieutenant Colonel, 57 NY Infantry, Sept. 17, 1862. Contused GSW left breast, Fredericksburg, VA, Dec. 11, 1862.

Alford B. Chapman
Massachusetts MOLLUS Collection, USAMHI. Published by E. Anthony, 501 Broadway, New York, from Photographic Negative in Brady's National Portrait Gallery.

Edmund Cobb Charles
US Military Academy Library. Charles D. Fredricks & Co., "Specialite," 587 Broadway, New York.

Colonel, 57 NY Infantry, April 24, 1863. GSW Wilderness, VA, May 5, 1864.

Born: Aug. 1, 1835 New York City, NY
Died: May 5, 1864 KIA Wilderness, VA
Occupation: Merchant dealing in fancy goods
Miscellaneous: Resided New York City, NY
Buried: Green-Wood Cemetery, Brooklyn, NY (Section 169, Lots 13800-13803)
References: Gilbert Frederick. *The Story of a Regiment*. Chicago, IL, 1895. Obituary, *New York Tribune*, May 12, 1864. Military Service File, National Archives. Letters Received, Volunteer Service Branch, Adjutant General's Office, File I74(VS)1863, National Archives.

Edmund Cobb Charles

Lieutenant Colonel, 25 NY Infantry, May 21, 1861. Resigned Oct. 4, 1861. Colonel, 42 NY Infantry, Dec. 18, 1861. GSW left groin, White Oak Swamp, VA, June 30, 1862. Captured White Oak Swamp, VA, June 30, 1862. Confined Libby Prison, Richmond, VA. Paroled July 17, 1862. Discharged for disability, March 17, 1863, due to effects of wound.

Born: 1821? NY
Died: April 25, 1863 New York City, NY
Miscellaneous: Resided Eastchester, Westchester Co., NY; and New York City, NY
Buried: Green-Wood Cemetery, Brooklyn, NY (Section K, Lot 13501)
References: Obituary, *New York Times*, April 27, 1863. William J. Tenney. *Military and Naval History of the Rebellion in the United States*. New York City, NY, 1865. Military Service File, National Archives.

*Edmund Cobb Charles
Donald K. Ryberg Collection.*

Above: *Edmund Cobb Charles
Courtesy of Dave Zullo. Charles D.
Fredricks & Co., "Specialite," 587
Broadway, New York.*

Right: *Edmund Cobb Charles
Massachusetts MOLLUS Collection,
USAMHI. Published by E. Anthony, 501
Broadway, New York, from Photo-
graphic Negative in Brady's National
Portrait Gallery.*

Harvey Strong Chatfield

Private, Co. G, 7 NY State Militia, April 26, 1861. Honorably mustered out, June 3, 1861. Captain, Co. K, 43 NY Infantry, Aug. 30, 1861. Resigned July 16, 1862. Captain, Co. A, 78 NY Infantry, Aug. 1, 1863. Captain, Co. B, 78 NY Infantry, Oct. 20, 1863. Lieutenant Colonel, 78 NY Infantry, Nov. 30, 1863. Lieutenant Colonel, 102 NY Infantry, July 12, 1864. Colonel, 102 NY Infantry, Jan. 7, 1865. Honorably mustered out, July 21, 1865.

Born: July 15, 1837 Laurens, Otsego Co., NY
Died: Nov. 2, 1901 New York City, NY
Education: Attended Rensselaer Polytechnic Institute, Troy, NY. Graduated New York University Law School, 1860.
Occupation: Lawyer
Miscellaneous: Resided New York City, NY; Hoosick Falls, Rensselaer Co., NY, 1872-77; and Arlington, Hudson Co., NJ, 1878-84
Buried: Woodlands Cemetery, Cambridge, NY (Section T, Lots 18-20)
References: Pension File, National Archives. Death notice, *New York Times*, Nov. 4, 1901.

Harvey Strong Chatfield
Courtesy of Gil Barrett. Brady's National Photographic Portrait Gallery, 352 Pennsylvania Avenue, Washington, DC.

Above: *Harvey Strong Chatfield*
Roger D. Hunt Collection, USAMHI. J. Gurney & Son, Photographic Artists, 707 Broadway, New York.

Left: *Harvey Strong Chatfield*
Courtesy of the author.

George Foote Chester

Private, Co. H, 71 NY State Militia, April 21, 1861. Honorably mustered out, July 30, 1861. Captain, Co. D, 53 NY Infantry, Oct. 26, 1861. Lieutenant Colonel, 53 NY Infantry, Feb. 24, 1862. Honorably mustered out, March 24, 1862. Colonel, 101 NY Infantry, July 25, 1862. Honorably mustered out, Dec. 24, 1862.

Born: Jan. 28, 1828 Lawrenceville, Gwinnett Co., GA
Died: Dec. 19, 1889 San Mateo, FL
Education: Graduated Yale University, New Haven, CT, 1846
Occupation: School teacher and lawyer before war. Lawyer and petroleum dealer after war.

Offices/Honors: One of the founders of the Delta Kappa Epsilon fraternity
Miscellaneous: Resided New York City, NY; Titusville, Crawford Co., PA; Cleveland, OH; and San Mateo, Putnam Co., FL
Buried: San Mateo Cemetery, San Mateo, FL
References: *Obituary Record of Graduates of Yale College Deceased During the Academical Year Ending June 1890.* Pension File and Military Service File, National Archives. *Catalogue of the Delta Kappa Epsilon Fraternity. Biographical and Statistical.* New York City, NY, 1890.

Peter J. Claassen

Captain, Co. I, 83 NY Infantry, July 16, 1861. Acting AIG, Staff of Major Gen. Nathaniel P. Banks. Resigned May 22, 1862 for "personal reasons." Colonel, 132 NY Infantry, July 23, 1862. Honorably mustered out, June 29, 1865.

Born: 1827? Arnheim, Netherlands
Died: Dec. 29, 1896 Brooklyn, NY
Education: Attended University of Heidelberg, Germany
Occupation: Engaged in the printing business in Chicago, IL, 1866-73, and Canton, Stark Co., OH, 1873-75. Then removed to Brooklyn, NY, where he was a banker and stock broker.
Miscellaneous: Resided Brooklyn, NY, 1875-96. Sentenced to prison for misappropriation of funds after the failure of the Sixth National Bank, of which he was a director, he was pardoned by President Grover Cleveland in 1893.

George Foote Chester
Roger D. Hunt Collection, USAMHI. R. A. Lewis, 152 Chatham Street, New York.

Peter J. Claassen
Roger D. Hunt Collection, USAMHI. J. Gurney & Son, Photographic Artists, 707 Broadway, New York.

Buried: Original interment, Green-Wood Cemetery, Brooklyn, NY. Removed from Green-Wood Cemetery, June 1, 1897. Final resting place unknown.

References: Obituary, *New York Herald*, Jan. 1, 1897. Pension File, National Archives. Obituary, *New York Times*, Jan. 1, 1897. Letters Received, Volunteer Service Branch, Adjutant General's Office, File R629(VS)1862, National Archives.

Charles Henry Clark

Colonel, 54 NY National Guard, July 26, 1864. Honorably mustered out, Nov. 10, 1864.

Born: June 11, 1817 Saybrook, CT
Died: Nov. 20, 1873 Rochester, NY
Occupation: Lawyer
Offices/Honors: Mayor of Rochester, NY, 1858
Miscellaneous: Resided Rochester, Monroe Co., NY
Buried: Mount Hope Cemetery, Rochester, NY (Section E, Lot 47)
References: Blake McKelvey. "Rochester Mayors Before the Civil War," *Rochester History*, Vol. 26, No. 1 (Jan. 1964). Obituary, *Rochester Union and Advertiser*, Nov. 21, 1873. Kathlyne K. Viele. *Viele Records, 1613-1913*. New York City, NY, 1913.

Robert Bruce Clark

Lieutenant Colonel, 13 NY State Militia, May 17, 1861. Honorably mustered out, Aug. 6, 1861. Colonel, 13 NY National Guard, May 28, 1862. Honorably mustered out, Sept. 12, 1862.

Born: Nov. 20, 1823 Elizabeth, NJ
Died: March 9, 1896 Brooklyn, NY
Occupation: Civil engineer and real estate broker
Miscellaneous: Resided Brooklyn, NY
Buried: Green-Wood Cemetery, Brooklyn, NY (Section 61, Lot 747)
References: Pension File, National Archives. Obituary, *Brooklyn Daily Eagle*, March 9, 1896. James De Mandeville, compiler. *History of the 13th Regiment, N.G., S.N.Y.* New York City, NY, 1894.

Robert Bruce Clark
Michael J. McAfee Collection.

Robert Bruce Clark
History of the 13th Regiment, N.G., S.N.Y.

Robert Bruce Clark
Michael J. McAfee Collection.

William W. Clarke
Roger D. Hunt Collection, USAMHI. Finley & Son, Photographers, Canandaigua, NY.

William W. Clarke

Captain, Co. B, 85 NY Infantry, Aug. 29, 1861. Lieutenant Colonel, 85 NY Infantry, March 24, 1863. *Colonel*, 85 NY Infantry, May 15, 1865. Honorably mustered out, June 27, 1865.

Born: June 22, 1826 Naples, NY
Died: April 26, 1897 Brooklyn, NY
Occupation: Farmer and US Customs official
Miscellaneous: Resided Naples, Ontario Co., NY; Canandaigua, Ontario Co., NY; Brooklyn, NY; and New York City, NY
Offices/Honors: Sheriff of Ontario Co., NY, 1867-70
Buried: Rose Ridge Cemetery, Naples, NY
References: Pension File, National Archives. Obituary, *Naples Record*, April 28, 1897. *Diary of Caroline Cowles Richards, 1852-1872*. N.p., 1908. Wayne Mahood. *The Plymouth Pilgrims: A History of the 85th New York Infantry in the Civil War.* Hightstown, NJ, 1989.

William W. Clarke
Roger D. Hunt Collection, USAMHI. Finley & Sons, Photographers, Main Street, Canandaigua, NY.

William W. Clarke
Diary of Caroline Cowles Richards, 1852-1872.

William Bloomfield Coan
USAMHI. R. A. Lewis, 152 Chatham Street, New York.

William Bloomfield Coan

Private, Co. I, 7 NY State Militia, May 13, 1861. Honorably mustered out, June 3, 1861. Captain, Co. E, 48 NY Infantry, Aug. 27, 1861. Major, 48 NY Infantry, July 18, 1863. Lieutenant Colonel, 48 NY Infantry, June 9, 1864. Colonel, 48 NY Infantry, Dec. 3, 1864. Commanded 2 Brigade, 2 Division, 10 Army Corps, Army of the James, July 2, 1864-Aug. 28, 1864. GSW scalp, Fort Fisher, NC, Jan. 15, 1865. Commanded 2 Brigade, 2 Division, 10 Army Corps, Department of North Carolina, March 27, 1865-April 5, 1865, and June 9, 1865-July 18, 1865. Commanded 2 Division, 10 Army Corps, July 18, 1865-Aug. 1, 1865. Honorably mustered out, Sept. 1, 1865. Bvt. Colonel, USV, March 13, 1865, for gallant and meritorious conduct at the storming of Fort Fisher, NC.

Born: Oct. 12, 1830 Exeter, Penobscot Co., ME
Died: Jan. 28, 1877 Lawrence, MA
Occupation: Restaurant keeper before war. Grocer after war.
Miscellaneous: Resided New York City, NY; and Lawrence, Essex Co., MA
Buried: Bellevue Cemetery, Lawrence, MA (Section 5, Lot 30)
References: Abraham J. Palmer. *History of the 48th Regiment New York State Volunteers*. Brooklyn, NY, 1885. James M. Nichols. *Perry's Saints; or, the Fighting Parson's Regiment in the War of the Rebellion*. Boston, MA, 1886. Ruth C. Fulton. *Coan Genealogy*. Portsmouth, NH, 1982. Military Service File, National Archives.

William Bloomfield Coan
Courtesy of Gil Barrett.

William Bloomfield Coan
Courtesy of the author. C. D. Fredricks & Co., 587 Broadway, New York.

William Bloomfield Coan
Courtesy of Gil Barrett. C. D. Fredricks & Co., 587 Broadway, New York.

John Samuel Cocks

Colonel, 40 NY Infantry, June 14, 1861. Resigned June 29, 1861, "on account of mutual dissatisfaction between himself and some of his officers."

Born: 1813 NY

Died: April 5, 1863 Brooklyn, NY

Occupation: Wood turner

Offices/Honors: NY State Assembly, 1855

Miscellaneous: Resided New York City, NY; and Brooklyn, NY

Buried: Green-Wood Cemetery, Brooklyn, NY (Sections 157/158, Lot 14387)

References: George W. Cocks. *History and Genealogy of the Cock-Cocks-Cox Family*. New York City, NY, 1914. Death notice, *New York Herald*, April 7, 1863. *Report Annual Reunion and Dinner of the Old Guard Association, 12th Regiment, N. G. S. N. Y.* New York City, NY, 1894. Fred C. Floyd. *History of the 40th (Mozart) Regiment New York Volunteers*. Boston, MA, 1909.

John Samuel Cocks
Report Annual Reunion and Dinner of the Old Guard Association, 12th Regiment, N. G. S. N. Y.

Matthias W. Cole

Colonel, 52 NY National Guard, June 19, 1863. Honorably mustered out, July 25, 1863.

Born: Feb. 10, 1825 Brooklyn, NY
Died: April 13, 1891 Brooklyn, NY
Other Wars: Mexican War (Quartermaster Sergeant, 3 US Dragoons)
Occupation: Clerk in Brooklyn municipal tax office
Offices/Honors: Deputy Registrar of Arrears
Miscellaneous: Resided Brooklyn, NY
Buried: Evergreens Cemetery, Brooklyn, NY (Prospect Hill Section, Lot 89, unmarked)
References: Obituary, *Brooklyn Daily Eagle*, April 14, 1891. Pension File, National Archives.

Clinton Gilbert Colgate

Private, Co. C, 7 NY State Militia, April 30, 1861. Honorably mustered out, June 3, 1861. Major, 15 NY Engineers, June 25, 1861. Lieutenant Colonel, 15 NY Engineers, Sept. 14, 1861. Colonel, 15 NY Engineers, Dec. 12, 1862. Honorably mustered out, June 25, 1863.

Born: Sept. 25, 1834 New York City, NY
Died: Nov. 25, 1886 New York City, NY
Occupation: Purser on ocean steamer before war. US Internal Revenue service after war.
Offices/Honors: Assistant Assessor of Internal Revenue, 1870
Miscellaneous: Resided New York City, NY
Buried: Green-Wood Cemetery, Brooklyn, NY (Section 83, Lot 3361, unmarked)
References: Truman Abbe and Hubert A. Howson, compilers. *Robert Colgate, The Immigrant*. New Haven, CT, 1941. Pension File, National Archives. Obituary, *New York Daily Tribune*, Nov. 27, 1886.

Spencer Wallace Cone

Colonel, 61 NY Infantry, Oct. 26, 1861. Discharged April 14, 1862, upon "adverse report of a Board of Examination," which reported that his "management of the business and economy of his regiment is not as it should be, nor do his officers have confidence in his general capacity either in the field or camp for the reason that they believe him to

Clinton Gilbert Colgate
Massachusetts MOLLUS Collection, USAMHI. Published by E. Anthony, 501 Broadway, New York, from Photographic Negative in Brady's National Portrait Gallery.

lack self reliance and the ability to command men." Captain, Commissary of Subsistence, Staff of Brig. Gen. William Hall, NY National Guard, June 18, 1863. Honorably mustered out, July 23, 1863.

Born: May 25, 1819 Alexandria, VA
Died: Jan. 21, 1888 New York City, NY
Education: Attended New York University
Occupation: Journalist and poet
Miscellaneous: Resided New York City, NY
Buried: Green-Wood Cemetery, Brooklyn, NY (Section 171, Lot 11581, unmarked)
References: William Whitney Cone, compiler. *Some Account of the Cone Family in America.* Topeka, KS, 1903. Military Service File, National Archives. Letters Received, Volunteer Service Branch, Adjutant General's Office, File W157(VS)1862, National Archives. Sophia (Smith) Martin. *Mack Genealogy.* Rutland, VT, 1903.

Felix Confort

Lieutenant Colonel, Enfants Perdus, Independent Battalion, NY Infantry, April 4, 1862. *Colonel*, Enfants Perdus, Independent Battalion, NY Infantry, Jan. 17, 1863. Resigned May 9, 1863, due to "the bad spirit reigning amongst the offic-

ers" and also due to "the invincible difficulty of the English language ... so that even the Regulations remain a riddle to me."

Born: 1812? France
Died: March 14, 1870 Washington, DC
Other Wars: Crimean War
Occupation: Military service of France
Buried: Soldiers Home National Cemetery, Washington, DC (Section I, Grave 5664)
References: Death Notice, *Washington Daily Morning Chronicle*, March 15, 1870. Military Service File, National Archives. Letters Received, Volunteer Service Branch, Adjutant General's Office, File N165(VS)1862, National Archives.

Anthony Conk

Colonel, 139 NY Infantry, July 28, 1862. Resigned July 29, 1863, "on account of pressing private business."

Born: Oct. 7, 1822 NJ
Died: Aug. 9, 1894 Brooklyn, NY
Occupation: Carpenter
Miscellaneous: Resided Brooklyn, NY
Buried: Green-Wood Cemetery, Brooklyn, NY (Section 84, Lot 9995)
References: Obituary, *Brooklyn Daily Eagle*, Aug. 10, 1894. Pension File, National Archives.

Anthony Conk
Courtesy of Dave Zullo.

Frederick Augustus Conkling
Courtesy of Brian Caplan. American Porcelain Photographic Company, 653 Broadway, New York.

Frederick Augustus Conkling
Collection of The New-York Historical Society. Published by E. Anthony, 501 Broadway, New York, from Photographic Negative in Brady's National Portrait Gallery.

Freeman Conner (in the uniform of the prewar US Zouave Cadets)
Michael J. McAfee Collection.

Frederick Augustus Conkling

Colonel, 84 NY National Guard, July 3, 1863. Honorably mustered out, Aug. 4, 1863. Colonel, 84 NY National Guard, July 13, 1864. Honorably mustered out, Oct. 29, 1864.

Born: Aug. 22, 1816 Canajoharie, NY
Died: Sept. 18, 1891 New York City, NY
Occupation: Dry goods merchant, banker and politician
Offices/Honors: NY State Assembly, 1854, 1859-60. US House of Representatives, 1861-63.
Miscellaneous: Resided New York City, NY. Brother of US Senator Roscoe Conkling.
Buried: Green-Wood Cemetery, Brooklyn, NY (Sections 152/158, Lot 17959)
References: *Biographical Directory of the American Congress.* Obituary, *New York Tribune*, Sept. 19, 1891.

Freeman Conner

1 Lieutenant, Co. D, 11 NY Infantry, April 20, 1861. Captain, Co. D, 44 NY Infantry, Aug. 12, 1861. Major, 44 NY Infantry, July 4, 1862. Lieutenant Colonel, 44 NY Infantry, July 14, 1862. GSW right arm, Fredericksburg, VA, Dec. 13, 1862. Discharged for disability caused by wounds, April 3, 1863. Lieutenant Colonel, 44 NY Infantry, May 12, 1863. *Colonel*, 44 NY Infantry, Aug. 27, 1863. GSW left breast, Laurel Hill, VA, May 8, 1864. Honorably mustered out, Oct. 11, 1864.

Born: March 2, 1836 Exeter, NH
Died: March 28, 1906 Chicago, IL
Occupation: Commission merchant and farmer
Miscellaneous: Resided Exeter, Rockingham Co., NH; Chicago, IL; and Valparaiso, Porter Co., IN
Buried: Graceland Cemetery, Valparaiso, IN (Clear View Section, Lot 135)

Freeman Conner
Roger D. Hunt Collection, USAMHI. Black & Case, Photographic Artists,
163 & 173 Washington Street, Boston, MA.

References: Pension File and Military Service File, National
Archives. Obituary, *Chicago Daily Tribune*, March 30,
1906. *Memorials of Deceased Companions of the
Commandery of Illinois, MOLLUS*, From July 1, 1901 to
Dec. 31, 1911. Chicago, IL, 1912.

Freeman Conner (postwar)
Memorials of Deceased Companions of the Commandery of Illinois, MOLLUS.

Freeman Conner (seated,
center) with Officers of the
44th New York
Ronn Palm Collection.

Joseph Speed Conrad

1 Lieutenant, 2 US Infantry, May 14, 1861. Assistant Commissary of Subsistence, Staff of Brig. Gen. Nathaniel Lyon, June-Aug. 1861. GSW Wilson's Creek, MO, Aug. 10, 1861. Captain, 2 US Infantry, Nov. 1, 1861. Lieutenant Colonel, Additional ADC, May 5, 1862. Honorably mustered out of volunteer service, Jan. 21, 1864. Acting AAG, 1 Brigade, 1 Division, 5 Army Corps, Army of the Potomac, April 20-June 5, 1864. *Colonel*, 7 NY Heavy Artillery, June 13, 1864. Declined. Acting Judge Advocate, Staff of Major Gen. Winfield S. Hancock, June 6-Sept. 3, 1864. Bvt. Colonel, USA, March 13, 1865, for gallant and meritorious services in the campaign under Gen. W. S. Hancock in 1864.

Born: Aug. 23, 1833 Ithaca, NY

Died: Dec. 4, 1891 Fort Randall, SD

Education: Attended Dickinson College, Carlisle, PA. Graduated Union College, Schenectady, NY, 1853. Graduated US Military Academy, West Point, NY, 1857.

Occupation: Regular Army (Colonel, 21 US Infantry, Feb. 24, 1891)

Buried: City Cemetery, Ithaca, NY

References: Bernard W. Conrad, Jr. *Conrad Family Histories*. Raleigh, NC, 1998. George W. Cullum. *Biographical Register of the Officers and Graduates of the US Military Academy*. Third Edition. Boston and New York, 1891. *Annual Reunion*, Association of the Graduates of the US Military Academy, 1892. Obituary, *Omaha Morning World Herald*, Dec. 6, 1891. Obituary, *Army and Navy Journal*, Dec. 12, 1891. *National Cyclopedia of American Biography*. Letters Received, Appointment, Commission and Personal Branch, Adjutant General's Office, File 3218(ACP)1874, National Archives.

Joseph Speed Conrad (1857)
US Military Academy Library.

Right: *Joseph Speed Conrad*
Courtesy of the author. Beardsley Bros., Gallery of Art, 73 Owego Street, Ithaca, NY.

Joseph Speed Conrad
Courtesy of Stephen B. Rogers. Beardsley Bros., Gallery of Art, 73 Owego Street, Ithaca, NY.

Joseph Speed Conrad
Courtesy of the author. Beardsley Bros., Art Gallery, 71 & 73 Owego Street, Ithaca, NY.

Erastus Cooke

Colonel, 156 NY Infantry, Aug. 23, 1862. Discharged for disability, March 28, 1863, due to severe fracture of left shoulder caused by fall aboard steamer while embarking at Key West, FL.

Born: Sept. 3, 1818 Laurens, Otsego Co., NY
Died: June 20, 1885 Brooklyn, NY
Occupation: Lawyer and judge
Miscellaneous: Resided Kingston, NY; and Brooklyn, NY. Brother-in-law of Bvt. Brig. Gen. Theodore B. Gates.
Buried: Wiltwyck Cemetery, Kingston, NY
References: Obituary, *Brooklyn Daily Eagle*, June 20, 1885. Pension File and Military Service File, National Archives.

Joseph Speed Conrad (postwar)
Courtesy of David M. Neville.

Erastus Cooke (1867)
Collection of The New-York Historical Society. Churchill & Denison, No. 522 Broadway, Albany, NY.

Erastus Cooke
Collection of The New-York Historical Society. George A. Vallet, Head of Wall Street, Kingston, NY.

Erastus Cooke (1867)
Courtesy of the author. Jeffers & McDonnald, No. 519 Broadway, Albany, NY.

John Coonan

1 Lieutenant, Co. I, 69 NY State Militia, April 20, 1861. Honorably mustered out, Aug. 3, 1861. Captain, Co. I, 69 NY State Militia, May 26, 1862. Honorably mustered out, Sept. 3, 1862. Captain, Co. I, 182 NY Infantry, Nov. 8, 1862. Shell wound left leg, Reams' Station, VA, Aug. 25, 1864. Lieutenant Colonel, 182 NY Infantry, Sept. 15, 1864. *Colonel*, 182 NY Infantry, April 19, 1865. Honorably mustered out, July 15, 1865.

Born: 1833? Ireland
Died: June 4, 1898 New York City, NY
Occupation: Carpenter and mechanic before war. Chief clerk, Board of Emigration, and foreman in New York City street cleaning department after war.
Miscellaneous: Resided New York City, NY; and Brooklyn, NY

Buried: Calvary Cemetery, Long Island City, NY (Section 4, Range 5, Plot W)
References: Pension File, National Archives. Obituary, *New York Herald,* June 6, 1898. Letters Received, Volunteer Service Branch, Adjutant General's Office, File C1239(VS)1863, National Archives.

John Joseph Coppinger

Captain, 14 US Infantry, Sept. 30, 1861. GSW 2nd Bull Run, VA, Aug. 30, 1862. *Colonel*, 189 NY Infantry, Dec. 31, 1864. Commission revoked. Colonel, 15 NY Cavalry, Jan. 19, 1865. Honorably mustered out of volunteer service, June 29, 1865.

Born: Oct. 11, 1834 Cove of Cork, County Cork, Ireland
Died: Nov. 4, 1909 Washington, DC
Other Wars: Captain, Irish Battalion of St. Patrick, Papal Army, 1860 (Wounded at Spoleto). Spanish American War (Major Gen., USV).

John Joseph Coppinger
US Military Academy Library. J. E. McClees, Artist, 910 Chestnut Street, Philadelphia, PA.

John Joseph Coppinger (postwar)
Frederick H. Meserve. Historical Portraits. Courtesy of New York State Library.

John Joseph Coppinger (1898)
District of Columbia MOLLUS Collection, USAMHI.

Joseph Walker Corning (1861)
Collection of The New-York Historical Society.

Occupation: Regular Army (Brig. Gen., retired Oct. 11, 1898)

Miscellaneous: Resided Washington, DC. Son-in-law of Senator and Presidential candidate James G. Blaine.

Buried: Arlington National Cemetery, Arlington, VA (Section 2, Lot 859)

References: Letters Received, Appointment, Commission and Personal Branch, Adjutant General's Office, File 2319(ACP)1871, National Archives. Walter A. Copinger, editor. *History of the Copingers or Coppingers of the County of Cork*. Manchester and London, 1884. Constance Wynn Altshuler. *Cavalry Yellow & Infantry Blue*. Tucson, AZ, 1991.

Joseph Walker Corning

Captain, Co. B, 33 NY Infantry, May 9, 1861. Lieutenant Colonel, 33 NY Infantry, Oct. 3, 1861. Commanded 3 Brigade, 2 Division, 6 Army Corps, Army of the Potomac, July–

Joseph Walker Corning
Roger D. Hunt Collection, USAMHI. J. P. Vail, Photographer, Palmyra, NY.

Aug. 1862. Honorably mustered out, June 2, 1863. Major, 111 NY Infantry, Sept. 29, 1864. *Colonel*, 194 NY Infantry, Jan. 27, 1865.

Born: Nov. 4, 1814 Yarmouth, Nova Scotia
Died: June 29, 1890 Palmyra, NY
Occupation: Agricultural and mercantile pursuits early in life. Practiced law after 1855.
Offices/Honors: Postmaster, Ontario, NY, 1841-45. NY State Assembly, 1861. Postmaster, Palmyra, NY, 1889-90.
Miscellaneous: Resided Clayton, Jefferson Co., NY, 1834-37; Ontario, Wayne Co., NY, 1837-47; and Palmyra, Wayne Co., NY, after 1847
Buried: Palmyra Cemetery, Palmyra, NY
References: William D. Murphy. *Biographical Sketches of the State Officers and Members of the Legislature of the State of New York in 1861*. New York City, NY, 1861. Obituary, *Rochester Union and Advertiser*, June 30, 1890. Obituary, *Wayne Democratic Press*, July 2, 1890. David W. Judd. *The Story of the 33rd N. Y. S. Vols: or Two Years Campaigning in Virginia and Maryland*. Rochester, NY, 1864.

Charles Robert Coster

Private, Co. K, 7 NY State Militia, May 14, 1861. Honorably mustered out, June 3, 1861. 1 Lieutenant, 12 US Infantry, June 27, 1861. GSW right leg, Gaines Mill, VA, June 27, 1862. Captain, 12 US Infantry, Aug. 30, 1862. Colonel, 134 NY Infantry, Oct. 8, 1862. Commanded 1 Brigade, 2

Charles Robert Coster
Massachusetts MOLLUS Collection, USAMHI.

Division, 11 Army Corps, Army of the Potomac, June 10, 1863-July 1863. Resigned from volunteer service, Nov. 4, 1863, due to "urgent private affairs requiring my immediate and entire attention" and also due to the reduced strength of the regiment. Resigned from regular service, Dec. 31, 1863. Provost Marshal, 6 District of New York, May 18, 1864. Resigned May 6, 1865.

Born: Dec. 18, 1839 New York City, NY
Died: Dec. 23, 1888 New York City, NY
Occupation: Stock broker and real estate agent
Offices/Honors: US Collector of Internal Revenue, 1869-77. US Pension Agent, 1878-86.
Miscellaneous: Resided New York City, NY. Brother of Colonel John H. Coster.
Buried: St. Peters Episcopal Churchyard, Westchester, Bronx, NY (Family mausoleum)
References: Obituary, *Army and Navy Journal*, Dec. 29, 1888. Henry Whittemore. *History of George Washington Post 103, G. A. R.* Detroit, MI, 1885. Pension File, National Archives. Obituary, *New York Herald*, Dec. 25, 1888. George W. Conklin. *Under the Crescent and Star: The 134th New York Volunteer Infantry in the Civil War*. Port Reading, NJ, 2000. Katharine Bagg Hastings. "William James (1771-1832) of Albany, NY, and His Descendants," *New York Genealogical and Biographical Record*, Vol. 55, No. 2 (April 1924). Letters Received, Volunteer Service Branch, Adjutant General's Office, File N441(VS)1862, National Archives.

John Henry Coster

Private, Co. K, 7 NY State Militia, April 26, 1861. Honorably mustered out, June 3, 1861. Captain, Co. F, 1 NY Infantry, Aug. 28, 1861. GSW jaw, Glendale, VA, June 30, 1862. Captured Glendale, VA, June 30, 1862. Confined at Libby Prison, Richmond, VA. Paroled July 22, 1862. Discharged for disability, March 3, 1863, due to the effects of his wound. *Colonel*, 181 NY Infantry, March 24, 1864. No men recruited and authority as colonel revoked. 1 Lieutenant, Co. H, 6 CA Infantry, Sept. 20, 1865. Honorably mustered out, Oct. 25, 1865. 1 Lieutenant, Co. I, 7 CA Infantry, Nov. 18, 1865. Honorably mustered out, March 31, 1866. Captain, Co. C, 1 AZ Infantry, April 1, 1866. Honorably mustered out, June 13, 1866.

Born: Nov. 26, 1835 New York City, NY

Died: Dec. 7, 1895 New York City, NY

Occupation: Architect before war. Regular Army (Captain, 8 US Cavalry, retired June 26, 1882).

Offices/Honors: Long associated with the American Jockey Club, he became its secretary in 1880

Miscellaneous: Resided New York City, NY. Brother of Colonel Charles R. Coster.

Buried: Green-Wood Cemetery, Brooklyn, NY (Section 157, Lot 14301)

References: Obituary Circular, Whole No. 495, New York MOLLUS. Charlotte Goldthwaite, compiler. *Boardman Genealogy*. Hartford, CT, 1895. Military Service File, National Archives. Obituary, *New York Herald*, Dec. 8, 1895. Letters Received, Volunteer Service Branch, Adjutant General's Office, File C267(VS)1863, National Archives.

David Smith Cowles

Colonel, 128 NY Infantry, July 19, 1862. Commanded 1 Brigade, 2 Division, 19 Army Corps, Department of the Gulf, May 27, 1863. Shell wound "through the body," Port Hudson, LA, May 27, 1863.

Born: Feb. 25, 1817 North Canaan, CT

Died: May 27, 1863 KIA Port Hudson, LA

Education: Attended Yale University, New Haven, CT (Class of 1839)

Occupation: Lawyer

Miscellaneous: Resided Hudson, Columbia Co., NY

Buried: City Cemetery, Hudson, NY

References: Calvin D. Cowles. *The Genealogy of the Cowles Families in America*. New Haven, CT, 1929. Franklin Ellis. *History of Columbia County, NY*. Philadelphia, PA, 1878. Pension File, National Archives. David H. Hanaburgh. *History of the 128th Regiment, New York Volunteers in the Late Civil War*. Poughkeepsie, NY, 1894.

David Smith Cowles
Roger D. Hunt Collection, USAMHI. Bendann Brothers' Galleries of Photography, 205 Baltimore Street, Baltimore, MD.

David Smith Cowles
Roger D. Hunt Collection, USAMHI. F. Forshew, Photographer, Hudson, NY.

George Clarence Cram

Captain, 3 US Cavalry, May 14, 1861. Captain, 6 US Cavalry, Aug. 3, 1861. *Colonel*, 22 NY Cavalry, Aug. 13, 1864. Did not join regiment, because Colonel Crooks, who had been dishonorably discharged, was restored to his command.

Born: 1830? NY
Died: Aug. 22, 1869 Stamford, CT
Occupation: Regular Army (Major, 4 US Cavalry, resigned Jan. 26, 1869)
Miscellaneous: Resided New York City, NY
Buried: Green-Wood Cemetery, Brooklyn, NY (Section 74, Lot 18997, unmarked)
References: Obituary, *New York Times*, Aug. 26, 1869. Letters Received, Commission Branch, Adjutant General's Office, File C11(CB)1869, National Archives.

Levin Crandell

Lieutenant Colonel, 125 NY Infantry, Aug. 27, 1862. Captured Harper's Ferry, WV, Sept. 15, 1862. Paroled Sept. 16, 1862. Colonel, 125 NY Infantry, July 3, 1863. GSW face, Petersburg, VA, June 16, 1864. Discharged for disability, Nov. 29, 1864, due to chronic diarrhea.

Born: Dec. 22, 1826 Easton, NY
Died: June 16, 1907 Jamaica, NY
Occupation: Bookkeeper and accountant
Miscellaneous: Resided Troy, Rensselaer Co., NY; New York City, NY, 1865-69; Brooklyn, NY, 1869-83; Hicksville, Nassau Co., NY, 1883-85; and Jamaica, Queens Co., NY, 1885-1907
Buried: Cypress Hills National Cemetery, Brooklyn, NY (Section 2, Grave 6564)

George Clarence Cram
Meade Album, Civil War Library & Museum, Philadelphia, PA.

Levin Crandell
Michael J. McAfee Collection. Schoonmaker, 282 River Street, Troy, NY.

Levin Crandell
New York State Military Museum and Veterans Research Center. Schoonmaker, Troy, NY.

Levin Crandell (postwar)
A Regimental History, The 125th New York State Volunteers.

References: Pension File, National Archives. Ezra D. Simons. *A Regimental History, The 125th New York State Volunteers.* New York City, NY, 1888. John C. Crandall. *Elder John Crandall of Rhode Island and His Descendants.* New Woodstock, NY, 1949.

James Creney

1 Lieutenant, Co. F, 95 NY Infantry, Oct. 15, 1861. Captain, Co. F, 95 NY Infantry, Feb. 20, 1862. Lieutenant Colonel, 95 NY Infantry, April 14, 1863. *Colonel*, 95 NY Infantry, June 3, 1864. GSW left leg, Petersburg, VA, June 18, 1864. GSW left hip, Hatcher's Run, VA, Feb. 6, 1865. Honorably mustered out, July 16, 1865. Bvt. Colonel, USV, March 13, 1865, for gallant and meritorious services in front of Petersburg, VA.

James Creney
Lance W. Ingmire Collection. F. M. Yeager, Reading, PA.

Born: Feb. 14, 1834 Hudson, NY

Died: March 2, 1882 Brooklyn, NY

Occupation: Lawyer before war. Assistant Chief of Ordnance at the New York Arsenal after war.

Miscellaneous: Resided Haverstraw, Rockland Co., NY; and Brooklyn, NY

Buried: St. Peter's Cemetery, Haverstraw, NY

References: Pension File, National Archives. Obituary, *Brooklyn Daily Eagle*, March 3, 1882. Town Clerk's Register of Soldiers, Haverstraw, Rockland Co., NY, New York State Archives.

Marriott N. Croft

Captain, Co. A, 40 NY Infantry, June 21, 1861. Honorably discharged, Nov. 28, 1861. *Colonel*, 3 Regiment Empire Brigade (later 163 NY Infantry), Aug. 1862. Succeeded as colonel by Colonel Francis H. Braulik.

Born: 1822?

Died: March 18, 1866 Washington, DC

Other Wars: Mexican War (1 Lieutenant, Co. G, 1 NY Volunteers)

Occupation: Seaman

Miscellaneous: Resided Brooklyn, NY; and New York City, NY

Buried: Brooklyn, NY?

References: Pension File, National Archives. Death notice, *New York Herald*, March 22, 1866. New York City Directory, 1862.

Samuel J. Crooks

Colonel, 8 NY Cavalry, Nov. 28, 1861. Resigned Feb. 21, 1862. Private, Unassigned, 33 NY Infantry, Aug. 26, 1862. Honorably mustered out, Dec. 22, 1862. Colonel, 22 NY Cavalry, Sept. 24, 1863. Captured Reams' Station, VA, June 30, 1864. Confined at Richmond, VA; Macon, GA; and Columbia, SC. Paroled Dec. 10, 1864. Dishonorably discharged, July 22, 1864, for "violation of the 49th Article of War, in occasioning a false alarm in the army with which he was serving," in the Wilderness, VA, May 7, 1864. His dishonorable discharge was revoked, March 23, 1865, and he was honorably discharged, to date March 21, 1865.

Born: 1827? Richmond, Staten Island, NY

Died: May 27, 1892 New York City, NY

Occupation: Lawyer

Miscellaneous: Resided Nunda, Livingston Co., NY; Rochester, NY; and New York City, NY

Buried: St. Andrews Cemetery, New Berlin, NY (unmarked)

References: Pension File and Military Service File, National Archives. Brian A. Bennett. "Escape from Harpers Ferry," *Civil War*, Vol. 10, No. 3 (May-June 1992). H. Wells Hand, editor. *Centennial History of the Town of Nunda, NY*. Rochester, NY, 1908.

William J. Cropsey

Colonel, 70 NY National Guard, Feb. 23, 1863. Regiment saw service in Brooklyn during the New York Draft Riots, July 1863.

Born: Feb. 24, 1826 New Utrecht, NY

Died: March 25, 1912 Brooklyn, NY

Occupation: Held a position in New York Custom House for 18 years

Offices/Honors: Postmaster, Fort Hamilton, NY, 1875-82

Miscellaneous: Resided New York City, NY; and New Utrecht, Kings Co., NY

Buried: Green-Wood Cemetery, Brooklyn, NY (Section 103, Lot 19476, unmarked)

References: Henry I. Hazelton. *The Boroughs of Brooklyn and Queens*. New York and Chicago, 1925. Obituary, *Brooklyn Daily Eagle*, March 26, 1912. Charlotte R. Bangs. *Reminiscences of Old New Utrecht and Gowanus*. N.p., 1912.

Edgar Montgomery Cullen

Edgar Montgomery Cullen (1882)
The Public Service of the State of New York.

Edgar Montgomery Cullen (postwar)
The New York Red Book.

2 Lieutenant, 1 US Infantry, March 24, 1862. 1 Lieutenant, 1
US Infantry, Sept. 29, 1863. Colonel, 96 NY Infantry, Dec.
26, 1862. Commanded 1 Brigade, 1 Division, 18 Army
Corps, Army of the James, June 18-July 12, 1864. Com-
manded 2 Brigade, 1 Division, 18 Army Corps, July 31-
Sept. 27, 1864 and Sept. 29-Dec. 3, 1864. Commanded 1
Brigade, 3 Division, 24 Army Corps, Army of the James,
Jan. 16-March 21, 1865. Resigned from volunteer service,
March 21, 1865. Resigned from regular service, April 9,
1865.

Born: Dec. 4, 1843 Brooklyn, NY

Died: May 23, 1922 Brooklyn, NY

Education: Attended Rensselaer Polytechnic Institute, Troy,
NY. Graduated Columbia University, New York City, NY,
1860.

Occupation: Lawyer and judge

Offices/Honors: NY Supreme Court Justice, 1881-1900. Associate Judge, NY Court of Appeals, 1900-04. Chief Judge,
NY Court of Appeals, 1904-13.

Miscellaneous: Resided Brooklyn, NY

Buried: Green-Wood Cemetery, Brooklyn, NY (Sections 82/
83, Lots 1808/29915)

References: *National Cyclopedia of American Biography.*
Obituary, *New York Times*, May 24, 1922. Henry I.
Hazelton. *The Boroughs of Brooklyn and Queens.* New
York and Chicago, 1925. William Kreutzer. *Notes and
Observations Made During Four Years of Service with the
98th New York Volunteers in the War of 1861.* Philadel-
phia, PA, 1878. Military Service File, National Archives.
Paul A. Chadbourne, editor. *The Public Service of the State
of New York.* New York City, NY, 1882. Edgar L. Murlin.
The New York Red Book. Albany, NY, 1896.

Francis Markoe Cummins

Captain, Co. A, 1 IA Infantry, May 14, 1861. Honorably mustered out, Aug. 21, 1861. Lieutenant Colonel, 6 IA Infantry, Aug. 30, 1861. Dismissed May 20, 1862 for "being
intoxicated in the early part of the action" at Shiloh "and
utterly unfit to perform any duty." Lieutenant Colonel, 124
NY Infantry, Aug. 16, 1862. Colonel, 124 NY Infantry,
July 2, 1863. Shell wound thigh, Gettysburg, PA, July 2,
1863. GSW right leg, Wilderness, VA, May 6, 1864. Dis-

Francis Markoe Cummins
Massachusetts MOLLUS Collection, USAMHI. Brady's National Photographic
Portrait Gallery, Broadway & Tenth Street, New York.

Francis Markoe Cummins
Massachusetts MOLLUS Collection, USAMHI. Brady's National Photographic
Portrait Gallery, Broadway & Tenth Street, New York.

Francis Markoe Cummins
William Howard Collection, USAMHI. Lawrence, Photographer, Newburgh,
NY.

charged for disability, Sept. 19, 1864, due to wounds received in action.

Born: June 29, 1822 Florida, Orange Co., NY

Died: March 26, 1884 Goshen, NY

Education: Attended Lafayette College, Easton, PA (Class of 1840)

Other Wars: Mexican War (Captain, 10 US Infantry)

Occupation: Miller and farmer

Miscellaneous: Resided Muscatine, Muscatine Co., IA; and Goshen, Orange Co., NY

Buried: Slate Hill Cemetery, Goshen, NY

References: Edmund J. Raus, Jr. *A Generation on the March: The Union Army at Gettysburg*. Gettysburg, PA, 1996. Military Service File, National Archives. Obituary, *Middletown Daily Press*, March 26, 1884. Charles H. Weygant. *History of the 124th Regiment New York State Volunteers*. Newburgh, NY, 1877. Charles J. LaRocca, editor. *This Regiment of Heroes*. N.p., 1991.

Leonard Douglas Hay Currie

Captain, AAG, Staff of Brig. Gen. William F. Smith, Sept. 30, 1861. Resigned July 26, 1862. Colonel, 133 NY Infantry, Sept. 24, 1862. GSW both arms, Port Hudson, LA, June 14, 1863. Honorably mustered out, June 6, 1865.

Born: March 6, 1832 London, England

Died: Jan. 3, 1907 London, England

Education: Attended Winchester College, Winchester, Hampshire, England

Other Wars: Crimean War (GSW foot, Battle of the Alma)

Occupation: English army officer (Captain, 19 Regiment of Foot)

Leonard Douglas Hay Currie (seated center; with wife, Harriet, seated right; Capt. John Schuyler Crosby, kneeling right; and Lt. Col. William S. Abert, standing right)
Civil War Library & Museum, Philadelphia, PA.

Leonard Douglas Hay Currie
Roger D. Hunt Collection, USAMHI. G. L. Collis, Photographer, 68 Cornhill,
E. C., London, England.

Miscellaneous: Resided Ventnor, Isle of Wight, England; and London, England

Buried: Ventnor Cemetery, Ventnor, Isle of Wight, England

References: M. L. Ferrar. *Officers of the Green Howards, Alexandra, Princess of Wales's Own (Yorkshire Regiment)*. Belfast, Ireland, 1931. Obituary, *London Times*, Jan. 4, 1907. Obituary, *The Paddington, Kensington and Bayswater Chronicle*, Jan. 5, 1907. Obituary, *Isle of Wight Mercury and Ventnor Gazette*, Jan. 5, 1907. Military Service File, National Archives.

Lionel Jobert d'Epineuil

Colonel, 53 NY Infantry, Oct. 16, 1861. Awaiting trial on charges of "incompetency, conduct unbecoming an officer and a gentleman, conduct prejudicial to good order and military discipline, willfully destroying military stores, and disobedience of orders," he was mustered out, March 11, 1862, and his demoralized regiment disbanded.

Leonard Douglas Hay Currie (postwar)
Massachusetts MOLLUS Collection, USAMHI.

George Frederick d'Utassy

Colonel, 39 NY Infantry, May 28, 1861. Cashiered May 29, 1863, on charges of "unlawfully selling and disposing of Government horses for his own benefit and conduct prejudicial to good order and military discipline, such as opening private letters, selling appointments, causing muster rolls to be altered, presenting to the United States and receiving payment of a false and fraudulent account amounting to $3265.40, and permitting the members of the band to draw pay for pretended services as private soldiers."

Born: Nov. 6, 1827 Buda Pesth, Hungary
Died: May 2, 1892 Wilmington, DE (accidental asphyxiation by gas)
Other Wars: Hungarian War of Independence, 1848-49, and Crimean War
Occupation: Teacher of languages and life insurance agent
Miscellaneous: Resided New York City, NY; Cincinnati, OH; and Baltimore, MD. Original name was David Strasser. Known as Frederick George d'Utassy during Civil War.

Lionel Jobert d'Epineuil
Michael J. McAfee Collection.

Born: 1830? France
Died: ?
Occupation: Clerk, US Treasury Department, and civil engineer. Editor of *The Scientific Journal,* 1868-70. Returned to France in 1870.
Miscellaneous: Resided Washington, DC, and Philadelphia, PA. In describing d'Epineuil, the wife of Lieutenant Colonel Antoine Joseph Vignier de Monteil of the 53rd New York said he "gives himself as an old officer of the Navy and of the Marines in France, but who was never anything but a sailor who deserted when at Haiti and had then the command of a boat of one kind or the other for His Most Gracious Majesty Faustin the First."
Buried: ?
References: Military Service File, National Archives. Letters Received, Volunteer Service Branch, Adjutant General's Office, Files V2(VS)1862 and W379(VS)1862, National Archives. Gerald E. Wheeler and A. Stuart Pitts. "The 53rd New York: A Zoo-Zoo Tale," *New York History,* Vol. 37, No. 3 (Oct. 1956).

George Frederick d'Utassy
Courtesy of Gil Barrett. Brady's National Photographic Portrait Gallery, 352 Pennsylvania Avenue, Washington, DC.

Buried: Loudon Park Cemetery, Baltimore, MD (Edgewood Section, Lots 93-96)

References: Obituary, *Philadelphia Public Ledger*, May 4, 1892. Obituary, *Baltimore Sun*, May 2-3, 1892. Letters Received, Volunteer Service Branch, Adjutant General's Office, File D740(VS)1862, National Archives. John M. Pellicano. *Conquer or Die, The 39th New York Volunteer Infantry: Garibaldi Guard.* Flushing, NY, 1996. Michael Bacarella. *Lincoln's Foreign Legion, The 39th New York Infantry, The Garibaldi Guard.* Shippensburg, PA, 1996. Edmund Vasvary. *Lincoln's Hungarian Heroes.* Washington, DC, 1939.

Right: *George Frederick d'Utassy (right, with Major Charles Wiegand) Massachusetts MOLLUS Collection, USAMHI.*

George Frederick d'Utassy
Massachusetts MOLLUS Collection, USAMHI. Brady's National Photographic Portrait Gallery, 352 Pennsylvania Avenue, Washington, DC.

Right: *George Frederick d'Utassy*
Massachusetts MOLLUS Collection, USAMHI.

George Frederick d'Utassy (with the Hungarian flag) Massachusetts MOLLUS Collection, USAMHI. Brady's National Photographic Portrait Gallery, Broadway & Tenth Street, New York.

George Erskine Danforth

Colonel, Cherry Valley Regiment, Sept. 1861. Regiment consolidated with 76 NY Infantry, Jan. 14, 1862. *Colonel*, 134 NY Infantry, July 9, 1862. Organized regiment, but did not enter service.

Born: July 5, 1818 Middleburgh, NY
Died: April 22, 1881 Middleburgh, NY
Education: Attended Union College, Schenectady, NY (Class of 1839)

Occupation: Tannery operator and manufacturer
Offices/Honors: Brig. Gen., New York State Militia
Miscellaneous: Resided Middleburgh, Schoharie Co., NY. Son-in-law of New York Governor William C. Bouck. Brother-in-law of Colonel Gabriel Bouck (18 WI Infantry).
Buried: Middleburgh Cemetery, Middleburgh, NY
References: William E. Roscoe. *History of Schoharie County, NY*. Syracuse, NY, 1882. Obituary, *Schoharie Union*, April 28, 1881. Obituary, *Schoharie Republican*, April 28, 1881. John J. May, compiler. *Danforth Genealogy*. Boston, MA, 1902.

George Frederick d'Utassy (left, with Lt. Col. Alexander Repetti, and the Hungarian, American and Italian flags)
Massachusetts MOLLUS Collection, USAMHI. Brady's National Photographic Portrait Gallery, Broadway & Tenth Street, New York.

Jared Mansfield Davies

Major, 5 NY Infantry, May 10, 1861. Colonel, 2 NY Cavalry, Aug. 1, 1861. Discharged for disability, Dec. 6, 1862, due to "chronic dysentery attended with intestinal ulceration."

Born: Dec. 21, 1828 West Point, NY
Died: Oct. 12, 1908 Burlington, VT
Education: Attended New York University, New York City, NY. Attended Harvard University Law School, Cambridge, MA.
Occupation: Lawyer
Miscellaneous: Resided New York City, NY; Fishkill-on-the-Hudson, Dutchess Co., NY; and Burlington, VT. First cousin of Major Gen. Henry E. Davies. Nephew of Brig. Gen. Thomas A. Davies.
Buried: St. Lukes Episcopal Churchyard, Beacon, NY
References: Henry E. Davies. *Davies Memoir: A Genealogical and Biographical Monograph on the Family and Descendants of John Davies of Litchfield, CT.* N.p., 1895. Obituary, *Burlington Free Press*, Oct. 13, 1908. Military Service File, National Archives. Letters Received, Volunteer Service Branch, Adjutant General's Office, File D961(VS)1862, National Archives.

Benjamin Franklin Davis

Captain, 1 US Dragoons, July 30, 1861. Captain, 1 US Cavalry, Aug. 3, 1861. Lieutenant Colonel, 1 CA Cavalry, Aug. 19, 1861. Resigned from volunteer service, Nov. 1, 1861. Colonel, 8 NY Cavalry, June 6, 1862. Commanded 5 Brigade, Cavalry Division, Army of the Potomac, Sept. 1862-Nov. 1862. Commanded 1 Brigade, 1 Division, Cavalry Corps, Army of the Potomac, Dec. 15, 1862-May 27, 1863 and June 6-9, 1863. Commanded 1 Division, Cavalry Corps, Army of the Potomac, May 27-June 6, 1863. GSW head, Beverly Ford, VA, June 9, 1863.

Born: Feb. 1832 AL
Died: June 9, 1863 KIA Beverly Ford, VA
Education: Graduated US Military Academy, West Point, NY, 1854
Other Wars: Mexican War (Private, Co. E, Anderson's Battalion MS Rifles)
Occupation: Regular Army (Captain, 1 US Cavalry)

Jared Mansfield Davies
Roger D. Hunt Collection, USAMHI.

Benjamin Franklin Davis
Meade Album, Civil War Library & Museum, Philadelphia, PA.

Miscellaneous: Resided Los Angeles, CA. Widely known by the nickname "Grimes."

Buried: Post Cemetery, West Point, NY (Section 26, Row A, Grave 8)

References: George W. Cullum. *Biographical Register of the Officers and Graduates of the US Military Academy*. Third edition. Boston and New York, 1891. Henry L. Abbot. *Half Century of a West Point Class, 1850 to 1854*. Boston, MA, N.d. US Military Academy Cadet Application Papers, National Archives. Letters Received, Volunteer Service Branch, Adjutant General's Office, File N298(VS)1862, National Archives. Mexican War Service File, National Archives.

Jacob J. DeForest
USAMHI. D. Woodworth, No. 444 Broadway, Albany, NY.

Uriah L. Davis

Colonel, 85 NY Infantry, Nov. 7, 1861. Discharged for disability, Feb. 8, 1862, due to "ill health and physical prostration."

Born: Oct. 27, 1812 Austerlitz, Columbia Co., NY

Died: July 24, 1897 Callery, Butler Co., PA

Occupation: Farmer and lumberman

Offices/Honors: Town Supervisor, Austerlitz, Columbia Co., NY, 1847. Sheriff of Allegany Co., NY, 1867-70.

Miscellaneous: Resided Spencertown, Columbia Co., NY; Bolivar, Allegany Co., NY; and Angelica, Allegany Co., NY. First cousin of Colonel Edward Frisby.

Buried: Angelica Cemetery, Angelica, NY (Lot 358)

References: Military Service File, National Archives. Obituary, *Wellsville Daily Reporter*, July 30, 1897. Edward S. Frisbee. *Frisbee-Frisbie Genealogy*. Rutland, VT, 1926. Wayne Mahood. *The Plymouth Pilgrims: A History of the 85th New York Infantry in the Civil War*. Hightstown, NJ, 1989.

Jacob J. De Forest

Lieutenant Colonel, 81 NY Infantry, Dec. 20, 1861. GSW left breast, Fair Oaks, VA, May 31, 1862. Colonel, 81 NY Infantry, July 7, 1862. Commanded 1 Brigade, 2 Division, 18 Army Corps, Department of the South, March 6, 1863-April 16, 1863. Discharged for disability, to date March 30, 1863. Discharge revoked and restored to command, April 28, 1863. Commanded 1 Brigade, 1 Division, 18 Army Corps, Army of the James, April 28, 1864-May 1, 1864. Discharged for disability, Sept. 1, 1864, due to "chronic diarrhea and debility, the result of remittent fever."

Born: Oct. 10, 1820 Duanesburgh, NY

Died: March 13, 1904 Rotterdam, NY

Occupation: Carpenter and builder

Miscellaneous: Resided Duanesburgh, Schenectady Co., NY; and Albany, NY

Buried: Prospect Hill Cemetery, Guilderland, NY

References: Pension File, National Archives. G. Howell and W. Munsell. *History of the County of Schenectady, NY*. New York City, NY, 1886. Letters Received, Volunteer Service Branch, Adjutant General's Office, File N123(VS) 1863, National Archives.

Jacob J. DeForest
New York State Military Museum and
Veterans Research Center. D. Woodworth,
No. 444 Broadway, Albany, NY.

Jacob J. DeForest
Courtesy of Michael Albanese.

Jacob J. DeForest
New York State Military Museum and Veterans Research
Center.

Othneil De Forest

Colonel, 5 NY Cavalry, Oct. 1, 1861. Commanded 3 Brigade, Cavalry Division, 22 Army Corps, Department of Washington, April 7, 1863-June 26, 1863. Dismissed March 29, 1864, for "presenting false and fraudulent accounts against the government." Dismissal revoked, March 14, 1866, and he was restored to rank as Colonel, 5 NY Cavalry, to date Sept. 3, 1864.

Born: Aug. 13, 1826 NY
Died: Dec. 16, 1864 New York City, NY (congestion of the brain)
Education: Graduated Yale University, New Haven, CT, 1847
Occupation: Broker
Miscellaneous: Resided Philadelphia, PA; and New York City, NY
Buried: Woodlands Cemetery, Philadelphia, PA (Section C, Lots 424-426)
References: Pension File and Military Service File, National Archives. *Obituary Record of Graduates of Yale College Deceased During the Academical Year Ending in July 1865.* Louis N. Boudrye. *Historic Records of the 5th New York Cavalry, 1st Ira Harris Guard.* Albany, NY, 1865. John W. De Forest. *The De Forests of Avesnes (and of New Netherland).* New Haven, CT, 1900.

Peter Degive

Colonel, 29 NY Infantry, Sept. 10, 1863. Organization discontinued Oct. 14, 1863.

Born: ?
Died: ?
Occupation: Hotelkeeper
Buried: ?
References: New York City Directory, 1861. Frederick Phisterer, compiler. *New York in the War of the Rebellion, 1861 to 1865.* Third Edition. Albany, NY, 1912.

Chauncey Mitchell Depew

Colonel, 172 NY Infantry, Aug. 1862. Succeeded by Colonel John P. Jenkins, Sept. 10, 1862.

Born: April 23, 1834 Peekskill, NY
Died: April 5, 1928 New York City, NY
Education: Graduated Yale University, New Haven, CT, 1856
Occupation: Lawyer and railway president
Offices/Honors: NY State Assembly, 1862-63. US Senate, 1899-1911.
Miscellaneous: Resided Peekskill, Westchester Co., NY; and New York City, NY

Othneil DeForest
Historic Records of the 5th New York Cavalry, 1st Ira Harris Guard.

Chauncey Mitchell Depew (postwar)
Frederick H. Meserve. Historical Portraits. Courtesy of New York State Library.

Chauncey Mitchell Depew (postwar)
Frederick H. Meserve. Historical Portraits. Courtesy of New York State Library.

Louis Palma di Cesnola
Courtesy of Gil Barrett. J. Gurney & Son, 707 Broadway, New York.

Buried: Hillside Cemetery, Peekskill, NY

References: *Dictionary of American Biography. History of the Academic Class of 1856, Yale University, to 1896.* Boston, MA, 1897. Chauncey M. Depew. *My Memories of Eighty Years.* New York City, NY, 1922. *Biographical Directory of the American Congress.*

Louis Palma di Cesnola

Major, 11 NY Cavalry, Sept. 11, 1861. Lieutenant Colonel, 11 NY Cavalry, Feb. 22, 1862. Resigned June 20, 1862, complaining that "Colonel J. B. Swain is as ignorant of any military knowledge as a new recruit." Colonel, 4 NY Cavalry, Sept. 11, 1862. Commanded Cavalry Brigade, 11 Army Corps, Army of the Potomac, Dec. 1862-Jan. 1863. Dismissed Feb. 2, 1863, for "having been detected in forwarding to the North stolen property belonging to the United States." His dismissal was revoked and he was restored to his command, March 3, 1863, upon evidence that the revolvers sent to his wife were forwarded to officers home on recruiting duty. Commanded 1 Brigade, 2 Division, Cavalry Corps, Army of the Potomac, May 20, 1863-June 11, 1863. Sabre wound head and GSW left arm, Aldie, VA, June 17, 1863. Captured Aldie, VA, June 17, 1863. Confined Libby Prison, Richmond, VA. Paroled March 21, 1864. Commanded 2 Brigade, 1 Division, Cavalry Corps, Army of the Shenandoah, Aug. 6, 1864-Aug. 30, 1864. Honorably mustered out, Sept. 4, 1864.

Born: June 29, 1832 Rivarolo Canavese, Piedmont, Italy

Died: Nov. 20, 1904 New York City, NY

Education: Attended Royal Military Academy, Cherasco, Italy

Other Wars: Crimean War (ADC, Staff of Gen. Ansaldi)

Occupation: Early in life an officer in Sardinian army. Coming to US in 1858, he taught languages before war. Archaeologist, collector of antiquities, and author after war.

Louis Palma di Cesnola (postwar)
Military Order Congress Medal of Honor Legion of the United States.

Christian Friedrich Dickel
Michael J. McAfee Collection. J. Brill, 204 Chatham Square, New York.

Offices/Honors: US Consul, Cyprus, 1865-76. Director of the Metropolitan Museum of Art, New York City, NY, 1879-1904. Medal of Honor, Aldie, VA, June 17, 1863. "Was present, in arrest, when, seeing his regiment fall back, he rallied his men, accompanied them, without arms, in a second charge, and in recognition of his gallantry was released from arrest. He continued in the action at the head of his regiment until he was desperately wounded and taken prisoner."

Miscellaneous: Resided New York City, NY

Buried: Kensico Cemetery, Valhalla, NY (Section 6, Tecumseh Plot, Lot 1145)

References: Elizabeth McFadden. *The Glitter and the Gold.* New York City, NY, 1971. *Dictionary of American Biography.* Pension File and Military Service File, National Archives. St. Clair A. Mulholland. *Military Order Congress Medal of Honor Legion of the United States.* Philadelphia, PA, 1905. Letters Received, Volunteer Service Branch, Adjutant General's Office, File B168(VS)1863, National Archives.

Christian Friedrich Dickel

Colonel, 4 NY Cavalry, Nov. 1, 1861. Discharged for disability, Sept. 10, 1862, due to acute bronchitis and erysipelas of the face.

Born: Aug. 1808 Germany

Died: Sept. 18, 1880 Wood-Ridge, NJ

Occupation: Proprietor of a riding academy

Miscellaneous: Resided Wood-Ridge, Bergen Co., NJ; and New York City, NY

Buried: Maple Grove Park Cemetery, Hackensack, NJ (marker illegible)

References: Pension File and Military Service File, National Archives. Obituary, *New York Herald*, Sept. 20, 1880.

John W. Dininny
Roger D. Hunt Collection, USAMHI. Charles D. Fredricks & Co., "Specialite,"
587 Broadway, New York.

Adolphus Dobke
Everitt Bowles Collection. T. F. Saltsman, Photographer, Cor. Union & Col-
lege Streets, Nashville, TN.

John W. Dininny

Major, 141 NY Infantry, Sept. 12, 1862. Colonel, 141 NY Infantry, Feb. 11, 1863. Discharged for disability, June 1, 1863, due to failing eyesight.

Born: June 23, 1820 Oneonta, NY
Died: Nov. 1, 1894 Addison, NY
Education: Graduated Genesee Wesleyan Seminary, Lima, NY, 1842
Occupation: Lawyer
Miscellaneous: Resided Addison, Steuben Co., NY
Buried: Addison Rural Cemetery, Addison, NY
References: Irwin W. Near. *A History of Steuben County and Its People.* Chicago, IL, 1911. Pension File, National Archives. Obituary, *Addison Advertiser*, Nov. 1, 1894. Obituary, *Corning Daily Journal*, Nov. 2, 1894.

Adolphus Dobke

Captain, Co. D, 45 NY Infantry, Sept. 2, 1861. Major, 45 NY Infantry, June 15, 1862. Shell wound right leg, 2nd Bull Run, VA, Aug. 29, 1862. Lieutenant Colonel, 45 NY Infantry, May 11, 1863. *Colonel*, 45 NY Infantry, Jan. 22, 1864. Lieutenant Colonel, 58 NY Infantry, June 30, 1865. Honorably mustered out, Oct. 1, 1865.

Born: April 18, 1821 (or April 9, 1822) Germany
Died: March 29, 1904 Jersey City, NJ
Occupation: Policeman and shipping clerk
Miscellaneous: Resided New York City, NY; and Jersey City, NJ
Buried: Lutheran Cemetery, Middle Village, Queens, NY (Map 3A, Koltes Post Plot, Row 8, Grave 4)
References: Pension File, National Archives. Obituary, *Newark Advertiser*, March 31, 1904.

John Augustus Dodge

Colonel, 75 NY Infantry, Nov. 14, 1861. Discharged for disability, July 21, 1862, due to general debility caused by remittent fever.

Born: Oct. 16, 1818 near Poughkeepsie, NY
Died: Nov. 28, 1881 New York City, NY
Occupation: Merchant before war. Mower and reaper manufacturer and banker after war.
Miscellaneous: Resided Auburn, Cayuga Co., NY, to 1873; Danbury, CT, 1873-74; and New York City, NY, 1874-81
Buried: Fort Hill Cemetery, Auburn, NY (Glen Alpine Section, Lot 36)
References: Obituary, *New York Times*, Nov. 30, 1881. Pension File, National Archives. Theron R. Woodward. *Descendants of Tristram Dodge*. Chicago, IL, 1904. Henry and James Hall. *Cayuga in the Field, A Record of the 19th New York Volunteers, All the Batteries of the 3rd New York Artillery, and 75th New York Volunteers*. Auburn, NY, 1873.

Stephen Augustus Dodge

Colonel, 87 NY Infantry, Nov. 19, 1861. GSW left thigh, Fair Oaks, VA, May 31, 1862. Captured Fair Oaks, VA, May 31, 1862. Confined Libby Prison, Richmond, VA. Paroled July 17, 1862. Honorably mustered out, Sept. 6, 1862, upon consolidation of regiment with 40 NY Infantry.

Born: Sept. 24, 1822 Brooklyn, NY
Died: May 6, 1917 Brooklyn, NY
Occupation: Decorative painter before war. Real estate agent and stock broker after war.
Miscellaneous: Resided New York City, NY; Brooklyn, NY; Jersey City, NJ; Spring Valley, Rockland Co., NY; and Freehold, Monmouth Co., NJ
Buried: Evergreens Cemetery, Brooklyn, NY (Mount Lebanon Section, Lots 41-42)
References: Pension File, National Archives. Theron R. Woodward. *Descendants of Tristram Dodge*. Chicago, IL, 1904. Obituary, *Brooklyn Daily Eagle*, May 8, 1917. Erroneous Obituary, *New York Daily Tribune*, June 5, 1862. Letters Received, Volunteer Service Branch, Adjutant General's Office, Files D546(VS)1862 and E125(VS)1862, National Archives.

John Augustus Dodge
Massachusetts MOLLUS Collection, USAMHI. Published by E. Anthony, 501 Broadway, New York, from Photographic Negative in Brady's National Portrait Gallery.

John Augustus Dodge (postwar)
Courtesy of Henry Deeks. L. S. Upham, 77 Genesee Street, Auburn, NY.

Dudley Donnelly

Colonel, 28 NY Infantry, May 18, 1861. Commanded 1 Brigade, 1 Division, 5 Army Corps, Army of the Potomac, March 13, 1862-April 4, 1862. Commanded 1 Brigade, 1 Division, Department of the Shenandoah, April 4, 1862-May 27, 1862. GSW groin, Cedar Mountain, VA, Aug. 9, 1862.

Born: Dec. 18, 1824 Cortland Co., NY
Died: Aug. 15, 1862 DOW Culpeper, VA
Occupation: Lawyer
Miscellaneous: Resided Lockport, Niagara Co., NY
Buried: Cold Spring Cemetery, Lockport, NY (Section K, Lot 18)
References: D. Williams Patterson. *John Stoddard of Wethersfield, CT, and His Descendants*. N.p., 1873. Charles W. Boyce. *A Brief History of the 28th Regiment New York State Volunteers*. Buffalo, NY, 1896. Obituary, *Lockport Daily Journal and Courier*, Aug. 11, 1862. Pension File, National Archives.

Dudley Donnelly
Massachusetts MOLLUS Collection, USAMHI.

Thomas Donnelly Doubleday

Colonel, 4 NY Heavy Artillery, Nov. 1, 1861. Cashiered Dec. 28, 1862 for "drunkenness on duty and neglect of duty," but his sentence was remitted, and he was restored to command, despite a petition from many of the officers that he not be restored to command. "Having unreasonably failed to appear before the examining board, and after diligent inquiry by the board, having been found inefficient, incapable, and physically disqualified for his position," he was discharged, March 7, 1863.

Born: Feb. 18, 1816 Ballston Spa (or Albany), NY
Died: May 11, 1864 New York City, NY (accidentally killed; run over by a stage)
Occupation: Bookseller and stationer
Miscellaneous: Resided Port Richmond, Staten Island, NY. Brother of Major Gen. Abner Doubleday and Bvt. Brig. Gen. Ulysses Doubleday.
Buried: Staten Island Cemetery, West New Brighton, Staten Island, NY (Lot 165)
References: Margaret B. Curfman. *Doubleday Families of America*. Wichita, KS, 1972. Military Service File, National Archives. Hyland C. Kirk. *Heavy Guns and Light: A History of the 4th New York Heavy Artillery*. New York City, NY, 1890. Letters Received, Volunteer Service Branch, Adjutant General's Office, File H118(VS)1862, National Archives.

Thomas Donnelly Doubleday
Massachusetts MOLLUS Collection, USAMHI.

Thomas Donnelly Doubleday
Massachusetts MOLLUS Collection, USAMHI.

Thomas Donnelly Doubleday
Massachusetts MOLLUS Collection, USAMHI.

Jeremiah Clinton Drake

Captain, Co. G, 49 NY Infantry, Aug. 30, 1861. Colonel, 112 NY Infantry, Sept. 2, 1862. Commanded 1 Brigade, Vodges' Division, Northern District, Department of the South, Jan. 15, 1864-Feb. 25, 1864. Commanded 1 Brigade, 2 Division, District of Florida, Department of the South, Feb. 28, 1864-March 11, 1864. Commanded 2 Division, District of Florida, Department of the South, March 11, 1864-April 20, 1864. Commanded 2 Brigade, 3 Division, 10 Army Corps, Army of the James, May 2-28, 1864. Commanded 2 Brigade, 3 Division, 18 Army Corps, Army of the James, May 30, 1864-June 1, 1864. GSW bowels, Cold Harbor, VA, June 1, 1864.

Born: April 19, 1824 Salisbury, Herkimer Co., NY
Died: June 2, 1864 DOW Cold Harbor, VA
Education: Graduated University of Rochester (NY), 1852
Occupation: Baptist clergyman
Miscellaneous: Resided Churchville, Monroe Co., NY; Panama, Chautauqua Co., NY; and Westfield, Chautauqua Co., NY
Buried: Westfield Cemetery, Westfield, NY

Jeremiah Clinton Drake
Roger D. Hunt Collection, USAMHI.

References: William L. Hyde. *History of the 112th Regiment NY Volunteers*. Fredonia, NY, 1866. Andrew W. Young. *History of Chautauqua County, NY*. Buffalo, NY, 1875.

William Findlay Drum

Private, Co. F, 2 OH Infantry, April 17, 1861. Honorably mustered out, July 31, 1861. 2 Lieutenant, 2 US Infantry, Aug. 5, 1861. Captain, 2 US Infantry, May 1, 1863. Lieutenant Colonel, 5 NY Veteran Infantry, April 1, 1865. Colonel, 5 NY Veteran Infantry, May 29, 1865. Honorably mustered out, Aug. 21, 1865.

Born: Nov. 16, 1833 Fort Columbus, New York Harbor, NY
Died: July 4, 1892 Fort Yates, ND
Education: Attended US Military Academy, West Point, NY (Class of 1854)
Occupation: Regular Army (Lieutenant Colonel, 12 US Infantry, Dec. 8, 1886)
Miscellaneous: Resided Springfield, Clark Co., OH. Nephew of Bvt. Brig. Gen. Richard C. Drum.
Buried: Arlington National Cemetery, Arlington, VA (Section 3, Lot 1774)
References: William H. Powell and Edward Shippen, editors. *Officers of the Army and Navy (Regular) Who Served in the Civil War*. Philadelphia, PA, 1892. Pension File, National Archives.

William Findlay Drum
Officers of the Army and Navy (Regular) Who Served in the Civil War.

Charles Durkee

Lieutenant Colonel, 98 NY Infantry, Jan. 10, 1862. Colonel, 98 NY Infantry, July 4, 1862. Resigned Feb. 25, 1863, "in the interest of harmony among the officers."

Born: Jan. 9, 1827 Burke, Franklin Co., NY
Died: Jan. 6, 1879 Malone, NY
Occupation: Merchant engaged in the drug business and later in general merchandising
Miscellaneous: Resided Malone, Franklin Co., NY. Kreutzer described him as, "Dutch in his name, ... Dutch in his features, size and shape."
Buried: Morningside Cemetery, Malone, NY
References: Frederick J. Seaver. *Historical Sketches of Franklin County, NY*. Albany, NY, 1918. Pension File, National Archives. Obituary, *Malone Palladium*, Jan. 9, 1879. William Kreutzer. *Notes and Observations Made During Four Years of Service with the 98th New York Volunteers in the War of 1861*. Philadelphia, PA, 1878. Letters Received, Volunteer Service Branch, Adjutant General's Office, File M2060(VS)1862, National Archives.

William Findlay Drum
State Archives, Connecticut State Library. R. W. Addis, Photographer, McClees Gallery, 308 Penna. Ave., Washington, DC.

Richard Cornell Duryea (postwar)
US Military Academy Library. S. B. Duryea, 253 Fulton Street, Brooklyn, NY.

Richard Cornell Duryea

Captain, 1 US Artillery, May 14, 1861. Colonel, 7 NY Heavy Artillery, Dec. 26, 1864. Commanded 2 Brigade, 1 Division, 2 Army Corps, Army of the Potomac, Jan. 29, 1865-Feb. 17, 1865. Honorably mustered out of volunteer service, July 3, 1865.

Born: Sept. 9, 1830 Queens Co., NY
Died: Jan. 23, 1902 Grand Haven, MI
Education: Graduated US Military Academy, West Point, NY, 1853
Occupation: Regular Army (Captain, 1 US Artillery, honorably mustered out, Dec. 15, 1870). Manufacturer in Brooklyn, NY; and later Inspector of Harbors and Harbor Works in Michigan.
Miscellaneous: Resided Brooklyn, NY; Cheboygan, Cheboygan Co., MI; and Grand Haven, Ottawa Co., MI, 1881-1902
Buried: Lake Forest Cemetery, Grand Haven, MI (Block 18, Lot 19, family marker)
References: *Annual Reunion*, Association of the Graduates of the US Military Academy, 1902. Pension File, National Archives. Robert Keating. *Carnival of Blood: The Civil War Ordeal of the 7th New York Heavy Artillery*. Baltimore, MD, 1998.

William Dutton

Colonel, 98 NY Infantry, Jan. 23, 1862

Born: Jan. 14, 1823 Watertown, CT
Died: July 4, 1862 New York City, NY (typhoid fever)
Education: Graduated US Military Academy, West Point, NY, 1846
Occupation: Resigning from the army several months after graduation, he spent several years as a school principal and then became a farmer and tile and brick manufacturer
Offices/Honors: NY State Assembly, 1852
Miscellaneous: Resided Huron, Wayne Co., NY. Described by Kreutzer as "a brave, friendly, impulsive man; a little too excitable for cool command."
Buried: Glenside Cemetery, Wolcott, NY
References: Lewis H. Clark. *Military History of Wayne County, NY*. Sodus, NY, 1884. George W. Cullum. *Biographical Register of the Officers and Graduates of the US Military Academy*. Third Edition. Boston and New York, 1891. William Kreutzer. *Notes and Observations Made During Four Years of Service with the 98th New York Volunteers in the War of 1861*. Philadelphia, PA, 1878. Pension File, National Archives.

William Dutton
New York State Military Museum and Veterans Research Center.

Augustus Wade Dwight

Captain, Co. E, 122 NY Infantry, July 8, 1862. Lieutenant Colonel, 122 NY Infantry, Aug. 28, 1862. GSW leg slight, Winchester, VA, Sept. 19, 1864. GSW right wrist, Cedar Creek, VA, Oct. 19, 1864. *Colonel, 122 NY Infantry, Jan. 27, 1865.* Shell wound head, Fort Stedman, VA, March 25, 1865.

Born: Feb. 22, 1827 Halifax, VT

Died: March 25, 1865 KIA near Petersburg, VA

Education: Attended Yale University, New Haven, CT (Class of 1854)

Occupation: Lawyer

Miscellaneous: Resided Syracuse, Onondaga Co., NY

Buried: Oakwood Cemetery, Syracuse, NY (Section 56, GAR Plot, Grave 61)

References: Benjamin W. Dwight. *History of the Descendants of John Dwight of Dedham, MA.* New York City, NY, 1874. Charles H. Leeds, compiler. *Academic Class of Fifty-Four Yale University, 1854-96.* Stamford, CT, 1896. David B. Swinfen. *Ruggles' Regiment: The 122nd New York Volunteers in the American Civil War.* Hanover, NH, 1982.

Augustus Wade Dwight
Roger D. Hunt Collection, USAMHI. George K. Knapp & Co., Successors to Taber Brothers, No. 6 Franklin Buildings, East Genesee Street, Syracuse, NY.

Augustus Wade Dwight
Roger D. Hunt Collection, USAMHI.

Augustus Wade Dwight
Roger D. Hunt Collection, USAMHI. Bonta & Curtiss, Successor to B. F. Howland & Co., No. 4 Franklin Buildings, East Genesee Street, Syracuse, NY.

Charles Chauncey Dwight

Captain, Co. D, 75 NY Infantry, Sept. 17, 1861. Acting AAG, Staff of Brig. Gen. Lewis G. Arnold, May-Sept. 1862. Captain, AAG, USV, June 11, 1862. Colonel, 160 NY Infantry, Sept. 6, 1862. Provost Marshal General, Department of the Gulf, Jan. 11-June 3, 1863. Commanded 3 Brigade, 1 Division, 19 Army Corps, Department of the Gulf, Jan. 20-Feb. 15, 1864. Acting AIG, Staff of Major Gen. William B. Franklin, Feb.-May, 1864. Commissioner for the exchange of prisoners of war, New Orleans, LA, May 24, 1864-March 18, 1865. Resigned, May 25, 1865, because "the war is ended" and also to enable the promotion of Captain Henry P. Underhill.

Born: Sept. 15, 1830 Richmond, Berkshire Co., MA
Died: April 8, 1902 Auburn, NY
Education: Graduated Williams College, Williamstown, MA, 1850
Occupation: Lawyer and judge
Offices/Honors: Justice, NY Supreme Court, 1868-1902
Miscellaneous: Resided Auburn, Cayuga Co., NY. First cousin of Colonel James F. Dwight (11 MO Cavalry).
Buried: Stockbridge Cemetery, Stockbridge, MA
References: Benjamin W. Dwight. *History of the Descendants of John Dwight of Dedham, MA.* New York City, NY, 1874. Joel H. Monroe. *Historical Records of 120 Years.* Auburn, NY, 1913. Military Service File, National Archives. Letters Received, Volunteer Service Branch, Adjutant General's Office, File D594(VS)1862, National Archives.

Charles Chauncey Dwight
Courtesy of Steve Meadow. Brady's National Photographic Portrait Gallery, Broadway & Tenth Street, New York.

Charles Chauncey Dwight (standing left; with Major Lewis E. Carpenter)
Massachusetts MOLLUS Collection, USAMHI.

Charles Chauncey Dwight
Roger D. Hunt Collection, USAMHI. Anderson's Photographic Gallery, 61 Camp Street, New Orleans, LA.

Charles Chauncey Dwight (1867)
Roger D. Hunt Collection, USAMHI. Jeffers & McDonnald, No. 519 Broadway, Albany, NY.

Garret W. Dyckman

Captain, Co. A, 1 NY Infantry, April 23, 1861. Lieutenant Colonel, 1 NY Infantry, May 7, 1861. Colonel, 1 NY Infantry, Sept. 10, 1861. Discharged Oct. 9, 1862, on the recommendation of Governor Edwin D. Morgan and Brig. Gen. David B. Birney, for "inefficiency as evidenced by the demoralized condition" of his regiment.

Born: May 30, 1814 Cortlandtown, Westchester Co., NY
Died: May 22, 1868 New York City, NY
Other Wars: Mexican War (Major, 1 NY Volunteers, severely wounded in shoulder at Churubusco, MX)
Occupation: Merchant and accountant
Offices/Honors: NY State Assembly, 1858. Register of New York County, NY.
Miscellaneous: Resided New York City, NY. One of the most prominent competitors for the gold box bequeathed by General Andrew Jackson to the bravest soldier from New York City.

Garret W. Dyckman (1857)
Harper's Weekly, Vol. 1, No. 40 (Oct. 3, 1857).

Buried: Cedar Hill Cemetery, Montrose, NY

References: H. Dorothea Romer and Helen B. Hartman. *Jan Dyckman of Harlem and His Descendants*. New York City, NY, 1981. Obituary, *New York Herald*, May 24-25, 1868. Military Service File, National Archives. Obituary, *Peekskill Messenger*, May 28, 1868. Letters Received, Volunteer Service Branch, Adjutant General's Office, File N448(VS)1862, National Archives. "Major Garrett Dyckman and the Gold Box Which He Did Not Get," *Harper's Weekly,* Vol. 1, No. 40 (Oct. 3, 1857). William D. Murphy. *Biographical Sketches of the State Officers and Members of the Legislature of the State of New York in 1858*. Albany, NY, 1858.

John Henry Edson

Major, 1 MA Cavalry, Nov. 4, 1861. Resigned Jan. 7, 1862. Lieutenant Colonel, 10 VT Infantry, Sept. 1, 1862. Resigned Oct. 16, 1862. *Colonel*, 3 NY Infantry, Dec. 31, 1864. Never joined regiment since the low strength of the regiment did not permit the mustering of a colonel.

Born: Jan. 18, 1830 Brooklyn, NY

Died: Feb. 11, 1914 Elizabeth, NJ

Education: Graduated US Military Academy, West Point, NY, 1853

Occupation: Regular Army (2 Lieutenant, Mounted Rifles, resigned Sept. 1, 1860). Clerk, Provost Marshal General's Bureau, Washington, DC, 1863-64. Oil and mining company superintendent, 1864-66. Chemical manufacturer, 1867-69. New York Custom House employee, 1870-79.

Miscellaneous: Resided Elizabeth, NJ. Brother-in-law of Bvt. Brig. Gen. James V. Bomford.

Buried: Evergreen Cemetery, Hillside, NJ (Section G, Lot 67)

References: Jarvis B. Edson. *Edsons in England and America*. New York City, NY, 1903. *Annual Reunion*, Association of the Graduates of the US Military Academy, 1914. George W. Cullum. *Biographical Register of the Officers and Graduates of the US Military Academy*. Third Edition. Boston and New York, 1891. Obituary, *New York Herald,* Feb. 13, 1914.

John Henry Edson (postwar)
Annual Reunion, Association of the Graduates of the US Military Academy, 1914.

Ephraim Elmer Ellsworth
Beverly H. Kallgren Collection, USAMHI.

Ephraim Elmer Ellsworth
Massachusetts MOLLUS Collection, USAMHI. Brady's National Photographic
Portrait Gallery, Broadway & Tenth Street, New York.

Ephraim Elmer Ellsworth

Colonel, 11 NY Infantry, May 7, 1861. GSW breast, Alexandria, VA, May 24, 1861.

Born: April 11, 1837 Malta, Saratoga Co., NY
Died: May 24, 1861 KIA Alexandria, VA
Occupation: Law student. Commanded the prewar US Zouave Cadets of Chicago.
Miscellaneous: Resided Chicago, IL
Buried: Hudson View Cemetery, Mechanicville, NY
References: Ruth Painter Randall. *Colonel Elmer Ellsworth: A Biography of Lincoln's Friend and First Hero of the Civil War.* Boston and Toronto, 1960. *Exercises Connected With the Unveiling of the Ellsworth Monument.* Albany, NY, 1875. Nathaniel B. Sylvester. *History of Saratoga County, NY.* Philadelphia, PA, 1878.

Ephraim Elmer Ellsworth
Massachusetts MOLLUS Collection, USAMHI. Brady's National Photographic
Portrait Gallery, Broadway & Tenth Street, New York.

Frederic Ely Embick

2 Lieutenant, Co. A, 11 PA Infantry, April 24, 1861. 1 Lieutenant, Co. A, 11 PA Infantry, June 24, 1861. Honorably mustered out, July 31, 1861. Major, 50 NY Engineers, Aug. 23, 1861. Lieutenant Colonel, 106 NY Infantry, Sept. 30, 1862. Colonel, 106 NY Infantry, Aug. 4, 1863. Dismissed Sept. 14, 1863, for "violation of the 6th Article of War, in behaving himself with contempt or disrespect toward his commanding officer, through a series of disrespectful communications, and for insubordinate conduct," in refusing to allow the detail of a private from his regiment as forage master. Disability resulting from dismissal removed, Dec. 14, 1863. Recommissioned as colonel to date Dec. 15, 1863, but never mustered because the regiment was below minimum strength.

Ephraim Elmer Ellsworth
Civil War Library & Museum, Philadelphia, PA.

Ephraim Elmer Ellsworth
Gil Barrett Collection, USAMHI.

Ephraim Elmer Ellsworth
Michael J. McAfee Collection.

Born: Dec. 21, 1834 Lebanon, PA

Died: Sept. 10, 1913 New York City, NY

Education: Attended US Military Academy, West Point, NY (Class of 1860)

Occupation: Lumber merchant and real estate agent

Miscellaneous: Resided Williamsport, Lycoming Co., PA; and New York City, NY

Buried: Wildwood Cemetery, Williamsport, PA

References: Pension File and Military Service File, National Archives. Obituary, *Williamsport Sun*, Sept. 12, 1913. Obituary, *New York Times*, Sept. 12, 1913. Ed Malles, editor. *Bridge Building in Wartime: Colonel Wesley Brainerd's Memoir of the 50th New York Volunteer Engineers*. Knoxville, TN, 1997. Letters Received, Volunteer Service Branch, Adjutant General's Office, File E468(VS)1863, National Archives.

Ephraim Elmer Ellsworth
Massachusetts MOLLUS Collection, USAMHI.

William Emerson
Mike Waskul Collection. Hopkins & Son, Photographers, Albion, NY.

William Emerson

Colonel, 151 NY Infantry, Sept. 3, 1862. Commanded 1 Brigade, 3 Division, 6 Army Corps, Army of the Shenandoah, Aug. 6, 1864-Nov. 1864. Honorably mustered out, Dec. 21, 1864.

Born: March 8, 1825 Rochester, NY
Died: May 10, 1894 Rochester, NY
Occupation: Lumber merchant. Later operated a cotton batten mill and a large ice business.
Miscellaneous: Resided Rochester, Monroe Co., NY
Buried: Mount Hope Cemetery, Rochester, NY (Range 3, Lot 58)
References: Obituary, *Rochester Union and Advertiser*, May 11, 1894. Obituary, *Rochester Democrat and Chronicle*, May 11, 1894. Pension File, National Archives. Helena A. Howell, compiler. *Chronicles of the 151st Regiment New York State Volunteer Infantry*. Albion, NY, 1911.

William Emerson (postwar)
National Archives.

Richard C. Enright

Lieutenant Colonel, 63 NY Infantry, Aug. 30, 1861. Colonel, 63 NY Infantry, Nov. 2, 1861. Discharged Jan. 21, 1862 upon "adverse report of a Board of Examination." Order discharging him was amended, Oct. 20, 1866, "so as to honorably discharge him, to date Feb. 5, 1862, he having subsequently appeared before said Board and passed a satisfactory examination, and the vacancy resulting from his discharge having been filled."

Born: 1835? County Kerry, Ireland
Died: Feb. 10, 1911 New York City, NY
Occupation: Clerk
Offices/Honors: Deputy Clerk in the office of the Clerk of Oneida Co., NY, before war
Miscellaneous: Resided Utica, Oneida Co., NY; Brooklyn, NY, 1862-70; Cincinnati, OH, 1870-85; New York City, NY, 1885-90; Omaha, NE, 1890-91; Chicago, IL, 1891-1905; and New York City, NY, 1905-11
Buried: Holy Cross Cemetery, Brooklyn, NY (St. Peter's Section, Range A, Plot 30, unmarked)
References: Pension File and Military Service File, National Archives. Death certificate. Letters Received, Volunteer Service Branch, Adjutant General's Office, File M288(VS)1861, National Archives. David P. Conyngham. *The Irish Brigade and Its Campaigns.* Boston, MA, 1869.

David Morris Evans

Musician, Co. A, 35 NY Infantry, June 11, 1861. 1 Sergeant, Co. I, 35 NY Infantry. 1 Lieutenant, Adjutant, 35 NY Infantry, Oct. 28, 1861. Major, 35 NY Infantry, Jan. 1, 1863. Lieutenant Colonel, 35 NY Infantry, Feb. 9, 1863. Honorably mustered out, June 5, 1863. 1 Lieutenant, Adjutant, 20 NY Cavalry, July 2, 1863. Lieutenant Colonel, 20 NY Cavalry, Oct. 13, 1863. Colonel, 20 NY Cavalry, April 1, 1865. Honorably mustered out, July 31, 1865.

Born: Feb. 21, 1831 New Castle, Emlyn, Wales
Died: May 8, 1924 Minneapolis, MN
Education: Attended Williams College, Williamstown, MA (Class of 1856)
Occupation: Lawyer and journalist. After the war held a responsible position in US Mint at Philadelphia for 15 years

Above Right: David Morris Evans
Roger D. Hunt Collection, USAMHI. B. F. Evans, No. 14 Main Street, Norfolk, VA.
Right: David Morris Evans (seated center; with Capt. Henry C. Chittenden, left; and Major John B. Preston, right)
Roger D. Hunt Collection, USAMHI. B. F. Evans, No. 14 Main Street, Norfolk, VA.

and then spent later years as clerk in Minneapolis Post Office.

Offices/Honors: President, Redfield (SD) College

Miscellaneous: Resided Philadelphia, PA; and Minneapolis, MN

Buried: Lakewood Cemetery, Minneapolis, MN (Section 21, Lot 667)

References: Pension File, National Archives. Obituary Circular, Whole No. 924, Minnesota MOLLUS. Obituary, *Minneapolis Morning Tribune,* May 10, 1924.

William Everdell, Jr.

Colonel, 23 NY National Guard, June 18, 1863. Honorably mustered out, July 22, 1863.

William Everdell, Jr. (November 1863)
Courtesy of Ed Italo. Augustus Morand, 297 Fulton Street, Brooklyn, NY.

Above Right: *William Everdell, Jr.*
Massachusetts MOLLUS Collection, USAMHI. Published by E. Anthony, 501 Broadway, New York, from Photographic Negative in Brady's National Portrait Gallery.
Right: *William Everdell, Jr. (November 1863)*
Michael J. McAfee Collection. Augustus Morand, 297 Fulton Street, Brooklyn, NY.

Born: May 6, 1822 New York City, NY
Died: Nov. 5, 1912 Brooklyn, NY
Occupation: Engaged in the engraving and printing business
Offices/Honors: President of the Brooklyn Institute, 1870-78
Miscellaneous: Resided Brooklyn, NY
Buried: Green-Wood Cemetery, Brooklyn, NY (Section 167, Lot 16843)
References: Obituary, *Brooklyn Daily Eagle*, Nov. 5, 1912.

James Fairman

Captain, Co. B, 10 NY Infantry, April 26, 1861. Discharged May 28, 1861. *Colonel*, 73 NY Infantry, Aug. 16, 1861. Due to a conflict with Colonel William R. Brewster over the colonelcy, he resigned Nov. 30, 1861. Colonel, 96 NY Infantry, March 5, 1862. Discharged for disability, Sept. 25, 1862, due to ill health caused by disease of the bladder and urinary organs.

Above & Above Right: *James Fairman*
Massachusetts MOLLUS Collection, USAMHI.
Right: *James Fairman (postwar)*
Lafayette Post 140 GAR Collection, Civil War Library & Museum, Philadelphia, PA.

Noah Lane Farnham
US Military Academy Library.

Noah Lane Farnham
Massachusetts MOLLUS Collection, USAMHI. Brady's National Photographic
Portrait Gallery, 352 Pennsylvania Avenue, Washington, DC.

Born: April 6, 1825 Glasgow, Scotland

Died: March 12, 1904 New York City, NY

Occupation: Artist and landscape painter. Later in life became a prominent art critic and lecturer.

Miscellaneous: Resided New York City, NY; Scranton, Lackawanna Co., PA; and San Francisco, CA

Buried: Evergreens Cemetery, Brooklyn, NY (Greenwood Shade Section, Lot 203, unmarked)

References: George C. Groce and David H. Wallace. *The New-York Historical Society's Dictionary of Artists in America, 1564-1860.* New Haven and London, 1957. Circular, Whole No. 272, California MOLLUS. Will probated, *New York Times*, March 27, 1904. Pension File, Department of Veterans Affairs. Military Service File, National Archives. Thomas P. Lowry. *Tarnished Eagles: The Courts-Martial of Fifty Union Colonels and Lieutenant Colonels.* Mechanicsburg, PA, 1997. Letters Received, Volunteer Service Branch, Adjutant General's Office, File F388(VS)1862, National Archives.

Noah Lane Farnham

1 Lieutenant, Co. B, 7 NY State Militia, April 26, 1861. Lieutenant Colonel, 11 NY Infantry, May 7, 1861. *Colonel*, 11 NY Infantry, June 4, 1861. GSW head, Bull Run, VA, July 21, 1861.

Born: June 6, 1829 Haddam, CT

Died: Aug. 14, 1861 DOW Washington, DC

Occupation: Merchant tailor

Offices/Honors: Assistant Engineer, New York City Fire Department, 1855-59

Miscellaneous: Resided New York City, NY

Buried: Grove Street Cemetery, New Haven, CT (Spruce Avenue, Tier 9, Lot 62)

References: William J. Tenney. *Military and Naval History of the Rebellion in the United States.* New York City, NY, 1865. John Gilmary Shea, editor. *The Fallen Brave.* New York City, NY, 1861. Obituary, *New York Herald*, Aug. 15, 1861.

Alonzo Ferguson

1 Lieutenant, Adjutant, 121 NY Infantry, July 21, 1862. 1 Lieutenant, Adjutant, 152 NY Infantry, Sept. 2, 1862. Lieutenant Colonel, 152 NY Infantry, Oct. 13, 1862. Colonel, 152 NY Infantry, Jan. 10, 1863. Discharged for disability, Nov. 23, 1863, due to "dyspepsia and kidney complaint attended with pain and weakness in the lumbar region."

Born: March 19, 1820 Nassau, Rensselaer Co., NY
Died: April 3, 1912 Westwood, Bergen Co., NJ
Occupation: Hardware merchant and manufacturer before war. Hardware merchant and insurance agent after war.
Miscellaneous: Resided Buffalo, NY; Cobleskill, Schoharie Co., NY; and New York City, NY
Buried: Rural Cemetery, Albany, NY (Section 26, Lot 118)
References: *Biographical Review of the Leading Citizens of Schoharie, Schenectady, and Greene Counties, NY.* Boston, MA, 1899. William E. Roscoe. *History of Schoharie County, NY.* Syracuse, NY, 1882. Pension File, National Archives.

John Fisk

Colonel, 2 NY Mounted Rifles, July 2, 1863. Discharged for disability, Dec. 5, 1864, due to "chronic diarrhea and dropsical swelling of the feet." Colonel, 2 NY Mounted Rifles, March 9, 1865. Discharged May 18, 1865, upon "adverse report of a Board of Examination," which cited his "gross ignorance and entire inefficiency as an officer."

Born: Nov. 30, 1802 Brookfield, Madison Co., NY
Died: Jan. 10, 1891 Suspension Bridge, Niagara Co., NY
Occupation: Civil engineer and canal contractor
Miscellaneous: Resided Suspension Bridge, Niagara Co., NY; and Washington, DC
Buried: Cold Spring Cemetery, Lockport, NY (Section D, Lot 93)
References: Circular, Whole No. 888, California MOLLUS. Frederick C. Pierce. *Fiske and Fisk Family.* Chicago, IL, 1896. Pension File, National Archives. Obituary, *Lockport Union*, Jan. 10, 1891. Obituary, *Niagara Falls Gazette*, Jan. 14, 1891.

Alonzo Ferguson
New York State Military Museum and Veterans Research Center. Anson's, 589 Broadway, Opposite Metropolitan Hotel, New York.

Alonzo Ferguson
Courtesy of the author. S. J. Thompson, Photographist, No. 519 Broadway, Albany, NY.

Hugh C. Flood

1 Lieutenant, Co. A, 69 NY State Militia, May 26, 1862. Honorably mustered out, Sept. 3, 1862. 1 Lieutenant, Adjutant, 155 NY Infantry, Sept. 11, 1862. Major, 155 NY Infantry, Nov. 8, 1862. Lieutenant Colonel, 155 NY Infantry, March 27, 1863. *Colonel*, 155 NY Infantry, Nov. 3, 1863. GSW abdomen, Spotsylvania, VA, May 18, 1864. Discharged for disability, Oct. 13, 1864, due to effects of wound in abdomen.

Born: 1832? Ireland
Died: Nov. 5, 1864 New York City, NY
Occupation: Liquor merchant
Miscellaneous: Resided New York City, NY
Buried: Holy Cross Cemetery, Brooklyn, NY
References: Pension File, National Archives. Death notice, *New York Herald*, Nov. 7, 1864.

Hugh C. Flood
Massachusetts MOLLUS Collection, USAMHI. Brady's National Photographic Portrait Gallery, Broadway & Tenth Street, New York.

Elbridge G. Floyd

Captain, Co. C, 3 NY Infantry, April 20, 1861. Major, 3 NY Infantry, Sept. 20, 1862. Lieutenant Colonel, 3 NY Infantry, May 23, 1863. GSW left leg, Drewry's Bluff, VA, May 16, 1864. *Colonel*, 3 NY Infantry, June 14, 1864. Discharged for disability, Dec. 7, 1864, due to effects of wound of left leg.

Born: March 4, 1837 Lebanon, NH
Died: March 24, 1917 Omaha, NE
Occupation: Mechanic (grate and fender maker) before war. Manager and later proprietor of the famous Diamond Saloon and Gambling House in Omaha.
Miscellaneous: Resided Albany, NY, to 1869; and Omaha, NE, after 1869. Brother of Colonel Horace W. Floyd (3 VT Infantry). William Lord, 40 MA Infantry, was awarded Medal of Honor for rescuing Floyd when he was wounded at Drewry's Bluff.
Buried: Prospect Hill Cemetery, Omaha, NE (Lot 590, 1st Addition, unmarked)
References: Obituary, *Omaha Morning World-Herald*, March 25, 1917. Pension File, National Archives.

David S. Forbes

Colonel, 68 NY National Guard, June 25, 1863. Honorably mustered out, July 29, 1863.

Born: Feb. 11, 1817 Greene, Chenango Co., NY
Died: May 31, 1904 Fredonia, NY
Occupation: Merchant and grain elevator operator
Miscellaneous: Resided Fredonia, Chautauqua Co., NY; and Buffalo, NY. Father-in-law of Commander William B. Cushing of the US Navy.
Buried: Forest Hill Cemetery, Fredonia, NY (Section V, Lot 56)
References: Butler F. Dilley, editor. *Biographical and Portrait Cyclopedia of Chautauqua County, NY*. Philadelphia, PA, 1891. Pension File, National Archives. Obituary, *The Grape Belt and Chautauqua Farmer*, May 31, 1904. Obituary, *Fredonia Censor*, June 8, 1904.

Following Page, Below Left: *James Prentice Foster*
History of the 128th Regiment, New York Volunteers in the Late Civil War. F. Forshew, Photographer, Hudson, NY.

David S. Forbes (postwar)
Fredonia Censor, June 8, 1904.

James Prentice Foster

Captain, Co. L, 5 NY Cavalry, Oct. 31, 1861. Major, 128 NY
    Infantry, Aug. 29, 1862. Lieutenant Colonel, 128 NY In-
    fantry, May 27, 1863. *Colonel*, 128 NY Infantry, Dec. 18,
    1863. GSW right leg, Red River, LA, May 5, 1864. Dis-
    missed Nov. 17, 1864, for "neglect of duty, conduct preju-
    dicial to good order and military discipline, and breach of
    arrest." Disability resulting from dismissal removed Jan.
    24, 1865. Dismissal revoked, March 23, 1867, and he was
    honorably discharged as of date of dismissal.

Born: Nov. 27, 1830 Athens, NY

Died: Aug. 15, 1904 Geneva, NY

Occupation: Merchant before war. Instructor to the Onondaga
    Indians, 1867-70. Episcopal clergyman after 1870.

Offices/Honors: Collector of the Port, Wilmington, NC, 1866

Miscellaneous: Resided Athens, NY, 1854-61; Wilmington,
    NC, 1865-67; Syracuse, NY, 1867-72; Cortland, NY, 1872-
    75; Pulaski, NY, 1875-78; Newark, NY, 1878-81; Sodus,
    NY, 1881-84; and Geneva, Ontario Co., NY, 1884-1904

Buried: Washington Street Cemetery, Geneva, NY (Section J,
    Lot 20)

References: Pension File and Military Service File, National
    Archives. Lewis H. Clark. *Military History of Wayne
    County, NY.* Sodus, NY, 1884. Obituary, *Geneva Daily
    Times,* Aug. 16, 1904. David H. Hanaburgh. *History of the
    128th Regiment, New York Volunteers in the Late Civil
    War.* Poughkeepsie, NY, 1894.

James Prentice Foster
Roger D. Hunt Collection, USAMHI. F. Forshew, Photographer, Hudson, NY.

Henry Thomas Fowler

Lieutenant Colonel, 63 NY Infantry, Nov. 4, 1861. GSW right
   arm, Antietam, MD, Sept. 17, 1862. Colonel, 63 NY Infantry, Oct. 25, 1862. Discharged for disability, July 4,
   1863, due to effects of wound received at Antietam.

Born: Nov. 13, 1819 CT
Died: Jan. 19, 1877 Guilford, CT
Occupation: Agent
Miscellaneous: Resided Brooklyn, NY; and Guilford, New
   Haven Co., CT. Brother of Lt. Col. Douglas Fowler, 17
   CT Infantry.
Buried: Alderbrook Cemetery, Guilford, CT
References: Alvan Talcott, compiler. *Families of Early
   Guilford, CT*. Baltimore, MD, 1984. Pension File, National
   Archives. David P. Conyngham. *The Irish Brigade and Its
   Campaigns*. Boston, MA, 1869.

Henry Thomas Fowler (center)
Massachusetts MOLLUS Collection, USAMHI.

Henry Thomas Fowler
US Military Academy
Library.

Watson A. Fox (postwar)
Lafayette Post 140 GAR Collection, Civil War Library & Museum, Philadel-
phia, PA.

Watson A. Fox

Colonel, 74 NY National Guard, June 19, 1863. Honorably mustered out, Aug. 3, 1863. Colonel, 74 NY National Guard, Nov. 20, 1863. Honorably mustered out, Dec. 16, 1863.

Born: Jan. 17, 1819 Erie Co., NY
Died: Jan. 20, 1896 New York City, NY
Occupation: Grocery and ship chandlery business before war. Engaged in marine transportation and marine insurance after war.
Miscellaneous: Resided Buffalo, NY; and New York City, NY, after 1883
Buried: Forest Lawn Cemetery, Buffalo, NY (Section F, Lot 99)
References: Obituary, *Buffalo Morning Express*, Jan. 22, 1896. *Souvenir 74th Regiment NGSNY*. Buffalo, NY, 1899. Henry P. Phelps. *The Grand Army of the Republic (Department of New York) Personal Records*. New York City, NY, 1896.

James Leslie Fraser

Lieutenant Colonel, 47 NY Infantry, Sept. 14, 1861. Colonel, 47 NY Infantry, Aug. 5, 1862. Commanded US Forces, Hilton Head, SC, 10 Army Corps, Department of the South, Oct. 5-20, 1862. Discharged for disability, March 17, 1863, due to "diabetes and disease of the liver."

Born: 1825? Ireland
Died: July 7, 1866 New York City, NY (pistol shot wound received during an altercation at his restaurant)
Occupation: Restaurant keeper
Miscellaneous: Resided New York City, NY
Buried: Green-Wood Cemetery, Brooklyn, NY (Section 180, Lot 13152, unmarked)
References: Obituary, *New York Herald*, July 9, 1866. Pension File and Military Service File, National Archives.

James Leslie Fraser
Massachusetts MOLLUS Collection, USAMHI.

James Leslie Fraser
Roger D. Hunt Collection, USAMHI. J. H. Bigelow, 212 Broadway, New York.

Edward Frisby

Colonel, 30 NY Infantry, May 21, 1861. GSW head, Bull Run, VA, Aug. 30, 1862.

Born: Aug. 3, 1809 Trenton, NY
Died: Aug. 30, 1862 KIA Bull Run, VA
Occupation: Early in life a hatter, he later became a livery stable keeper
Offices/Honors: Joined NY State Militia at the age of 18, eventually serving as Brigadier General, 11 Brigade, 3 Division, 1856-60
Miscellaneous: Resided Albany, NY. First cousin of Colonel Uriah L. Davis.
Buried: Rural Cemetery, Albany, NY (Section 20, Lot 7)
References: Edward S. Frisbee. *The Frisbee-Frisbie Genealogy*. Rutland, VT, 1926. Rufus W. Clark. *The Heroes of Albany*. Albany, NY, 1867. Obituary, *Albany Evening Journal*, Sept. 8, 1862.

James Madison Fuller

Colonel, 105 NY Infantry, March 26, 1862. Resigned Aug. 2, 1862, "having been informed that a large number of the line officers have expressed a want of confidence in my ability to lead them into action."

Born: October 4, 1807 Kirby, Caledonia Co., VT
Died: April 12, 1891 Saranac, MI
Occupation: Methodist clergyman
Miscellaneous: Resided Lowell, Kent Co., MI; East Saginaw, Saginaw Co., MI; Detroit, MI; and Saranac, Ionia Co., MI
Buried: South Boston Cemetery, near Saranac, MI
References: Pension File, National Archives. Death notice, *Grand Rapids Telegram-Herald*, April 15, 1891. *Detroit Annual Conference, Methodist Episcopal Church, Thirty-Sixth Session*. 1891.

Edward Frisby
Meade Album, Civil War Library & Museum, Philadelphia, PA.

Edward Frisby
Courtesy of Dave Zullo.

William S. Fullerton

Colonel, 19 NY Cavalry, July 25, 1862. Resigned Sept. 3, 1862.

Born: 1806? Sparta, NY
Died: April 1, 1874 Sparta, NY
Occupation: Farmer
Offices/Honors: NY State Assembly, 1846-47. Major Gen.,
NY State Militia.
Miscellaneous: Resided Sparta, Livingston Co., NY.
Buried: Old Sparta Burying Ground, Sparta, NY (unmarked)
References: Gordon W. Fullerton. *The Fullertons, Fullartons,
and Fullingtons of North America.* N.p., 1986. Obituary,
Dansville Advertiser, April 9, 1874. Military Service File,
National Archives.

Augustus Funk

2 Lieutenant, Co. C, 38 NY Infantry, May 7, 1861. 1 Lieutenant, Co. C, 38 NY Infantry, Aug. 6, 1861. Captain, Co. H,
38 NY Infantry, Jan. 11, 1862. GSW left arm,
Williamsburg, VA, May 5, 1862. GSW left thigh, 2nd Bull
Run, VA, Aug. 29, 1862. Discharged for disability, Dec. 4,
1862, on account of wounds. Major, 38 NY Infantry, Jan.
19, 1863. Honorably mustered out, June 22, 1863. Authorized as *Colonel*, 38 NY Infantry (Reorganizing), June 23,
1863. Reorganization discontinued, Oct. 14, 1863. Colonel, 39 NY Infantry, Nov. 13, 1863. Commanded 3 Brigade, 3 Division, 2 Army Corps, Army of the Potomac,
Feb. 10-March 25, 1864. GSW left leg, Wilderness, VA,
May 6, 1864. Commanded 3 Brigade, 1 Division, 2 Army
Corps, March 25, 1865. GSW right hip, Boydton Plank
Road, VA, March 31, 1865. Commanded 3 Brigade, 1 Division, 2 Army Corps, May 28-June 28, 1865. Honorably
mustered out, July 1, 1865.

Born: Nov. 27, 1841 FL
Died: Oct. 18, 1883 New York City, NY
Occupation: Hotelkeeper and clerk in Adjutant General's Of-
fice, Washington, DC. Regular Army (1 Lieutenant, RQM,
41 US Infantry, resigned Nov. 20, 1868).
Offices/Honors: Brig. Gen., NY National Guard
Miscellaneous: Resided Washington, DC; and New York City,
NY
Buried: Woodlawn Cemetery, New York City, NY (Section
77, Fern Plot, Lot 7595)
References: Pension File and Military Service File, National
Archives. Obituary, *New York Herald*, Oct. 19, 1883.
Obituary, *New York Times*, Oct. 23, 1883. John M.
Pellicano. *Conquer or Die, The 39th New York Volunteer*

Augustus Funk
New York State Military Museum and Veterans Research Center. Hallett &
Brother, 134 & 136 Bowery, Near Grand Street, New York.

Infantry: Garibaldi Guard. Flushing, NY, 1996. Michael
Bacarella. *Lincoln's Foreign Legion, The 39th New York
Infantry, The Garibaldi Guard.* Shippensburg, PA, 1996.

Augustus Funk (postwar)
National Archives.

Haviland Gifford
New York State Military Museum and Veterans Research Center. R. W. Addis, Photographer, 308 Penna. Avenue, Washington, DC.

Haviland Gifford (postwar)
History of the 93rd Regiment New York Volunteer Infantry.

Robert P. Gibson

Colonel, 12 NY Heavy Artillery, March 31, 1863. Regiment did not complete organization and his authority as colonel was revoked, June 22, 1863.

Born: April 3, 1819 New York City, NY
Died: Dec. 27, 1890 New York City, NY
Education: Graduated Princeton (NJ) University, 1840. Graduated New York College of Medicine, 1855.
Occupation: Physician
Miscellaneous: Resided New York City, NY. Lineal descendant of Peter Stuyvesant.
Buried: St. Mark's-in-the-Bowery Churchyard, New York City, NY
References: Obituary, *New York Times*, Dec. 28, 1890.

Haviland Gifford

1 Lieutenant, Adjutant, 93 NY Infantry, Jan. 22, 1862. GSW right arm, Wilderness, VA, May 5, 1864. Lieutenant Colonel, 93 NY Infantry, Feb. 3, 1865. *Colonel*, 93 NY Infantry, March 1, 1865. Honorably mustered out, June 29, 1865.

Born: Feb. 24, 1820 Easton, Washington Co., NY
Died: April 3, 1901 Crawfordsville, IN
Occupation: Farmer
Miscellaneous: Resided Easton, Washington Co., NY; Augusta, Kalamazoo Co., MI; Warren, Marion Co., MO; and Crawfordsville, Montgomery Co., IN
Buried: Prairie Home Cemetery, Climax, Kalamazoo Co., MI
References: Pension File, National Archives. David H. King, A. Judson Gibbs, and Jay H. Northup, compilers. *History of the 93rd Regiment New York Volunteer Infantry*. Milwaukee, WI, 1895. Obituary, *Crawfordsville Journal*, April 4, 1901. Jane B. Welling. *They Were Here Too*. Vol. 3. N.p., 1971.

John Gittermann

1 Lieutenant, Co. C, 29 NY Infantry, May 13, 1861. Captain, Co. C, 29 NY Infantry, Aug. 2, 1861. Acting AAG, Staff of Colonel Gustave P. Cluseret, May 11-June 8, 1862. GSW right shoulder and right lung, Cross Keys, VA, June 8, 1862. Acting ADC, Staff of Brig. Gen. Carl Schurz, Aug. 9-Sept. 3, 1862. Acting ADC, Staff of Brig. Gen. Adolph von Steinwehr, Jan. 20-March 29, 1863. Discharged for disability, May 6, 1863, due to wounds. *Colonel*, 29 NY Infantry, July 25, 1863. Succeeded by Colonel Peter Degive, Sept. 10, 1863. Captain, 20 VRC, Aug. 19, 1863. Captain,

Co. D, 4 VRC, Dec. 14, 1863. Discharged for disability, July 4, 1864, due to "tuberculosis of the lungs."

Born: 1826? Germany
Died: Feb. 6, 1866 Rock Island, IL
Miscellaneous: Resided New York City, NY; and Cedar Rapids, Linn Co., IA
Buried: Chippiannock Cemetery, Rock Island, IL (South Public Lot 3, Grave 18)
References: Pension File and Military Service File, National Archives. Letters Received, Volunteer Service Branch, Adjutant General's Office, File G303(VS)1863, National Archives.

Abel Godard

Captain, Co. K, 60 NY Infantry, Sept. 25, 1861. Major, 60 NY Infantry, Sept. 16, 1862. Discharged for disability, Dec. 13, 1862, due to chronic diarrhea. Colonel, 60 NY Infantry, Dec. 30, 1862. Discharged for disability, Sept. 13, 1864, due to chronic diarrhea.

Born: June 26, 1835 Richville, NY
Died: July 25, 1891 Richville, NY
Education: Graduated University of Rochester (NY), 1859. Graduated Albany (NY) Law School, 1861.
Occupation: Real estate agent and banker
Offices/Honors: NY State Senate, 1866-67. NY State Assembly, 1882-83.
Miscellaneous: Resided Richville, St. Lawrence Co., NY
Buried: Wayside Cemetery, Richville, NY
References: Obituary, *Gouverneur Free Press*, Aug. 5, 1891. Winfred R. Goddard, Jr. *The Goddards of Granby, CT*. San Diego, CA, 1985. Pension File, National Archives. Paul A. Chadbourne, editor. *The Public Service of the State of New York*. New York City, NY, 1882. Richard Eddy. *History of the 60th Regiment New York State Volunteers*. Philadelphia, PA, 1864.

Abel Godard
Ogdensburg (NY) Public Library. Courtesy of Jeff Kowalis.

Abel Godard (1882)
The Public Service of the State of New York.

William Bingham Goodrich

Captain, Co. A, 60 NY Infantry, Sept. 11, 1861. Lieutenant Colonel, 60 NY Infantry, Oct. 8, 1861. Colonel, 60 NY Infantry, May 1, 1862. Commanded 3 Brigade, 2 Division, 12 Army Corps, Army of the Potomac, Sept. 12-17, 1862. GSW right breast, Antietam, MD, Sept. 17, 1862.

Born: Dec. 1, 1821 Wilna, Jefferson Co., NY
Died: Sept. 17, 1862 KIA Antietam, MD
Other Wars: Mexican War (Private, Easton's Battalion, MO Infantry)
Occupation: Lawyer and newspaper publisher
Miscellaneous: Resided Canton, St. Lawrence Co., NY
Buried: Green-Wood Cemetery, Brooklyn, NY (Section 165, Lot 30802)
References: Richard Eddy. *History of the 60th Regiment New York State Volunteers.* Philadelphia, PA, 1864. Pension File, National Archives. Samuel W. Durant. *History of St. Lawrence County, NY.* Philadelphia, PA, 1878.

William Bingham Goodrich
Meade Album, Civil War Library & Museum, Philadelphia, PA.

Benjamin Frank Gott

Captain, Co. C, 57 NY Infantry, Nov. 12, 1861. Discharged for disability, June 14, 1862, due to "a disease of the kidneys and liver." Lieutenant Colonel, 174 NY Infantry, Oct. 15, 1862. Colonel, 174 NY Infantry, Oct. 17, 1863. Honorably discharged, Feb. 17, 1864, upon consolidation of 174 NY Infantry with 162 NY Infantry.

Born: Jan. 1, 1834 Newark, NJ
Died: July 12, 1904 Upper Montclair, NJ
Occupation: Merchant engaged in jewelry business
Offices/Honors: Appointed Commissioner of the Board of Charities and Correction for Kings County, NY, in 1885, he served two full terms, during one of which he was President of the Board
Miscellaneous: Resided Brooklyn, NY
Buried: Green-Wood Cemetery, Brooklyn, NY (Section 178, Lot 13143)
References: Obituary, *New York Times*, July 13, 1904. Pension File and Military Service File, National Archives. Philip P. Gott. *Ancestors and Descendants of an Ohio Gott Family.* Fort Lauderdale, FL, 1972. Obituary, *Brooklyn Daily Eagle*, July 13, 1904. Letters Received, Volunteer Service Branch, Adjutant General's Office, File G850(VS)1863, National Archives.

Charles Gould

Colonel, 176 NY Infantry, Sept. 4, 1862. Succeeded by Colonel Mark Hoyt, Oct. 2, 1862.

Born: Sept. 30, 1811 Litchfield, CT
Died: Sept. 8, 1870 Europe
Occupation: Broker
Miscellaneous: Resided New York City, NY
Buried: Green-Wood Cemetery, Brooklyn, NY (Section 32, Lots 14750-14751)
References: James G. Mumford. *Mumford Memoirs.* Boston, MA, 1900. W. A. Croffut and John M. Morris. *The Military and Civil History of Connecticut During the War of 1861-65.* New York City, NY, 1869. Clarence W. Bowen. *The History of Woodstock, CT: Genealogies of Woodstock Families.* Norwood, MA, 1935.

Charles Gould
The Military and Civil History of Connecticut During the War of 1861-65.

William S. Grantsynn
Michael Albanese Collection.

William S. Grantsynn

Captain, Co. H, 140 NY Infantry, Aug. 30, 1862. GSW left leg, Wilderness, VA, May 5, 1864. Lieutenant Colonel, 140 NY Infantry, Aug. 8, 1864. Colonel, 140 NY Infantry, Jan. 24, 1865. Honorably mustered out, June 3, 1865.

Born: May 30, 1832 Steuben Co., NY
Died: Dec. 17, 1907 Chicago, IL
Occupation: Civil engineer
Offices/Honors: City Surveyor, Rochester, NY, 1869-75
Miscellaneous: Resided Rochester, NY; Scottville, Mason Co., MI; and Chicago, IL
Buried: Pleasant Plains Township Cemetery, near Baldwin, Lake Co., MI
References: Pension File, National Archives. Obituary, *Rochester Democrat and Chronicle*, Dec. 24, 1907. Brian A. Bennett. *Sons of Old Monroe: A Regimental History of Patrick O'Rorke's 140th New York Volunteer Infantry.* Dayton, OH, 1992.

Charles Osborn Gray

Lieutenant Colonel, 96 NY Infantry, March 5, 1862. Colonel, 96 NY Infantry, Sept. 25, 1862. GSW breast, Kinston, NC, Dec. 14, 1862.

Born: March 24, 1839 Warrensburg, NY
Died: Dec. 14, 1862 KIA Kinston, NC
Education: Attended Rensselaer Polytechnic Institute, Troy, NY (Class of 1859)
Occupation: School teacher
Miscellaneous: Resided Warrensburg, Warren Co., NY
Buried: Warrensburg Cemetery, Warrensburg, NY (Section A, Circle)
References: Obituary, *Glens Falls Messenger*, Dec. 26, 1862. Samuel Burhans, Jr., compiler. *Burhans Genealogy.* New York City, NY, 1894. Town Clerk's Register of Soldiers, Warrensburg, Warren Co., NY, New York State Archives. Obituary, *Troy Daily Whig*, Dec. 22, 1862. Winslow C. Watson. *The Military and Civil History of the County of Essex, New York.* Albany, NY, 1869.

Charles Osborn Gray
Courtesy of the author.

Charles Osborn Gray
The Military and Civil History of the County of Essex, New York.

Charles Osborn Gray
New York State Military Museum and Veterans Research Center.

Nelson Winch Green

Colonel, 76 NY Infantry, Oct. 29, 1861. Arrested upon charges
of "conduct amounting to insanity" preferred by the officers of his regiment, he was discharged June 3, 1862, upon
adverse report of a Board of Examination, which con-
cluded, "... so excitable is his mind, and so uncontrollable
are his impulses, that they do not consider him a fit person
to command a regiment." By Special Order dated Sept. 9,
1867, his discharge was revoked, and his resignation was
accepted to date June 3, 1862.

Born: July 30, 1819 Pike, Wyoming Co., NY
Died: May 12, 1907 Stoneham, MA
Education: Attended US Military Academy, West Point, NY
(Class of 1843)
Occupation: Newspaper editor and author
Miscellaneous: Resided Cortland, NY; Springfield, Hampden
Co., MA; Amherst, Hampshire Co., MA; and Stoneham,
Middlesex Co., MA

Buried: Lindenwood Cemetery, Stoneham, MA

References: Pension File, National Archives. Abram P. Smith. *History of the 76th Regiment New York Volunteers.* Cortland, NY, 1867. Letters Received, Volunteer Service Branch, Adjutant General's Office, File M250(VS)1862, National Archives.

David Elmore Gregory

Private, Co. H, 71 NY State Militia, April 21, 1861. Honorably mustered out, July 30, 1861. 1 Lieutenant, Adjutant, 61 NY Infantry, Oct. 17, 1861. GSW right arm, White Oak Swamp, VA, June 30, 1862. Captured White Oak Swamp, VA, June 30, 1862. Paroled July 19, 1862. Lieutenant Colonel, 144 NY Infantry, Sept. 28, 1862. Colonel, 144 NY Infantry, May 24, 1863. Resigned Oct. 24, 1863, on account of "family affliction," specifically the illness of his wife.

Born: Jan. 1, 1836 Albany, NY

Died: Jan. 30, 1893 New York City, NY

Occupation: Clerk, salesman, and telegraph company superintendent

Miscellaneous: Resided New York City, NY. First cousin of Bvt. Brig. Gen. Lewis Benedict and Colonel Spencer H. Stafford (73 USCT).

Buried: Rural Cemetery, Albany, NY (Section 3, Lot 28)

References: Pension File and Military Service File, National Archives. Grant Gregory. *Ancestors and Descendants of Henry Gregory.* Provincetown, MA, 1938. Obituary, *New York Times*, Feb. 3, 1893. Letters Received, Volunteer Service Branch, Adjutant General's Office, File A430(VS)1862, National Archives.

Nelson Winch Green
History of the 76th Regiment New York Volunteers.

David Elmore Gregory
Roger D. Hunt Collection, USAMHI. J. Gurney & Son, Photographic Artists, 707 Broadway, New York.

John Augustus Griswold
Frederick H. Meserve. Historical Portraits. Courtesy of New York State Library.

John Augustus Griswold

Colonel, 125 NY Infantry, July 28, 1862. Resigned Aug. 22, 1862.

Born: Nov. 11, 1818 Nassau, Rensselaer Co., NY
Died: Oct. 31, 1872 Troy, NY
Occupation: Iron manufacturer and banker
Offices/Honors: US House of Representatives, 1863-69
Miscellaneous: Resided Troy, Rensselaer Co., NY. Nephew of Major General John E. Wool.
Buried: Oakwood Cemetery, Troy, NY (Section C, Griswold vault)
References: Nathaniel B. Sylvester. *History of Rensselaer County, NY*. Philadelphia, PA, 1880. *Dictionary of American Biography. National Cyclopedia of American Biography.* William H. Barnes. *The Fortieth Congress of the United States: Historical and Biographical.* New York City, NY, 1869. Henry Hall, editor. *America's Successful Men of Affairs.* New York City, NY, 1895.

William Thomas Campbell Grower

Captain, Co. D, 17 NY Infantry, May 20, 1861. Major, 17 NY Infantry, May 10, 1862. GSW leg 2nd Bull Run, VA, Aug. 30, 1862. Discharged for disability, Feb. 14, 1863, due to wounds. Discharge revoked, March 25, 1863. Honorably mustered out, June 2, 1863. *Colonel*, 17 NY Veteran Infantry, June 3, 1863. Commanded 3 Brigade, 4 Division, 16 Army Corps, Army of the Tennessee, July 21, 1864-Aug. 20, 1864. GSW side and groin, Jonesboro, GA, Sept. 1, 1864.

Born: 1839? Leeds, England
Died: Sept. 3, 1864 DOW Atlanta, GA
Occupation: Bank teller
Miscellaneous: Resided New York City, NY
Buried: Green-Wood Cemetery, Brooklyn, NY (Section 98, Lot 15301)
References: Pension File and Military Service File, National Archives. *Proceedings of the Third Brigade Association, First Division, Fifth Army Corps.* Record 3. New York City, NY, 1900. Letters Received, Volunteer Service Branch, Adjutant General's Office, File B389(VS)1863, National Archives. Obituary, *New York Times,* Sept. 20, 1864.

John Augustus Griswold
History of Rensselaer County, NY.

*William Thomas Campbell Grower
Roger D. Hunt Collection, USAMHI. Brady's
National Photographic Portrait Gallery, 352
Pennsylvania Avenue, Washington, DC.*

*William Thomas Campbell Grower
Roger D. Hunt Collection, USAMHI. E.
M. Douglass, Artist, 324 Fulton St.,
Brooklyn, NY.*

*William Thomas Campbell Grower
Roger D. Hunt Collection, USAMHI. Anson's, 589 Broadway, Opposite Metropolitan Hotel, New York.*

Nicholas Grumbach

Captain, Co. B, 149 NY Infantry, Sept. 2, 1862. Major, 149 NY Infantry, July 3, 1864. Lieutenant Colonel, 149 NY Infantry, May 11, 1865. *Colonel*, 149 NY Infantry, June 7, 1865. Honorably mustered out, June 12, 1865. Bvt. Colonel, USV, March 13, 1865, for faithful and highly meritorious services since September, 1862, and particularly during the campaigns of Atlanta and Georgia.

Born: Jan. 30, 1835 Detroit, MI
Died: July 5, 1912 Syracuse, NY
Occupation: Cigar manufacturer before war. Real estate and insurance agent after war.
Miscellaneous: Resided Syracuse, Onondaga Co., NY
Buried: Woodlawn Cemetery, Syracuse, NY (Section 22, Lot 3)
References: Dwight H. Bruce, editor. *Onondaga's Centennial: Gleanings of a Century.* Boston, MA, 1896. Obituary, *Syracuse Post-Standard*, July 6, 1912. Pension File, National Archives. George K. Collins. *Memoirs of the 149th Regiment New York Volunteer Infantry.* Syracuse, NY, 1891.

George Murray Guion

Captain, Co. A, 33 NY Infantry, May 9, 1861. Lieutenant Colonel, 148 NY Infantry, Sept. 14, 1862. GSW Antietam, MD, Sept. 17, 1862. Colonel, 148 NY Infantry, Oct. 26, 1863. Commanded 2 Brigade, 2 Division, 18 Army Corps, Army of the James, Aug. 26, 1864-Sept. 19, 1864. Commanded 1 Brigade, 2 Division, 18 Army Corps, Sept. 30, 1864-Oct. 16, 1864. Resigned Oct. 16, 1864 on account of "family matters of the most vital importance."

Born: June 28, 1836 Meriden, CT
Died: Nov. 9, 1910 Colorado Springs, CO
Occupation: Engaged in the drug business
Offices/Honors: Brig. Gen., NY National Guard. County Treasurer, Seneca Co., NY.
Miscellaneous: Resided Seneca Falls, Seneca Co., NY, to 1891; Chicago, IL, 1891-1906; Colorado Springs, CO, 1906-10
Buried: Evergreen Cemetery, Colorado Springs, CO (Block 53, Lot 63)
References: J. Marshall Guion, IV. *Descendants of Louis Guion, Huguenot.* Olean, NY, 1976. Obituary, *Colorado Springs Gazette*, Nov. 10, 1910. Obituary, *Chicago Daily Tribune,* Nov. 10, 1910. Military Service File, National Archives. *Memorials of Deceased Companions of the Commandery of Illinois, MOLLUS.* From July 1, 1901 to Dec. 31, 1911. Chicago, IL, 1912. Letters Received, Volunteer Service Branch, Adjutant General's Office, File P791(VS)1862, National Archives.

Nicholas Grumbach (postwar)
Memoirs of the 149th Regiment New York Volunteer Infantry.

George Murray Guion
Paul Russinoff Collection.

George Murray Guion
Paul Russinoff Collection.

George Murray Guion (right, with brother, John M. Guion)
Paul Russinoff Collection.

George Murray Guion (postwar)
Memorials of Deceased Companions of the Commandery of Illinois, MOLLUS.

George Murray Guion
Paul Russinoff Collection.

138

George B. Hall
Massachusetts MOLLUS Collection, USAMHI.

George B. Hall

Colonel, 71 NY Infantry, July 18, 1861. Commanded 2 Brigade, 2 Division, 3 Army Corps, Army of the Potomac, Sept. 5-Dec. 24, 1862. Discharged for disability, April 28, 1863, due to chronic hepatitis and acute dysentery.

Born: July 15, 1825
Died: May 24, 1864 Brooklyn, NY
Other Wars: Mexican War (Captain, Co. A, 1 NY Volunteers)
Occupation: Employee of New York City Inspector's Department
Miscellaneous: Resided Brooklyn, NY. Took part in William Walker's filibustering expedition to Nicaragua.
Buried: Green-Wood Cemetery, Brooklyn, NY (Section 68, Lots 3942/3943)
References: William J. Tenney. *Military and Naval History of the Rebellion in the United States.* New York City, NY, 1865. Obituary, *Brooklyn Daily Eagle*, May 26 and 30, 1864. Military Service File, National Archives. Letters Received, Volunteer Service Branch, Adjutant General's Office, File M821(VS) 1863, National Archives.

Henry Hills Hall

Lieutenant Colonel, 4 NY Heavy Artillery, Dec. 30, 1861. Colonel, 4 NY Heavy Artillery, May 25, 1863. Commanded 4 Brigade, Defenses South of the Potomac, 22 Army Corps, Department of Washington, July 2, 1863-Aug. 5, 1863. Resigned Aug. 5, 1863, in response to an adverse report from a Board of Examination.

Born: March 25, 1816 Boston, MA
Died: March 29, 1893 Brooklyn, NY
Other Wars: Mexican War (2 Lieutenant, Shivor's Independent Co., TX Volunteers)
Occupation: Accountant, employed for many years in the Arrears Department of the Brooklyn city government
Miscellaneous: Resided Brooklyn, NY
Buried: Sleepy Hollow Cemetery, Tarrytown, NY (Section 47, Plot 3524)
References: Pension File, National Archives. Hyland C. Kirk. *Heavy Guns and Light: History of the 4th New York Heavy Artillery.* New York City, NY, 1890. Obituary, *New York Tribune*, March 31, 1893. Obituary, *Brooklyn Daily Eagle*, March 31, 1893. Letters Received, Volunteer Service Branch, Adjutant General's Office, File H887(VS)1863, National Archives.

Henry Hills Hall
Roger D. Hunt Collection, USAMHI.

Henry Hills Hall
Massachusetts MOLLUS Collection, USAMHI.

Henry Hills Hall
Roger D. Hunt Collection, USAMHI.

Henry Hills Hall
Massachusetts MOLLUS Collection, USAMHI.

Henry Hills Hall
Massachusetts MOLLUS Collection, USAMHI.

Thomas Spencer Hall

Captain, Co. E, 92 NY Infantry, Oct. 30, 1861. Major, 92 NY
Infantry, Jan. 8, 1862. *Colonel*, 92 NY Infantry, Dec. 27,
1862. Honorably mustered out, June 10, 1863.

Born: Aug. 20, 1826 Norfolk, NY
Died: March 25, 1898 La Canada, Los Angeles Co., CA
Education: Attended Yale University, New Haven, CT. Graduated University of Vermont, Burlington, VT, 1850.
Occupation: Merchant and miller before war. US Internal Revenue official and rancher after war.
Miscellaneous: Resided Norfolk, St. Lawrence Co., NY, to 1873; and Los Angeles and La Canada, Los Angeles Co., CA, after 1873
Buried: Evergreen Cemetery, Los Angeles, CA (Section G, Lot 84)

References: Pension File and Military Service File, National Archives. Obituary Circular, Whole No. 541, California MOLLUS. Obituary, *Los Angeles Times*, March 27, 1898. Letters Received, Volunteer Service Branch, Adjutant General's Office, File H1268(VS)1863, National Archives.

Charles Hamilton

Sergeant, Co. I, 5 NY Infantry, May 9, 1861. Corporal, Co. I, 5 NY Infantry, Aug. 6, 1861. Major, 110 NY Infantry, Sept. 2, 1862. Colonel, 110 NY Infantry, Dec. 10, 1863. Commanded District of Key West and Tortugas, Department of the Gulf, Aug. 16-Oct. 15, 1864, Dec. 1864-Jan. 1865, and June-Aug. 1865. Honorably mustered out, Aug. 28, 1865.

Born: Sept. 15, 1828 Brighton, MA
Died: June 5, 1873 Doctortown, GA
Occupation: Lumber merchant
Miscellaneous: Resided Canandaigua, Ontario Co., NY; New York City, NY; Burlington, Chittenden Co., VT; and Doctortown, Wayne Co., GA
Buried: Bridport Cemetery, Bridport, VT
References: Pension File and Military Service File, National Archives. Research files of Norman F. Rau.

Charles Hamilton
Roger D. Hunt Collection, USAMHI.

Charles Hamilton
Courtesy of Norman F. Rau.

Theodore Burns Hamilton

Captain, Co. G, 33 NY Infantry, May 22, 1861. Captured Gaines' Mill, VA, June 27, 1862. Confined Libby Prison, Richmond, VA. Paroled Aug. 12, 1862. Lieutenant Colonel, 62 NY Infantry, Dec. 27, 1862. GSW Marye's Heights, VA, May 3, 1863. Assistant Provost Marshal, 1 Division, Department of West Virginia, Feb.-March 1864. GSW right leg, Spotsylvania, VA, May 9, 1864. Honorably mustered out, June 29, 1864. *Colonel*, 62 NY Infantry, June 30, 1864. Muster out revoked, July 16, 1864. GSW Winchester, VA, Sept. 19, 1864. Honorably mustered out, Aug. 30, 1865. Bvt. Colonel, USV, Aug. 1, 1864, for gallant services in the battle of the Wilderness and Spotsylvania Court House, VA.

Born: 1836 New York City, NY
Died: Nov. 23, 1893 Queens, Long Island, NY
Occupation: Law student before war. Custom House broker and iron merchant after war.

Miscellaneous: Resided Plainfield, NJ; and Queens, Long Island, NY.
Buried: Sleepy Hollow Cemetery, Tarrytown, NY (Section 24, Plot 483)
References: Pension File, National Archives. Obituary, *New York Tribune*, Nov. 25, 1893. Edmund J. Raus, Jr. *A Generation on the March: The Union Army at Gettysburg.* Gettysburg, PA, 1996.

Herbert von Hammerstein

Captain, Co. A, 8 NY Infantry, April 23, 1861. Major, Additional ADC, Staff of Major Gen. George B. McClellan, Sept. 20, 1861. Honorably discharged, March 31, 1863. Lieutenant Colonel, 78 NY Infantry, May 30, 1863. Colonel, 78 NY Infantry, July 30, 1863. Colonel, 102 NY Infantry, July 12, 1864. Discharged for disability, Jan. 7, 1865.

Born: Dec. 20, 1835 Hildesheim, Hanover, Germany
Died: ?
Occupation: Officer in Austrian Army before war. Sergeant, Co. E, 2 US Cavalry, July 17, 1865-Aug. 14, 1867.
Miscellaneous: Resided Washington, DC. While serving after the war in the US Cavalry, he had both legs frozen during a snowstorm (and subsequently amputated), after which he returned to Austria and died.
Buried: ?
References: Wilhelm Kaufmann. *The Germans in the American Civil War.* Translated by Steven Rowan and edited by Don Heinrich Tolzmann with Werner D. Mueller and Robert E. Ward. Carlisle, PA, 1999. Letters Received, Commission Branch, Adjutant General's Office, File H793(CB)1866, National Archives. Military Service File, National Archives.

Otto Harhaus

Captain, Co. G, 2 NY Cavalry, Aug. 13, 1861. Major, 2 NY Cavalry, March 1, 1862. Lieutenant Colonel, 2 NY Cavalry, June 16, 1863. Colonel, 2 NY Cavalry, Sept. 18, 1863. Honorably mustered out, Sept. 10, 1864.

Born: 1826?
Died: ?
Miscellaneous: Resided New York City, NY
Buried: ?
References: Military Service File, National Archives.

Gabriel Theodore Harrower

Colonel, 161 NY Infantry, Sept. 6, 1862. Resigned Nov. 25, 1863, due to "personal reasons" including the settlement of his father's estate.

Born: Sept. 25, 1816 Chenango Co., NY

Died: Aug. 15, 1895 Lawrenceville, PA

Occupation: Farmer and lumber merchant

Offices/Honors: Sheriff of Steuben Co., NY, 1853-56. NY State Senate, 1872-73.

Miscellaneous: Resided Lindley, Steuben Co., NY; and Lawrenceville, Tioga Co., PA. Brother of Colonel Henry G. Harrower.

Buried: Lawrenceville Cemetery, Lawrenceville, PA

References: William H. McElroy and Alex. McBride. *Life Sketches of Executive Officers and Members of the Legislature of the State of New York*. Albany, NY, 1873. Irwin W. Near. *A History of Steuben County and Its People*. Chicago, IL, 1911. Obituary, *Corning Daily Journal*, Aug. 16, 1895. Pension File, National Archives. William E. Jones. *The Military History of the 161st New York Volunteer Infantry*. Bath, NY, 1865.

Otto Harhaus
Roger D. Hunt Collection, USAMHI.

McClellan and Staff (From left: Major Herbert von Hammerstein, Colonel Edward H. Wright, Lt. Col. Paul von Radowitz, Capt. William F. Biddle, Lt. Col. Albert V. Colburn, Capt. Charles R. Lowell, Major Gen. George B. McClellan, Lt. Col. Edward McK. Hudson, Capt. William S. Abert, Capt. Arthur McClellan)
Library of Congress.

Gabriel Theodore Harrower (1872)
Courtesy of Robert D. Marcus. R. E. Churchill, Photographer, 520 Broadway, Albany, NY.

Henry George Harrower

Captain, Co. F, 86 NY Infantry, Oct. 7, 1861. *Colonel*, 161 NY Infantry, March 3, 1864. Honorably mustered out, Oct. 12, 1864.

Born: June 17, 1830 Lindley, Steuben Co., NY
Died: Jan. 12, 1911 Elmira, NY
Occupation: Farmer and lumberman
Miscellaneous: Resided Lindley, Steuben Co., NY; Marshfield, Wood Co., WI; Wilkes-Barre, Luzerne Co., PA; and Elmira, Chemung Co., NY. Brother of Colonel Gabriel T. Harrower.
Buried: Presho Cemetery, Presho, Steuben Co., NY
References: Pension File, National Archives. Obituary, *Elmira Star-Gazette*, Jan. 12, 1911. Obituary, *Corning Evening Leader*, Jan. 13, 1911. Henry C. Bradsby, editor. *History of Luzerne County, PA*. Chicago, IL, 1893.

Louis F. Hartmann

Captain, Co. A, 29 NY Infantry, Sept. 29, 1861. Major, 29 NY Infantry, May 5, 1862. Lieutenant Colonel, 29 NY Infantry, June 9, 1862. Colonel, 29 NY Infantry, April 14, 1863. GSW left shoulder, Chancellorsville, VA, May 2, 1863. Honorably mustered out, June 20, 1863.

Born: 1821 Braunschweig, Germany
Died: April 15, 1876 Milwaukee, WI
Occupation: Merchant
Miscellaneous: Resided New York City, NY; and Milwaukee, WI
Buried: Forest Home Cemetery, Milwaukee, WI (Section 4, Block 17, Lot 5)
References: Pension File, National Archives.

Louis F. Hartmann
Courtesy of Jacqueline T. Eubanks.

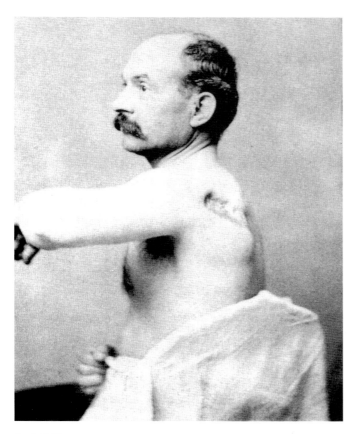

Louis F. Hartmann
National Archives.

Samuel Gilbert Hatheway, Jr.
(prewar)
Elmira (NY) Sunday Telegram,
March 10, 1940.

Samuel Gilbert Hatheway, Jr.

Colonel, 141 NY Infantry, Sept. 11, 1862. Resigned Feb. 11, 1863, upon receiving an order to appear before a Board of Examination, "he never having drilled his regiment in battalion drill and also having contrary to orders neglected regimental and company inspections."

Born: Jan. 18, 1810 Freetown, Cortland Co., NY
Died: April 16, 1864 Solon, Cortland Co., NY
Education: Attended Homer (NY) Academy. Graduated Union College, Schenectady, NY, 1831.
Occupation: Lawyer
Offices/Honors: NY State Assembly, 1842-43
Miscellaneous: Resided Solon, Cortland Co., NY; and Elmira, Chemung Co., NY
Buried: Hatheway Family Cemetery, Solon, NY
References: Elizabeth S. Versailles, compiler. *Hathaways of America.* Northampton, MA, 1970. *A Record of the Members of the Kappa Alpha Society, 1825-1913.* Ithaca, NY, 1913. Military Service File, National Archives. Obituary, *Ithaca Citizen and Democrat*, April 26, 1864. Biographical sketch, *Elmira Sunday Telegram*, March 10, 1940.

Samuel Gilbert Hatheway, Jr.
Massachusetts MOLLUS Collection, USAMHI.

William W. Hayt

1 Lieutenant, Adjutant, 23 NY Infantry, May 16, 1861. Honorably mustered out, May 22, 1863. Colonel, 189 NY Infantry, Oct. 1, 1864.

Born: Jan. 9, 1824 Ithaca, NY
Died: Nov. 8, 1864 City Point, VA (congestion of the brain)
Occupation: Lumber merchant
Miscellaneous: Resided Corning, Steuben Co., NY; and Albany, NY
Buried: Hope Cemetery, Corning, NY
References: Pension File, National Archives. Obituary, *Corning Journal*, Nov. 10, 1864. Irwin W. Near. *A History of Steuben County and Its People.* Chicago, IL, 1911. William H. Rogers. *History of the 189th Regiment of New York Volunteers.* New York City, NY, 1865.

William Brown Hayward

Colonel, 60 NY Infantry, Oct. 25, 1861. Resigned Jan. 8, 1862, due to "considerations of a private nature." Lieutenant Colonel, 102 NY Infantry, March 4, 1862. Resigned July 16, 1862, due to "circumstances of a private and important nature."

Born: May 1818 Baltimore, MD
Died: Jan. 26, 1888 Philadelphia, PA
Occupation: Regular Army (Sergeant, 1 US Artillery, July 21, 1837; resigned Dec. 31, 1842, as 1 Lieutenant, 8 US Infantry). Dry goods merchant, dry goods purchasing agent and insurance broker.
Offices/Honors: Assistant Superintendent of the Philadelphia Tract and Mission Society at his death.
Miscellaneous: Resided New York City, NY; Chicago, IL; and Philadelphia, PA
Buried: Mount Vernon Cemetery, Philadelphia, PA (Section B, Lot 195 1/2, unmarked)
References: Pension File, National Archives. Richard Eddy. *History of the 60th Regiment New York State Volunteers.* Philadelphia, PA, 1864. Obituary, *Philadelphia Public Ledger*, Jan. 28, 1888.

William W. Hayt
Roger D. Hunt Collection, USAMHI. Moulton & Larkin, Photographers, 114, 116 & 118 Water St., Elmira, NY.

William Brown Hayward (postwar)
Unknown Philadelphia newspaper, Jan. 28, 1888.

Benjamin Lucius Higgins (postwar)
Syracuse Standard, Nov. 20, 1891.

Erastus Dutton Holt
Meade Album, Civil War Library & Museum, Philadelphia, PA.

Benjamin Lucius Higgins

Captain, Co. A, 86 NY Infantry, Aug. 26, 1861. Major, 86 NY Infantry, Jan. 23, 1863. Lieutenant Colonel, 86 NY Infantry, May 3, 1863. Colonel, 86 NY Infantry, June 12, 1863. Shell wound left side, Gettysburg, PA, July 2, 1863. GSW both thighs, Mine Run, VA, Nov. 27, 1863. Discharged for disability, June 25, 1864, due to wounds.

Born: Oct. 14, 1826 Brewster, MA
Died: Nov. 19, 1891 Syracuse, NY
Occupation: Wholesale liquor merchant and photographer
Offices/Honors: Chief engineer, Syracuse Fire Department, before war. US Internal Revenue gauger, 1867-75.
Miscellaneous: Resided Syracuse, Onondaga Co., NY
Buried: Oakwood Cemetery, Syracuse, NY (Section 3, Lot 45)
References: Mrs. Sarah Sumner Teall. *Onondaga's Part in the Civil War.* Syracuse, NY, 1915. William M. Beauchamp. *Past and Present of Syracuse and Onondaga County, NY.* New York and Chicago, 1908. Obituary, *Syracuse Standard*, Nov. 20, 1891.

John Calvin Holley

Colonel, 143 NY Infantry, Aug. 14, 1862. *Lieutenant Colonel*, 143 NY Infantry, Oct. 11, 1862. Did not enter service.

Born: Nov. 27, 1823 Amenia, Dutchess Co., NY
Died: Jan. 29, 1868 Monticello, NY
Occupation: Hotelkeeper
Miscellaneous: Resided Monticello, Sullivan Co., NY
Buried: Rock Ridge Cemetery, Monticello, NY
References: James E. Quinlan. *History of Sullivan County, NY.* Liberty, NY, 1873. Obituary, *Monticello Republican Watchman*, Feb. 7, 1868.

Erastus Dutton Holt

Private, Co. K, 6 MA Infantry, May 4, 1861. Honorably mustered out, Aug. 2, 1861. 1 Lieutenant, Co. I, 49 NY Infantry, Sept. 6, 1861. Captain, Co. I, 49 NY Infantry, Oct. 12, 1861. Lieutenant Colonel, 49 NY Infantry, July 27, 1864. *Colonel*, 49 NY Infantry, Aug. 20, 1864. GSW head, Petersburg, VA, April 2, 1865. Bvt. Colonel, USV, Oct. 19, 1864, for gallant and meritorious services at the battles of the Wilderness and Spotsylvania Court House, and in the Shenandoah Valley.

Born: March 12, 1832 Sheridan, Chautauqua Co., NY

Died: April 7, 1865 DOW City Point, VA

Education: Attended Fredonia (NY) Academy

Miscellaneous: Resided Boston, MA; and Forestville, Chautauqua Co., NY

Buried: Forest Hill Cemetery, Fredonia, NY (Section C, Lot 99)

References: Daniel S. Durrie. *Genealogical History of the Holt Family in the United States.* Albany, NY, 1864. Obituary, *Fredonia Censor*, April 12, 1865. Frederick D. Bidwell. *History of the 49th New York Volunteers.* Albany, NY, 1916.

George Faulkner Hopper

Captain, Co. H, 10 NY Infantry, April 26, 1861. Major, 10 NY Infantry, April 26, 1863. Lieutenant Colonel, 10 NY Infantry, Jan. 5, 1864. *Colonel*, 10 NY Infantry, Jan. 5, 1865. Honorably mustered out, June 30, 1865.

Born: April 26, 1824 New York City, NY

Died: Aug. 4, 1891 Paskack, NJ

Occupation: Paperhanger and volunteer fireman before war. Superintendent of various departments of the New York City Post Office after war.

Offices/Honors: Vice President of the Association of Exempt Firemen

Miscellaneous: Resided New York City, NY. Popularly known as "Uncle George."

Buried: Green-Wood Cemetery, Brooklyn, NY (Section 62, Lot 4362)

References: Obituary circular, Whole No. 353, New York MOLLUS. George H. Washburn. *A Complete Military History and Record of the 108th Regiment New York Volunteers.* Rochester, NY, 1894. Pension File, National Archives. Charles W. Cowtan. *Services of the 10th New York Volunteers (National Zouaves) in the War of the Rebellion.* New York City, NY, 1882. Edmund J. Raus, Jr. *A Generation on the March: The Union Army at Gettysburg.* Gettysburg, PA, 1996. Obituary, *New York Herald*, Aug. 6, 1891.

William A. Howard

Colonel, 1 NY Marine Artillery, Sept. 1, 1861. Discharged March 28, 1863. Colonel, 13 NY Heavy Artillery, May 11, 1863. Honorably mustered out, July 4, 1865.

Born: Sept. 7, 1807 North Yarmouth, ME

Died: Nov. 18, 1871 Greenport, NY

George Faulkner Hopper
New York State Military Museum and Veterans Research Center. R. A. Lewis, 152 Chatham Street, New York.

Occupation: Midshipman, USN, Jan. 1, 1825. Resigned, April 12, 1832. Captain, US Revenue Cutter Service, Dec. 19, 1837. In 1848 the German Confederacy appointed him second in command of the fleet on the Weser, and he there constructed a navy yard and dock and remained in charge until the breaking up of the fleet. Resumed commission in Revenue Cutter Service after the Civil War, and was detailed on special duty to raise the American flag over our new possessions in Alaska.

Miscellaneous: Resided Greenport, Suffolk Co., NY. Described as "a handsome, plausible man with a breezy salt-water manner and in neat semi-nautical attire."

Buried: Boston, MA

References: Obituary, *Greenport Republican Watchman*, Dec. 2, 1871. Augustus W. Corliss. *Old Times in North Yarmouth, Maine.* Vol. 3, No. 2 (April 1879). Silas W. Burt. *My Memoirs of the Military History of the State of New York.* Albany, NY, 1902. *Appletons' Cyclopedia of American Biography.* Obituary, *New York Herald*, Nov. 29, 1871. Florence Kern. *The United States Revenue Cutters in the Civil War.* Bethesda, MD, N.d. Letters Received, Volunteer Service Branch, Adjutant General's Office, File H183(VS)1862, National Archives.

William A. Howard
Massachusetts MOLLUS Collection, USAMHI. Published by E. Anthony, 501
Broadway, New York, from Photographic Negative in Brady's National Por-
trait Gallery.

William A. Howard
Massachusetts MOLLUS Collection, USAMHI. Published by E. Anthony, 501
Broadway, New York, from Photographic Negative in Brady's National Por-
trait Gallery.

Mark Hoyt

Colonel, 176 NY Infantry, Oct. 2, 1862. Organized regiment, but resigned before regiment left state.

Born: May 5, 1835 Stamford, CT

Died: Dec. 30, 1896 New York City, NY

Occupation: Leather merchant

Miscellaneous: Resided New York City, NY

Buried: Woodland Cemetery, Stamford, CT (Section C, Lots 5-8)

References: David W. Hoyt. *Genealogical History of the Hoyt, Haight, Hight Families*. Providence, RI, 1871. Obituary, *New York Tribune*, Dec. 31, 1896. Thomas W. Herringshaw. *Herringshaw's Encyclopedia of American Biography of the Nineteenth Century*. Chicago, IL, 1905. Henry Hall, editor. *America's Successful Men of Affairs*. New York City, NY, 1895.

Mark Hoyt (postwar)
America's Successful Men of Affairs.

Edward McKeever Hudson

Colonel, 4 NY Infantry, April 25, 1861. Declined. Captain, 14 US Infantry, May 14, 1861. Lieutenant Colonel, Additional ADC, Sept. 28, 1861. ADC, Staff of Major Gen. George B. McClellan, Aug. 8, 1861-March 31, 1863. Honorably mustered out of volunteer service, March 31, 1863. GSW right thigh, Wilderness, VA, May 5, 1864. Acting AIG, Department of the Missouri, Aug.-Dec., 1864.

Born: 1826? CT
Died: July 20, 1892 Washington, DC
Education: Graduated US Military Academy, West Point, NY, 1849
Occupation: Regular Army (Major, 15 US Infantry, retired Dec. 15, 1870)
Miscellaneous: Resided Stamford, CT; New York City, NY; and Washington, DC. Brother of Colonel Henry W. Hudson.
Buried: Arlington National Cemetery, Arlington, VA (Section 1, Lot 65)
References: George W. Cullum. *Biographical Register of the Officers and Graduates of the US Military Academy.* Third Edition. Boston and New York, 1891. *Annual Reunion*, Association of the Graduates of the US Military Academy, 1893. Obituary, *Washington Post,* July 22, 1892. Letters Received, Appointment, Commission and Personal Branch, Adjutant General's Office, File 1642(ACP)1872, National Archives.

Edward McKeever Hudson
Massachusetts MOLLUS Collection, USAMHI.

Henry Wadsworth Hudson

Lieutenant Colonel, 82 NY Infantry, Nov. 29, 1861. Colonel, 82 NY Infantry, May 26, 1862. Commanded 1 Brigade, 2 Division, 2 Army Corps, Army of the Potomac, May 1-3, 1863. Dismissed May 20, 1863. Dismissal revoked Aug. 13, 1863. Colonel, 82 NY Infantry, Aug. 18, 1863. Commanded 1 Brigade, 2 Division, 2 Army Corps, Army of the Potomac, Dec. 10, 1863-Jan. 2, 1864. Honorably mustered out, June 25, 1864. *Colonel*, 59 NY Infantry, July 18, 1864. Commission revoked, Sept. 24, 1864.

Edward McKeever Hudson
Massachusetts MOLLUS Collection, USAMHI. Brady's National Photographic Portrait Gallery, Broadway & Tenth Street, New York.

Robert Savage Hughston
Massachusetts MOLLUS Collection, USAMHI.

Born: March 28, 1816
Died: May 21, 1889 Syracuse, NY
Occupation: Foreman in paper mill before war. Salesman after war.
Miscellaneous: Resided North Manchester, Hartford Co., CT; New York City, NY; and Syracuse, Onondaga Co., NY. Brother of Colonel Edward McK. Hudson.
Buried: Old North Burying Ground, Hartford, CT (Section K, Lot 21)
References: Pension File and Military Service File, National Archives. Henry K. Olmsted, compiler. *Genealogy of the Olmsted Family in America.* New York City, NY, 1912.

Robert Savage Hughston

Colonel, 144 NY Infantry, Aug. 17, 1862. Commanded Hughston's Brigade, Gurney's Division, 7 Army Corps, Department of Virginia, April 17, 1863-May 4, 1863. Resigned May 24, 1863 in order to resume his duties as clerk of Delaware Co., NY, having accepted the appointment of colonel "with a view only of raising the regiment and bringing it into the field." Resignation approved with comment, "He is an excellent gentleman but not a good military officer."

Born: 1813? NY
Died: June 19, 1873 Sidney, NY
Occupation: US Treasury Department clerk after war.
Offices/Honors: County clerk, Delaware Co., NY, 1858-64
Miscellaneous: Resided Delhi, Delaware Co., NY; and Unadilla, Otsego Co., NY
Buried: St. Matthews Episcopal Churchyard, Unadilla, NY
References: Pension File and Military Service File, National Archives. Obituary, *Delhi Republican*, July 5, 1873.

Harmon Daniel Hull

Captain, Co. A, 5 NY Infantry, April 25, 1861. Major, 5 NY Infantry, Sept. 3, 1861. *Colonel*, 165 NY Infantry, Sept. 4, 1862. Lieutenant Colonel, 5 NY Infantry, Sept. 26, 1862. Discharged Dec. 30, 1862, to enable him to accept colonelcy of 165 NY Infantry, but did not enter service since the regiment never reached full strength (only six companies formed).

Born: Aug. 1, 1835 Volney, Oswego Co., NY
Died: June 6, 1902 New York City, NY
Occupation: Commission merchant
Offices/Honors: Special US Treasury Agent, 1889-93
Miscellaneous: Resided New York City, NY
Buried: Arlington National Cemetery, Arlington, VA (Section 3, Lot 1405)
References: Obituary Circular, Whole No. 755, New York MOLLUS. Pension File, National Archives. Obituary, *New York Times,* June 8, 1902. Obituary, *New York Herald*, June 8, 1902.

Walter Clarke Hull

Private, Co. I, 37 NY Infantry, Dec. 5, 1861. Corporal, Co. I, 37 NY Infantry, June 18, 1862. 1 Sergeant, Co. I, 37 NY Infantry, Aug. 5, 1862. 2 Lieutenant, Co. K, 37 NY Infantry, Sept. 13, 1862. Acting ADC, Staff of Major Gen. George Stoneman, Nov. 1862-May 1863. Captain, ADC, USV, May 19, 1863. Captain, Co. L, 2 NY Cavalry, July 13, 1863. GSW Hanover Court House, VA, May 28, 1864. Captain, Co. A, 2 NY Cavalry, Aug. 29, 1864. Major, 2 NY Cavalry, Sept. 10, 1864. Colonel, 2 NY Cavalry, Nov. 1, 1864. GSW Nineveh, VA, Nov. 12, 1864.

Walter Clarke Hull
Roger D. Hunt Collection, USAMHI.

Walter Clarke Hull
New York State Military Museum and Veterans Research Center.

Born: April 8, 1843 Angelica, NY

Died: Nov. 12, 1864 KIA Nineveh, near Cedar Creek, VA

Occupation: Clerk

Miscellaneous: Resided Ellicottville, Cattaraugus Co., NY

Buried: Forest Lawn Cemetery, Buffalo, NY (Section 3, Lot 18)

References: Charles H. Weygant, compiler. *The Hull Family in America*. N.p., 1913. A. Milburn Petty. "History of the 37th Regiment, New York Volunteers," *Journal of the American Irish Historical Society*, Vol. 31 (1937). Pension File and Military Service File, National Archives.

Walter Clarke Hull
Roger D. Hunt Collection, USAMHI. P. B. Marvin, Photographer, Addis Gallery, 308 Penna. Avenue, Washington, DC.

Lewis Webb Husk
Courtesy of Gil Barrett. Fowler, 77 Genesee Street, Auburn, NY, S. L. Upham, Artist.

Lewis Webb Husk

Captain, Co. G, 111 NY Infantry, Aug. 15, 1862. Major, 111 NY Infantry, May 5, 1864. Lieutenant Colonel, 111 NY Infantry, Aug. 20, 1864. *Colonel*, 111 NY Infantry, Feb. 25, 1865. Honorably mustered out, June 4, 1865. Bvt. Colonel, USV, April 9, 1865, for conspicuous gallantry in the engagement near Boydton Plank Road, VA; for efficient services on all subsequent occasions, and for particularly meritorious services during the campaign terminating with the surrender of the insurgent army under General Robert E. Lee.

Born: July 30, 1834 Owasco, NY
Died: March 20, 1911 Auburn, NY
Occupation: Book binder before war. Salesman after war.
Miscellaneous: Resided Auburn, Cayuga Co., NY; St. Louis, MO; Albany, NY; and Waukesha, Waukesha Co., WI
Buried: Fort Hill Cemetery, Auburn, NY (Linden View Section, Lot 105)
References: Obituary Circular, Whole No. 487, Wisconsin MOLLUS. Obituary, *Auburn Semi-Weekly Journal*, March 21, 1911. *The Union Army*. Vol. 8 (New York Edition). Madison, WI, 1908.

James Francis Xavier Huston

Captain, Co. E, 82 NY Infantry, May 21, 1861. Lieutenant Colonel, 82 NY Infantry, May 26, 1862. *Colonel*, 82 NY Infantry, May 20, 1863. GSW head and leg, Gettysburg, PA, July 2, 1863.

Born: Jan. 7, 1818 Ireland
Died: July 2, 1863 KIA Gettysburg, PA
Occupation: Clerk
Miscellaneous: Resided New York City, NY
Buried: Calvary Cemetery, Long Island City, NY (Section 4, Range 23, Plot O)
References: Pension File, National Archives. Edmund J. Raus, Jr. *A Generation on the March: The Union Army at Gettysburg*. Gettysburg, PA, 1996.

Lewis Webb Husk (postwar)
Sal Alberti/James Lowe Collection. Horton, Albany, NY.

James Francis Xavier Huston
Meade Album, Civil War Library & Museum, Philadelphia, PA.

Joseph Hyde

1 Lieutenant, Co. H, 125 NY Infantry, Aug. 19, 1862. Captured Harper's Ferry, WV, Sept. 15, 1862. Paroled Sept. 16, 1862. Captain, Co. H, 125 NY Infantry, July 17, 1863. Acting AIG, Staff of Brig. Gen. Joshua T. Owen, Aug. 15, 1863-Feb. 10, 1864. Major, 125 NY Infantry, Nov. 18, 1863. Lieutenant Colonel, 125 NY Infantry, May 8, 1864. *Colonel*, 125 NY Infantry, Jan. 20, 1865. Honorably mustered out, June 5, 1865.

Born: June 5, 1821 Washington Co., NY

Joseph Hyde
A Regimental History, The 125th New York State Volunteers.

Died: Aug. 14, 1900 Los Angeles, CA
Occupation: Civil engineer. Superintendent of the Lillie Safe Works for several years before the war.
Miscellaneous: Resided Troy, Rensselaer Co., NY; Stockton, San Joaquin Co., CA; and Los Angeles, CA
Buried: Los Angeles National Cemetery, Los Angeles, CA (Section 5, Row G, Grave 20)
References: Pension File, National Archives. Obituary Circular, Whole No. 591, California MOLLUS. Circular, Whole No. 212, California MOLLUS. William H. Ward, editor. *Records of Members of the Grand Army of the Republic.* San Francisco, CA, 1886. Ezra D. Simons. *A Regimental History, The 125th New York State Volunteers.* New York City, NY, 1888.

Charles Henry Innes

Colonel, 36 NY Infantry, June 11, 1861. Accidental GSW right leg, Washington, DC, July 15, 1861. Commanded 1 Brigade, 1 Division, 4 Army Corps, Army of the Potomac, May 31, 1862-June 7, 1862. Resigned July 6, 1862, "by reason of ill health," due to "camp fever" contracted during the Peninsula campaign.

Born: Feb. 23, 1823 New York City, NY
Died: June 14, 1888 New York City, NY
Other Wars: Mexican War (Captain, Co. H, 1 NY Volunteers)

David Ireland

1 Lieutenant, Adjutant, 79 NY Infantry, June 1, 1861. Captain, 15 US Infantry, Aug. 5, 1861. Colonel, 137 NY Infantry, Sept. 13, 1862. Commanded 3 Brigade, 2 Division, 12 Army Corps, Army of the Cumberland, Oct. 29, 1863-Jan. 27, 1864 and Feb. 9, 1864-April 14, 1864. Commanded 2 Division, 12 Army Corps, Jan. 27, 1864-Feb. 9, 1864. Commanded 3 Brigade, 2 Division, 20 Army Corps, Army of the Cumberland, April 14, 1864-May 15, 1864 and June 6-Sept. 9, 1864. GSW Resaca, GA, May 15, 1864.

Born: May 13, 1833 Scotland
Died: Sept. 10, 1864 Atlanta, GA (dysentery)
Occupation: Tailor
Miscellaneous: Resided New York City, NY; and Binghamton, Broome Co., NY
Buried: Spring Forest Cemetery, Binghamton, NY
References: Pension File, National Archives. Oliver S. Phelps and A. T. Servin. *The Phelps Family of America.* Pittsfield, MA, 1899. Obituary, *Broome Weekly Republican*, Sept. 14, 1864. Letters Received, Volunteer Service Branch, Adjutant General's Office, File I846(VS)1863, National Archives.

Allan Hyre Jackson

Captain, Co. G, 91 NY Infantry, Oct. 1, 1861. Major, 134 NY Infantry, Dec. 19, 1862. Lieutenant Colonel, 134 NY Infantry, Jan. 22, 1863. *Colonel*, 134 NY Infantry, Nov. 4, 1863. GSW right hand, Peach Tree Creek, GA, July 20, 1864. Honorably mustered out, June 10, 1865.

Born: Jan. 24, 1835 Gilboa, Schoharie Co., NY
Died: Aug. 22, 1911 Schenectady, NY
Education: Graduated Union College, Schenectady, NY, 1853. Graduated Harvard University Law School, Cambridge, MA, 1856.
Occupation: Lawyer before war. Regular Army (Major, Paymaster, retired Oct. 29, 1898).
Miscellaneous: Resided Schenectady, NY
Buried: Vale Cemetery, Schenectady, NY (Section M-3, Lot 68)
References: Obituary, *Schenectady Union-Star*, Aug. 22, 1911. Pension File, National Archives. George W. Conklin. *Under the Crescent and Star: The 134th New York Volunteer Infantry in the Civil War.* Port Reading, NJ, 2000. Obituary, *Union Alumni Monthly,* Vol. 1, No. 1 (Nov. 1911).

David Ireland
Bruce P. Bonfield Collection. Brady's National Photographic Portrait Gallery, Broadway & Tenth Street, New York.

Occupation: Clerk and US Customs Inspector before war. Canvasser, ice dealer, and surveyor after war.
Miscellaneous: Resided New York City, NY
Buried: Moravian Cemetery, New Dorp, Staten Island, NY (Section O, Lot 235, unmarked)
References: Pension File and Military Service File, National Archives. Obituary, *New York Times,* June 15, 1888. Letters Received, Volunteer Service Branch, Adjutant General's Office, File J95(VS)1863, National Archives.

Allan Hyre Jackson
Special Collections, Schaffer Library, Union College.

Allan Hyre Jackson
Courtesy of Dave Zullo. J. N. Wilson, Photographer, South East Corner, Broughton & Whitaker Streets, Savannah, GA.

Allan Hyre Jackson
Courtesy of Dave Zullo. Webster & Bro., Louisville, KY.

Allan Hyre Jackson
Roger D. Hunt Collection, USAMHI. Henry Ulke, 278 Pennsylvania Avenue, Washington, DC 1865.

Allan Hyre Jackson
Courtesy of Dave Zullo. Webster & Bro., Louisville, KY.

Allan Hyre Jackson
Courtesy of Dave Zullo.

Allan Hyre Jackson and Wife, Mary
Courtesy of Dave Zullo.

Allan Hyre Jackson and Family
Courtesy of Dave Zullo. James Hinds, Photographist, 129 State Street,
Schenectady, NY.

William Ayrault Jackson
Courtesy of Henry Deeks.

William Ayrault Jackson

Colonel, 18 NY Infantry, May 13, 1861

Born: March 29, 1832 Schenectady, NY
Died: Nov. 11, 1861 Washington, DC (bilious remittent fever)
Education: Graduated Union College, Schenectady, NY, 1851
Occupation: Lawyer (law partner of Bvt. Brig. Gen. Frederick Townsend)
Offices/Honors: Inspector General, State of New York, 1861
Miscellaneous: Resided Schenectady, NY; and Albany, NY
Buried: Vale Cemetery, Schenectady, NY (Section X, Union College Plot, Lot 10)
References: *Memoir of William A. Jackson.* Albany, NY, 1862. *Record of the Jackson Family.* Philadelphia, PA, 1878. Albert A. Pomeroy. *History and Genealogy of the Pomeroy Family.* Toledo, OH, 1912. Rufus W. Clark. *The Heroes of Albany.* Albany, NY, 1867. *Catalogue of the Sigma Phi.* N.p., 1915.

Edward Christopher James
New York State Military Museum and Veterans Research Center. James M. Dow, Photographist, Ogdensburg, NY.

Edward Christopher James

1 Lieutenant, Adjutant, 50 NY Engineers, Aug. 19, 1861. Major, 60 NY Infantry, May 1, 1862. Lieutenant Colonel, 106 NY Infantry, Aug. 29, 1862. Colonel, 106 NY Infantry, Sept. 30, 1862. Discharged for disability, Aug. 4, 1863, due to the continuing effects of "external hemorrhoids and prolapsis ani."

Born: May 1, 1841 Ogdensburg, NY
Died: March 24, 1901 Palm Beach, FL
Education: Attended Walnut Hill Academy, Geneva, NY
Occupation: Lawyer
Miscellaneous: Resided Ogdensburg, St. Lawrence Co., NY; and New York City, NY
Buried: Ogdensburg Cemetery, Ogdensburg, NY (Range 10, Lot 27)

References: *Representative Men of New York.* New York City, NY, 1898. *Dictionary of American Biography.* Obituary, *New York Times*, March 25, 1901. Military Service File, National Archives.

David Tuttle Jenkins

1 Lieutenant, Adjutant, 146 NY Infantry, Aug. 18, 1862. Major, 146 NY Infantry, Sept. 17, 1862. Lieutenant Colonel, 146 NY Infantry, Oct. 11, 1862. Colonel, 146 NY Infantry, July 23, 1863. Commanded 3 Brigade, 2 Division, 5 Army Corps, Army of the Potomac, Jan. 1864-Feb. 15, 1864. GSW head and body, Wilderness, VA, May 5, 1864.

Born: May 4, 1836 Vernon, NY
Died: May 5, 1864 KIA Wilderness, VA
Education: Attended Rensselaer Polytechnic Institute, Troy, NY (Class of 1857)
Occupation: Surveyor and lawyer
Miscellaneous: Resided Vernon, Oneida Co., NY
Buried: Wilderness, VA (Body never recovered). Cenotaph at Vernon Cemetery, Vernon, NY
References: *"The Highest Praise of Gallantry," Memorials of David T. Jenkins and James E. Jenkins.* New Material by Patrick A. Schroeder. Daleville, VA, 2001. Mary G. Brainard, compiler. *Campaigns of the 146th Regiment New York State Volunteers.* New York City, NY, 1915. *Under the Maltese Cross, Antietam to Appomattox, Campaigns 155th Pennsylvania Volunteers.* Pittsburgh, PA, 1910.

Above Left: *David Tuttle Jenkins*
Under the Maltese Cross, Antietam to Appomattox, Campaigns 155th Penn-sylvania Volunteers.
Left: *David Tuttle Jenkins*
Massachusetts MOLLUS Collection, USAMHI.

John P. Jenkins

1 Lieutenant, Adjutant, 27 NY Infantry, May 21, 1861. Resigned Oct. 16, 1861. *Colonel*, 3 Regiment Eagle Brigade, Dec. 5, 1861. Incomplete regiment merged into 95 NY Infantry, March 6, 1862. *Colonel*, 172 NY Infantry, Sept. 10, 1862. Organization discontinued, Nov. 20, 1862. Lieutenant Colonel, 17 NY National Guard, July 8, 1863. Honorably mustered out, Aug. 13, 1863.

Born: April 12, 1827 NJ
Died: March 19, 1871 St. Augustine, FL
Occupation: Lawyer
Offices/Honors: County Clerk, Westchester Co., NY, 1855-58. County Register, Westchester Co., NY, 1858-61.
Miscellaneous: Resided White Plains, Westchester Co., NY
Buried: Rural Cemetery, White Plains, NY
References: Elizabeth G. Fuller, compiler. *Lives Well Spent: Westchester County Obituaries and Death Notices in the Eastern State Journal.* Elmsford, NY, 1994.

John P. Jenkins
William Gladstone Collection.

Edwin Sherman Jenney

Captain, Co. I, 3 NY Infantry, April 24, 1861. Resigned Oct. 3, 1861 to organize a light artillery battery. Captain, Battery F, 3 NY Light Artillery, Nov. 25, 1861. Major, 3 NY Light Artillery, Jan. 1, 1863. Judge Advocate, Staff of Major Gen. John J. Peck, Aug. 1863-Aug. 1864. Colonel, 185 NY Infantry, Sept. 19, 1864. Resigned Feb. 3, 1865, due to "the irreparable injury to my future prospects, which my remaining in service would cause," and also due to the approaching death of an aunt with whom he lived.

Born: Sept. 5, 1840 Poughkeepsie, NY
Died: June 28, 1900 Union Springs, NY
Education: Attended Hamilton College, Clinton, NY. Attended Princeton (NJ) University.
Occupation: Lawyer
Offices/Honors: Quartermaster General, State of NY, 1882-84
Miscellaneous: Resided Syracuse, Onondaga Co., NY
Buried: Oakwood Cemetery, Syracuse, NY (Section 27, Lot 55)
References: Susan C. Tufts. *The Descendants of John Jenney of Plymouth, MA.* N.p., 1942. Obituary, *Syracuse Post-Standard*, June 30, 1900. Pension File, National Archives. Letters Received, Volunteer Service Branch, Adjutant General's Office, File S471(VS)1862, National Archives.

Edwin Sherman Jenney (1883)
Roger D. Hunt Collection, USAMHI. W. V. Ranger & Co., Portraits, 43 S. Salina Street, Syracuse, NY.

Nathan J. Johnson

Captain, Co. I, 93 NY Infantry, Dec. 11, 1861. Lieutenant Colonel, 115 NY Infantry, April 15, 1864. Arrested May 24, 1864, upon charges of being "under the influence of intoxicating drink" and using "harsh, profane, disrespectful and abusive language addressed to his senior officer" on the advanced picket line at Bermuda Hundred, VA, May 20, 1864. Charges withdrawn and released from arrest, July 29, 1864. GSW arm, Deep Bottom, VA, Aug. 16, 1864. GSW right shoulder, Chaffin's Farm, VA, Sept. 29, 1864. GSW slight, Fort Fisher, NC, Jan. 15, 1865. Commanded 3 Brigade, 2 Division, 24 Army Corps, Department of North Carolina, Jan. 15, 1865-Feb. 14, 1865. Colonel, 115 NY Infantry, April 29, 1865. Honorably mustered out, June 17, 1865. Bvt. Colonel, USV, March 13, 1865, for gallant and meritorious conduct at the storming of Fort Fisher, NC.

Born: Aug. 22, 1822 Granville, NY
Died: Oct. 10, 1884 Broadalbin, NY
Education: Graduated Union College, Schenectady, NY, 1844
Occupation: Lawyer and newspaper editor
Offices/Honors: County judge, Fulton Co., NY
Miscellaneous: Resided Johnstown, Fulton Co., NY, 1847-60; Ballston Spa, Saratoga Co., NY, 1865-72; Granville, Washington Co., NY; New York City, NY; Soldiers Home, Bath, NY; Soldiers Home, Hampton, VA; and Broadalbin, Fulton Co., NY

Edwin Sherman Jenney (1883)
Massachusetts MOLLUS Collection, USAMHI.

Nathan J. Johnson
Roger D. Hunt Collection, USAMHI. P. B. Marvin, Photographer, Addis Gallery, 308 Penna. Avenue, Washington, DC.

Nathan J. Johnson
Courtesy of Henry Deeks. P. B. Marvin, Photographer, The Addis Gallery, 308 Penna. Avenue (Bet. 9th & 10th Sts.), Washington, DC.

Buried: Broadalbin Cemetery, Broadalbin, NY

References: David H. King, A. Judson Gibbs, and Jay H. Northup, compilers. *History of the 93rd Regiment New York Volunteer Infantry.* Milwaukee, WI, 1895. Pension File and Military Service File, National Archives. Obituary, *Gloversville Intelligencer,* Oct. 16, 1884. James H. Clark. *The Ironhearted Regiment: Being an Account of the Battles, Marches and Gallant Deeds Performed by the 115th Regiment NY Volunteers.* Albany, NY, 1865. *Catalogue of the Sigma Phi.* N.p., 1915.

William Johnson

Colonel, 148 NY Infantry, Aug. 20, 1862. Discharged for disability, Oct. 26, 1863, due to ill health caused by chronic diarrhea.

Born: Dec. 8, 1821 Williamstown, MA

Died: Oct. 11, 1875 Seneca Falls, NY

Occupation: Manufacturer of woolen goods, railroad and canal contractor, gun manufacturer, and banker

Offices/Honors: NY State Assembly, 1861. NY State Senate, 1872-75.

Miscellaneous: Resided Seneca Falls, Seneca Co., NY; Trenton, NJ, 1864-65; and New York City, NY, 1867-71

Buried: Restvale Cemetery, Seneca Falls, NY

References: *History of Seneca County, NY, 1786-1876.* Philadelphia, PA, 1876. Pension File, National Archives. William H. McElroy and Alex. McBride. *Life Sketches of Executive Officers and Members of the Legislature of the State of New York.* Albany, NY, 1873. Obituary, *Seneca Falls Reveille,* Oct. 15, 1875. Letters Received, Volunteer Service Branch, Adjutant General's Office, File J1(VS)1863, National Archives.

Frank Jones

1 Sergeant, Co. A, 71 NY State Militia, May 3, 1861. 1 Lieutenant, Adjutant, 31 NY Infantry, May 24, 1861. Colonel, 31 NY Infantry, Sept. 13, 1862. Acting AAG, 3 Brigade, 1 Division, 6 Army Corps, Army of the Potomac, Oct.-Dec. 1862. Honorably mustered out, June 4, 1863.

Born: April 24, 1832 Boston, MA

Died: March 15, 1916 Washington, DC

Above Right: *William Johnson (1861)*
Collection of The New-York Historical Society.
Right: *William Johnson (1872)*
Courtesy of Robert D. Marcus. R. E. Churchill, Photographer, 520 Broadway, Albany, NY.

Occupation: Clerk, US Treasury Department, 1863-81. Clerk, US War Department, 1881-1916, serving after 1890 in the War Records Division of the Adjutant General's Office.

Miscellaneous: Resided New York City, NY; and Washington, DC. Known as an athlete in his younger days, he took an active interest in outdoor sports, especially boating and baseball.

Buried: Arlington National Cemetery, Arlington, VA (Section 2, Lot 3630)

References: Pension File, National Archives. Obituary, *Washington Evening Star*, March 15, 1916. Letters Received, Volunteer Service Branch, Adjutant General's Office, File N720(VS)1862, National Archives.

Schuyler F. Judd

Colonel, 106 NY Infantry, June 30, 1862. Discharged for disability, Sept. 30, 1862, due to severe diarrhea and intermittent fever.

Schuyler F. Judd
New York State Military Museum and Veterans Research Center.

Born: Sept. 8, 1811 NY
Died: Aug. 9, 1864 Ogdensburg, NY
Occupation: Auctioneer
Miscellaneous: Resided Ogdensburg, St. Lawrence Co., NY
Buried: Ogdensburg Cemetery, Ogdensburg, NY (Range 12, Lot 57)
References: Military Service File, National Archives. Death notice, *Ogdensburg Daily Journal*, Aug. 11, 1864. Letters Received, Volunteer Service Branch, Adjutant General's Office, File N711(VS)1862, National Archives.

Edward Ernst Reinhold Kapff

Lieutenant Colonel, 7 NY Infantry, April 23, 1861. Colonel, 7 NY Infantry, July 3, 1861. Discharged for disability, Feb. 8, 1862, due to injuries to his head and face incurred in a fall from his horse.

Born: 1810? Germany
Died: Aug. 14, 1869 Stuttgart, Germany
Occupation: Captain in the Army of Wurttemberg. Restaurant operator.
Miscellaneous: Resided New York City, NY, to 1868; and Stuttgart, Wurttemberg, Germany
Buried: New Cemetery, Stuttgart, Germany
References: Pension File, National Archives. *Appletons' Annual Cyclopedia and Register of Important Events of the Year 1869.* New York City, NY, 1870.

Henry Morris Karples

Private, Co. E, 12 NY State Militia, June 11, 1861. Honorably mustered out, Aug. 5, 1861. 1 Lieutenant, Co. E, 52 NY Infantry, March 9, 1862. Captain, Co. E, 52 NY Infantry, Oct. 7, 1862. Major, 52 NY Infantry, July 2, 1863. GSW left breast and scrotum, Spotsylvania, VA, May 18, 1864. Lieutenant Colonel, 52 NY Infantry, May 18, 1864. *Colonel*, 52 NY Infantry, Nov. 9, 1864. Honorably mustered out, July 1, 1865.

Born: 1838? Austria
Died: June 16, 1892 New York City, NY
Occupation: Regular Army (2 Lieutenant, 37 US Infantry, cashiered June 9, 1868). Clerk and oil inspector after war.
Miscellaneous: Resided New York City, NY. Imprisoned in 1871 for obtaining monies from the US Treasury by means of false, forged and fraudulent vouchers.
Buried: Evergreens Cemetery, Brooklyn, NY (Orient Hill Section, Lot 265, unmarked)

References: M. Francis Dowley. *History and Honorary Roll of the 12th Regiment, N.G.S.N.Y.* New York City, NY, 1869. Pension File, National Archives. Letters Received, Appointment, Commission and Personal Branch, Adjutant General's Office, File 2009(ACP)1871, National Archives. Death Certificate.

Oliver Keese, Jr.

1 Lieutenant, RQM, 118 NY Infantry, July 16, 1862. Lieutenant Colonel, 118 NY Infantry, Aug. 21, 1862. Colonel, 118 NY Infantry, July 8, 1863. Discharged for disability, Sept. 16, 1864, due to chronic rheumatism.

Born: July 9, 1830 Keeseville, NY
Died: Jan. 24, 1889 Titusville, PA
Occupation: Merchant before war. Oil producer and iron manufacturer after war.
Offices/Honors: Treasurer of Crawford Co., PA, 1888-89.
Miscellaneous: Resided Keeseville, Clinton Co., NY; and Titusville, Crawford Co., PA
Buried: Evergreen Cemetery, Keeseville, NY
References: Obituary, *Titusville Morning Herald*, Jan. 25, 1889. Pension File, National Archives.

Oliver Keese, Jr.
Roger D. Hunt Collection, USAMHI.

Oliver Keese, Jr.
Courtesy of Thomas Harris. R. A. Lewis, 152 Chatham Street, New York.

Patrick Kelly

Captain, Co. E, 69 NY State Militia, April 20, 1861. Honorably mustered out, Aug. 3, 1861. Captain, 16 US Infantry, Oct. 26, 1861. Lieutenant Colonel, 88 NY Infantry, Sept. 14, 1861. Colonel, 88 NY Infantry, Sept. 22, 1862. Commanded 2 Brigade, 1 Division, 2 Army Corps, Army of the Potomac, Dec. 20, 1862-Feb. 18, 1863, May 8, 1863-Jan. 12, 1864, and June 3, 1864-June 16, 1864. GSW Petersburg, VA, June 16, 1864.

Patrick Kelly
Above: *New York State Military Museum and Veterans Research Center.*
Above Left: *Meade Album, Civil War Library & Museum, Philadelphia, PA.*
Left: *US Military Academy Library.*

Born: 1822 Castlehacket, Tuam, County Galway, Ireland

Died: June 16, 1864 KIA Petersburg, VA

Occupation: Farmer before coming to United States in 1849

Miscellaneous: Resided Castlehacket, Tuam, County Galway, Ireland; and New York City, NY

Buried: Calvary Cemetery, Long Island City, NY (Section 4, Range 5, Plot H)

References: *Dedication of the New York Auxiliary State Monument on the Battlefield of Gettysburg.* Albany, NY, 1926. David P. Conyngham. *The Irish Brigade and Its Campaigns.* Boston, MA, 1869. Obituary, *Irish American*, July 2, 1864.

William D. Kennedy

Colonel, 42 NY Infantry, June 22, 1861

Born: Aug. 26, 1818 Baltimore, MD

Died: July 22, 1861 Washington, DC (congestion of the brain)

Occupation: Merchant in the wholesale paint business

Offices/Honors: Elected Grand Sachem of the Tammany Society, 1861

Miscellaneous: Resided New York City, NY. Brother of New York City Police Superintendent John A. Kennedy.

Buried: Cypress Hills Cemetery, Brooklyn, NY (Section 6, Lot 1525)

References: *Proceedings of the Democratic Republican General Committee of the City of New York Relative to the Death of Colonel William D. Kennedy.* N.p., N.d. Pension File, National Archives. Obituary, *New York Herald*, July 23, 1861.

James E. Kerrigan

Colonel, 25 NY Infantry, May 21, 1861. Dismissed Feb. 21, 1862, on various charges including "habitual neglect of duty, conduct to the prejudice of good order and military discipline, violation of the 44th article of war, and disobedience of orders."

Born: Dec. 25, 1830 New York City, NY

Died: Nov. 1, 1899 Brooklyn, NY

Other Wars: Mexican War (Private, Co. D, 1 NY Volunteers)

Occupation: Trunk maker and cotton broker

Offices/Honors: US House of Representatives, 1861-63

Miscellaneous: Resided New York City, NY

Buried: St. Raymonds Cemetery, New York City, NY (Section 3, Range 4, Plot 15, unmarked)

References: Obituary, *New York Times*, Nov. 3, 1899. Pension File and Military Service File, National Archives. Letters Received, Volunteer Service Branch, Adjutant General's Office, File K81(VS)1862, National Archives. Thomas P. Lowry. *Tarnished Eagles: The Courts-Martial of Fifty Union Colonels and Lieutenant Colonels.* Mechanicsburg, PA, 1997. *Biographical Directory of the American Congress.*

George C. Kibbe

Private, Co. B, 11 NY Infantry, May 7, 1861. Sergeant, Co. F, 11 NY Infantry, Sept. 1, 1861. 2 Lieutenant, Co. C, 11 NY Infantry, Feb. 15, 1862. Honorably mustered out, June 2, 1862. 2 Lieutenant, Co. C, 6 NY Heavy Artillery, Aug. 16, 1862. 1 Lieutenant, Co. C, 6 NY Heavy Artillery, Dec. 13, 1862. Captain, Co. C, 6 NY Heavy Artillery, Jan. 26, 1863. Major, 6 NY Heavy Artillery, Sept. 30, 1864. Lieutenant Colonel, 6 NY Heavy Artillery, Dec. 1, 1864. Colonel, 6 NY Heavy Artillery, Jan. 10, 1865. Honorably mustered out, June 28, 1865.

Born: Feb. 19, 1834 CT

Died: March 18, 1892 Port Richmond, Staten Island, NY

Occupation: Deputy Surveyor, New York Custom House, and later shipyard superintendent

Miscellaneous: Resided Brooklyn, NY; and Port Richmond, Staten Island, NY.

Buried: Fair Ridge Cemetery, Chappaqua, NY (Section 2, Lot 275)

George C. Kibbe (1884)
USAMHI. Moreno & Loper, No. 4 East Fourteenth Street, New York.

References: Obituary, *Brooklyn Daily Eagle*, March 26, 1892. Obituary, *New York Tribune*, March 20, 1892. Pension File, National Archives. Doreen P. Hanna, compiler. *Kibbe Genealogical Notes*. Skowhegan, ME, 1972.

Hale Kingsley

Captain, Co. R, 25 NY State Militia, May 4, 1861. Honorably mustered out, Aug. 4, 1861. Captain, Co. R, 25 NY National Guard, May 31, 1862. Resigned July 21, 1862. *Colonel*, 163 NY Infantry, July 11, 1862. Declined.

Born: Feb. 18, 1824 Boston, MA
Died: Oct. 22, 1881 Albany, NY
Occupation: Lawyer
Miscellaneous: Resided Albany, NY
Buried: Rural Cemetery, Albany, NY (Section 16, Lot 6, unmarked)
References: Obituary, *Albany Evening Journal*, Oct. 22, 1881.

Jacob Krettner

Colonel, 65 NY National Guard, June 18, 1863. Returned home on account of sickness, June 22, 1863.

Born: 1810? Strasburg, Germany
Died: April 13, 1870 Buffalo, NY
Occupation: Insurance agent
Miscellaneous: Resided Buffalo, NY
Buried: Lakeside Memorial Park, Hamburg, NY
References: Obituary, *Buffalo Commercial Advertiser*, April 14, 1870. *Annual Report of the Adjutant General, Dec. 31, 1863*. Albany, NY, 1864. Research files of Benedict R. Maryniak.

William Kreutzer

Captain, Co. F, 98 NY Infantry, Oct. 28, 1861. Acting AAG, Staff of Colonel William W. H. Davis, Jan. 4, 1863-Sept. 1, 1863. Lieutenant Colonel, 98 NY Infantry, Feb. 25, 1863. GSW right knee, Cold Harbor, VA, June 3, 1864. *Colonel*, 98 NY Infantry, June 3, 1864. Commanded 1 Brigade, 3 Division, 24 Army Corps, Department of North Carolina, Jan. 15-16, 1865. Provost Marshal, Richmond, VA, April 4, 1865-Aug. 31, 1865. Honorably mustered out, Aug. 31, 1865.

Born: Sept. 11, 1828 Benton, Yates Co., NY
Died: May 27, 1901 Lyons, NY
Education: Graduated Genesee College, Lima, NY, 1852. Attended Auburn (NY) Theological Seminary.
Occupation: School teacher before war. Lawyer and hardware merchant after war.
Miscellaneous: Resided Lyons, Wayne Co., NY
Buried: Rural Cemetery, Lyons, NY (Lot 254, unmarked)
References: Pension File, National Archives. Obituary, *Wayne Democratic Press*, May 29, 1901. Obituary, *Rochester Democrat and Chronicle*, May 28, 1901. Obituary Circular, Whole No. 692, New York MOLLUS. Frank Smalley, editor. *Alumni Record and General Catalogue of Syracuse University, 1872-1910, Including Genesee College, 1852-1871, and Genesee Medical College, 1835-1872*. Syracuse, NY, 1911. William Kreutzer. *Notes and Observations Made During Four Years of Service With the 98th New York Volunteers in the War of 1861*. Philadelphia, PA, 1878.

William Kreutzer (postwar)
Wayne County, NY, Historian's Office. Charles Ravell, Photographer, Lyons, NY.

William Kreutzer (postwar)
Wayne County, NY, Historian's Office.

William Ladew
A Brief History of the 34th Regiment
New York State Volunteers.

William Ladew

Colonel, 34 NY Infantry, May 30, 1861. Resigned March 20, 1862, due to "business of a private character and continued ill health."

Born: Feb. 2, 1823 Ulster Co., NY

Died: April 26, 1880 New York City, NY

Occupation: Railroad contractor, tannery superintendent, and stone quarry operator

Miscellaneous: Resided Kingston, Ulster Co., NY; Gray, Herkimer Co., NY; Jersey City, NJ; and New York City, NY

Buried: Hudler Cemetery, near Mount Tremper, Ulster Co., NY

References: Louis N. Chapin. *A Brief History of the 34th Regiment New York State Volunteers*. New York City, NY, 1903. Pension File, National Archives. Obituary, *Kingston Daily Freeman*, April 29, 1880.

James Lake

Private, Co. A, 1 RI Detached Militia, May 2, 1861. Honorably mustered out, Aug. 2, 1861. Major, Additional ADC, April 11, 1862. ADC, Staff of Major Gen. Ambrose E. Burnside. Resigned July 16, 1862. Captain, Co. G, 17 NY Veteran Infantry, Oct. 14, 1863. Lieutenant Colonel, 17 NY Veteran Infantry, Sept. 3, 1864. *Colonel*, 17 NY Veteran Infantry, Jan. 3, 1865. GSW left leg and scrotum, Averasboro, NC, March 16, 1865. Honorably mustered out, July 13, 1865.

James Lake (seated center)
Massachusetts MOLLUS Collection, USAMHI.

Born: June 20, 1837 OH

Died: Feb. 10, 1873 Jersey City, NJ

Miscellaneous: Resided New York City, NY, to 1868; and Jersey City, NJ, 1868-73

Buried: Wooster Cemetery, Wooster, OH (Section 9, Lot 292)

References: Pension File, National Archives. Obituary, *New York Times*, Feb. 14, 1873. Letters Received, Adjutant General's Office, File L204(AGO)1862, National Archives. Letters Received, Commission Branch, Adjutant General's Office, File L339(CB)1863, National Archives.

James Crandall Lane

Major, 102 NY Infantry, January 1, 1862. Lieutenant Colonel, 102 NY Infantry, July 16, 1862. Commanded 2 Brigade, 2 Division, 12 Army Corps, Army of the Potomac, Sept. 17, 1862-Oct. 28, 1862. Colonel, 102 NY Infantry, Dec. 13, 1862. GSW right arm, Gettysburg, PA, July 3, 1863. Honorably discharged, July 12, 1864, by reason of consolidation of the regiment with 78 NY Infantry.

Born: July 23, 1823 New York City, NY

Died: Dec. 12, 1888 New York City, NY

Occupation: Civil engineer engaged in the service of the US Coast Survey and also in railroad construction

Miscellaneous: Resided Brooklyn, NY; and New York City, NY

Buried: Woodlawn Cemetery, New York City, NY (Section 56, Highland Plot, Lot 6509, unmarked)

James Crandall Lane
Roger D. Hunt Collection, USAMHI. Published by E. Anthony, 501 Broadway, New York, from Photographic Negative in Brady's National Portrait Gallery.

References: *National Cyclopedia of American Biography*. Paul F. Mottelay and T. Campbell-Copeland, editors. *The Soldier in our Civil War*. New York City, NY, 1886. Obituary, *New York Tribune*, Dec. 14, 1888. Pension File, National Archives. Letters Received, Volunteer Service Branch, Adjutant General's Office, File L575(VS) 1863, National Archives.

Above: *James Crandall Lane (postwar)*
National Archives.
Above Right: *James Crandall Lane*
Frederick H. Meserve. Historical Portraits. Courtesy of New York State Library.

Jacob H. Lansing

Captain, Co. C, 86 NY Infantry, Aug. 31, 1861. Major, 86 NY Infantry, May 3, 1863. Lieutenant Colonel, 86 NY Infantry, June 12, 1863. GSW left arm, North Anna, VA, May 24, 1864. *Colonel*, 86 NY Infantry, June 25, 1864. Honorably mustered out, Nov. 14, 1864.

Born: March 9, 1824 Albany, NY
Died: Nov. 8, 1885 Corning, NY
Occupation: Jeweler
Offices/Honors: Brig. Gen., NY National Guard, 1866-77
Miscellaneous: Resided Albany, NY; and Corning, Steuben Co., NY
Buried: Hope Cemetery, Corning, NY
References: Irwin W. Near. *A History of Steuben County and Its People*. Chicago, IL, 1911. Obituary, *Corning Journal*, Nov. 12, 1885. Pension File, National Archives.

Jacob H. Lansing
Jeff Kowalis Collection. W. J. Moulton, Elmira, NY.

Henry Martyn Lazelle (1872)
Courtesy of Henry Deeks. E. L. Eaton, Omaha, NE.

Above: *Henry Martyn Lazelle (1886)*
Courtesy of Henry Deeks. Partridge's Western Headquarters, Opposite the Post Office, Portland, OR.
Right: *Henry Martyn Lazelle (postwar)*
Frederick H. Meserve. Historical Portraits. Courtesy of New York State Library.

Henry Martyn Lazelle

Captain, 8 US Infantry, June 11, 1861. Acting Assistant Commissary General of Prisoners, Washington, DC, June 4, 1862-Sept. 16, 1863. Colonel, 16 NY Cavalry, Oct. 14, 1863. Commanded Independent Cavalry Brigade, 22 Army Corps, Department of Washington, Feb.-April, 1864 and July-Oct. 1864. Resigned volunteer commission, Oct. 19, 1864. Acting AIG, Staff of Major Gen. Frederick Steele, Jan. 6, 1865-Feb. 12, 1865. Assistant Provost Marshal General, Military Division of West Mississippi, Feb. 12, 1865-July 9, 1865.

Born: Sept. 8, 1832 Enfield, MA
Died: July 21, 1917 Georgeville, Quebec, Canada
Education: Graduated US Military Academy, West Point, NY, 1855
Occupation: Regular Army (Colonel, 18 US Infantry, retired Nov. 26, 1894; Brigadier General, retired April 23, 1904)
Miscellaneous: Resided Seattle, WA; Boston, MA; and Georgeville, Quebec, Canada. In charge of the publication of *War of the Rebellion: Official Records of the Union and Confederate Armies*, 1887-89.
Buried: Lazelle Family Cemetery, Cedar Lodge Road, Georgeville, Quebec, Canada
References: George W. Cullum. *Biographical Register of the Officers and Graduates of the US Military Academy*. Third Edition. Boston and New York, 1891. *Annual Reunion*, Association of the Graduates of the US Military Academy, 1918. Pension File, National Archives.

Marshall Lefferts

Colonel, 7 NY State Militia, April 26, 1861. Honorably mustered out, June 3, 1861. Colonel, 7 NY National Guard, May 25, 1862. Honorably mustered out, Sept. 5, 1862. Colonel, 7 NY National Guard, June 16, 1863. Honorably mustered out, July 20, 1863.

Born: Jan. 15, 1821 Brooklyn, NY
Died: July 3, 1876 near Newark, NJ
Occupation: Iron manufacturer and telegraph construction engineer before war. Telegraph company executive after war.
Miscellaneous: Resided New York City, NY
Buried: Green-Wood Cemetery, Brooklyn, NY (Section 8, Lots 7363-7366)

Above and Above Right: *Marshall Lefferts*
Massachusetts MOLLUS Collection, USAMHI. Brady's National Photographic Portrait Gallery, 352 Pennsylvania Avenue, Washington, DC.
Right: *Marshall Lefferts*
Courtesy of Richard F. Carlile. Brady's National Photographic Portrait Gallery, 352 Pennsylvania Avenue, Washington, DC.

Marshall Lefferts
Massachusetts MOLLUS Collection, USAMHI.

Marshall Lefferts
National Archives. Brady's National Photographic Portrait Gallery, 352 Pennsylvania Avenue, Washington, DC.

References: *National Cyclopedia of American Biography. Dictionary of American Biography.* Emmons Clark. *History of the 7th Regiment of New York, 1806-1889.* New York City, NY, 1890. Teunis G. Bergen. *Genealogy of the Lefferts Family.* Albany, NY, 1878. Obituary, *New York Times*, July 4, 1876.

Right: *Marshall Lefferts*
Michael J. McAfee Collection. J. Gurney & Son, Photographic Artists, 707 Broadway, New York.

Eugene LeGal

Colonel, 55 NY National Guard, June 24, 1863. Honorably mustered out, July 27, 1863.

Born: 1816? Bretagne, France
Died: March 20, 1872 New York City, NY
Occupation: Bookkeeper
Miscellaneous: Resided New York City, NY
Buried: New York Bay Cemetery, Jersey City, NJ (Section M-South, Lot 443, unmarked)
References: Obituary, *New York Times*, March 23, 1872. Funeral, *New York Tribune*, March 25, 1872.

John Cockey Lemmon

Colonel, 10 NY Cavalry, Nov. 25, 1861. Facing charges of "incompetency as a commander" and being "a habitual liar to such an extent that many of his officers would not believe him under oath," he tendered his resignation and was honorably discharged, April 3, 1863, on account of disability due to "severe rheumatic pains in the hips, knees and ankles" and "chronic nephritis with edema of the legs."

Born: July 13, 1806 Seneca Co., NY
Died: Feb. 12, 1875 Washington, DC
Education: Attended Hobart College, Geneva, NY
Occupation: Miller and US Government clerk
Miscellaneous: Resided Buffalo, NY; and Washington, DC
Buried: Forest Lawn Cemetery, Buffalo, NY (Section 6, Lot 7, unmarked)
References: Noble D. Preston. *History of the 10th Regiment of Cavalry, New York State Volunteers*. New York City, NY, 1892. Pension File and Military Service File, National Archives. Letters Received, Volunteer Service Branch, Adjutant General's Office, File L205(VS)1863, National Archives. George A. Rummel, III. *72 Days at Gettysburg*. Shippensburg, PA, 1997.

Eugene LeGal
Michael J. McAfee Collection. J. Gurney & Son, Photographic Artists, 707 Broadway, New York.

John Cockey Lemmon
History of the 10th Regiment of Cavalry, New York State Volunteers.

Charles McKnight Leoser (1861)
US Military Academy Library.

Charles McKnight Leoser

2 Lieutenant, 2 US Dragoons, May 6, 1861. 1 Lieutenant, Adjutant, 11 NY Infantry, May 7, 1861. Major, 11 NY Infantry, June 15, 1861. 1 Lieutenant, 2 US Cavalry, Aug. 8, 1861. Colonel, 11 NY Infantry, Aug. 15, 1861. Resigned volunteer commission, April 17, 1862. GSW right side, Beverly Ford, VA, June 9, 1863. Captain, 2 US Cavalry, June 9, 1863. Captured Trevilian Station, VA, June 11, 1864. Confined Libby Prison, Richmond, VA; Macon, GA; and Charleston, SC. Paroled Sept. 12, 1864. Exchanged Jan. 15, 1865. Staff of Major Gen. Alfred T. A. Torbert. Provost Marshal General, Army of the Shenandoah, May 1865. Resigned Oct. 19, 1865, because "affairs of the most urgent nature imperatively demand my presence at home."

Born: Aug. 4, 1839 Reading, PA
Died: Feb. 23, 1896 Larchmont Manor, NY
Education: Graduated US Military Academy, West Point, NY, May 1861

Occupation: Merchant and publisher
Miscellaneous: Resided Reading, Berks Co., PA; and New York City, NY
Buried: Post Cemetery, West Point, NY (Section 15, Row A, Grave 7)
References: Pension File, National Archives. Mary Elizabeth Sergent. *They Lie Forgotten.* Middletown, NY, 1986. *Annual Reunion*, Association of the Graduates of the US Military Academy, 1896. Obituary Circular, Whole No. 504, New York MOLLUS. George W. Cullum. *Biographical Register of the Officers and Graduates of the US Military Academy.* Third Edition. Boston and New York, 1891. Letters Received, Volunteer Service Branch, Adjutant General's Office, File W1019(VS)1862, National Archives.

Charles McKnight Leoser
Courtesy of Patrick A. Schroeder. Charles D. Fredricks & Co., "Specialite," 587 Broadway, New York.

Charles McKnight Leoser (1864)
Courtesy of Patrick A. Schroeder.

Charles McKnight Leoser (postwar)
Annual Reunion, Association of the Graduates of the US Military Academy, 1896. W. Kurtz, Madison Square, New York City.

Charles Lewis

Private, Co. K, 14 NY Infantry, May 17, 1861. Sergeant, Co. K, 14 NY Infantry, Jan. 1, 1862. GSW Gaines' Mill, VA, June 27, 1862. 1 Lieutenant, Co. G, 159 NY Infantry, Oct. 14, 1862. Captain, Co. C, 159 NY Infantry, March 6, 1863. GSW Port Hudson, LA, June 14, 1863. Major, 176 NY Infantry, Dec. 21, 1863. Lieutenant Colonel, 176 NY Infantry, Nov. 14, 1864. *Colonel*, 176 NY Infantry, Oct. 18, 1865. Commanded District of Columbus, 2 Division, Department of Georgia, Jan.-Feb. 1866. Honorably mustered out, April 27, 1866. Bvt. Colonel, USV, March 13, 1865, for distinguished services and conspicuous gallantry at Cedar Creek, VA, October 19, 1864.

Born: July 1, 1831
Died: Dec. 31, 1878 New York City, NY (Committed suicide by jumping overboard from a ferry boat in New York Harbor)
Occupation: Bookkeeper and superintendent of woolen mills
Miscellaneous: Resided Stottsville, Columbia Co., NY
Buried: City Cemetery, Hudson, NY

References: Obituary, *New York Times*, Jan. 2, 1879. Pension File and Military Service File, National Archives. Obituary, *Hudson Evening Register*, Jan. 2, 1879.

George W. Lewis

Captain, Co. G, 13 NY Infantry, May 1, 1861. Captain, Co. K, 3 NY Cavalry, Sept. 1, 1861. Major, 3 NY Cavalry, Sept. 17, 1861. Lieutenant Colonel, 3 NY Cavalry, Dec. 27, 1862. Colonel, 3 NY Cavalry, June 15, 1864. Commanded 1 Brigade, Cavalry Division, Army of the James, Oct. 23, 1864-Nov. 5, 1864. Honorably mustered out, July 12, 1865.

Born: 1826? Waterloo, NY
Died: Jan. 5, 1896 Quincy, IL
Miscellaneous: Resided Rochester, NY; Suffolk, VA; and Chicago, IL
Buried: Soldiers Home Cemetery, Quincy, IL
References: Pension File, National Archives. Death Notice, *Chicago Daily Tribune*, Jan. 7, 1896.

George W. Lewis
Roger D. Hunt Collection, USAMHI. B. F. Evans, No. 14 Main Street, Norfolk, VA.

James Lewis

Captain, Co. C, 144 NY Infantry, Sept. 1, 1862. Lieutenant Colonel, 144 NY Infantry, May 24, 1863. Colonel, 144 NY Infantry, Sept. 25, 1864. Honorably mustered out, June 25, 1865.

Born: May 23, 1836 Hamden, Delaware Co., NY
Died: Oct. 28, 1899 Joliet, IL
Education: Graduated Amherst (MA) College, 1861. Graduated Union Theological Seminary, New York City, NY, 1868.
Occupation: Presbyterian clergyman
Miscellaneous: Resided Delhi, Delaware Co., NY; Humboldt, Allen Co., KS; Howell, Livingston Co., MI; and Joliet, Will Co., IL
Buried: Elmwood Cemetery, Detroit, MI (Section B, Lot 62)
References: James H. McKee. *Back in War Times: History of the 144th Regiment, New York Volunteer Infantry*. Unadilla, NY, 1903. *Memorials of Deceased Companions of the Commandery of Illinois, MOLLUS,* From May 8, 1879 to July 1, 1901. Chicago, IL, 1901. *Portrait and Biographical Album of Will County, IL*. Chicago, IL, 1890.

Above: *James Lewis*
Massachusetts MOLLUS Collection, USAMHI.
Right: *James Lewis*
Roger D. Hunt Collection, USAMHI. Tolles & Seely, Photographists, 38 & 40 Owego Street, Ithaca, NY.

James Lewis (postwar)
Back in War Times: History of the 144th Regiment, New York Volunteer Infantry.

Henry Frederick Liebenau

Sergeant Major, 71 NY State Militia, April 20, 1861. Honorably mustered out, July 30, 1861. 1 Lieutenant, Co. E, 53 NY Infantry, July 7, 1862. Honorably mustered out, Sept. 13, 1862. *Colonel,* Seymour Light Infantry, Dec. 4, 1862. Incomplete regiment merged into 178 NY Infantry, June 22, 1863. *Colonel,* 25 NY Cavalry, Sept. 14, 1863. His muster as colonel was prohibited, "he having been charged with accepting money for recommending persons for commissions" in his regiment.

Born: May 26, 1833 PA
Died: May 2, 1901 New York City, NY
Occupation: Postal clerk before war. Night inspector, New York Custom House, journalist with the New York Star and finally Inspector, New York City Department of Public Works, after war.
Miscellaneous: Resided New York City, NY
Buried: Woodlawn Cemetery, New York City, NY (Section 66, Poplar Plot, Lot 5605)

References: Pension File, National Archives. Thomas S. Townsend. *Honors of the Empire State in the War of the Rebellion.* New York City, NY, 1889. Letters Received, Commission Branch, Adjutant General's Office, File C27(CB)1868, National Archives. LeRoy P. Graf and Ralph W. Haskins, editors. *The Papers of Andrew Johnson.* Vol. 14. Knoxville, TN, 1967.

Charles Edward Livingston

Major, 92 NY Infantry, Dec. 20, 1861. Major, 76 NY Infantry, Jan. 7, 1862. Captured Groveton, VA, Aug. 29, 1862. Paroled Sept. 1, 1862. Lieutenant Colonel, 76 NY Infantry, Nov. 20, 1862. Acting AIG, Staff of Major Gen. Abner Doubleday, Dec. 1862-July 1863. Colonel, 76 NY Infantry, June 25, 1863. Honorably discharged, Dec. 1, 1864, by reason of "reduced command."

Born: Oct. 1837
Died: Jan. 4, 1893 Thomasville, GA
Education: Attended US Military Academy, West Point, NY (Class of 1860)
Miscellaneous: Resided Philadelphia, PA; and Thomasville, Thomas Co., GA

Charles Edward Livingston (left, at Gettysburg Reunion, Sept. 8, 1886)
Jeff Kowalis Collection.

Buried: St. John's Reformed Churchyard, Upper Red Hook, Dutchess Co., NY

References: Pension File and Military Service File, National Archives. Death notice, *Red Hook Journal*, Jan. 13, 1893. John Watts DePeyster. *Address Delivered Wednesday, 28th November, 1866, in Feller's Hall, Madalin, Township of Red Hook, Dutchess Co., NY, Upon the Occasion of the Inauguration of a Monument Erected by This Immediate Neighborhood (Tivoli-Madalin) to her Defenders.* New York City, 1867. Abram P. Smith. *History of the 76th Regiment New York Volunteers.* Cortland, NY, 1867.

William Kenneth Logie

Captain, Co. E, 141 NY Infantry, Sept. 11, 1862. Lieutenant Colonel, 141 NY Infantry, March 7, 1863. Colonel, 141 NY Infantry, June 1, 1863. GSW left breast, Peach Tree Creek, GA, July 20, 1864.

William Kenneth Logie
Roger D. Hunt Collection, USAMHI.

Born: 1837? LA

Died: July 20, 1864 KIA Peach Tree Creek, GA

Education: Attended Hobart College, Geneva, NY. Graduated Union College, Schenectady, NY, 1857.

Occupation: Lawyer

Miscellaneous: Resided Geneva, Ontario Co., NY; and Corning, Steuben Co., NY

Buried: Washington Street Cemetery, Geneva, NY (Section H, Lot 107)

References: Irwin W. Near. *A History of Steuben County and Its People.* Chicago, IL, 1911. Obituary, *Geneva Gazette*, Aug. 5, 1864. Obituary, *Corning Journal*, July 28, 1864. "The Logie Memorial," *The Shield of Theta Delta Chi*, Vol. 7, No. 3 (Sept. 1891).

Newton Bosworth Lord

Captain, Co. K, 35 NY Infantry, May 9, 1861. Major, 35 NY Infantry, June 3, 1861. Colonel, 35 NY Infantry, Aug. 10, 1861. Resigned Feb. 9, 1863, on account of "business affairs." Colonel, 20 NY Cavalry, Sept. 30, 1863. Commanded Defenses of Norfolk and Portsmouth (VA), Oct. 1864. Commanded 1 Brigade, Cavalry Division, Department of Virginia, March 11-20, 1865. Resigned March 23, 1865, since "he could not humiliate himself so much as to appear" before a board of officers ordered to assemble to examine into his "capacity, qualifications, propriety of conduct, and efficiency."

Born: Jan. 1, 1832 Brownville, NY

Died: April 15, 1890 Santiago, Chile

Occupation: Foundryman before war. Railroad construction engineer after war.

Miscellaneous: Resided Brownville, Jefferson Co., NY; New York City, NY; and Santiago, Chile

Buried: Santiago, Chile. Cenotaph in Brownville Cemetery, Brownville, NY.

References: Kenneth Lord. *Genealogy of the Descendants of Thomas Lord.* N.p., 1946. Pension File, National Archives. Albert D. Shaw. *A Full Report of the First Reunion and Banquet of the 35th New York Volunteers.* Watertown, NY, 1888. Letters Received, Volunteer Service Branch, Adjutant General's Office, File L283(VS)1862, National Archives. Thomas P. Lowry. *Tarnished Eagles: The Courts-Martial of Fifty Union Colonels and Lieutenant Colonels.* Mechanicsburg, PA, 1997.

Newton Bosworth Lord
Roger D. Hunt Collection, USAMHI.

Newton Bosworth Lord
Massachusetts MOLLUS Collection, USAMHI.

Newton Bosworth Lord
Roger D. Hunt Collection, USAMHI.

Ephraim A. Ludwick

Captain, Co. K, 112 NY Infantry, Sept. 2, 1862. Major, 112 NY Infantry, June 1, 1864. GSW right arm (amputated), Chaffin's Farm, VA, Sept. 29, 1864. Lieutenant Colonel, 112 NY Infantry, Nov. 26, 1864. Colonel, 112 NY Infantry, Jan. 18, 1865. Honorably mustered out, June 13, 1865.

Born: April 8, 1836 Pittsburgh, PA
Died: Sept. 27, 1887 San Francisco, CA
Education: Graduated Allegheny College, Meadville, PA, 1862
Occupation: Methodist clergyman
Offices/Honors: Superintendent, NY State Soldiers' Home, 1867-69. Chaplain, NHDVS, Milwaukee, WI, 1870-73. Chaplain, Sailors' Home, San Francisco, CA, 1880-87.
Miscellaneous: Resided Dunkirk, Chautauqua Co., NY; and San Francisco, CA
Buried: San Francisco National Cemetery, San Francisco, CA (Section OS, Plot 43, Grave 1)

Ephraim A. Ludwick
Donald K. Ryberg Collection. A. F. Wells, Silver Creek, NY.

Ephraim A. Ludwick
Donald K. Ryberg Collection.

Ephraim A. Ludwick
Roger D. Hunt Collection, USAMHI.

References: Pension File, National Archives. William H. Ward, editor. *Records of Members of the Grand Army of the Republic.* San Francisco, CA, 1886. William L. Hyde. *History of the 112th Regiment New York Volunteers.* Fredonia, NY, 1866.

Thomas Lynch

Captain, Co. B, 69 NY State Militia, April 20, 1861. Honorably mustered out, Aug. 3, 1861. Captain, Co. B, 69 NY National Guard, June 20, 1862. Honorably mustered out, Sept. 3, 1862. Colonel, 77 NY National Guard, Aug. 2, 1864. Honorably mustered out, Nov. 9, 1864.

Born: March 16, 1835 Ireland
Died: Sept. 24, 1907 Bath, NY
Occupation: Merchant
Miscellaneous: Resided New York City, NY; Hampton, VA; and Bath, Steuben Co., NY
Buried: Bath National Cemetery, Bath, NY (Section H, Row 37, Grave 13)
References: Pension File, National Archives.

Ephraim A. Ludwick (seated right, as Aide de Camp on the Staff of Governor Reuben E. Fenton, 1868)
Donald K. Ryberg Collection. J. H. Abbott, No. 480 Broadway, Albany, NY.

William A. Lynch

1 Lieutenant, Co. I, 42 NY Infantry, June 28, 1861. Captain, Co. K, 42 NY Infantry, Nov. 1, 1861. Summarily dismissed April 23, 1862, for being "more than useless" and for being "absent for insufficient cause." Dismissal revoked May 16, 1862. GSW stomach, Antietam, MD, Sept. 17, 1862. Lieutenant Colonel, 42 NY Infantry, March 16, 1863. *Colonel*, 42 NY Infantry, Oct. 14, 1863. GSW right leg, Cold Harbor, VA, June 3, 1864. Honorably mustered out, July 13, 1864.

Born: 1836? New York City, NY
Died: Aug. 5, 1874 New York City, NY
Occupation: Painter before war. Painter and saloon keeper after war.
Miscellaneous: Resided New York City, NY
Buried: Green-Wood Cemetery, Brooklyn, NY (Section 2, Lot 7517, unmarked)

References: Pension File, National Archives. Obituary, *New York Times*, Aug. 6, 1874. Letters Received, Volunteer Service Branch, Adjutant General's Office, File L180(VS)1862, National Archives. Obituary, *New York Herald*, Aug. 6, 1874.

George Lyons

Colonel, 8 NY State Militia, April 25, 1861. Honorably mustered out, Aug. 2, 1861.

Born: Nov. 10, 1810 NY
Died: Dec. 5, 1878 Morrisania, NY
Occupation: Merchant
Offices/Honors: Served as colonel of the 8 NY State Militia, 1854-61, after commanding the State Fencibles for 18 years
Miscellaneous: Resided New York City, NY
Buried: Green-Wood Cemetery, Brooklyn, NY (Section 67, Lot 2193)
References: Obituary, *New York Herald*, Dec. 9, 1878.

George Lyons
Massachusetts MOLLUS Collection, USAMHI. Brady's National Photographic Portrait Gallery, 352 Pennsylvania Avenue, Washington, DC.

James Alexander Magruder

Major, 15 NY Engineers, Oct. 23, 1861. Lieutenant Colonel, 15 NY Engineers, Dec. 12, 1862. Honorably mustered out, July 8, 1863. *Colonel, 2 NY Engineers, July 22, 1863.* Recruiting for regiment discontinued and authority as colonel revoked, Oct. 9, 1863.

Born: Jan. 16, 1816 Georgetown, DC
Died: June 15, 1897 Georgetown, DC
Occupation: Commission merchant
Offices/Honors: Collector of the Port, Georgetown, DC
Miscellaneous: Resided Georgetown, DC
Buried: Oak Hill Cemetery, Washington, DC (Lot 175)
References: Obituary, *Washington Evening Star*, June 16, 1897. Pension File, National Archives. Letters Received, Volunteer Service Branch, Adjutant General's Office, Files M1317(VS) 1863 and M2191(VS) 1863, National Archives.

George Lyons
Massachusetts MOLLUS Collection, USAMHI. Published by E. Anthony, 501 Broadway, New York, from Photographic Negative in Brady's National Portrait Gallery.

George Lyons (seated; with Major Obed F. Wentworth, left; and Capt. Joshua M. Varian, right)
Sal Alberti/James Lowe Collection. Published by E. Anthony, 501 Broadway, New York, from Photographic Negative in Brady's National Portrait Gallery.

Joachim Maidhof

Colonel, 11 NY National Guard, May 28, 1862. Honorably mustered out, Sept. 16, 1862. Colonel, 11 NY National Guard, June 16, 1863. Honorably mustered out, July 20, 1863.

Born: June 10, 1827 Aschaffenburg, Bavaria, Germany
Died: Aug. 29, 1906 New York City, NY
Occupation: Operated a dress trimming business. Later connected with the Ninth National Bank.
Miscellaneous: Resided New York City, NY
Buried: Woodlawn Cemetery, New York City, NY (Section 98, Oak Hill Plot, Lot 8687)
References: Obituary, *New York Times*, Aug. 30, 1906. Pension File, National Archives.

James Edward Mallon

Private, Co. D, 7 NY State Militia, April 26, 1861. Honorably mustered out, June 3, 1861. 2 Lieutenant, Co. K, 40 NY Infantry, Aug. 1, 1861. 1 Lieutenant, Co. K, 40 NY Infantry, Sept. 13, 1861. 1 Lieutenant, Adjutant, 40 NY Infantry, Dec. 3, 1861. 1 Lieutenant, Co. A, 40 NY Infantry, April 9, 1862. Acting AAG and Ordnance Officer, Staff of Major Gen. Philip Kearny, May-Aug. 1862. GSW Fair Oaks, VA, May 31, 1862. Major, 42 NY Infantry, Aug. 2, 1862. Provost Marshal, Staff of Major Gen. Edwin V. Sumner, Dec. 1862-Jan. 1863. Provost Marshal, Staff of Major Gen. Darius N. Couch, Feb.-March 1863. Colonel, 42 NY Infantry, March 17, 1863. Commanded 3 Brigade, 2 Division, 2 Army Corps, Army of the Potomac, July 18-27, 1863 and Oct. 1-14, 1863. GSW stomach, Bristoe Station, VA, Oct. 14, 1863.

Born: Sept. 12, 1836 Brooklyn, NY
Died: Oct. 14, 1863 KIA Bristoe Station, VA
Occupation: Wholesale commission business. Flour broker on Produce Exchange.
Miscellaneous: Resided Brooklyn, NY. Brother-in-law of Colonel Edward J. Riley.
Buried: Holy Cross Cemetery, Brooklyn, NY (Select Ground, Range 2, Plot 16)
References: Pension File and Military Service File, National Archives. Obituary, *New York Times*, Oct. 21, 1863. Fred C. Floyd. *History of the 40th (Mozart) Regiment New York Volunteers*. Boston, MA, 1909. Francis A. Walker. *History of the Second Army Corps in the Army of the Potomac*. New York City, NY, 1887. Obituary, *Irish American*, Oct. 24, 1863.

James Edward Mallon
Massachusetts MOLLUS Collection, USAMHI. Published by E. Anthony, 501 Broadway, New York, from Photographic Negative in Brady's National Portrait Gallery.

William Lester Markell

Major, 8 NY Cavalry, Nov. 28, 1861. Lieutenant Colonel, 8 NY Cavalry, March 23, 1863. Colonel, 8 NY Cavalry, June 9, 1863. GSW left hand, Funkstown, MD, July 10, 1863. Resigned Feb. 27, 1864, due to "business interests."

Born: Jan. 15, 1836 Manheim Centre, NY
Died: Feb. 13, 1916 Syracuse, NY
Occupation: Merchant and manufacturer before war. Clerk after war.
Miscellaneous: Resided Rochester, NY, to 1886; Albany, NY, 1886-1909; and Syracuse, Onondaga Co., NY, 1909-16
Buried: Oakwood Cemetery, Syracuse, NY (Section 60, Lot 176)
References: Pension File, National Archives. Obituary, *Syracuse Post-Standard*, Feb. 14, 1916.

Henry Patchen Martin

Lieutenant Colonel, 71 NY State Militia, May 3, 1861. Colonel, 71 NY State Militia, June 3, 1861. Honorably mustered out, July 31, 1861. Colonel, 71 NY National Guard, May 28, 1862. Honorably mustered out, Sept. 2, 1862.

Born: Nov. 13, 1827 New York City, NY

Died: Oct. 10, 1906 Brooklyn, NY

Occupation: Made a fortune in real estate. Also engaged for a time in the sale of pianos.

Miscellaneous: Resided Brooklyn, NY

Buried: Green-Wood Cemetery, Brooklyn, NY (Section 92, Lot 8154, family mausoleum)

References: Obituary, *Brooklyn Daily Eagle*, Oct. 11, 1906. Obituary, *New York Times*, Oct. 11, 1906. Henry Whittemore. *History of the 71st Regiment N. G. S. N. Y.* New York City, NY, 1886. Augustus T. Francis. *History of the 71st Regiment, N. G., N. Y.* New York City, NY, 1919.

Henry Patchen Martin Courtesy of Richard F. Carlile. J. Gurney & Son, Photographic Artists, 707 Broadway, New York.

Henry Patchen Martin Roger D. Hunt Collection, USAMHI. Charles D. Fredricks & Co., "Specialite," 587 Broadway, New York.

Henry Patchen Martin Courtesy of Richard F. Carlile. Charles D. Fredricks & Co., "Specialite," 587 Broadway, New York.

Henry Patchen Martin
Courtesy of Alan J. Sessarego.

Henry Patchen Martin
Roger D. Hunt Collection, USAMHI. C. D. Fredricks & Co., 587 Broadway,
New York.

Joel O. Martin

1 Lieutenant, Co. H, 17 NY Infantry, May 10, 1861. Captain,
Co. H, 17 NY Infantry, Oct. 24, 1861. GSW face, 2nd Bull
Run, VA, Aug. 30, 1862. Dismissed Feb. 22, 1863, for
"worthlessness and engaging in the sutler business while
on recruiting service." 1 Lieutenant, Adjutant, 17 NY Veteran Infantry, June 10, 1863. *Lieutenant Colonel*, 17 NY
Veteran Infantry, July 1, 1863. Major, 17 NY Veteran Infantry, Oct. 14, 1863. Lieutenant Colonel, 17 NY Veteran
Infantry, May 10, 1864. *Colonel*, 17 NY Veteran Infantry,
Sept. 3, 1864. Discharged for disability, Jan. 4, 1865, due
to chronic diarrhea contracted in the Peninsular Campaign.

Henry Patchen Martin (postwar)
Lafayette Post 140 GAR Collection, Civil War Library & Museum, Philadelphia, PA.

Born: Dec. 7, 1835 NY

Died: July 2, 1877 Indianapolis, IN (committed suicide by stabbing himself twenty times with a pocket knife)

Occupation: Lawyer and insurance agent. Secretary of the Masonic Mutual Benefit Society of Indiana at his death.

Miscellaneous: Resided Norwich, Chenango Co., NY; and Indianapolis, IN.

Buried: Crown Hill Cemetery, Indianapolis, IN (Section 13, Lot 46)

References: Obituary, *Indianapolis Sentinel*, July 3, 1877. Obituary, *Chenango Semi-Weekly Telegraph*, July 11, 1877. Military Service File, National Archives. Letters Received, Volunteer Service Branch, Adjutant General's Office, File B130(VS)1863, National Archives.

Joel Whitney Mason

1 Lieutenant, Adjutant, 6 NY State Militia, May 14, 1861. Honorably mustered out, July 31, 1861. Colonel, 6 NY National Guard, June 22, 1863. Honorably mustered out, July 22, 1863.

Born: Oct. 30, 1821 Princeton, MA

Died: July 5, 1894 Hunter, NY

Occupation: Furniture manufacturer

Offices/Honors: New York City Police Commissioner, 1880-84

Miscellaneous: Resided New York City, NY

Buried: Green-Wood Cemetery, Brooklyn, NY (Section 26, Lot 5675)

References: Obituary, *New York Times*, July 6, 1894. Obituary, *New York Tribune*, July 6, 1894. Mason Family Bible. "Mr. Wheeler's Successor," *New York Times*, May 26, 1880.

Roderick Nicol Matheson

Colonel, 32 NY Infantry, May 22, 1861. GSW right leg, Crampton's Gap, MD, Sept. 14, 1862.

Born: 1826 Inverness, Scotland

Died: Oct. 2, 1862 DOW Burkittsville, MD

Occupation: Farmer and school teacher

Miscellaneous: Resided New York City, NY; San Francisco, CA; and Healdsburg, Sonoma Co., CA

Buried: Oak Mound Cemetery, Healdsburg, CA

Above Right: *Joel Whitney Mason*
Roger D. Hunt Collection, USAMHI.
Right: *Roderick Nicol Matheson*
Courtesy of the author. R. W. Addis, Photographer, McClees Gallery, 308 Penna. Avenue, Washington, DC.

Roderick Nicol Matheson
Massachusetts MOLLUS Collection, USAMHI.

Roderick Nicol Matheson
Courtesy of Healdsburg Museum and Historical Society.

References: Obituary, *New York Times*, April 18, 1906. Letters Received, Volunteer Service Branch, Adjutant General's Office, File M1056(VS)1862, National Archives. Simon Wolf. *The American Jew as Patriot, Soldier and Citizen.* Philadelphia, PA, 1895.

Waters W. McChesney

Colonel, 10 NY Infantry, May 2, 1861. Discharged for disability, Sept. 1, 1861, due to "valvular disease of the heart." Colonel, 134 IL Infantry, May 31, 1864. Honorably mustered out, Oct. 25, 1864.

Born: Oct. 30, 1838 Troy, NY
Died: April 19, 1865 Chicago, IL
Occupation: Clerk and bookkeeper
Miscellaneous: Resided Chicago, IL
Buried: Oakwood Cemetery, Troy, NY (Section D-1, Lot 69)
References: Pension File and Military Service File, National Archives. Paul W. Prindle and Katherine E. Schultz. *The McChesney Family of Rensselaer County, NY.* Annville, PA, 1969. Charles W. Cowtan. *Services of the 10th New York Volunteers (National Zouaves) in the War of the Rebellion.* New York City, NY, 1882. Letters Received, Volunteer Service Branch, Adjutant General's Office, File M155(VS)1862, National Archives.

References: *An Illustrated History of Sonoma County, CA.* Chicago, IL, 1889. Timothy J. Reese. *Sealed With Their Lives: The Battle of Crampton's Gap.* Baltimore, MD, 1998. Pension File, National Archives.

William Mayer

1 Lieutenant, Co. K, 8 NY Infantry, April 23, 1861. 2 Lieutenant, Co. C, 8 NY Infantry, Oct. 1, 1861. 1 Lieutenant, Co. C, 8 NY Infantry, Jan. 1, 1862. Resigned June 30, 1862. *Colonel, 171 NY Infantry, Sept. 2, 1862.* Lieutenant Colonel, 171 NY Infantry, Sept. 26, 1862. Discharged Nov. 19, 1862 upon consolidation of incomplete regiment with 175 NY Infantry.

Born: 1834 Vienna, Austria
Died: April 17, 1906 Berlin, Germany
Occupation: Newspaper editor and publisher
Buried: Berlin, Germany?

Waters W. McChesney
Roger D. Hunt Collection, USAMHI.

Waters W. McChesney
Courtesy of Richard F. Carlile. Brady's National Photographic Portrait Gallery, Broadway & Tenth Street, New York.

John H. McCunn

Colonel, 37 NY Infantry, May 28, 1861. Having been judged by most of the officers of the regiment as "wholly incompetent to command the regiment," he resigned Aug. 31, 1861, citing the lessening of his authority due to the finding of a court martial and related remarks by Major Gen. McClellan.

Born: 1825 Londonderry, Ireland
Died: July 6, 1872 New York City, NY
Occupation: Lawyer and judge

Waters W. McChesney
Massachusetts MOLLUS Collection, USAMHI. Brady's National Photographic Portrait Gallery, Broadway & Tenth Street, New York.

John H. McCunn
New York State Military Museum and Veterans Research Center.

John H. McCunn
Collection of The New-York Historical Society. Published by E. Anthony, 501 Broadway, New York, from Photographic Negative in Brady's National Portrait Gallery.

Offices/Honors: Judge of the New York Superior Court. Accused of gross wrongdoing, he was removed from office, July 2, 1872, and died of pneumonia four days later.

Miscellaneous: Resided New York City, NY

Buried: Calvary Cemetery, Long Island City, NY (Section 7, Range 12, Plot W)

References: Franklin B. Hough. *American Biographical Notes.* Albany, NY, 1875. Obituary, *New York Times*, July 7, 1872. Charges against, *New York Times*, April 21, 1872. Military Service File, National Archives. Obituary, *New York Daily Tribune*, July 8, 1872. A. Milburn Petty. "History of the 37th Regiment, New York Volunteers," *Journal of the American Irish Historical Society*, Vol. 31 (1937). Thomas P. Lowry. *Tarnished Eagles: The Courts-Martial of Fifty Union Colonels and Lieutenant Colonels.* Mechanicsburg, PA, 1997.

Peter McDermott

Major, 71 NY Infantry, July 18, 1861. Discharged Aug. 1, 1861. Colonel, 170 NY Infantry, July 17, 1862. With charges pending against him, he resigned, Jan. 4, 1863, in consequence of his impaired health and in order to promote "a more harmonious working of the general details of the regiment, and the welfare of the service."

Born: May 22, 1824 Albany, NY

Died: March 14, 1905 Hampton, VA

Other Wars: Mexican War (Sergeant, Co. A, 1 OH Infantry)

Occupation: US Customs inspector and iron worker

Miscellaneous: Resided Brooklyn, NY; Washington, DC; Scranton, Lackawanna Co., PA; and Hampton, VA

Buried: Cathedral Cemetery, Scranton, PA (GAR Plot, Section 9)

References: Pension File and Military Service File, National Archives.

Andrew N. McDonald

Captain, Co. B, 106 NY Infantry, Aug. 12, 1862. Major, 106 NY Infantry, Aug. 4, 1863. Lieutenant Colonel, 106 NY Infantry, June 1, 1864. GSW left leg and left temple, Cold Harbor, VA, June 1, 1864. Captured Cold Harbor, VA, June 1, 1864. Confined at Macon, GA, and Columbia, SC. Escaped Dec. 13, 1864. Colonel, 106 NY Infantry, Dec. 20, 1864. Honorably mustered out, June 22, 1865.

Born: 1836 NY

Died: March 2, 1885 Jersey City, NJ

Occupation: Chemist and pharmacist before war. Engaged in wholesale drug business after war.

Miscellaneous: Resided Ogdensburg, St. Lawrence Co., NY, 1856-59 and 1865-68; Brockville, Ontario, 1859-62; and Jersey City, NJ, 1868-85

Buried: Green Hill Cemetery, Amsterdam, NY

References: Pension File, National Archives. Obituary, *Amsterdam Daily Democrat*, March 6, 1885.

Christopher R. McDonald

Private, Co. K, 8 NY State Militia, April 25, 1861. Honorably mustered out, Aug. 2, 1861. 1 Lieutenant, Co. D, 47 NY Infantry, Aug. 28, 1861. Captain, Co. D, 47 NY Infantry, Dec. 14, 1861. Major, 47 NY Infantry, July 7, 1863. Lieutenant Colonel, 47 NY Infantry, Sept. 29, 1863. GSW right leg and back, Cold Harbor, VA, June 1, 1864. GSW right shoulder, Chaffin's Farm, VA, Sept. 29, 1864. Colonel, 47 NY Infantry, Oct. 27, 1864. Honorably mustered out, Aug. 30, 1865.

Born: 1831 Washington Co., NY

Died: Oct. 16, 1874 New York City, NY

Occupation: Salesman and clerk

Miscellaneous: Resided New York City, NY

Buried: Cypress Hills National Cemetery, Brooklyn, NY (Section 1, Grave 3662)

References: Obituary, *New York Herald*, Oct. 18, 1874. Pension File, National Archives. Letters Received, Volunteer Service Branch, Adjutant General's Office, File I646(VS)1862, National Archives.

Archibald Livingston McDougall

Colonel, 123 NY Infantry, July 23, 1862. Commanded 1 Brigade, 1 Division, 12 Army Corps, Army of the Potomac, May 18, 1863-July 26, 1863. GSW leg (amputated), Dallas, GA, May 25, 1864.

Born: July 9, 1817 Greenwich, NY

Died: June 23, 1864 DOW Chattanooga, TN

Occupation: Lawyer

Miscellaneous: Resided Salem, Washington Co., NY

Buried: Evergreen Cemetery, Salem, NY

References: *Dedication of the New York Auxiliary State Monument on the Battlefield of Gettysburg.* Albany, NY, 1926. Pension File, National Archives. Obituary, *Salem Press*, July 5, 1864. Henry C. Morhous. *Reminiscences of the 123rd Regiment, New York State Volunteers.* Greenwich,

Archibald L. McDougall
Courtesy of Michael Russert. G. W. Rider, Salem, NY.

NY, 1879. Kenneth A. Perry, compiler. *"We Are In A Fight Today," The Civil War Diaries of Horace P. Mathews & King S. Hammond.* Bowie, MD, 2000.

William McEvily

Colonel, 155 NY Infantry, Oct. 10, 1862. Discharged for disability, Nov. 3, 1863, due to sunstroke incurred July 20, 1863.

Born: 1829 Louisburgh, County Mayo, Ireland

Died: March 25, 1889 New York City, NY

Occupation: Architect and builder

Miscellaneous: Resided New York City, NY

Buried: Calvary Cemetery, Long Island City, NY (Section 7, Range 11, Plot II)

References: Military Service File, National Archives. Obituary, *New York Times*, March 26, 1889. Letters Received, Volunteer Service Branch, Adjutant General's Office, File M1420(VS) 1863, National Archives.

Archibald L. McDougall
Courtesy of Michael Russert. G. W. Rider, Salem, NY.

James Bedell McKean

Colonel, 77 NY Infantry, Oct. 14, 1861. Discharged for disability, July 27, 1863, due to "ulceration of the bowels" resulting from physical exhaustion and fever contracted in the Peninsular Campaign.

Born: Aug. 5, 1821 Hoosick, Rensselaer Co., NY (or Bennington, VT)
Died: Jan. 5, 1879 Salt Lake City, UT
Occupation: Lawyer and judge
Offices/Honors: US House of Representatives, 1859-63. Chief Justice, Utah Territory Supreme Court, 1870-75.
Miscellaneous: Resided Saratoga Springs, Saratoga Co., NY; and Salt Lake City, UT

Above Right: *William McEvily*
Courtesy of Henry Deeks. J. Gurney & Son, Photographic Artists, 707 Broadway, New York.
Right: *William McEvily*
Roger D. Hunt Collection, USAMHI. Charles D. Fredricks & Co., "Specialite," 587 Broadway, New York.

Buried: Mount Olivet Cemetery, Salt Lake City, UT (Section O, Lot 142)

References: *Biographical Directory of the American Congress.* Military Service File, National Archives. Obituary, *New York Tribune*, Jan. 9, 1879. George T. Stevens. *Three Years in the Sixth Corps*. Albany, NY, 1866. Nathaniel B. Sylvester. *History of Saratoga County, NY*. Philadelphia, PA, 1878. Obituary, *Salt Lake Daily Tribune*, Jan. 7, 1879. *Report of the 43rd Annual Reunion of the Survivors Association of the 77th Regiment New York State Infantry Volunteers of 1861-65*. N.p., 1915.

Above: *James Bedell McKean*
Massachusetts MOLLUS Collection, USAMHI.
Above Right: *James Bedell McKean*
Report of the 43rd Annual Reunion of the Survivors Association of the 77th Regiment New York State Infantry Volunteers of 1861-65.
Right: *James Bedell McKean (postwar)*
Frederick H. Meserve. Historical Portraits. Courtesy of New York State Library.

James Power McMahon

Captain, Co. K, 69 NY Infantry, Nov. 17, 1861. Staff of Brig.
Gen. Thomas F. Meagher, March-June 1862. Provost Marshal, Staff of Major Gen. Israel B. Richardson, June-Oct.
1862. Lieutenant Colonel, 155 NY Infantry, Oct. 21, 1862.
Colonel, 164 NY Infantry, March 23, 1863. GSW Cold
Harbor, VA, June 3, 1864, "pierced by 14 or 15 bullets."

Born: 1836 County Wexford, Ireland
Died: June 3, 1864 KIA Cold Harbor, VA
Education: Attended St. John's College, Fordham, NY
Occupation: Lawyer
Miscellaneous: Resided Buffalo, NY
Buried: St. Agnes Cemetery, Utica, NY (Section 64, Lot 1)
References: Research Files of Benedict R. Maryniak. Obituary, *Brooklyn Daily Eagle*, June 14, 1864. Obituary, *Army and Navy Journal*, June 25, 1864. Pension File and Military Service File, National Archives. Obituary, *Irish American*, June 18, 1864.

James Power McMahon
Massachusetts MOLLUS Collection, USAMHI.

James Power McMahon
Courtesy of Olaf. Philp & Solomons' Metropolitan Gallery, 332 Pennsylvania Avenue, Washington, DC.

James Power McMahon
Jack McCormack Collection.

Camp of the 164th New York Infantry (James P. McMahon, seated center)
Massachusetts MOLLUS Collection, USAMHI.

Officers of the 164th & 170th New York Infantry (From left, Unknown Officer; Col. James P. McMahon, 164th New York; Capt. Hugh F. Olone, 170th New York; Lt. Col. Michael C. Murphy, 170th New York; 1 Lt. Edward McCaffrey, 164th New York; 2 Lt. Michael J. Eagan, 170th New York; Unknown Officer; 2 Lt. Thomas Montgomery, 170th New York; Unknown Officer)
Massachusetts MOLLUS Collection, USAMHI.

John Eugene McMahon

Colonel, 164 NY Infantry, Aug. 8, 1862

Born: 1833 Ireland
Died: March 11, 1863 Buffalo, NY (consumption)
Education: Graduated St. John's College, Fordham, NY, 1851
Occupation: Lawyer
Miscellaneous: Resided Buffalo, NY
Buried: St. Agnes Cemetery, Utica, NY (Section 64, Lot 1)
References: Research Files of Benedict R. Maryniak. Pension File and Military Service File, National Archives.

Duncan McMartin

Colonel, 153 NY Infantry, Sept. 5, 1862. Discharged for disability, April 21, 1863, due to "disease of the lungs tending to consumption."

Born: Feb. 24, 1817 Fulton Co., NY
Died: July 6, 1894 Beaman, Grundy Co., IA
Education: Attended Harvard University Law School, Cambridge, MA
Occupation: Lawyer and farmer
Miscellaneous: Resided Hagaman's Mills, near Amsterdam, Montgomery Co., NY; and Beaman, Grundy Co., IA
Buried: Woodland Cemetery, Des Moines, IA (Block 17, Lot 23)
References: Military Service File, National Archives. *Portrait and Biographical Record of Jasper, Marshall and Grundy Counties, Iowa.* Chicago, IL, 1894.

Andrew Thomas McReynolds

Colonel, 1 NY Cavalry, June 15, 1861. Commanded 4 Brigade, Cavalry Division, Army of the Potomac, Sept.-Oct. 1862. Commanded Post of Martinsburg, WV, Defenses of the Upper Potomac, 8 Army Corps, Middle Department, Jan.-March 1863. Commanded 3 Brigade, 2 Division, 8 Army Corps, March-June 1863. Honorably mustered out, June 15, 1864.

Born: Dec. 25, 1808 Dungannon, County Tyrone, Ireland
Died: Nov. 25, 1898 Muskegon, MI
Other Wars: Mexican War (Captain, 3 US Dragoons) (Shell wound left arm, Mexico City, MX, Aug. 20, 1847)
Occupation: Lawyer
Offices/Honors: MI House of Representatives, 1840. MI State Senate, 1847.

The McMahon Brothers (Martin Thomas, left; John Eugene, center; James Power, right)
Jack McCormack Collection.

Duncan McMartin (postwar)
Portrait and Biographical Record of Jasper, Marshall and Grundy Counties, Iowa.

Miscellaneous: Resided Detroit, MI; and Grand Rapids, Kent Co., MI

Buried: Fulton Street Cemetery, Grand Rapids, MI (Block 12, Lot 18)

References: William M. Sweeny. "General Andrew Thomas McReynolds, Hero of the Mexican and Civil Wars," *Journal of the American Irish Historical Society*, Vol. 25 (1926). Obituary, *Grand Rapids Herald*, Nov. 26, 1898. Military Service File, National Archives. *American Biographical History of Eminent and Self-Made Men*. Michigan Volume. Cincinnati, OH, 1878.

Above: *Andrew Thomas McReynolds (1847)*
Journal of the American Irish Historical Society, Vol. 25 (1926).
Above Right and Right: *Andrew Thomas McReynolds*
Massachusetts MOLLUS Collection, USAMHI.

Andrew Thomas McReynolds
Massachusetts MOLLUS Collection, USAMHI. Published by E. Anthony, 501 Broadway, New York, from Photographic Negative in Brady's National Portrait Gallery.

Andrew Thomas McReynolds
Massachusetts MOLLUS Collection, USAMHI. Published by E. Anthony, 501 Broadway, New York, from Photographic Negative in Brady's National Portrait Gallery.

Robert Burnett Merritt

1 Lieutenant, Co. A, 75 NY Infantry, Oct. 2, 1861. Lieutenant Colonel, 75 NY Infantry, Oct. 21, 1861. Colonel, 75 NY Infantry, July 21, 1862. Commanded 3 Brigade, 1 Division, 19 Army Corps, Department of the Gulf, July 10, 1863-Jan. 20, 1864. Commanded 2 Brigade, 2 Division, 19 Army Corps, June 27, 1864-July 2, 1864. Discharged for disability, Sept. 20, 1864, due to chronic diarrhea and acute bronchitis.

Born: May 1840 Grant Co., WI
Died: Dec. 7, 1900 New York City, NY
Education: Attended US Military Academy, West Point, NY (Class of 1862)
Occupation: Notary Public
Buried: Kensico Cemetery, Valhalla, NY (Section 8, Mohegan Plot, Lot A, Range 2, Grave 2, unmarked)
References: Pension File, National Archives. Henry and James Hall. *Cayuga in the Field, A Record of the 19th New York*

Robert Burnett Merritt
Roger D. Hunt Collection, USAMHI. Wm. Frank Browne, Photographer, Kilpatrick's Div. Hd. Qrs., 5th Mich. Cav.

Robert Burnett Merritt (background center; with Brig. Gen. Godfrey Weitzel, foreground; New Orleans, LA, March 1863) Massachusetts MOLLUS Collection, USAMHI.

Jeremiah V. Meserole
Courtesy of Jacqueline T. Eubanks.

Volunteers, All the Batteries of the 3rd New York Artillery, and 75th New York Volunteers. Auburn, NY, 1873.

Jeremiah V. Meserole

Sergeant, Co. D, 7 NY State Militia, April 26, 1861. Honorably mustered out, June 3, 1861. Colonel, 47 NY National Guard, May 27, 1862. Honorably mustered out, Sept. 1, 1862. Colonel, 47 NY National Guard, June 17, 1863. Honorably mustered out, July 23, 1863.

Born: Oct. 23, 1833 New York City, NY
Died: Aug. 13, 1908 Far Rockaway, Long Island, NY
Occupation: Surveyor and bank president
Offices/Honors: Brig. Gen., NY National Guard, 1868-76
Miscellaneous: Resided New York City, NY
Buried: Green-Wood Cemetery, Brooklyn, NY (Section 140, Lot 27020)
References: Obituary, *New York Tribune*, Aug. 14, 1908. Obituary, *New York Times*, Aug. 14, 1908.

Francis Charles Miller

Captain, Co. C, 24 NY Infantry, May 1, 1861. Major, 147 NY Infantry, Sept. 23, 1862. Lieutenant Colonel, 147 NY Infantry, Feb. 4, 1863. GSW head, Gettysburg, PA, July 1, 1863. Colonel, 147 NY Infantry, Nov. 5, 1863. GSW left side, Wilderness, VA, May 5, 1864. Captured Wilderness, VA, May 5, 1864. Confined at Lynchburg, VA; Macon, GA; Savannah, GA; Charleston, SC; and Columbia, SC. Paroled Dec. 10, 1864. Honorably mustered out, June 7, 1865.

Born: 1830 Herkimer Co., NY
Died: Aug. 17, 1878 Oneida, NY
Occupation: Carpenter and builder before war. Lumber merchant after war.
Miscellaneous: Resided Oswego, NY; and Oneida, Madison Co., NY.
Buried: Glenwood Cemetery, Oneida, NY
References: Obituary, *Oneida Dispatch*, Aug. 23, 1878. Pension File, National Archives.

Francis Charles Miller
New York State Military Museum and Veterans Research Center.

Charles Austin Milliken
Courtesy of the author. J. H. Abbott, No. 480 Broadway, Albany, NY.

Timothy Wadsworth Miller

Colonel, 153 NY Infantry, Aug. 23, 1862. Succeeded by Colonel Duncan McMartin, Sept. 5, 1862.

Born: Sept. 27, 1823 Johnstown, NY
Died: Feb. 9, 1872 Johnstown, NY
Education: Attended Union College, Schenectady, NY (Class of 1848)
Occupation: Merchant and banker
Miscellaneous: Resided Johnstown, Fulton Co., NY
Buried: Johnstown Cemetery, Johnstown, NY
References: Frank E. Miller. *A Genealogy of the Family of Millers*. Syracuse, NY, 1925. Obituary, *Gloversville Intelligencer*, Feb. 15, 1872. Henry C. Johnson, editor. *Tenth General Catalogue of the Psi Upsilon Fraternity*. Bethlehem, PA, 1888.

Charles Austin Milliken

Private, Co. C, 43 NY Infantry, Sept. 16, 1861. Sergeant Major, 43 NY Infantry, Sept. 23, 1861. 2 Lieutenant, Co. C, 43 NY Infantry, Nov. 6, 1861. GSW shoulder, Lee's Mills, VA, April 28, 1862. 1 Lieutenant, Adjutant, 43 NY Infantry, July 16, 1862. GSW Spotsylvania, VA, May 12, 1864. Major, 43 NY Infantry, July 13, 1864. Lieutenant Colonel, 43 NY Infantry, Sept. 21, 1864. GSW Cedar Creek, VA, Oct. 19, 1864. GSW face (slight), Petersburg, VA, March 25, 1865. *Colonel*, 43 NY Infantry, May 7, 1865. Honorably mustered out, June 27, 1865. Bvt. Colonel, USV, Oct. 19, 1864, for gallant and meritorious services in the present campaign before Richmond, VA, and in the Shenandoah Valley.

Born: 1836? ME
Died: Aug. 31, 1867 Galveston, TX (yellow fever)
Occupation: Assistant foreman in newspaper office
Miscellaneous: Resided Wasioja, Dodge Co., MN; Albany, NY; and Galveston, TX
Buried: Old City Cemetery, Galveston, TX
References: Military Service File, National Archives. Gideon T. Ridlon. *History of the Families Millingas and Millanges of Saxony and Normandy*. Lewiston, ME, 1907.

Simon Hosack Mix
Massachusetts MOLLUS Collection, USAMHI. Brady's National Photographic
Portrait Gallery, Broadway & Tenth Street, New York.

Simon Hosack Mix
Seward Osborne Collection. Brady's National Photographic Portrait Gallery,
Broadway & Tenth Street, New York.

Simon Hosack Mix

Lieutenant Colonel, 3 NY Cavalry, Aug. 16, 1861. Colonel, 3 NY Cavalry, April 8, 1862. Authorized as *Colonel*, 23 NY Cavalry, Oct. 27, 1862. Never joined regiment, which failed to complete organization. Commanded Cavalry Brigade, 18 Army Corps, Department of North Carolina, May-July 1863. Chief of Cavalry, Staff of Major Gen. John J. Peck, March 5, 1864-April 28, 1864. Commanded 1 Brigade, Cavalry Division, Army of the James, April 28, 1864-June 15, 1864. GSW and captured, Petersburg, VA, June 15, 1864.

Born: Feb. 25, 1825 Johnstown, NY

Died: June 15, 1864 DOW Petersburg, VA

Education: Attended Schoharie (NY) Academy

Occupation: Newspaper editor

Miscellaneous: Resided Schoharie, Schoharie Co., NY

Buried: Petersburg, VA (Body never recovered). Cenotaph in Old Stone Fort Cemetery, Schoharie, NY.

References: William E. Roscoe. *History of Schoharie County, NY.* Syracuse, NY, 1882. George H. Warner, compiler. *Military Records of Schoharie County Veterans of Four Wars.* Albany, NY, 1891. Pension File and Military Service File, National Archives. Edward A. Hagan. *Hot Whisky for Five: Schoharie County and the Civil War.* Cobleskill, NY, 1985. Arthur B. Gregg. "Simon Hosack Mix - The Story of a Short Life," *Schoharie County Historical Review,* Vol. 25, No. 2 (Fall-Winter 1961).

Joseph Anton Moesch
US Military Academy Library.

Joseph Anton Moesch
Americana Image Gallery Collection, USAMHI.

Joseph Anton Moesch

1 Sergeant, Co. B, 9 NY State Militia, May 27, 1861. Captain, Co. B, 83 NY Infantry, Oct. 11, 1861. GSW Fredericksburg, VA, Dec. 13, 1862. Lieutenant Colonel, 83 NY Infantry, Jan. 18, 1863. Colonel, 83 NY Infantry, Oct. 13, 1863. GSW Wilderness, VA, May 6, 1864.

Born: Aug. 13, 1829 (or Oct. 26, 1827) Eiken, Canton Aargau, Switzerland
Died: May 6, 1864 KIA Wilderness, VA
Occupation: Baker and clerk
Miscellaneous: Resided New York City, NY
Buried: Fredericksburg National Cemetery, Fredericksburg, VA
References: George A. Hussey, historian, and William Todd, editor. *History of the 9th Regiment NYSM-NGSNY (83rd NY Volunteers).* New York City, NY, 1889. Edmund J. Raus, Jr. *A Generation on the March: The Union Army at Gettysburg.* Gettysburg, PA, 1996. Pension File, National Archives.

James Monroe, Jr.

Colonel, 22 NY National Guard, May 28, 1862

Born: Feb. 10, 1820 Albemarle Co., VA
Ded: July 31, 1862 Harpers Ferry, WV (typhoid fever)
Other Wars: Mexican War (Captain, 6 US Infantry)
Occupation: Regular Army (2 Lieutenant, 6 US Infantry, Aug. 17, 1837; resigned May 9, 1855 as Captain, 6 US Infantry)
Miscellaneous: Resided New York City, NY
Buried: Holy Cross Cemetery, Brooklyn, NY
References: George W. Wingate. *History of the 22nd Regiment of the New York National Guard.* New York City, NY, 1896. Pension File, National Archives.

Henry Moore

Colonel, 47 NY Infantry, Sept. 14, 1861. Resigned Aug. 5, 1862 due to "physical incapacity to perform the duties devolving upon me in the field at the present time." Colonel, 47 NY Infantry, March 17, 1863. GSW left arm and right leg, Olustee, FL, Feb. 20, 1864. Honorably mustered out, Oct. 27, 1864.

James Monroe, Jr.
Roger D. Hunt Collection, USAMHI. Broadbent & Co., 912 & 914 Chestnut Street, Philadelphia, PA.

James Monroe, Jr.
History of the 22nd Regiment of the New York National Guard.

Born: 1825? New York City, NY

Died: Jan. 2, 1904 Yonkers, NY

Occupation: Engaged in the sash and blind business and later in the real estate business

Miscellaneous: Resided New York City, NY; Pleasantville, Westchester Co., NY; and Yonkers, Westchester Co., NY

Buried: Probably Kensico Cemetery, Valhalla, NY (Section 11, Tecumseh Plot, Lot 44) with his wife Sarah E. Moore, who was buried there Oct. 15, 1898. Cemetery records show that Henry Moore is buried in the same grave as Sarah E. Moore, but the date of burial is listed as Aug. 21, 1893. There is no marker for either Henry or Sarah Moore.

References: Pension File, National Archives. Obituary, *Yonkers Statesman*, Jan. 4, 1904.

Henry Moore
New York State Military Museum and Veterans Research Center.

Above: *Henry and Sarah Moore*
Roger D. Hunt Collection, USAMHI. Original photo enhanced by Michael Stretch.
Right: *Roger D. Hunt Collection, USAMHI. S. A. Cooley, Photographer, 10th Army Corps, Beaufort, SC.*

Joseph S. Morgan

Major, 13 NY State Militia, May 17, 1861. Honorably mustered out, Aug. 6, 1861. Colonel, 90 NY Infantry, Nov. 27, 1861. Commanded 1 Brigade, 4 Division, 19 Army Corps, Department of the Gulf, May 30, 1863-July 13, 1863. Dismissed April 19, 1864 for "conduct unbecoming an officer and a gentleman." Disability resulting from dismissal removed, Oct. 13, 1864.

Born: 1822? Brooklyn, NY
Died: Nov. 2, 1907 Cleveland, OH
Occupation: Hotelkeeper before war. Agent after war with interests in mining in the West.
Miscellaneous: Resided Brooklyn, NY, to 1877; Los Angeles, CA; Tucson, AZ; and Cleveland, OH
Buried: Lake View Cemetery, Cleveland, OH (Section 14, Lot 237, unmarked)
References: Pension File and Military Service File, National Archives. Obituary, *Cleveland Plain Dealer,* Nov. 3, 1907.

Lewis Gouverneur Morris

Colonel, 135 NY Infantry (later 6 NY Heavy Artillery), Aug. 14, 1862. Succeeded by Colonel William H. Morris, Sept. 2, 1862.

Born: Aug. 19, 1808 Claverack, NY
Died: Sept. 19, 1900 Fordham, NY
Occupation: Gentleman farmer
Offices/Honors: President of the NY State Agricultural Society
Miscellaneous: Resided Fordham, Westchester Co., NY
Buried: St. Anne's Episcopal Church, Mott Haven, Bronx, New York City, NY
References: Margherita Arlina Hamm. *Famous Families of New York.* New York and London, 1902. J. Thomas Scharf. *History of Westchester County, NY.* Philadelphia, PA, 1886. Obituary, *New York Times,* Sept. 20, 1900.

Joseph S. Morgan
Roger D. Hunt Collection, USAMHI.

Lewis Gouverneur Morris (postwar)
Famous Families of New York.

Lewis Owen Morris

Captain, 1 US Artillery, April 21, 1861. Colonel, 7 NY Heavy
Artillery, Aug. 1, 1862. Commanded 2 Brigade, Defenses
North of the Potomac, Military District of Washington,
Oct. 1862-Feb. 1863. Commanded 2 Brigade, Defenses
North of the Potomac, 22 Army Corps, Department of
Washington, Feb. 2, 1863-May 16, 1864. Commanded 4
Brigade, 1 Division, 2 Army Corps, Army of the Potomac,
June 3-4, 1864. GSW left shoulder, Cold Harbor, VA, June
4, 1864.

Born: Aug. 14, 1824 Albany, NY
Died: June 4, 1864 KIA Cold Harbor, VA
Other Wars: Mexican War (1 Lieutenant, 1 US Artillery)
Occupation: Regular Army (Captain, 1 US Artillery)
Miscellaneous: Resided Albany, NY. Great-grandson of Lewis
Morris, Signer of the Declaration of Independence. Brother
of Colonel Thomas F. Morris.
Buried: Rural Cemetery, Albany, NY (Section 9, Lot 1)
References: Rufus W. Clark. *The Heroes of Albany*. Albany,
NY, 1867. Frederick W. Pyne. *Descendants of the Signers
of the Declaration of Independence*. Camden, ME, 1998.
Robert Keating. *Carnival of Blood: The Civil War Ordeal
of the 7th New York Heavy Artillery*. Baltimore, MD, 1998.
Obituary, *New York Times,* June 9, 1864.

Lewis Owen Morris
Courtesy of Thomas Harris. B. Loeb & Co., Fort Reno, DC.

Lewis Owen Morris
Courtesy of Fred Jolly.

Lewis Owen Morris
Massachusetts MOLLUS Collection, USAMHI.

Orlando Harriman Morris

Major, 66 NY Infantry, Oct. 29, 1861. Colonel, 66 NY Infantry, Dec. 3, 1862. Commanded 3 Brigade, 1 Division, 2 Army Corps, Army of the Potomac, May 15, 1863-May 25, 1863. Contused GSW right side, Gettysburg, PA, July 2, 1863. Commanded 4 Brigade, 1 Division, 2 Army Corps, June 3, 1864. GSW heart, Cold Harbor, VA, June 3, 1864.

Born: 1835 NY

Died: June 3, 1864 KIA Cold Harbor, VA

Education: Graduated Columbia University, New York City, NY, 1854. Attended Harvard University Law School, Cambridge, MA.

Occupation: Lawyer

Miscellaneous: Resided New York City, NY; and Bergen Point, Hudson Co., NJ

Buried: Green-Wood Cemetery, Brooklyn, NY (Section 23, Lot 14520)

Orlando Harriman Morris
New York State Military Museum and Veterans Research Center.

Orlando Harriman Morris
Meade Album, Civil War Library & Museum, Philadelphia, PA.

References: Obituary, *Army and Navy Journal*, June 18, 1864.
William J. Tenney. *The Military and Naval History of the Rebellion in the United States*. New York City, NY, 1865.
Pension File and Military Service File, National Archives.
Obituary, *New York Times*, June 9, 1864.

Thomas Ford Morris

Lieutenant Colonel, 17 NY Infantry, May 18, 1861. Resigned May 9, 1862. *Colonel*, 93 NY Infantry, May 10, 1862. Commissioned to replace Colonel John S. Crocker, who had been captured near Yorktown, VA, April 23, 1862, he was not allowed to take command since "the absence of an officer taken prisoner does not create a vacancy."

Born: April 14, 1829 Albany, NY
Died: March 21, 1886 Yonkers, NY
Education: Attended Albany (NY) Academy
Occupation: Banker and stock broker

Thomas Ford Morris
Courtesy of Henry Deeks. Published by E. Anthony, 501 Broadway, New York, from Photographic Negative in Brady's National Portrait Gallery.

Miscellaneous: Resided Yonkers, Westchester Co., NY. Great-grandson of Lewis Morris, Signer of the Declaration of Independence. Brother of Colonel Lewis O. Morris.

Buried: Oakland Cemetery, Yonkers, NY (Section 2, Lot 125)

References: Obituary, *New York Tribune*, March 24, 1886. Obituary, *Yonkers Gazette*, March 27, 1886. Henry Whittemore. *History of George Washington Post 103, G. A. R.* Detroit, MI, 1885. Military Service File, National Archives. David H. King, A. Judson Gibbs, and Jay H. Northup, compilers. *History of the 93rd Regiment, New York Volunteer Infantry*. Milwaukee, WI, 1895. Letters Received, Volunteer Service Branch, Adjutant General's Office, File B827(VS)1862, National Archives.

Andrew Jackson Morrison

Colonel, 7 NY Cavalry, Nov. 6, 1861. Honorably mustered out, March 31, 1862. Volunteer ADC, Staff of Brig. Gen. Innis N. Palmer, May-Sept. 1862. GSW left hand, Oak Grove, VA, June 25, 1862. Colonel, 26 NJ Infantry, Sept. 16, 1862. Dismissed June 11, 1863, for "drunkenness on duty." Dismissal revoked, Feb. 6, 1864. Colonel, 3 NJ Cavalry, Nov. 4, 1863. Resigned Aug. 29, 1864, due to "reasons referring to the interests of the service and myself."

Born: Oct. 3, 1831 Argyle, Washington Co., NY

Died: Jan. 28, 1907 Troy, NY

Other Wars: Mexican War (Volunteer ADC to Capt. John Butler)

Occupation: Adventurer before war, participating in the abortive filibuster expeditions of Narciso Lopez and William Walker. Railway postal agent after war.

Miscellaneous: Resided West Troy, Albany Co., NY.

Buried: Rural Cemetery, Albany, NY (Section 105, Lot 447)

References: Alan A. Siegel. *For the Glory of the Union*. Rutherford, NJ, 1984. Pension File, National Archives. Obituary, *Albany Evening Journal*, Jan. 29, 1907.

Thomas Ford Morris
National Archives. Brady's National Photographic Portrait Gallery, Broadway & Tenth Street, New York.

Andrew Jackson Morrison
Massachusetts MOLLUS Collection, USAMHI.

Charles Beatty Morton

1 Lieutenant, Co. H, 13 NY State Militia, May 17, 1861. Honorably mustered out, Aug. 6, 1861. Captain, Co. H, 47 NY National Guard, May 27, 1862. Honorably mustered out, Sept. 1, 1862. Colonel, 173 NY Infantry, Sept. 22, 1862. Resigned March 5, 1863 on account of "inability to perform duties of the office."

Born: Feb. 2, 1833 Troy, NY

Died: Jan. 16, 1922 Brooklyn, NY

Occupation: Policeman before war. Municipal official after war.

Offices/Honors: NY State Assembly, 1872. Assistant Postmaster, Brooklyn, NY, 1877-84.

Miscellaneous: Resided Troy, Rensselaer Co., NY; and Brooklyn, NY, after 1855

Buried: Graham Cemetery, Hubbardsville, Madison Co., NY

References: Obituary, *Brooklyn Daily Eagle*, Jan. 16, 1922. Pension File, National Archives.

Thaddeus Phelps Mott

Captain, 3 Independent Battery, NY Light Artillery, June 17, 1861. Captain, 19 US Infantry, Oct. 29, 1861. GSW left thigh, White Oak Swamp, VA, June 30, 1862. Resigned volunteer commission, July 8, 1862, to report for duty with 19 US Infantry. Resigned regular commission, Jan. 30, 1863. Lieutenant Colonel, 14 NY Cavalry, Feb. 26, 1863. Colonel, 14 NY Cavalry, July 10, 1863. Dismissed Jan. 18, 1864, for "destroying property belonging to an inhabitant of the United States" and "conduct to the prejudice of good order and military discipline." Dismissal revoked, Dec. 18, 1865, and resignation accepted as of date of dismissal.

Born: Dec. 7, 1831 New York City, NY

Died: Nov. 23, 1894 Toulon, France

Education: Attended New York University, New York City, NY

Offices/Honors: US Minister to Costa Rica, 1867-68. Major General, Egyptian Army, 1869-75.

Miscellaneous: Resided New York City, NY; and Toulon, France

Charles Beatty Morton (1872)
Courtesy of Robert D. Marcus. R. E. Churchill, Photographer, 520 Broadway, Albany, NY.

Thaddeus Phelps Mott
Massachusetts MOLLUS Collection, USAMHI. Published by E. Anthony, 501 Broadway, New York, from Photographic Negative in Brady's National Portrait Gallery.

Thaddeus Phelps Mott
Massachusetts MOLLUS Collection, USAMHI.

Buried: Toulon, France?

References: Pension File and Military Service File, National
Archives. Obituary, *New York Tribune*, Nov. 25, 1894. John
H. Jones. *The Jones Family of Long Island*. New York
City, NY, 1907. William B. Hesseltine and Hazel C. Wolf.
The Blue and the Gray on the Nile. Chicago, IL, 1961.
Letters Received, Volunteer Service Branch, Adjutant
General's Office, File M68(VS)1862, National Archives.

Above Right: *Thaddeus Phelps Mott*
Massachusetts MOLLUS Collection, USAMHI. Published by E. Anthony, 501
Broadway, New York, from Photographic Negative in Brady's National Por-
trait Gallery.
Right: *Thaddeus Phelps Mott*
Massachusetts MOLLUS Collection, USAMHI.

John McLeod Murphy

Colonel, 15 NY Engineers, May 11, 1861. Resigned Dec. 12, 1862, in order to accept appointment in the US Navy. Acting Lieutenant, USN, Dec. 4, 1862. Commanded USS Carondelet, Mississippi Squadron, March-Oct. 1863. Resigned July 30, 1864.

Born: Feb. 14, 1827 North Castle, Westchester Co., NY

Died: June 1, 1871 New York City, NY

Education: Graduated US Naval Academy, Annapolis, MD, 1847

Other Wars: Mexican War (Midshipman, USN)

Occupation: Midshipman, USN, Feb. 18, 1841. Passed Midshipman, USN, Aug. 10, 1847. Resigned May 10, 1852. Civil engineer on transportation and municipal projects before war. Played a major role in the exploration and development of the Isthmus of Tehuantepec in southern Mexico. Engaged in various literary and engineering pursuits after war.

Offices/Honors: NY State Senate, 1860-61

Miscellaneous: Resided New York City, NY

Buried: Calvary Cemetery, Long Island City, NY (Section 5, Range 9, Plot Z)

References: Pension File and Military Service File, National Archives. William D. Murphy. *Biographical Sketches of the State Officers and Members of the Legislature of the State of New York in 1861.* New York City, NY, 1861. Obituary, *New York Herald*, June 2, 1871.

Mathew Murphy

2 Lieutenant, Co. G, 69 NY State Militia, April 20, 1861. Honorably mustered out, Aug. 3, 1861. Lieutenant Colonel, 69 NY National Guard, May 26, 1862. Honorably mustered out, Sept. 3, 1862. Colonel, 182 NY Infantry, Nov.

John McLeod Murphy
Massachusetts MOLLUS Collection, USAMHI. Published by E. Anthony, 501 Broadway, New York, from Photographic Negative in Brady's National Portrait Gallery.

Mathew Murphy
Massachusetts MOLLUS Collection, USAMHI. Brady's National Photographic Portrait Gallery, Broadway & Tenth Street, New York.

8, 1862. Commanded 3 Brigade, 1 Division, 7 Army Corps, Department of Virginia, April 9-July 11, 1863. Commanded 2 Brigade, Tyler's Division, 22 Army Corps, Department of Washington, Jan.-March 1864 and April-May 1864. GSW arm, Spotsylvania, VA, May 18, 1864. Commanded 2 Brigade, 2 Division, 2 Army Corps, Army of the Potomac, June 26-Oct. 27, 1864 and Nov. 27, 1864-Feb. 5, 1865. GSW right knee, Hatcher's Run, VA, Feb. 5, 1865.

Born: Dec. 20, 1839 Ballisodare, County Sligo, Ireland
Died: April 16, 1865 DOW City Point, VA
Occupation: School principal
Miscellaneous: Resided New York City, NY
Buried: Calvary Cemetery, Long Island City, NY (Section 4, Range 3, Plot V)
References: William J. Tenney. *Military and Naval History of the Rebellion in the United States.* New York City, NY, 1865. Pension File, National Archives. Obituary, *Irish American*, April 29, 1865. Death notice and obituary, *New York Herald*, April 22 and 24, 1865.

Homer Augustus Nelson

Colonel, 167 NY Infantry, Sept. 3, 1862. Regiment failed to complete organization and was merged into the 159 NY Infantry. *Colonel*, 159 NY Infantry, Nov. 1, 1862. Resigned Nov. 25, 1862.

Born: Aug. 31, 1829 Poughkeepsie, NY
Died: April 25, 1891 Poughkeepsie, NY
Occupation: Lawyer and judge
Offices/Honors: US House of Representatives, 1863-65. NY Secretary of State, 1867-70. NY State Senate, 1882-83.
Miscellaneous: Resided Poughkeepsie, Dutchess Co., NY
Buried: Poughkeepsie Rural Cemetery, Poughkeepsie, NY (Section C, Lots 8-10)
References: *Biographical Directory of the American Congress.* Obituary, *Poughkeepsie Daily Eagle*, April 27, 1891. *Commemorative Biographical Record of the Counties of Dutchess and Putnam, NY.* Chicago, IL, 1897.

Homer Augustus Nelson (1867)
Courtesy of William Hallam Webber.

Homer Augustus Nelson (1867)
Courtesy of the author. Jeffers & McDonnald, No. 519 Broadway, Albany, NY.

David J. Nevin
Roger D. Hunt Collection, USAMHI.

David J. Nevin

Captain, Co. D, 62 NY Infantry, June 30, 1861. Lieutenant Colonel, 62 NY Infantry, Oct. 1, 1861. Colonel, 62 NY Infantry, May 31, 1862. Commanded 3 Brigade, 3 Division, 6 Army Corps, Army of the Potomac, July 1-4, 1863. Honorably mustered out, June 29, 1864.

Born: 1828 York, PA
Died: Oct. 24, 1880 New York City, NY
Occupation: Wholesale coal merchant
Miscellaneous: Resided New York City, NY
Buried: Rosedale Cemetery, Orange, NJ (Old Part, Lot 600, unmarked)
References: Obituary, *New York Herald*, Oct. 25, 1880. *Dedication of the New York Auxiliary State Monument on the Battlefield of Gettysburg*. Albany, NY, 1926. Pension File, National Archives.

William Northedge

Major, 59 NY Infantry, Oct. 23, 1861. Lieutenant Colonel, 59 NY Infantry, Sept. 17, 1862. Colonel, 59 NY Infantry, Jan. 8, 1863. Dismissed June 27, 1863, on charges of drunkenness, breach of arrest, and "offering violence to the commanding officer of his regiment while he himself was under arrest." Volunteer ADC, Staff of Brig. Gen. James L. Kiernan, Aug.-Oct. 1863. Sergeant, Co. H, 1 US Veteran Volunteers, Feb. 16, 1865. Honorably mustered out, July 21, 1866.

Born: Feb. 22, 1806 Aboard steamer on Lake Champlain, NY
Died: May 11, 1868 Washington, DC
Occupation: Confectioner and policeman before war. Clerk after war.
Miscellaneous: Resided Montreal, Canada; New Haven, CT; New York City, NY; Troy, NY; Albany, NY; and Washington, DC. Deserted his first wife and subsequently married two other women.
Buried: Congressional Cemetery, Washington, DC (Range 96, Site 88)
References: Pension File and Military Service File, National Archives. "Shepherd's Millions," *New York Herald*, May 29, 1877. Letters Received, Volunteer Service Branch, Adjutant General's Office, File N195(VS) 1863, National Archives.

William Northedge
Courtesy of Henry Deeks. Brady's National Photographic Portrait Gallery, Broadway & Tenth Street, New York.

Charles Cooper Nott

Captain, Co. E, 5 IA Cavalry, Aug. 28, 1861. Lieutenant Colonel, 131 NY Infantry, Aug. 14, 1862. Colonel, 176 NY Infantry, Dec. 31, 1862. Captured Brashear City, LA, June 23, 1863. Confined at Camp Ford, Tyler, TX. Paroled July 22, 1864. Honorably mustered out, Aug. 8, 1864.

Born: Sept. 16, 1827 Schenectady, NY
Died: March 6, 1916 New York City, NY
Education: Graduated Union College, Schenectady, NY, 1848
Occupation: Lawyer, judge and author
Offices/Honors: Associate Justice, US Court of Claims, 1865-96. Chief Justice, US Court of Claims, 1896-1905.
Miscellaneous: Resided New York City, NY
Buried: Williams College Cemetery, Williamstown, MA
References: Andrew V. V. Raymond. *Union University: Its History, Influence, Characteristics and Equipment.* New York City, NY, 1907. *National Cyclopedia of American Biography.* Timothy Hopkins. *John Hopkins of Cambridge, MA, and Some of His Descendants.* N.p., 1932. Military Service File, National Archives. Obituary, *New York Times,* March 7, 1916. Obituary, *Union Alumni Monthly,* Vol. 5, No. 8 (June 1916). Charles C. Nott. *Sketches of the War, a Series of Letters to the North Moore Street School of New York.* New York City, NY, 1863. Charles C. Nott. *Sketches in Prison Camps, a Continuation of Sketches of the War.* New York City, NY, 1865.

Charles Cooper Nott (postwar)
Union University: Its History, Influence, Characteristics and Equipment.

Henry F. O'Brien

Captain, Co. H, 155 NY Infantry, Oct. 12, 1862. Honorably discharged, Feb. 6, 1863. *Colonel,* 11 NY Infantry, June 27, 1863.

Born: 1823? Ireland
Died: July 14, 1863 New York City, NY (Brutally murdered by a mob in New York City Draft Riots)
Miscellaneous: Resided New York City, NY
Buried: Calvary Cemetery, Long Island City, NY (Section 1 West, Avenue E, Plot 10, unmarked)
References: Military Service File, National Archives. Adrian Cook. *The Armies of the Streets: The New York City Draft Riots of 1863.* Lexington, KY, 1974. Iver Bernstein. *The New York City Draft Riots.* New York and Oxford, 1990.

Henry F. O'Brien
New York State Military Museum and Veterans Research Center.

John O'Mahony

Colonel, 99 NY National Guard, Aug. 2, 1864. Honorably
   mustered out, Nov. 9, 1864.

Born: 1816 Mitchelstown, County Cork, Ireland
Died: Feb. 6, 1877 New York City, NY
Education: Attended Trinity College, University of Dublin,
   Ireland
Occupation: Newspaper editor and Irish Nationalist
Miscellaneous: Resided New York City, NY
Buried: Glasnevin Cemetery, Dublin, Ireland
References: *Dictionary of American Biography.* Obituary, *New
   York Tribune*, Feb. 8, 1877.

John O'Mahony
Massachusetts MOLLUS Collection, USAMHI.

John O'Mahony
Massachusetts MOLLUS Collection, USAMHI.

John O'Mahony
Massachusetts MOLLUS Collection, USAMHI.

Patrick Henry O'Rorke

2 Lieutenant, Corps of Engineers, June 24, 1861. Colonel, 140 NY Infantry, Sept. 8, 1862. 1 Lieutenant, Corps of Engineers, March 3, 1863. Commanded 3 Brigade, 2 Division, 5 Army Corps, Army of the Potomac, Dec. 1862-Jan. 1863 and Feb. 5, 1863-June 13, 1863. GSW neck, Gettysburg, PA, July 2, 1863.

Born: March 28, 1836 County Cavan, Ireland
Died: July 2, 1863 KIA Gettysburg, PA
Education: Graduated US Military Academy, West Point, NY, June 1861
Occupation: Student
Miscellaneous: Resided Rochester, NY
Buried: Holy Sepulchre Cemetery, Rochester, NY
References: Brian A. Bennett. *The Beau Ideal of a Soldier and a Gentleman.* Wheatland, NY, 1996. Oliver W. Norton. *The Attack and Defense of Little Round Top.* New York City, NY, 1913. Mary Elizabeth Sergent. *An Unremaining Glory.* Middletown, NY, 1997. Donald M. Fisher. "Born in Ireland, Killed at Gettysburg: The Life, Death, and Legacy of Patrick Henry O'Rorke," *Civil War History*, Vol. 39, No. 3 (Sept. 1993). Brian A. Bennett. *Sons of Old Monroe: A Regimental History of Patrick O'Rorke's 140th New York Volunteer Infantry.* Dayton, OH, 1992.

Patrick Henry O'Rorke
Michael Albanese Collection.

Patrick Henry O'Rorke
US Military Academy Library. Powelson, Photographer, 58 State Street, Rochester, NY.

Patrick Henry O'Rorke
Michael Albanese Collection.

Egbert Olcott
Massachusetts MOLLUS Collection, USAMHI.

Benjamin F. Onderdonk
Roger D. Hunt Collection, USAMHI. B. F. Evans & Son, 14 Main Street, Norfolk, VA.

Egbert Olcott

Private, Co. C, 44 NY Infantry, Sept. 9, 1861. 1 Lieutenant, Co. B, 25 NY Infantry, Nov. 21, 1861. Captain, Co. B, 25 NY Infantry, April 17, 1862. Major, 121 NY Infantry, Aug. 23, 1862. Lieutenant Colonel, 121 NY Infantry, April 10, 1863. GSW forehead, Wilderness, VA, May 6, 1864. Captured Wilderness, VA, May 6, 1864. Paroled Aug. 3, 1864. Colonel, 121 NY Infantry, July 4, 1864. Commanded 2 Brigade, 1 Division, 6 Army Corps, Army of the Shenandoah, Oct. 19, 1864-Nov. 3, 1864. Honorably mustered out, Dec. 13, 1864. Colonel, 121 NY Infantry, Jan. 6, 1865. Honorably mustered out, June 25, 1865. Bvt. Colonel, USV, Oct. 19, 1864, for distinguished gallantry in the battle of Cedar Creek, VA.

Born: Dec. 21, 1836 Cherry Valley, NY
Died: Feb. 23, 1882 Willard, Seneca Co., NY
Education: Attended Brown University, Providence, RI (Class of 1859)
Occupation: Regular Army (1 Lieutenant, 29 US Infantry, resigned March 26, 1868). Stock broker.
Miscellaneous: Resided Cherry Valley, Otsego Co., NY; and Brooklyn, NY
Buried: Cherry Valley Cemetery, Cherry Valley, NY
References: Pension File, National Archives. Isaac O. Best. *History of the 121st New York State Infantry.* Chicago, IL, 1921. Obituary, *Otsego Republican*, March 1, 1882. *Historical Catalogue of Brown University, 1764-1904.* Providence, RI, 1905.

Benjamin F. Onderdonk

1 Sergeant, Co. H, 5 NY Infantry, May 9, 1861. 1 Lieutenant, Co. A, 1 NY Mounted Rifles, Aug. 31, 1861. Captain, Co. A, 1 NY Mounted Rifles, Sept. 8, 1861. Major, 1 NY Mounted Rifles, July 5, 1862. Lieutenant Colonel, 1 NY Mounted Rifles, Aug. 13, 1862. Colonel, 1 NY Mounted Rifles, April 29, 1863. Dismissed July 19, 1864, for "drunkenness on duty and for intrigue and underhanded devices to accomplish the dismissal of an officer of his regiment." Disability resulting from dismissal removed, Oct. 19, 1864.

Born: May 2, 1834 NJ
Died: Feb. 25, 1903 Mountain View, NJ

Occupation: Drug brokerage business before war. Sash and blind maker, bookkeeper, and US Customs inspector after war.

Miscellaneous: Resided New York City, NY; Plainfield, Union Co., NJ; Dunellen, Union Co., NJ; New Brunswick, NJ; Jersey City, NJ; and Mountain View, Passaic Co., NJ

Buried: Reformed Dutch Churchyard, Pompton Plains, NJ

References: Pension File, National Archives. Letters Received, Volunteer Service Branch, Adjutant General's Office, File S1610(VS)1864, National Archives.

Jeremiah Palmer

Colonel, 2 NY Heavy Artillery, Oct. 17, 1861. Discharged Feb. 20, 1862, upon "adverse report of a Board of Examination." Lieutenant Colonel, 2 NY Heavy Artillery, March 14, 1862. Shell wound left shoulder, Petersburg, VA, June 19, 1864. Honorably mustered out, Dec. 7, 1864.

Born: 1819 Herkimer, NY

Died: March 16, 1903 Brooklyn, NY

Occupation: Contractor and builder

Miscellaneous: Resided Oriskany, Oneida Co., NY; and Brooklyn, NY

Buried: Green-Wood Cemetery, Brooklyn, NY (Section 86, Lot 31217, Grave 130)

References: Obituary, *Brooklyn Daily Eagle*, March 19, 1903. Pension File and Military Service File, National Archives.

Thomas Jefferson Parker

Colonel, 64 NY Infantry, Nov. 13, 1861. Commanded 1 Brigade, 1 Division, 2 Army Corps, Army of the Potomac, June 1-4, 1862. Resigned July 12, 1862.

Born: Aug. 17, 1813 Union Twp., Seneca Co., NY

Died: May 26, 1908 Gowanda, NY

Occupation: Merchant tailor before war. Mail contractor and Justice of the Peace after war.

Offices/Honors: Assistant Journal Clerk and Engrossing Clerk, NY State Assembly, 1872-73

Miscellaneous: Resided Gowanda, Cattaraugus Co., NY

Buried: Pine Hill Cemetery, Gowanda, NY (Section C, Lot 82)

References: *Presidents, Soldiers, Statesmen.* Western New York Edition. New York, Toledo and Chicago, 1899. Augustus G. Parker, compiler. *Parker in America, 1630-1910.* Buffalo, NY, 1911. Pension File and Military Service File, National Archives.

Thomas Jefferson Parker
Courtesy of Phil Palen.

Jeremiah Palmer
Roger D. Hunt Collection, USAMHI.

Thomas Jefferson Parker (left) and William Glenny (right) 1902
Courtesy of Stephen B. Rogers.

Theodore Weld Parmele
Roger D. Hunt Collection, USAMHI. M. H. Kimball, Photographer, 477 Broadway, New York.

Theodore Weld Parmele

Captain, Co. A, 37 NY National Guard, May 29, 1862. Major, 37 NY National Guard, June 17, 1862. Honorably mustered out, Sept. 2, 1862. Colonel, 174 NY Infantry, Oct. 3, 1862. Dismissed Oct. 17, 1863, "having been absent from his regiment without leave for three months." Dismissal revoked, Jan. 5, 1864, and he was honorably discharged for disability, due to spinal concussion caused by a fall from his horse, to date Dec. 7, 1863.

Born: June 24, 1833 New York City, NY
Died: May 14, 1893 New York City, NY
Occupation: Employed in the office of the Manhattan Gas Light Co. before war. Coal agent and civil engineer after war.
Offices/Honors: Superintendent, SC State Penitentiary
Miscellaneous: Resided Greenwich, Fairfield Co., CT; Staten Island, NY, 1863-69; Columbia, SC, 1869-78; and New York City, NY, 1878-93. Son-in-law of Bvt. Brig. Gen. Charles Roome.
Buried: Green-Wood Cemetery, Brooklyn, NY (Section 60, Lot 673, unmarked)
References: Pension File and Military Service File, National Archives. Dorothy H. Smallwood, editor. *Parmelee Data.* N.p., 1940.

Oliver Beale Peirce

Colonel, Mohawk Rangers, or Guards of Liberty and Union. Discharged Feb. 17, 1862, upon consolidation of regiment with 81 NY Infantry.

Born: Dec. 29, 1808 Berkshire, MA
Died: June 16, 1865 Butler Center, Wayne Co., NY
Occupation: Newspaper editor, temperance lecturer, text book author, and inventor
Miscellaneous: Resided Rome, Oneida Co., NY. Henry Ward Beecher once said of him that he was "like a locomotive with a full head of steam on, but no engineer aboard."
Buried: Rome Cemetery, Rome, NY (Section B, Lot 11)
References: Peirce family records, courtesy of Margaret L. Peirce. Obituary, *Utica Morning Herald and Gazette*, June 22, 1865. Obituary, *The Roman Citizen*, June 23, 1865. Obituary, *Rome Sentinel*, June 27, 1865.

Oliver Beale Peirce
Courtesy of Margaret L. Peirce.

Oliver Beale Peirce
Courtesy of Margaret L. Peirce.

Elias Peissner

Lieutenant Colonel, 119 NY Infantry, Aug. 9, 1862. Colonel, 119 NY Infantry, Sept. 1, 1862. GSW Chancellorsville, VA, May 2, 1863.

Born: Sept. 5, 1825 Vilseck, Bavaria

Died: May 2, 1863 KIA Chancellorsville, VA

Education: Graduated Gymnasium of Amberg, Germany, 1843. Attended University of Munich, Germany, 1843-48.

Occupation: Professor, German Language and Literature, Union College, Schenectady, NY, 1855-63

Miscellaneous: Resided Schenectady, NY

Buried: Riverside Cemetery, Fort Miller, NY

References: Pension File, National Archives. Larry Hart. *Through the Darkest Hour*. Scotia, NY, 1990. Adolf E. Zucker, editor. *The Forty-Eighters: Political Refugees of the German Revolution of 1848*. New York City, NY, 1950. *Catalogue of the Sigma Phi*. N.p., 1915. George H. Danton. "Elias Peissner," *Monatshefte fur Deutschen Unterricht*, Vol. 32, No. 7 (Nov. 1940).

Elias Peissner
Special Collections, Schaffer Library, Union College. Pendleton, Photographer, 5 Chatham Square, New York.

Elias Peissner
Special Collections, Schaffer Library, Union College.

Elias Peissner (1860)
Collection of The New-
York Historical Society.

Elias Peissner (1861)
Special Collections, Schaffer Library, Union College.

Elias Peissner (1862)
Special Collections, Schaffer Library,
Union College.

Elias Peissner
Roger D. Hunt Collection, USAMHI. James Hinds, Photographist, 129 State Street, Schenectady, NY.

Elias Peissner
Special Collections, Schaffer Library, Union College.

Right, Far Right: *Elias Peissner Special Collections, Schaffer Library, Union College.*

James H. Perry

Colonel, 48 NY Infantry, Oct. 26, 1861

Born: June 28, 1811 Plattekill, Ulster Co., NY

Died: June 18, 1862 Fort Pulaski, GA (apoplexy)

Education: Attended US Military Academy, West Point, NY (Class of 1837)

Other Wars: Texas War for Independence

Occupation: Methodist clergyman

Miscellaneous: Resided Newburgh, Orange Co., NY; Madison, New Haven Co., CT; Sag Harbor, NY; Bridgeport, CT; and Brooklyn, NY

Buried: Cypress Hills Cemetery, Brooklyn, NY (Section 3, Lot 272)

References: Abraham J. Palmer. *History of the 48th Regiment New York State Volunteers*. Brooklyn, NY, 1885. Pension File, National Archives. James M. Nichols. *Perry's Saints; or, the Fighting Parson's Regiment in the War of the Rebellion*. Boston, MA, 1886. Obituary, *Brooklyn Daily Eagle*, June 27, 1862. Obituary, *New York Daily Tribune*, June 28, 1862.

This Page: *James H. Perry*
Massachusetts MOLLUS Collection, USAMHI.

William Henry Pettes

Lieutenant Colonel, 50 NY Engineers, Sept. 18, 1861. Colonel, 50 NY Engineers, June 3, 1863. Honorably mustered out, July 5, 1865.

Born: Dec. 24, 1811 Windsor, VT
Died: Feb. 29, 1880 Fort Washington, MD
Education: Attended Norwich Military Academy, Middletown, CT. Graduated US Military Academy, West Point, NY, 1832.
Other Wars: Florida War
Occupation: 2 Lieutenant, 1 US Artillery, resigned Sept. 11, 1836. Civil engineer.
Miscellaneous: Resided Richland, Oswego Co., NY; and Buffalo, NY
Buried: Washington, DC?
References: William A. Ellis, editor. *History of Norwich University, 1819-1911*. Montpelier, VT, 1911. Ed Malles, editor. *Bridge Building in Wartime: Colonel Wesley Brainerd's Memoir of the 50th New York Volunteer Engineers*. Knoxville, TN, 1997. George W. Cullum. *Biographical Register of the Officers and Graduates of the US Military Academy*. Third Edition. Boston and New York, 1891.

William Henry Pettes
Massachusetts MOLLUS Collection, USAMHI.

William Henry Pettes
Massachusetts MOLLUS Collection, USAMHI.

William Henry Pettes
Massachusetts MOLLUS Collection, USAMHI.

John Pickell

Colonel, 13 NY Infantry, Aug. 17, 1861. Facing criticism from Brig. Gen. John H. Martindale for his "lack of aptitude in the management of his regiment," he resigned March 31, 1862.

Born: 1799 Dansville, NY
Died: Jan. 23, 1865 Dansville, NY
Education: Graduated US Military Academy, West Point, NY, 1822
Other Wars: Florida War (GSW right leg)
Occupation: 1 Lieutenant, Adjutant, 4 US Artillery, resigned Aug. 5, 1838. Coal company executive and newspaper editor.
Offices/Honors: MD House of Representatives, 1842-43
Miscellaneous: Resided Dansville, Livingston Co., NY; Baltimore, MD; and Frostburg, Allegany Co., MD
Buried: Greenmount Cemetery, Dansville, NY (Section P, Lots 5-6)
References: Obituary, *Dansville Advertiser*, Jan. 26, 1865. Military Service File, National Archives. George W. Cullum. *Biographical Register of the Officers and Graduates of the US Military Academy*. Third Edition. Boston and New York, 1891. Letters Received, Volunteer Service Branch, Adjutant General's Office, File M245(VS)1862, National Archives.

Alexander Piper

Captain, 3 US Artillery, May 14, 1861. Colonel, 10 NY Heavy Artillery, Dec. 31, 1862. Commanded 3 Brigade, Defenses North of the Potomac, 22 Army Corps, Department of Washington, April 14, 1863-March 26, 1864. Commanded 3 Brigade, Defenses South of the Potomac, 22 Army Corps, March 26, 1864-May 14, 1864. Commanded 2 Brigade, 3 Division, 18 Army Corps, Army of the James, June 5-9, 1864. Commanded 1 Brigade, 2 Division, 18 Army Corps, June 20-July 24, 1864. Honorably mustered out of volunteer service, July 6, 1865.

Alexander Piper
Courtesy of Henry Deeks. Hart's Arcade Photographic Gallery, Watertown, NY.

Alexander Piper
Roger D. Hunt Collection, USAMHI.

Alexander Piper (1868)
Courtesy of Howard Norton.

Alexander Piper (1872)
Courtesy of David M. Neville.

Alexander Piper (postwar)
Annual Reunion, Association of the Graduates of the US Military Academy,
1903.

Born: May 11, 1828 Harrisburg, PA

Died: Feb. 22, 1902 New York City, NY

Education: Graduated US Military Academy, West Point, NY,
1851

Occupation: Regular Army (Colonel, 5 US Artillery, retired
July 1, 1891)

Miscellaneous: Resided New York City, NY

Buried: Post Cemetery, West Point, NY (Section 22, Row A,
Grave 6)

References: *Annual Reunion,* Association of the Graduates of
the US Military Academy, 1903. Pension File, National
Archives.

Burr Baldwin Porter

Major, Additional ADC, USV, June 2, 1862. Assistant to Chief
of Staff, Staff of Major General John C. Fremont, June
1862. Colonel, 40 MA Infantry, Sept. 7, 1862. Commanded
2 Brigade, Abercrombie's Division, 22 Army Corps, Department of Washington, March 31-April 17, 1863. Commanded Porter's Brigade, Gurney's Division, 7 Army
Corps, Department of Virginia, April 17-May 4, 1863.
Commanded 2 Brigade, 2 Division, 4 Army Corps, Department of Virginia, May 4-July 15, 1863. Resigned July
21, 1863, due to "discontent unfitting me for command,
and pressing reasons of a family and private nature." Colonel, 26 NY Cavalry, Feb. 13, 1865. Colonel, 3 MA Cavalry, March 21, 1865. Commanded 1 Cavalry Brigade, 22
Army Corps, Department of Washington, June 1865. Honorably mustered out, July 21, 1865.

Born: Oct. 26, 1829 Montrose, PA

Died: Dec. 10, 1870 Josnes, France (KIA, Franco-Prussian War)

Education: Graduated Rutgers College, New Brunswick, NJ,
1849

Burr Baldwin Porter
Massachusetts MOLLUS Collection, USAMHI.

Burr Baldwin Porter
Massachusetts MOLLUS Collection, USAMHI.

Other Wars: Crimean War on staff of Omar Pasha of Turkey. Franco-Prussian War on staff of Gen. Chanzy of France.

Occupation: Lawyer

Miscellaneous: Resided Newark, NJ; and Boston, MA. Born Burr Baldwin, he was adopted by his uncle, P. H. Porter.

Buried: Forest Hills Cemetery, Jamaica Plain, MA (Rhododendron Path, Lot 1558)

References: Charles C. Baldwin. *The Baldwin Genealogy From 1500 to 1881.* Cleveland, OH, 1881. James K. Ewer. *The Third Massachusetts Cavalry in the War For the Union.* Maplewood, MA, 1903. Military Service File, National Archives. Letters Received, Volunteer Service Branch, Adjutant General's Office, File M1584(VS) 1863, National Archives.

Above Right: *Burr Baldwin Porter*
Massachusetts MOLLUS Collection, USAMHI.
Right: *Officers of the 8th New York Heavy Artillery (Adjutant Edwin L. Blake, left; Col. Peter A. Porter, center; Surgeon James M. Leet, right; at Headquarters, Fort Federal Hill, Baltimore, MD, 1862)*
Casualties by Battles and by Names in the 8th New York Heavy Artillery.

Peter Augustus Porter

Colonel, 129 NY Infantry, July 7, 1862. Colonel, 8 NY Heavy Artillery, Dec. 19, 1862. Commanded 2 Brigade, Maryland Heights Division, Army of West Virginia, July 10, 1863-Aug. 3, 1863. Commanded 2 Separate Brigade, 8 Army Corps, Middle Department, Jan. 20, 1864-May 10, 1864. GSW neck and heart, Cold Harbor, VA, June 3, 1864.

Born: July 14, 1827 Black Rock, near Buffalo, NY
Died: June 3, 1864 KIA Cold Harbor, VA
Education: Graduated Harvard University, Cambridge, MA, 1845. Attended University of Heidelberg, Germany.
Occupation: Gentleman of leisure
Offices/Honors: NY State Assembly, 1862
Miscellaneous: Resided Niagara Falls, Niagara Co., NY. Half-Brother of CSA Brig. Gen. John B. Grayson. First cousin of CSA Major General John C. Breckinridge.
Buried: Oakwood Cemetery, Niagara Falls, NY (Section 3C, Lot 141)
References: Edward T. Williams. *Niagara County, NY, 1821-1921.* Chicago, IL, 1921. Thomas W. Higginson. *Harvard Memorial Biographies.* Cambridge, MA, 1866. William J. Hoppin and Frederic S. Cozzens. *Proceedings of the Century Association in Honor of the Memory of Brig. Gen. James S. Wadsworth and Colonel Peter A. Porter.* New York City, NY, 1865. Malcolm W. Bryan, III. *The Breckinridges of Virginia and Their Kentucky Kin.* N.p., 1994. James M. Hudnut. *Casualties by Battles and by Names in the 8th New York Heavy Artillery, August 22, 1862-June 5, 1865, Together With a Review of the Service of the Regiment Fifty Years After Muster-in.* New York City, NY, 1913.

Henry Langdon Potter

Lieutenant Colonel, 71 NY Infantry, July 18, 1861. GSW left leg, Oak Grove, VA, June 25, 1862. GSW left wrist and hand, Bristoe Station, VA, Aug. 27, 1862. Colonel, 71 NY Infantry, May 1, 1863. Shell wound left leg, Gettysburg, PA, July 1, 1863. Dismissed Dec. 31, 1864, on a charge of

Peter Augustus Porter
Niagara County, NY, 1821-1921.

Peter Augustus Porter
Casualties by Battles and by Names in the 8th New York Heavy Artillery.

"conduct prejudicial to good order and military discipline" involving complicity to defraud a soldier of his bounty. Pardoned by President Lincoln "in view of the imperfect and conflicting testimony and the merely circumstantial evidence," and honorably discharged to date, Dec. 31, 1864.

Born: March 26, 1828 Tyringham, MA
Died: March 29, 1907 Rahway, NJ
Occupation: Brewer and paper manufacturer before war. Lawyer and US customs inspector after war.
Miscellaneous: Resided New York City, NY; and Rahway, Union Co., NJ.
Buried: Rahway Cemetery, Rahway, NJ
References: Pension File, National Archives. Obituary, *New York Times*, March 31, 1907. Charles E. Potter, editor. *Genealogies of the Potter Families and Their Descendants in America.* Boston, MA, 1888. Thomas P. Lowry. *Tarnished Eagles: The Courts-Martial of Fifty Union Colonels and Lieutenant Colonels.* Mechanicsburg, PA, 1997.

James Neilson Potter

2 Lieutenant, Co. D, 82 PA Infantry, July 23, 1861. Acting ADC, Staff of Major Gen. Darius N. Couch, Sept. 28, 1862-May 1863. 1 Lieutenant, Co. D, 82 PA Infantry, Dec. 1, 1862. Captain, ADC, USV, April 25, 1863. ADC and Acting Judge Advocate, Staff of Major Gen. Darius N. Couch, May 1863-April 1864. Captain, Commissary of Subsistence, USV, March 2, 1864. Commissary of Subsistence, 1 Brigade, 2 Division, Cavalry Corps, Army of the Potomac, April 6, 1864-Feb. 1, 1865. *Colonel*, 146 NY Infantry, Dec. 31, 1864. Commission revoked. Resigned Feb. 1, 1865.

Born: Aug. 1841 Schenectady, NY
Died: July 22, 1906 Pau, France?
Occupation: Clerk and stock broker
Miscellaneous: Resided Philadelphia, PA; New York City, NY; and Pau, France. Half brother of Major Gen. Robert B. Potter.
Buried: Pau, France?
References: Frank H. Potter. *The Alonzo Potter Family.* Concord, NH, 1923. Charles E. Potter, editor. *Genealogies of the Potter Families and Their Descendants in America.* Boston, MA, 1888. Military Service File, National Archives. Letters Received, Commission Branch, Adjutant General's Office, File P550(CB)1863, National Archives.

George Watson Pratt

Colonel, 20 NY State Militia, April 23, 1861. Honorably mustered out, Aug. 2, 1861. Colonel, 20 NY State Militia, Oct. 3, 1861. Colonel, 80 NY Infantry, Dec. 7, 1861. GSW breast, 2nd Bull Run, VA, Aug. 30, 1862.

Born: April 18, 1830 Prattsville, NY
Died: Sept. 11, 1862 DOW Albany, NY
Education: Ph. D., University of Mecklenburg, Germany, 1850
Occupation: Leather manufacturer and tannery operator
Offices/Honors: NY State Senate, 1858-59
Miscellaneous: Resided Prattsville, Greene Co., NY; Kingston, Ulster Co., NY; and Esopus, Ulster Co., NY. Traveled extensively and engaged actively in literary pursuits. His library of more than 8000 volumes included an extensive collection of rare works on Oriental subjects.
Buried: Rural Cemetery, Albany, NY (Section 44, Lot 3)
References: Theodore B. Gates. *The War of the Rebellion.* New York City, NY, 1884. Rufus W. Clark. *The Heroes of Albany.* Albany, NY, 1867. Obituary, *Albany Evening Journal*, Sept. 13, 1862. William D. Murphy. *Biographical Sketches of the State Officers and Members of the Legislature of the State of New York in 1858.* Albany, NY, 1858. Frederick W. Chapman. *The Pratt Family: or the Descendants of Lieut. William Pratt, One of the First Settlers of Hartford and Saybrook.* Hartford, CT, 1864.

George Watson Pratt (prewar)
New York State Library Collection, USAMHI.

Above: *George Watson Pratt*
Roger D. Hunt Collection, USAMHI.
Above Left: *George Watson Pratt*
New York State Military Museum and Veterans Research Center.
Left: *George Watson Pratt*
Massachusetts MOLLUS Collection, USAMHI.

Edward Livingston Price

1 Lieutenant, Co. E, 74 NY Infantry, June 20, 1861. Ordnance Officer, Staff of Major Gen. Joseph Hooker, April–July 1862. Captain, Co. E, 74 NY Infantry, June 23, 1862. *Major*, 74 NY Infantry, July 20, 1862. Commission as major revoked, Nov. 1, 1862. Colonel, 145 NY Infantry, Feb. 4, 1863. GSW slight, Chancellorsville, VA, May 2, 1863. Dismissed Dec. 9, 1863, for "violation of orders, absence without leave, neglect of duty, all this while his regiment was in transit to the Department of the Cumberland, and for fraudulent conduct, employing enlisted men as servants and failing to make the deduction from his pay, as required by an act of Congress."

Born: Dec. 25, 1844 New York City, NY
Died: Feb. 4, 1922 Newark, NJ
Occupation: Lawyer
Offices/Honors: NJ State Assembly, 1866, 1868
Miscellaneous: Resided Newark, NJ. Uncle of Bvt. Brig. Gen. Francis Price, Jr.
Buried: Mount Pleasant Cemetery, Newark, NJ (Section T, Lot 24)
References: Francis B. Lee, editor. *Genealogical and Memorial History of the State of New Jersey*. New York City, NY, 1910. Obituary, *Newark Star-Eagle*, Feb. 4, 1922. Military Service File, National Archives. Samuel F. Bigelow and George J. Hagar, editors. *The Biographical Cyclopedia of New Jersey*. New York City, NY, 1909. Letters Received, Volunteer Service Branch, Adjutant General's Office, File P1112(VS)1862, National Archives.

Gilbert Gibson Prey
New York State Military Museum and Veterans Research Center.

Gilbert Gibson Prey

Captain, Co. F, 104 NY Infantry, Dec. 2, 1861. Major, 104 NY Infantry, Sept. 11, 1862. Lieutenant Colonel, 104 NY Infantry, Oct. 21, 1862. Colonel, 104 NY Infantry, Oct. 21, 1862. Captured Weldon Railroad, VA, Aug. 19, 1864. Confined at Libby Prison, Richmond, VA; Salisbury, NC; and Danville, VA. Paroled Feb. 22, 1865. Honorably discharged, March 3, 1865, due to "reduced state of his command."

Born: Aug. 12, 1822 St. Andrews, New Brunswick
Died: Feb. 6, 1903 Eagle, Wyoming Co., NY
Occupation: Farmer before war. Carpenter and joiner after war.
Miscellaneous: Resided Eagle, Wyoming Co., NY
Buried: Eagle Cemetery, Eagle, NY
References: *History of Wyoming County, NY*. New York City, NY, 1880. Pension File, National Archives. Town Clerk's Register of Soldiers, Eagle, Wyoming Co., NY, NY State Archives. Obituary, *Wyoming County Herald*, Feb. 13, 1903. Raymond G. Barber and Gary E. Swinson, editors. *The Civil War Letters of Charles Barber, Private, 104th New York Volunteer Infantry*. Torrance, CA, 1991.

Edward Livingston Price
Massachusetts MOLLUS Collection, USAMHI.

Edward Livingston Price (postwar)
Genealogical and Memorial History of the State of New Jersey.

Edward Pye
Massachusetts MOLLUS Collection, USAMHI. C. D. Fredricks & Co., 587 Broadway, New York.

Edward Pye

Captain, Co. F, 95 NY Infantry, Oct. 15, 1861. Major, 95 NY Infantry, March 6, 1862. Colonel, 95 NY Infantry, Oct. 9, 1863. GSW neck, Cold Harbor, VA, June 2, 1864

Born: Sept. 5, 1823 Clarkstown, Rockland Co., NY
Died: June 11, 1864 DOW Alexandria, VA
Education: Graduated Rutgers College, New Brunswick, NJ, 1844
Occupation: Lawyer and judge
Miscellaneous: Resided Haverstraw, Rockland Co., NY
Buried: Oak Hill Cemetery, Nyack, NY (Section R, Lots 1009-1010)
References: John H. Raven, compiler. *Catalogue of the Officers and Alumni of Rutgers College.* Trenton, NJ, 1916. David Cole, editor. *History of Rockland County, NY.* New York City, NY, 1884. Pension File, National Archives. Obituary, *Rockland County Journal*, June 18, 1864.

John B. Raulston

Captain, Co. H, 81 NY Infantry, Sept. 11, 1861. Provost Marshal, Yorktown, VA, Nov. 1862-April 1863. Acting AIG, Staff of Brig. Gen. Charles A. Heckman, May 1863-Nov. 1863. Lieutenant Colonel, 81 NY Infantry, Sept. 6, 1863. GSW Cold Harbor, VA, June 1864. *Colonel*, 81 NY Infantry, Sept. 1, 1864. Commanded 1 Brigade, 1 Division, 18 Army Corps, Army of the James, Sept. 29, 1864-Dec. 3, 1864. Commanded 1 Brigade, 3 Division, 24 Army Corps, Army of the James, Dec. 3, 1864-Jan. 15, 1865. Honorably mustered out, Jan. 15, 1865.

Born: June 14, 1839 Oswego, NY
Died: Feb. 28, 1893 Chicago, IL
Occupation: Druggist and Deputy Collector of Internal Revenue
Miscellaneous: Resided Petersburg, VA; Lynchburg, Campbell Co., VA; Roanoke, VA; Danville, Pittsylvania Co., VA; and Chicago, IL, 1886-93. Brother of Colonel William C. Raulston.
Buried: Oakwoods Cemetery, Chicago, IL (Section J, Division 1, Lot 423). Cenotaph in Riverside Cemetery, Oswego, NY (Section L, Lot 160).

John B. Raulston
Roger D. Hunt Collection, USAMHI. Gray's Gallery, Oswego, NY.

John B. Raulston
National Archives.

John B. Raulston
New York State Military Museum and Veterans Research Center.

John B. Raulston
Courtesy of Henry Deeks.

John B. Raulston
Courtesy of Margaret L. Peirce.

References: Pension File and Military Service File, National Archives. Obituary, *Oswego Daily Palladium*, March 1, 1893. Death notice, *Chicago Daily Tribune*, March 1, 1893.

William C. Raulston

Captain, Co. A, 81 NY Infantry, Sept. 11, 1861. Major, 81 NY Infantry, May 31, 1862. Lieutenant Colonel, 81 NY Infantry, July 7, 1862. Colonel, 24 NY Cavalry, Aug. 25, 1863. GSW right chest and right leg, Petersburg, VA, June 18, 1864. Commanded 2 Brigade, 3 Division, 9 Army Corps, Army of the Potomac, June 19, 1864. Captured Poplar Spring Church, VA, Sept. 30, 1864. Confined at Libby Prison, Richmond, VA; Salisbury, NC; and Danville, VA. GSW abdomen, Danville, VA, Dec. 10, 1864, while attempting to escape from prison.

Born: Nov. 15, 1832 Castle Fin, County Donegal, Ireland
Died: Dec. 16, 1864 DOW Danville, VA
Occupation: Merchant
Miscellaneous: Resided Southwest Oswego, NY. Brother of Colonel John B. Raulston.
Buried: Riverside Cemetery, Oswego, NY (Section L, Lot 160)
References: Pension File and Military Service File, National Archives. Charles McCool Snyder. *Oswego County, New York, in the Civil War.* N.p., 1962. Letters Received, Volunteer Service Branch, Adjutant General's Office, File D851(VS)1863, National Archives.

Above: *William C. Raulston*
National Archives.
Left: *John B. Raulston*
Thomas L. Jones Collection, USAMHI. J. R. Rockwell, Photographer, 13 1/2 Sycamore Street, Petersburg, VA.

William C. Raulston
Roger D. Hunt Collection, USAMHI. Gray's Gallery, No. 11 East Bridge Street, Oswego, NY.

William C. Raulston
Roger D. Hunt Collection, USAMHI. Gray's Gallery, No. 11 Bridge Street, Oswego, NY.

William C. Raulston
Edgar Frutchey Collection, USAMHI.

William C. Raulston
Courtesy of the author. Gray's Gallery, No. 11 East Bridge Street, Oswego, NY.

Horatio Blake Reed

2 Lieutenant, 5 US Artillery, May 14, 1861. 1 Lieutenant, 5 US Artillery, Sept. 19, 1863. Acting AAG, 1 Brigade, Horse Artillery, Army of the Potomac, Nov. 1863-Feb. 29, 1864. Lieutenant Colonel, 22 NY Cavalry, Sept. 13, 1864. Colonel, 22 NY Cavalry, Jan. 24, 1865. Honorably mustered out of volunteer service, Aug. 1, 1865.

Born: Jan. 22, 1837 Rockaway, Long Island, NY

Died: March 7, 1888 Togus, Kennebec Co., ME

Education: Attended Rensselaer Polytechnic Institute, Troy, NY

Occupation: Regular Army (1 Lieutenant, Adjutant, 5 US Artillery, resigned May 8, 1870). Lieutenant Colonel, Egyptian Army, 1874-75. Civil engineer.

Miscellaneous: Resided Newburgh, Orange Co., NY

Buried: St. George's Cemetery, Newburgh, NY (Lot 162, unmarked)

References: *Appletons' Cyclopedia of American Biography.* Obituary, *Daily Kennebec Journal*, March 9, 1888. Obituary, *Newburgh Daily Register*, March 8, 1888. Letters Received, Commission Branch, Adjutant General's Office, File R37(CB)1870, National Archives. William B. Hesseltine and Hazel C. Wolf. *The Blue and the Gray on the Nile.* Chicago, IL, 1961. Richard L. Hill. *A Biographical Dictionary of the Anglo-Egyptian Sudan.* Oxford, England, 1951.

Horatio Blake Reed
Courtesy of the author.

Horatio Blake Reed
Courtesy of Karl E. Sundstrom. J. H. & J. L. Abbott, "Specialite," 480 Broadway, Albany, NY.

Horatio Blake Reed
Courtesy of Henry Deeks. J. T. Upson, Buffalo, NY.

Captain Robertson, Commanding 1st Brigade, Horse Artillery, and Staff, Brandy Station, VA, Feb. 1864 (left to right, seated; Capt. William Goldie, AQM; Capt. James M. Robertson; Surgeon McGuigan; 1 Lt. Horatio B. Reed, Acting AAG) Massachusetts MOLLUS Collection, USAMHI.

Addison Gardiner Rice

Colonel, 154 NY Infantry, Aug. 19, 1862. Succeeded by Colonel Patrick H. Jones, Sept. 25, 1862.

Born: Dec. 29, 1821 Richfield Springs, NY

Died: Nov. 19, 1883 Buffalo, NY

Occupation: Lawyer

Offices/Honors: NY State Assembly, 1862

Miscellaneous: Resided Ellicottville, Cattaraugus Co., NY; and Buffalo, NY

Buried: Forest Lawn Cemetery, Buffalo, NY (Section CC, Lot 89, Grave 1748, unmarked)

References: Franklin Ellis. *History of Cattaraugus County, NY.* Philadelphia, PA, 1879. Obituary, *Buffalo Commercial Advertiser*, Nov. 19, 1883. William D. Murphy. *Biographical Sketches of the State Officers and Members of the Legislature of the State of New York in 1862 and '63.* Albany, NY, 1863. Mark H. Dunkelman and Michael J. Winey. *The Hardtack Regiment: An Illustrated History of the 154th Regiment, New York State Infantry Volunteers.* Rutherford, NJ, 1981.

Addison Gardiner Rice (postwar)
History of Cattaraugus County, NY.

Samuel Thomas Richards
Courtesy of Mr. Chamberlin.

Richard H. Richardson
Massachusetts MOLLUS Collection, USAMHI.

Samuel Thomas Richards

Colonel, 118 NY Infantry, July 7, 1862. Discharged for disability, July 8, 1863, due to acute rheumatism.

Born: Dec. 7, 1824 Warrensburg, NY
Died: Jan. 6, 1871 Warrensburg, NY
Education: Graduated Union College, Schenectady, NY, 1844
Occupation: Merchant and lumber manufacturer
Offices/Honors: Treasurer, Warren Co., NY, 1858-70. US Collector of Internal Revenue, 1867-69.
Miscellaneous: Resided Warrensburg, Warren Co., NY
Buried: Warrensburg Cemetery, Warrensburg, NY (Section D-Circle, Lot 3)
References: Obituary, *Glens Falls Messenger*, Jan. 13, 1871. Samuel Burhans, Jr., compiler. *Burhans Genealogy.* New York City, NY, 1894. Military Service File, National Archives. Henry C. Johnson, editor. *The Tenth General Catalogue of the Psi Upsilon Fraternity.* Bethlehem, PA, 1888. John L. Cunningham. *Three Years with the Adirondack Regiment: 118th New York Volunteer Infantry.* Norwood, MA, 1920.

Richard H. Richardson

Lieutenant Colonel, 26 NY Infantry, May 17, 1861. Colonel, 26 NY Infantry, Sept. 19, 1862. Honorably mustered out, May 28, 1863. *Captain*, 57 NY Infantry, Sept. 27, 1864. Declined. *Captain*, 80 NY Infantry, Sept. 29, 1864. Declined.

Born: March 29, 1830 NY
Died: March 18, 1869 near Deansville, Oneida Co., NY
Occupation: Bookkeeper and clothing salesman before war. Railroad construction foreman after war.
Miscellaneous: Resided Utica, Oneida Co., NY; Oriskany Falls, Oneida Co., NY; and Deansville, Oneida Co., NY
Buried: Forest Hill Cemetery, Utica, NY (Section 22C, Lot 2119)
References: Obituary, *Utica Morning Herald and Gazette*, March 20, 1869. Obituary, *Utica Daily Observer*, March 19, 1869. Pension File, National Archives.

Robert Mark Richardson

Lieutenant Colonel, 12 NY Infantry, June 19, 1861. Resigned Feb. 6, 1863, supposing that "a reduction of the number of field officers will not be unacceptable" due to the expected consolidation of the regiment. Colonel, 15 NY Cavalry, May 29, 1863. Commanded 2 Brigade, 1 Cavalry Division, Army of West Virginia, Sept. 15, 1864-Oct. 14, 1864. Resigned Jan. 17, 1865, since "my private business at home demands my immediate attention."

Born: 1817 Vernon, NY
Died: Dec. 7, 1902 Syracuse, NY
Education: Graduated Hamilton College, Clinton, NY, 1843
Occupation: Lawyer, and later clerk to committees of the NY State Legislature. Clerk of the finance committee of the NY State Senate, 1872-94.
Offices/Honors: Brig. Gen., New York State Militia
Miscellaneous: Resided Syracuse, Onondaga Co., NY
Buried: Oakwood Cemetery, Syracuse, NY (Section 41, Lot 7)
References: Obituary, *Syracuse Post-Standard*, Dec. 8, 1902. Obituary, *Syracuse Journal*, Dec. 8, 1902. Pension File, National Archives. Chauncey S. Norton. *"The Red Neck Ties;" or, History of the 15th New York Volunteer Cavalry*. Ithaca, NY, 1891. Letters Received, Volunteer Service Branch, Adjutant General's Office, File C1416(VS)1862, National Archives.

John Lafayette Riker
Courtesy of Richard F. Carlile. Published by E. Anthony, 501 Broadway, New York, from Photographic Negative from Brady's National Portrait Gallery.

John Lafayette Riker

Colonel, 62 NY Infantry, July 3, 1861. GSW Fair Oaks, VA, May 31, 1862.

Born: 1824?
Died: May 31, 1862 KIA Fair Oaks, VA
Occupation: Lawyer
Miscellaneous: Resided New York City, NY. An active and influential leader of the American party.
Buried: Green-Wood Cemetery, Brooklyn, NY (Section 164, Lots 16159-16160)
References: Pension File, National Archives. Obituary, death notice and funeral, *New York Daily Tribune*, June 5, 9-11, 1862. Obituary, *New York Times*, June 8, 1862. Thomas P. Lowry. *Tarnished Eagles: The Courts-Martial of Fifty Union Colonels and Lieutenant Colonels*. Mechanicsburg, PA, 1997.

Left: *Robert Mark Richardson (postwar)*
Courtesy of the author.

John Lafayette Riker
Massachusetts MOLLUS Collection, USAMHI.

John Lafayette Riker
Massachusetts MOLLUS Collection, USAMHI. Published by E. Anthony, 501 Broadway, New York, from Photographic Negative in Brady's National Portrait Gallery.

John Lafayette Riker
Massachusetts MOLLUS Collection, USAMHI.

John Lafayette Riker
Massachusetts MOLLUS Collection, USAMHI.

Edward Johns Riley

Colonel, 40 NY Infantry, June 14, 1861. Discharged for disability, June 5, 1862, due to the effects of a kick on the back of his head by his horse.

Born: March 29, 1831 New York City, NY
Died: Feb. 21, 1918 Brooklyn, NY
Occupation: United States and Canadian agent for an English wall paper house
Miscellaneous: Resided New York City, NY; and Brooklyn, NY. Brother-in-law of Colonel James E. Mallon.
Buried: Holy Cross Cemetery, Brooklyn, NY (Select Ground, Range 3, Plot 16)
References: Fred C. Floyd. *History of the 40th (Mozart) Regiment New York Volunteers.* Boston, MA, 1909. Obituary, *Brooklyn Daily Eagle*, Feb. 22, 1918. Pension File, National Archives.

Above: *Edward Johns Riley*
Massachusetts MOLLUS Collection, USAMHI. Brady's National Portrait Gallery. Published by E. & H. T. Anthony, 501 Broadway, New York.
Above Right: *(prewar, as officer in 8th New York State Militia)*
Michael J. McAfee Collection.
Right: *History of the 40th (Mozart) Regiment New York Volunteers.*

Benjamin Ringold
US Military Academy Library. Julius Brill, 204 Chatham Square, New York.

Wardwell Greene Robinson
Courtesy of Michael Albanese.

Benjamin Ringold

Captain, Co. A, 103 NY Infantry, Jan. 4, 1862. Major, 103 NY Infantry, April 4, 1862. Colonel, 103 NY Infantry, Sept. 15, 1862. GSW chest, Suffolk, VA, May 3, 1863

Born: June 6, 1828 Duoslingen, Wurtemberg, Germany
Died: May 3, 1863 DOW Suffolk, VA
Miscellaneous: Resided New York City, NY
Buried: Cypress Hills National Cemetery, Brooklyn, NY (Section 1, Grave 3846)
References: Orville S. Kimball. *History and Personal Sketches of Co. I, 103 New York State Volunteers, 1862-64*. Elmira, NY, 1900. Pension File, National Archives. Obituary, *New York Daily Tribune*, May 7, 1863.

Wardwell Greene Robinson

Colonel, 184 NY Infantry, Sept. 16, 1864. Honorably mustered out, June 29, 1865.

Born: Nov. 28, 1829 Mexico, NY
Died: Dec. 8, 1913 Oswego, NY
Occupation: Lawyer
Miscellaneous: Resided Oswego, NY
Buried: Riverside Cemetery, Oswego, NY (Section O, Lot 337)
References: Obituary, *Oswego Daily Palladium*, Dec. 9, 1913. Crisfield Johnson. *History of Oswego County, NY*. Philadelphia, PA, 1877. John C. Churchill, editor. *Landmarks of Oswego County*. Syracuse, NY, 1895. Wardwell G. Robinson. *History of the 184th Regiment New York State Volunteers*. Oswego, NY, 1895.

John Rorbach

Colonel, 104 NY Infantry, March 15, 1862. Discharged for disability, Oct. 21, 1862, due to chronic diarrhea and inflammation of the bowels.

Born: Dec. 8, 1826 Newton, NJ
Died: Nov. 29, 1899 Geneseo, NY
Occupation: Hardware merchant, and later lawyer
Miscellaneous: Resided Geneseo, Livingston Co., NY
Buried: Temple Hill Cemetery, Geneseo, NY (Section L, Lot 10)
References: *Biographical Review of the Leading Citizens of Livingston and Wyoming Counties, NY*. Boston, MA, 1895. Pension File, National Archives. Obituary, *Livingston Republican*, Nov. 30, 1899. Raymond G. Barber and Gary E. Swinson, editors. *The Civil War Letters of Charles Bar-*

ber, Private, 104th New York Volunteer Infantry. Torrance, CA, 1991.

Rudolph Rosa

Colonel, 46 NY Infantry, Sept. 16, 1861. GSW right thigh, Groveton, VA, Aug. 29, 1862. Discharged for disability, Dec. 17, 1862, due to "general debility and nervousness subsequent to a gunshot wound in the thigh."

Born: Feb. 5, 1824 Silesia, Germany
Died: June 29, 1901 Brooklyn, NY
Occupation: Officer in the engineering corps of the Prussian army. Later surveyor with US Coast Survey and civil engineer.
Miscellaneous: Resided Brooklyn, NY; and New York City, NY
Buried: Mount Olivet Cemetery, Brooklyn, NY (Lot 1 Adult, Grave 321)
References: Pension File and Military Service File, National Archives. Adolf E. Zucker, editor. *The Forty-Eighters: Political Refugees of the German Revolution of 1848.* New York City, NY, 1950. Wilhelm Kaufmann. *The Germans in the American Civil War.* Translated by Steven Rowan and edited by Don Heinrich Tolzmann with Werner D. Mueller and Robert E. Ward. Carlisle, PA, 1999.

Edwin Rose

Colonel, 81 NY Infantry, Sept. 25, 1861. Discharged for disability, July 7, 1862, due to recurrence of liver and heart disease caused by "exposure and fatigue incident to the battles on the Chickahominy River." Provost Marshal, 1st District of New York, 1862-64.

Born: Feb. 14, 1807 Bridgehampton, Long Island, NY
Died: Jan. 12, 1864 Jamaica, Long Island, NY
Education: Graduated US Military Academy, West Point, NY, 1830

Rudolph Rosa
Michael J. McAfee Collection.

Edwin Rose
Edgar Frutchey Collection, USAMHI.

Edwin Rose
Courtesy of Dr. Louisa B. Smith and Leonard L. Smith.

Edwin Rose
Courtesy of Dr. Louisa B. Smith and Leonard L. Smith.

Edwin Rose
Courtesy of Dr. Louisa B. Smith and Leonard L. Smith.

Occupation: Regular Army (1 Lieutenant, 3 US Artillery, resigned June 30, 1837) and farmer
Offices/Honors: NY State Assembly, 1848-49, 1857. US Collector of Customs, Sag Harbor, NY, 1849-53.
Miscellaneous: Resided Bridgehampton, Suffolk Co., NY
Buried: Hayground Cemetery, near Bridgehampton, NY
References: Pension File, National Archives. George W. Cullum. *Biographical Register of the Officers and Graduates of the US Military Academy.* Third Edition. Boston and New York, 1891. Obituary, *New York Herald*, Jan. 15, 1864. William S. Pelletreau and John H. Brown. *American Families of Historic Lineage.* Long Island Edition. New York City, NY, N.d.

George Ryan

1 Lieutenant, 7 US Infantry, April 22, 1861. 1 Lieutenant, Adjutant, 7 US Infantry, Sept. 1, 1861. Captain, 7 US Infantry, July 9, 1862. Acting AAG, Staff of Major Gen. George Sykes, Dec. 1, 1862-June 28, 1863. Acting AAG and Chief of Staff, Staff of Brig. Gen. Romeyn B. Ayres, June 28-July 17, 1863. Colonel, 140 NY Infantry, July 17, 1863.

George Ryan (1857)
US Military Academy Library.

George Ryan
Under the Maltese Cross, Antietam to Appomattox, Campaigns 155th Pennsylvania Volunteers.

George Ryan (1857)
US Military Academy Library.

Henry Wines Ryder (Seated, with 2 Lt. Thomas J. Hoyt)
Report Annual Reunion and Dinner of the Old Guard Association, 12th Regiment, N. G. S. N. Y.

Commanded 3 Brigade, 2 Division, 5 Army Corps, Army of the Potomac, Dec. 1863-Jan. 1864 and Feb. 15, 1864-March 23, 1864. GSW breast, Laurel Hill, VA, May 8, 1864.

Born: April 19, 1836 Medway, MA
Died: May 8, 1864 DOW Laurel Hill, VA
Education: Graduated US Military Academy, West Point, NY, 1857
Occupation: Regular Army (Captain, 7 US Infantry)
Miscellaneous: Resided Norfolk, Litchfield Co., CT
Buried: Holy Sepulchre Cemetery, Rochester, NY
References: Theron W. Crissey, compiler. *History of Norfolk, Litchfield County, CT*. Everett, MA, 1900. George W. Cullum. *Biographical Register of the Officers and Graduates of the US Military Academy*. Third Edition. Boston and New York, 1891. Brian A. Bennett. *Sons of Old Monroe: A Regimental History of Patrick O'Rorke's 140th New York Volunteer Infantry*. Dayton, OH, 1992. *Under the Maltese Cross, Antietam to Appomattox, Campaigns 155th Pennsylvania Volunteers*. Pittsburgh, PA, 1910.

Henry Wines Ryder

Captain, Co. E, 12 NY State Militia, May 2, 1861. Honorably mustered out, Aug. 5, 1861. Captain, Co. E, 12 NY Infantry, Jan. 29, 1862. Shell wound head, Groveton, VA, Aug. 29, 1862. Acting ADC, Staff of Brig. Gen. Daniel Butterfield, Nov.-Dec. 1862. Appointed Provost Marshal, 5 Army Corps, Army of the Potomac, March 24, 1863. Major, 12 NY Infantry, Jan. 1, 1864. Major, 5 NY Veteran Infantry, June 2, 1864. *Lieutenant Colonel*, 5 NY Veteran Infantry, June 1, 1864. Declined. *Colonel*, 5 NY Veteran Infantry, July 4, 1864. Declined. Lieutenant Colonel, 5 NY Veteran Infantry, April 1, 1865. Honorably mustered out, Aug. 21, 1865.

Born: Nov. 30, 1833 NY
Died: Dec. 1, 1910 Newark, NJ
Miscellaneous: Resided Newark, NJ
Buried: Green-Wood Cemetery, Brooklyn, NY (Section 119, Lot 9102)
References: *Report Annual Reunion and Dinner of the Old Guard Association, 12th Regiment, N. G. S. N. Y.* New York City, NY, 1894. Obituary, *Newark Evening News*, Dec. 2, 1910. Military Service File, National Archives. Fremont Rider, compiler. *Genealogy of the Rider (Ryder) Families*. Middletown, CT, 1959.

Henry Wines Ryder
Patrick A. Schroeder Collection.

Henry Wines Ryder (postwar)
Report Annual Reunion and Dinner of the Old Guard Association, 12th Regiment, N. G. S. N. Y.

Augustus B. Sage (seated; with Lt. Col. George W. Warner)
USAMHI. Bogardus, Photographer, 363 Broadway, New York.

James Ryder

Colonel, 18 NY National Guard, July 8, 1863. Honorably mustered out, Aug. 15, 1863.

Born: June 23, 1827 Southeast, NY
Died: Feb. 8, 1897 Danbury, CT
Education: Attended North Salem (NY) Academy
Occupation: Farmer and dry goods merchant
Offices/Honors: CT House of Representatives, 1882
Miscellaneous: Resided Southeast, Putnam Co., NY; Danbury, Fairfield Co., CT; Brooklyn, NY; and Norwalk, Fairfield Co., CT
Buried: Wooster Cemetery, Danbury, CT (Section C, Benedict Lot)
References: Obituary, *Danbury Evening News*, Feb. 9, 1897. Obituary, *New York Tribune*, Feb. 11, 1897. Fremont Rider, compiler. *Genealogy of the Rider (Ryder) Families.* Middletown, CT, 1959. William S. Pelletreau. *History of Putnam County, NY.* Philadelphia, PA, 1886.

Augustus B. Sage

Captain, Co. B, 170 NY Infantry, Sept. 6, 1862. Resigned Jan. 12, 1863, "on account of ill health." Captain, Co. A, 11 NY Infantry, July 13, 1863. *Colonel*, 11 NY Infantry, July 27, 1863. Organization discontinued, Oct. 1, 1863, and men transferred to 17 NY Veteran Infantry. Captain, Co. D, 17 NY Veteran Infantry, Oct. 1, 1863. "Not wishing to serve as captain in a regiment of which I had been colonel of a portion thereof," he immediately tendered his resignation, which was not accepted until March 7, 1864. *Major*, 178 NY Infantry, June 4, 1864.

Born: 1841? NY
Died: Feb. 19, 1874 New York City, NY
Occupation: Stationer
Miscellaneous: Resided New York City, NY
Buried: Green-Wood Cemetery, Brooklyn, NY (Section 127, Lot 2458, Grave 541, unmarked)
References: Death notice, *New York Herald*, Feb. 20, 1874. Military Service File, National Archives.

Augustus B. Sage
Courtesy of the author. G. W. Loud, Union Photographer, 132 Bowery, New York.

Clinton Hezekiah Sage
Roger D. Hunt Collection, USAMHI.

Clinton Hezekiah Sage
Roger D. Hunt Collection, USAMHI. Guay's Photographic Gallery, No. 8 St. Charles St., New Orleans, LA, L. I. Prince, Photographer.

Clinton Hezekiah Sage

Lieutenant Colonel, 110 NY Infantry, Aug. 19, 1862. Colonel, 110 NY Infantry, Feb. 4, 1863. Resigned Dec. 10, 1863, due to "private matters."

Born: June 23, 1825 Chittenango, NY

Died: Feb. 4, 1907 Norwich, NY

Occupation: Railroad contractor

Miscellaneous: Resided Kenton, Hardin Co., OH; and Norwich, Chenango Co., NY

Buried: Mount Adnah Cemetery, Fulton, NY (Section 7, Lot 33)

References: Obituary Circular, Whole No. 912, New York MOLLUS. Pension File, National Archives. Circular, Whole No. 852, New York MOLLUS. Obituary, *Norwich Sun*, Feb. 6, 1907.

Simeon Sammons

Colonel, 115 NY Infantry, July 19, 1862. Captured Harpers Ferry, WV, Sept. 15, 1862. Paroled Sept. 16, 1862. GSW right foot, Olustee, FL, Feb. 20, 1864. GSW left hip, Petersburg, VA, July 30, 1864. Discharged for disability, Jan. 4, 1865, due to the effects of his wounds.

Born: May 23, 1811 near Johnstown, NY
Died: March 19, 1881 near Fonda, NY
Occupation: Farmer
Offices/Honors: NY State Assembly, 1865
Miscellaneous: Resided Fonda, Montgomery Co., NY
Buried: Sammons Family Cemetery, near Fonda, NY
References: *History of Montgomery and Fulton Counties, NY.* New York City, NY, 1878. Military Service File, National Archives. Cuyler Reynolds, editor. *Hudson-Mohawk Genealogical and Family Memoirs.* New York City, 1911. Obituary, *Mohawk Valley Register*, March 25, 1881. Obituary, *Canajoharie Courier*, March 22, 1881. James H. Clark. *The Iron Hearted Regiment: Being an Account of the Battles, Marches and Gallant Deeds Performed by the 115th Regiment New York Volunteers.* Albany, NY, 1865.

Jonah Sanford

Colonel, 92 NY Infantry, Dec. 9, 1861. Resigned May 15, 1862, due to "a general debilitated condition of the system, which renders him entirely unfit for and incapable of performing any military duty whatever."

Simeon Sammons
Collection of The New-York Historical Society.

Jonah Sanford
New York State Military Museum and Veterans Research Center.

Simeon Sammons
Courtesy of Dave Zullo.

Born: Nov. 30, 1790 Cornwall, VT

Died: Dec. 25, 1867 Hopkinton, NY

Other Wars: War of 1812

Occupation: Lawyer and judge

Offices/Honors: NY State Assembly, 1829-30. US House of Representatives, 1830-31.

Miscellaneous: Resided Hopkinton, St. Lawrence Co., NY

Buried: Hopkinton-Fort Jackson Cemetery, Hopkinton, NY

References: Samuel W. Durant. *History of St. Lawrence County, NY*. Philadelphia, PA, 1878. Carlton E. Sanford. *Early History of the Town of Hopkinton, NY*. Boston, MA, 1903. *Biographical Directory of the American Congress*. Letters Received, Volunteer Service Branch, Adjutant General's Office, File S503(VS)1862, National Archives.

James Woodruff Savage

Major, ADC, Staff of Major Gen. John C. Fremont, Sept. 20, 1861-Nov. 19, 1861. Lieutenant Colonel, Additional ADC, USV, March 31, 1862. Colonel, 12 NY Cavalry, Nov. 20, 1863. Honorably mustered out, July 19, 1865.

Born: Feb. 2, 1826 Bedford, NH

Died: Nov. 22, 1890 Omaha, NE

Education: Attended Phillips Academy, Andover, MA. Graduated Harvard University, Cambridge, MA, 1847.

Occupation: Lawyer and district court judge

Miscellaneous: Resided New York City, NY; and Omaha, NE

Buried: Forest Lawn Cemetery, Omaha, NE (Section 21, Lot 223)

James Woodruff Savage
Courtesy of Steve Meadow. C. D. Fredricks & Co., 587 Broadway, New York.

References: James W. Savage and J. T. Bill. *History of the City of Omaha, NE*. New York City, NY, 1894. William H. Ward, editor. *Records of Members of the Grand Army of the Republic*. San Francisco, CA, 1886. Obituary, *Omaha Morning World-Herald*, Nov. 23, 1890.

Louis Schirmer

James Woodruff Savage
USAMHI. Charles D. Fredricks & Co., "Specialite," 587 Broadway, New York.

Louis Schirmer
Roger D. Hunt Collection, USAMHI. Henry Ulke, 278 Pennsylvania Avenue, Washington, DC.

1 Lieutenant, Co. H, 29 NY Infantry, May 18, 1861. 1 Lieutenant, 2 Independent Battery, NY Light Artillery, July 21, 1861. Captain, 2 Independent Battery, NY Light Artillery, Nov. 25, 1861. Lieutenant Colonel, 3 Battalion, NY Heavy Artillery, May 19, 1863. Lieutenant Colonel, 15 NY Heavy Artillery, Sept. 30, 1863. Colonel, 15 NY Heavy Artillery, Oct. 6, 1863. Commanded 4 Brigade, Defenses South of the Potomac, 22 Army Corps, Department of Washington, Nov. 5, 1863-Jan. 12, 1864 and Feb. 12-March 14, 1864. Shell wound back, Petersburg, VA, June 18, 1864. Dismissed Aug. 3, 1865, for "embezzlement and misapplication of money held in trust and belonging to enlisted men."

Born: 1832? Germany
Died: ?
Occupation: Produce dealer before war
Miscellaneous: Resided Memphis, Shelby Co., TN, before war
Buried: ?
References: Military Service File, National Archives. US Census, 1860, Memphis, TN. Albert G. Riddle. *Argument for the Defence in the Case of the United States vs. Colonel Louis Schirmer, 15th New York Heavy Artillery, Tried Before General Court-Martial.* Washington, DC, 1865.

Engelbert Schnepf

Captain, Co. K, 20 NY Infantry, May 3, 1861. Major, 20 NY Infantry, May 16, 1861. Lieutenant Colonel, 20 NY Infantry, April 28, 1862. Honorably mustered out, June 1, 1863. *Colonel, 20 NY Infantry, July 20, 1863. Reorganization of regiment failed, and the incomplete regiment was merged into 16 NY Cavalry, Oct. 14, 1863.

Born: Oct. 25, 1821 near Baden, Germany
Died: March 24, 1880 Brooklyn, NY
Occupation: Shoe merchant before war. Saloon keeper after war.
Miscellaneous: Resided Brooklyn, NY
Buried: Lutheran Cemetery, Middle Village, Queens, NY (Map 5, Lot 1051)
References: Obituary, *Brooklyn Daily Eagle*, March 27, 1880. Pension File, National Archives.

Christian Schwarzwaelder

Colonel, 5 NY State Militia, May 1, 1861. Honorably mustered out, Aug. 7, 1861.

Born: Dec. 13, 1813 Baden, Germany
Died: Nov. 24, 1888 New York City, NY
Occupation: Furniture merchant and banker
Miscellaneous: Resided New York City, NY
Buried: Green-Wood Cemetery, Brooklyn, NY (Section 117, Lots 213/35315)
References: Obituary, *New York Times*, Nov. 25, 1888.

William Marsh Searing

Major, 30 NY Infantry, May 21, 1861. Lieutenant Colonel, 30 NY Infantry, March 11, 1862. Colonel, 30 NY Infantry, Aug. 30, 1862. Commanded 1 Brigade, 1 Division, 1 Army Corps, Army of the Potomac, March 20, 1863-April 9, 1863. Honorably mustered out, June 18, 1863.

Born: Dec. 1, 1821 Saratoga Springs, NY
Died: March 2, 1895 Saratoga Springs, NY
Occupation: Lawyer
Miscellaneous: Resided Saratoga Springs, Saratoga Co., NY
Buried: Greenridge Cemetery, Saratoga Springs, NY (Old Portion, Section F, Lot 29)
References: Nathaniel B. Sylvester. *History of Saratoga County, NY*. Richmond, IN, 1893. Pension File, National Archives. Obituary, *Albany Evening Journal*, March 4, 1895.

William Marsh Searing (postwar)
National Archives.

Jesse Segoine

Jesse Segoine
Sal Alberti/James Lowe Collection.

Colonel, 111 NY Infantry, July 19, 1862. Discharged for disability, Jan. 3, 1863, due to hemorrhoids, general debility, and advancing age.

Born: Jan. 6, 1804 New York City, NY
Died: Aug. 13, 1895 Auburn, NY
Occupation: Furniture manufacturer
Offices/Honors: US Government storekeeper, 1880-85
Miscellaneous: Resided Auburn, Cayuga Co., NY; and Brooklyn, NY
Buried: Fort Hill Cemetery, Auburn, NY (Fort Allegan Section, Lot 77)
References: Pension File, National Archives. Obituary, *Auburn Bulletin*, Aug. 14, 1895. Joel H. Monroe. *Historical Records of 120 Years*. Auburn, NY, 1913.

Jesse Segoine
Courtesy of The Excelsior Brigade. D. Appleton & Co., 443 & 445 Broadway, New York, A. A. Turner, Photographer.

Jesse Segoine
Courtesy of The Excelsior Brigade. Harter's Fine Art Gallery, 83 Genesee Street, Auburn, NY.

Jesse Segoine (postwar)
Massachusetts MOLLUS Collection, USAMHI.

John Wright Shedd
New York State Military Museum and Veterans Research Center.

George Holden Selkirk

1 Lieutenant, Co. D, 49 NY Infantry, Sept. 6, 1861. 1 Lieutenant, Adjutant, 49 NY Infantry, May 31, 1862. Captain, Co. D, 49 NY Infantry, Oct. 4, 1862. GSW right side of spine, Spotsylvania, VA, May 12, 1864. Captain, Co. B, 49 NY Infantry, Sept. 17, 1864. Major, 49 NY Infantry, Oct. 28, 1864. Lieutenant Colonel, 49 NY Infantry, April 1, 1865. *Colonel*, 49 NY Infantry, April 3, 1865. Honorably mustered out, June 27, 1865.

Born: Feb. 10, 1835 Buffalo, NY
Died: May 18, 1925 Buffalo, NY
Occupation: Art student and sculptor before war. Newspaper editor after war.
Offices/Honors: Secretary and Treasurer of the Buffalo Park Department, 1887-1925
Miscellaneous: Resided Buffalo, NY
Buried: Forest Lawn Cemetery, Buffalo, NY (Section R, Lot 5)

References: *The Union Army*. New York Edition. Madison, WI, 1908. Pension File, National Archives. Obituary, *Buffalo Evening News*, May 19, 1925. Frederick D. Bidwell. *History of the 49th New York Volunteers*. Albany, NY, 1916.

John Wright Shedd

1 Lieutenant, Adjutant, 105 NY Infantry, Dec. 5, 1861. Major, 105 NY Infantry, March 26, 1862. GSW left leg, Antietam, MD, Sept. 17, 1862. Colonel, 105 NY Infantry, Oct. 6, 1862. Honorably discharged, March 19, 1863, upon consolidation of regiment with 94 NY Infantry.

Born: Nov. 1, 1808 Bethany, Genesee Co., NY
Died: March 22, 1881 LeRoy, NY
Occupation: Farmer
Miscellaneous: Resided LeRoy, Genesee Co., NY. First cousin of Bvt. Brig. Gen. Warren Shedd.
Buried: Machpelah Cemetery, LeRoy, NY
References: Frank E. Shedd. *Daniel Shed Genealogy*. Boston, MA, 1921. Pension File, National Archives. Town Clerk's Register of Soldiers, LeRoy, Genesee Co., NY, NY State Archives. Obituary, *Batavia Daily News*, March 22, 1881.

Eliakim Sherrill
Roger D. Hunt Collection, USAMHI.

Eliakim Sherrill
Scott Hilts Collection. J. G. Vail, Photographer, 6 Seneca Street, Geneva, NY.

John Pitts Sherburne

1 Lieutenant, 1 US Infantry, April 8, 1861. Captain, 19 US Infantry, Oct. 24, 1861. Major, AAG, July 17, 1862. Commanded District of Washington, 22 Army Corps, Department of Washington, Sept. 1863. Colonel, 11 NY Cavalry, March 1, 1864. Chief of Cavalry, Department of the Gulf, June 25, 1864-Sept. 8, 1864. Discharged from volunteer service, March 15, 1865, for disability resulting from "extensive nervous prostration."

Born: July 9, 1831 Portsmouth, NH
Died: Jan. 9, 1880 San Francisco, CA
Education: Attended US Military Academy, West Point, NY (Class of 1853)
Occupation: Regular Army (Major, AAG, honorably mustered out, Dec. 28, 1870) and US Customs Inspector
Miscellaneous: Resided Portsmouth, Rockingham Co., NH; Lexington, Los Angeles Co., CA; El Monte, Los Angeles Co., CA; and San Francisco, CA. Brother-in-law of Brig. Gen. Amiel W. Whipple.
Buried: San Francisco National Cemetery, San Francisco, CA (Section OSA, Plot 69)
References: Mary McDougall Gordon, editor. *Through Indian Country to California: John P. Sherburne's Diary of the Whipple Expedition, 1853-1854*. Stanford, CA, 1988. Military Service File, National Archives. Letters Received, Appointment, Commission and Personal Branch, Adjutant General's Office, File 1889(ACP)1871, National Archives.

Eliakim Sherrill

Colonel, 126 NY Infantry, July 15, 1862. GSW lower jaw, Maryland Heights, MD, Sept. 13, 1862. Captured Harper's Ferry, WV, Sept. 15, 1862. Paroled Sept. 16, 1862. Commanded 3 Brigade, 3 Division, 2 Army Corps, Army of the Potomac, July 2-3, 1863. GSW bowels, Gettysburg, PA, July 3, 1863.

Born: Feb. 16, 1813 Greenville, Greene Co., NY
Died: July 4, 1863 DOW Gettysburg, PA
Occupation: Tanner and farmer
Offices/Honors: US House of Representatives, 1847-49. NY State Senate, 1854-55.
Miscellaneous: Resided Shandaken, Ulster Co., NY; Brooklyn, NY, 1857-60; and Geneva, Ontario Co., NY, 1860-63
Buried: Washington Street Cemetery, Geneva, NY
References: Arabella M. Willson. *Disaster, Struggle, Triumph: The Adventures of 1000 "Boys in Blue"*. Albany, NY, 1870. Pension File, National Archives. Wayne Mahood. *"Writ-*

ten in Blood," A History of the 126th New York Infantry in the Civil War. Hightstown, NJ, 1997. *Biographical Directory of the American Congress.*

Louis Philipp Siebert

2 Lieutenant, Co. A, 4 NY Cavalry, Oct. 28, 1861. 1 Lieutenant, Co. A, 4 NY Cavalry, Jan. 1, 1862. 1 Lieutenant, Co. C, 1 NY Mounted Rifles, May 13, 1862. Captain, Co. B, 1 NY Mounted Rifles, July 7, 1862. Resigned March 15, 1863, for "private reasons." Captain, AAG, USV, May 22, 1863. AAG, 3 Division, Cavalry Corps, Army of the Potomac. *Colonel,* 2 NY Mounted Rifles, Dec. 31, 1864. Resigned Feb. 23, 1865, for "private reasons."

Born: March 27, 1831 Worms, Germany

Died: Nov. 26, 1914 Washington, DC

Occupation: Engaged in commercial pursuits

Miscellaneous: Resided New York City, NY, 1866-83; Europe, 1883-95; and Washington, DC, 1895-1914

Buried: Arlington National Cemetery, Arlington, VA (Section 1, Lot 430)

References: Pension File, National Archives. Obituary, *New York Times,* Nov. 27, 1914. Obituary, *Washington Evening Star,* Nov. 27, 1914.

Right: *Louis Philipp Siebert*
Courtesy of Henry Deeks. Glosser,
527 Broadway, New York.

Louis Philipp Siebert
Massachusetts MOLLUS Collection, USAMHI.

Lewis C. Skinner

1 Lieutenant, Co. A, 104 NY Infantry, Sept. 30, 1861. Major, 104 NY Infantry, March 15, 1862. Lieutenant Colonel, 104 NY Infantry, Sept. 11, 1862. *Colonel*, 104 NY Infantry, Oct. 21, 1862. Discharged for disability, Oct. 21, 1862, due to dislocation of right ankle and fracture of right leg caused by fall from his horse. Major, 8 VRC, Dec. 9, 1863. Lieutenant Colonel, 8 VRC, Aug. 13, 1864. Honorably mustered out, July 2, 1866.

Born: June 4, 1833 Nunda, NY
Died: March 26, 1904 Colorado Springs, CO
Occupation: Merchant and real estate agent. Later engaged in the sheep raising and wool growing industry.
Offices/Honors: County Commissioner, El Paso Co., CO, 1887-89
Miscellaneous: Resided Nunda, Livingston Co., NY; Chicago, IL; St. Paul, MN; and Colorado Springs, El Paso Co., CO, after 1878.
Buried: Oakwood Cemetery, Nunda, NY
References: Obituary, *Colorado Springs Gazette*, March 27, 1904. Pension File, National Archives.

William Johnson Slidell

1 Lieutenant, 16 US Infantry, May 14, 1861. Captain, 16 US Infantry, Nov. 19, 1861. Acting AIG, Staff of Brig. Gen. Frank Wheaton, March-Nov. 1863. Colonel, 144 NY Infantry, Dec. 29, 1863. Resigned from volunteer service, Sept. 25, 1864. Resigned from regular service, Oct. 19, 1865, since "the war is ended, and I do not care to remain in the Army in time of peace."

Born: Aug. 27, 1838 New Orleans, LA
Died: Feb. 6, 1881 Princeton, NJ
Education: Attended Williams College, Williamstown, MA (Class of 1858)
Occupation: Educated to be a lawyer, but "preferred the less ambitious life of a country gentleman."
Miscellaneous: Resided Princeton, NJ. Nephew of CSA diplomat John Slidell. Nephew of Commodore Matthew C. Perry. First cousin of Brig. Gen. Ranald S. Mackenzie.
Buried: Island Cemetery, Newport, RI (Lots 642-645)

Above Left: *Lewis C. Skinner*
Scott Hilts Collection. Charles D. Fredricks & Co., "Specialite," 587 Broadway, New York.
Left: *New York State Military Museum and Veterans Research Center.*

William Johnson Slidell
Back in War Times: History of the 144th Regiment, New York Volunteer Infantry.

References: *A Biographical Record of the Kappa Alpha Society in Williams College.* New York City, NY, 1881. Obituary, *New York World*, Feb. 18, 1881. Military Service File, National Archives. Obituary, *Trenton Daily State Gazette*, Feb. 9, 1881. Letters Received, Commission Branch, Adjutant General's Office, File S252(CB)1869, National Archives. Letters Received, Adjutant General's Office, File S557(AGO)1861, National Archives. James H. McKee. *Back in War Times: History of the 144th Regiment, New York Volunteer Infantry.* Unadilla, NY, 1903.

Abel Smith

Colonel, 13 NY State Militia, May 17, 1861. Honorably mustered out, Aug. 6, 1861.

Born: Feb. 8, 1813 NY
Died: Oct. 18, 1861 Mechanicville, NY (injuries received in an accident while boarding a train)
Occupation: Licorice manufacturer
Offices/Honors: Colonel, 13 NY State Militia, 1848-61
Miscellaneous: Resided Williamsburg, Kings Co., NY. Father of Lieutenant Colonel Abel Smith, Jr., of the 165 NY Infantry.
Buried: Evergreens Cemetery, Brooklyn, NY (Ivy Path Section, Lot 2)
References: Obituary, *Brooklyn Daily Eagle*, Oct. 21-23, 1861. James De Mandeville, compiler. *History of the 13th Regiment, N.G., S.N.Y.* New York City, NY, 1894. Obituary, *Harper's Weekly*, Vol. 5, No. 253 (Nov. 2, 1861).

Abel Smith
Courtesy of Henry Deeks.

Abel Smith
History of the 13th Regiment, N.G., S.N.Y.

Elisha Brown Smith

Colonel, 114 NY Infantry, July 21, 1862. GSW abdomen, bullet passing out through the spine, Port Hudson, LA, June 14, 1863.

Born: Feb. 17, 1817 Norwich, NY
Died: June 19, 1863 DOW Port Hudson, LA
Occupation: Farmer, agent and municipal official
Miscellaneous: Resided Norwich, Chenango Co., NY
Buried: Mount Hope Cemetery, Norwich, NY

Elisha Brown Smith
Roger D. Hunt Collection, USAMHI. Chamberlin, Norwich, NY.

References: Harris H. Beecher. *Record of the 114th Regiment New York State Volunteers*. Norwich, NY, 1866. Elias P. Pellet. *History of the 114th Regiment New York State Volunteers*. Norwich, NY, 1866.

Hiram Smith

Captain, Co. F, 13 NY Infantry, May 1, 1861. Resigned Sept. 25, 1861, in order to resume his duties as sheriff of Monroe Co., NY. *Colonel*, 140 NY Infantry, Aug. 20, 1862. Regiment raised under his authority, but he did not actually enter service as colonel.

Born: 1815? Moriah, Essex Co., NY
Died: Aug. 20, 1883 Brooklyn, NY
Occupation: Engaged in the grocery and provision business. Later entered the coal and iron trade.
Offices/Honors: Sheriff, Monroe Co., NY, 1859-62
Miscellaneous: Resided Rochester, Monroe Co., NY; and Brooklyn, NY
Buried: Mount Hope Cemetery, Rochester, NY (Range 2, Lot 157)
References: Obituary, *Rochester Union and Advertiser*, Aug. 21, 1883. Obituary, *Rochester Democrat and Chronicle*, Aug. 21, 1883. *History of Monroe County, NY*. Philadelphia, PA, 1877. Military Service File, National Archives.

John Fellows Smith
New York State Military Museum and Veterans Research Center.

John Fellows Smith

Captain, Co. A, 112 NY Infantry, July 21, 1862. Major, 112 NY Infantry, Jan. 11, 1863. Provost Marshal, Suffolk, VA, Feb. 8-Aug.1, 1863. Provost Marshal, Norfolk, VA, Oct. 28-Dec. 1863. Provost Marshal, Staff of Brig. Gen. Israel Vogdes, Feb. 27-March 30, 1864. Assistant Provost Marshal General, 10 Army Corps, Army of the James, Staff of Major Gen. Quincy A. Gillmore, May 13-June 12, 1864. Lieutenant Colonel, 112 NY Infantry, May 18, 1864. Colonel, 112 NY Infantry, June 1, 1864. GSW abdomen, Fort Fisher, NC, Jan. 15, 1865.

Born: Dec. 31, 1822 Jamestown, NY
Died: Jan. 18, 1865 DOW Fort Fisher, NC
Occupation: Lawyer
Miscellaneous: Resided Jamestown, Chautauqua Co., NY
Buried: Lake View Cemetery, Jamestown, NY (Highland Section, Lot 22)
References: William L. Hyde. *History of the 112th Regiment New York Volunteers.* Fredonia, NY, 1866. Military Service File, National Archives.

George Washington Snyder

1 Lieutenant, Corps of Engineers, July 1, 1860. Acting ADC, Staff of Brig. Gen. Samuel P. Heintzelman, July 1861. *Colonel*, 12 NY Infantry, Sept. 25, 1861. Declined.

Born: July 30, 1833 Richmondville, NY
Died: Nov. 17, 1861 Washington, DC (typhoid fever)
Education: Graduated Union College, Schenectady, NY, 1852. Graduated US Military Academy, West Point, NY, 1856.

Occupation: Regular Army (1 Lieutenant, Corps of Engineers)
Buried: Rural Cemetery, Cobleskill, NY
References: Edward A. Hagan. *Hot Whisky for Five: Schoharie County and the Civil War.* Cobleskill, NY, 1985. George W. Cullum. *Biographical Register of the Officers and Graduates of the US Military Academy.* Third Edition. Boston and New York, 1891. Joseph R. Brown, Jr. "A Schoharie County Hero," *Schoharie County Historical Review,* Vol. 15, No. 1 (May 1951). *Catalogue of the Sigma Phi.* N.p., 1915. Obituary, *Schoharie Republican,* Nov. 21, 1861.

James William Snyder

Captain, Co. A, 9 NY Heavy Artillery, Aug. 8, 1862. Major, 9 NY Heavy Artillery, Dec. 30, 1862. GSW right leg, Petersburg, VA, June 18, 1864. Lieutenant Colonel, 9 NY Heavy Artillery, Sept. 15, 1864. Colonel, 9 NY Heavy Artillery, Nov. 28, 1864. Honorably mustered out, July 6, 1865. Bvt. Colonel, USV, April 2, 1865, for gallant and meritorious services before Petersburg, VA.

Born: Jan. 8, 1830 Red Creek, Wayne Co., NY
Died: Oct. 28, 1914 Wichita, KS
Occupation: Farmer before war. Flour and grain business and later insurance agent after war.
Miscellaneous: Resided Buffalo, NY; Guthrie, Logan Co., OK; and Wichita, Sedgwick Co., KS
Buried: Highland Cemetery, Wichita, KS (Block 4, Lot 137)

Officers of the Garrison of Fort Sumter (left to right; Truman Seymour, Abner Doubleday, George W. Snyder, Robert Anderson, Jefferson C. Davis, Samuel W. Crawford)
Massachusetts MOLLUS Collection, USAMHI.

James William Snyder
Slavery and Four Years of War.

Clemens Soest
Courtesy of Jacqueline T. Eubanks.

Franklin Spalding (postwar)
Biographical and Portrait Cyclopedia of Niagara County, NY.

References: Pension File and Military Service File, National Archives. Alfred S. Roe. *The 9th New York Heavy Artillery.* Worcester, MA, 1899. Joseph W. Keifer. *Slavery and Four Years of War.* New York and London, 1900.

Clemens Soest

Captain, Co. F, 29 NY Infantry, May 21, 1861. Lieutenant Colonel, 29 NY Infantry, May 23, 1861. Colonel, 29 NY Infantry, June 9, 1862. GSW right arm, Groveton, VA, Aug. 29, 1862. Commanded 1 Brigade, 2 Division, 11 Army Corps, Army of the Potomac, Feb. 22, 1863-March 5, 1863 and March 28, 1863-April 12, 1863. Discharged for disability, April 13, 1863, due to rheumatism.

Born: 1826? Hanover, Germany
Died: March 22, 1884 Harrisburg, PA
Occupation: Civil engineer
Miscellaneous: Resided Philadelphia, PA; and Harrisburg, PA. His full christian name was Carl August Clemens Daniel Soest.
Buried: Chelten Hills Cemetery, Philadelphia, PA (Section B, Lot 515, unmarked)
References: Pension File, National Archives. Death notice, *Harrisburg Daily Patriot,* March 24, 1884.

Franklin Spalding

Colonel, 151 NY Infantry, Aug. 20, 1862. Succeeded by Colonel William Emerson, Sept. 3, 1862.

Born; Aug. 8, 1815 Lewiston, Niagara Co., NY
Died: Aug. 3, 1895 Niagara Falls, NY
Education: Attended Lewiston (NY) Academy
Occupation: Farmer and banker
Offices/Honors: Sheriff of Niagara Co., NY, 1845-48. US Collector of Customs, Suspension Bridge, NY, 1851 and 1861-69.
Miscellaneous: Resided Lewiston, Niagara Co., NY; and Niagara Falls, Niagara Co., NY
Buried: Village Cemetery, Lewiston, NY
References: Samuel T. Wiley and W. Scott Garner. *Biographical and Portrait Cyclopedia of Niagara County, NY.* Philadelphia, PA, 1892. Obituary, *Niagara Falls Gazette,* Aug. 3, 1895. Charles W. Spalding. *The Spalding Memorial.* Chicago, IL, 1897.

Edward A. Springsteed

1 Lieutenant, Co. D, 43 NY Infantry, Aug. 17, 1861. Captain, Co. I, 7 NY Heavy Artillery, Aug. 14, 1862. Major, 7 NY Heavy Artillery, Aug. 18, 1862. GSW back, Petersburg, VA, June 16, 1864. *Lieutenant Colonel*, 7 NY Heavy Artillery, July 25, 1864. *Colonel*, 7 NY Heavy Artillery, July 26, 1864. GSW Reams' Station, VA, Aug. 25, 1864.

Born: Jan. 31, 1840 Albany, NY
Died: Aug. 25, 1864 KIA Reams' Station, VA
Occupation: Student
Miscellaneous: Resided Albany, NY
Buried: Rural Cemetery, Albany, NY (Section 62, Lot 97)
References: Rufus W. Clark. *The Heroes of Albany.* Albany, NY, 1867. Robert Keating. *Carnival of Blood: The Civil War Ordeal of the 7th New York Heavy Artillery.* Baltimore, MD, 1998. Obituary, *Albany Evening Journal,* Aug. 31, 1864.

Chester W. Sternberg

1 Lieutenant, Adjutant, 21 NY Infantry, May 15, 1861. GSW left leg, 2nd Bull Run, VA, Aug. 30, 1862. Major, 21 NY Infantry, Sept. 24, 1862. Lieutenant Colonel, 21 NY Infantry, Dec. 8, 1862. Honorably mustered out, May 18, 1863. Received authority, May 21, 1863, as colonel, to reorganize 21 NY Infantry for three years' service. Authority withdrawn Sept. 30, 1863.

Born: 1829 Niagara Co., NY
Died: Nov. 24, 1874 Middletown, NY
Occupation: Shipping clerk in the service of the American Express Company
Miscellaneous: Resided Buffalo, NY; and New York City, NY
Buried: Forest Lawn Cemetery, Buffalo, NY (Section W, Lot 55)
References: Obituary, *Buffalo Daily Courier,* Nov. 26, 1874. J. Harrison Mills. *Chronicles of the 21st Regiment New York State Volunteers.* Buffalo, NY, 1867. Pension File, National Archives.

Edward A. Springsteed
Massachusetts MOLLUS Collection, USAMHI.

Chester W. Sternberg
Courtesy of Benedict R. Maryniak. W. M. Knight, 194 Main Street, Buffalo, NY.

William Oliver Stevens
Massachusetts MOLLUS Collection, USAMHI. Brady's National Photographic Portrait Gallery, Broadway & Tenth Street, New York.

William Oliver Stevens
Massachusetts MOLLUS Collection, USAMHI. Brady's National Photographic Portrait Gallery, Broadway & Tenth Street, New York.

Ambrose Stevens

Major, 46 NY Infantry, May 7, 1864. Lieutenant Colonel, 46 NY Infantry, May 25, 1864. Assigned to special service on the staff of Major Gen. John A. Dix, June 8, 1864. Engaged in Secret Service activities, including coverage of the Niagara Falls "Peace Conference" of July 1864. Colonel, 123 NY Infantry, July 1, 1864. Colonel, 176 NY Infantry, Feb. 20, 1865. Honorably mustered out, Sept. 12, 1865.

Born: March 27, 1807 Batavia, NY
Died: Dec. 10, 1880 Lexington, KY
Education: Attended Hobart College, Geneva, NY. Graduated Union College, Schenectady, NY, 1827.
Occupation: Lawyer and live stock breeder. At his death was the leading writer on the editorial staff of the *Live Stock Record*.
Offices/Honors: NY State Assembly, 1855
Miscellaneous: Resided Batavia, Genesee Co., NY; and Lexington, Fayette Co., KY
Buried: Batavia Cemetery, Batavia, NY (Lot 22, unmarked)
References: Obituary, *Batavia Daily News*, Dec. 13, 1880. Obituary, *Batavia Spirit of the Times*, Dec. 18, 1880. Obituary, *Lexington Daily Press*, Dec. 12, 1880. "Niagara's Rebel Visitors," *New York Times*, Dec. 30, 1880. Military Service File, National Archives.

William Oliver Stevens

Captain, Co. D, 72 NY Infantry, June 21, 1861. Major, 72 NY Infantry, June 25, 1861. Colonel, 72 NY Infantry, Sept. 8, 1862. GSW left breast, Chancellorsville, VA, May 3, 1863.

Born: Feb. 3, 1828 Belfast, ME
Died: May 4, 1863 DOW Chancellorsville, VA
Education: Attended Phillips Academy, Andover, MA. Graduated Harvard University, Cambridge, MA, 1848.
Occupation: Lawyer
Offices/Honors: District Attorney of Chautauqua Co., NY, 1859-61
Miscellaneous: Resided Dunkirk, Chautauqua Co., NY
Buried: Forest Hill Cemetery, Fredonia, NY (Section A, Lot 65)
References: Henri L. Brown. *History of the Third Regiment Excelsior Brigade, 72nd New York Volunteer Infantry*. Jamestown, NY, 1902. Thomas W. Higginson. *Harvard Memorial Biographies*. Cambridge, MA, 1866. Obituary, *Fredonia Advertiser*, May 8, 1863.

Charles Hoffman Stewart

Captain, Co. G, 19 NY Infantry, May 7, 1861. Major, 19 NY Infantry, Sept. 28, 1861. Lieutenant Colonel, 3 NY Light Artillery, Dec. 23, 1861. Chief Engineer, Staff of Major Gen. John G. Foster, Aug. 10, 1862-Dec. 31, 1862. Colonel, 3 NY Light Artillery, Jan. 1, 1863. Commanded Sub-District of New Berne, NC, Nov.-Dec. 1864. Chief of Artillery, District of Beaufort, NC, March 3-30, 1865. Chief of Artillery, Department of North Carolina, March 30-April 1865. Honorably mustered out, July 15, 1865.

Born: Oct. 27, 1828 Geneseo, NY
Died: May 19, 1874 Auburn, NY
Occupation: Crockery merchant
Miscellaneous: Resided Auburn, Cayuga Co., NY
Buried: Fort Hill Cemetery, Auburn, NY (Greenwood Section, Lot 32)
References: Obituary, *Auburn Daily Bulletin*, May 20, 1874. Pension File and Military Service File, National Archives. Joel H. Monroe. *Historical Records of 120 Years*. Auburn, NY, 1913. Henry Hall and James Hall. *Cayuga in the Field, A Record of the 19th New York Volunteers, All the Batteries of the 3rd New York Artillery, and 75th New York Volunteers*. Auburn, NY, 1873.

Charles Hoffman Stewart
Roger D. Hunt Collection, USAMHI. Evans' Photographic "Specialite," 77 Genesee St., Auburn, NY 1862.

John Wesley Stiles

Colonel, 9 NY State Militia, May 16, 1861. Colonel, 83 NY Infantry, Dec. 7, 1861. Commanded 3 Brigade, Banks' Division, Army of the Potomac, Aug. 17, 1861-Oct. 8, 1861. Commanded 3 Brigade, 2 Division, 3 Army Corps, Army of Virginia, Aug. 29, 1862-Sept. 2, 1862. Discharged for disability, Jan. 18, 1863, due to "the exposure and fatigue of the campaign to the Rapidan and subsequent battle of Bull Run" and also a severe attack of pleurisy.

Charles Hoffman Stewart
Massachusetts MOLLUS Collection, USAMHI.

John Wesley Stiles
Courtesy of Richard F. Carlile. J. Gurney & Son, Photographic Artists, 707 Broadway, New York.

Born: Jan. 31, 1811 New York City, NY

Died: Sept. 16, 1885 New York City, NY

Occupation: Engaged in the ship chandlery business before war. Became an inventor after war. His hydrostatic gauge won the gold medal in 1884 at the American Institute.

Miscellaneous: Resided New York City, NY

Buried: Green-Wood Cemetery, Brooklyn, NY (Section 61, Lot 17536)

References: Mary S. P. Guild. *The Stiles Family in America.* Albany, NY, 1892. Obituary, *New York Times*, Sept. 17, 1885. Military Service File, National Archives. George A. Hussey, historian, and William Todd, editor. *History of the 9th Regiment, N.Y.S.M., N.G.S.N.Y. (83rd New York Volunteers), 1845-1888.* New York City, NY, 1889. Letters Received, Volunteer Service Branch, Adjutant General's Office, File S1882(VS)1862, National Archives.

John Wesley Stiles
Massachusetts MOLLUS Collection, USAMHI. Published by E. Anthony, 501 Broadway, New York, from Photographic Negative in Brady's National Portrait Gallery.

John Russell Strang

2 Lieutenant, Co. G, 104 NY Infantry, March 6, 1862. 1 Lieutenant, Co. G, 104 NY Infantry, Sept. 12, 1862. Major, 104 NY Infantry, Oct. 21, 1862. Lieutenant Colonel, 104 NY Infantry, Nov. 7, 1863. GSW abdomen, Weldon Railroad, VA, Aug. 19, 1864. Captured Weldon Railroad, VA, Aug. 19, 1864. Confined at Libby Prison, Richmond, VA. Paroled Oct. 9, 1864. Commanded 1 Battalion, Paroled Prisoners, Camp Parole, MD. *Colonel*, 104 NY Infantry, March 3, 1865. Rejoined regiment April 10, 1865. Honorably mustered out, July 17, 1865.

Born: Jan. 8, 1840 Galt, Ontario, Canada

Died: Feb. 15, 1919 Riverside, CA

Education: Graduated Albany (NY) Law School, 1865

Occupation: Lawyer

Miscellaneous: Resided Geneseo, Livingston Co., NY, to 1905; and Riverside, Riverside Co., CA

Buried: Olivewood Cemetery, Riverside, CA (Section L, Division 2, Lot 9)

References: *Biographical Review of the Leading Citizens of Livingston and Wyoming Counties, NY.* Boston, MA, 1895. Pension File and Military Service File, National Archives. Obituary, *Riverside Enterprise*, Feb. 16, 1919.

John Russell Strang
Courtesy of Tom Molocea. W. V. Ranger, Photographic Artist, Over Howard &
Burts Store, Main Street, Geneseo, NY.

John Russell Strang
New York State Military Museum and Veterans Research Center. Moulton &
Larkin, Photographers, 114, 116 & 118 Water Street, Elmira, NY.

Stephen Williamson Stryker

1 Lieutenant, Co. B, 11 NY Infantry, April 20, 1861. Resigned
July 29, 1861. Colonel, 44 NY Infantry, Aug. 30, 1861.
Resigned July 4, 1862, amid rumors concerning his con-
duct at the battle of Hanover Court House, VA, May 27,
1862. Lieutenant Colonel, 18 NY Cavalry, Aug. 31, 1863.
Dismissed Nov. 1, 1864 for "perpetrating frauds upon the
Government in appropriating bounties of the State for col-
ored cooks enlisted in his regiment."

Born: Sept. 17, 1836 Harlingen, Somerset Co., NJ
Died: May 10, 1897 Chicago, IL
Occupation: Merchant and later Western agent of J. B. Stetson
& Co., Hatters, of Philadelphia
Miscellaneous: Resided Chicago, IL
Buried: Rosehill Cemetery, Chicago, IL (Section N, Lot 92)

Stephen Williamson Stryker
New York State Military Museum and Veterans Research Center.

References: William S. Stryker, compiler. *Genealogical Record of the Strycker Family*. Camden, NJ, 1887. Pension File and Military Service File, National Archives. Eugene A. Nash. *A History of the 44th Regiment, New York Volunteer Infantry, in the Civil War, 1861-1865*. Chicago, IL, 1911. Obituary, *Chicago Daily Tribune*, May 11, 1897. Letters Received, Volunteer Service Branch, Adjutant General's Office, File R375(VS)1862, National Archives.

Stephen Williamson Stryker
Hopewell Museum Collection, USAMHI.

Stephen Williamson Stryker
Hopewell Museum Collection, USAMHI.

Stephen Williamson Stryker
Hopewell Museum Collection, USAMHI. R. W. Addis, Photographer, McClees' Gallery, 308 Penna. Avenue, Washington, DC.

Stephen Williamson Stryker
Hopewell Museum Collection, USAMHI.

Stephen Williamson Stryker
Courtesy of the author.

Stephen Williamson Stryker
Donald K. Ryberg Collection.

Charles Beebe Stuart

Colonel, 50 NY Engineers, Aug. 15, 1861. Discharged for disability, June 3, 1863, due to "an almost total loss of voice" caused by a severe cold and acute lung infection.

Born: June 4, 1814 Chittenango Springs, NY
Died: Jan. 4, 1881 Cleveland, OH
Occupation: Civil engineer engaged in railroad and drydock construction
Offices/Honors: Engineer-in-Chief, US Navy, 1850-53
Miscellaneous: Resided Chicago, IL. Author of numerous works on civil engineering.
Buried: Oakwoods Cemetery, Chicago, IL (Section D, Division 1, Lot 54)
References: *Dictionary of American Biography.* Obituary, *Chicago Daily Tribune*, Jan. 5, 1881. Obituary, *New York Times*, Jan. 5, 1881. Pension File, National Archives.

Charles Beebe Stuart
Massachusetts MOLLUS Collection, USAMHI. Brady's National Photographic
Portrait Gallery, 352 Pennsylvania Avenue, Washington, DC.

James Anthony Suiter

Lieutenant Colonel, 34 NY Infantry, May 30, 1861. Colonel, 34 NY Infantry, March 20, 1862. Resigned Jan. 22, 1863, due to dissatisfaction at not being assigned to brigade command upon the promotion of his brigade commander.

Born: April 29, 1816 Herkimer, NY
Died: Jan. 10, 1906 Herkimer, NY
Other Wars: Mexican War (2 Lieutenant, Co. E, 1 NY Volunteers)
Occupation: Saddler and harness maker
Miscellaneous: Resided Herkimer, Herkimer Co., NY
Buried: Oak Hill Cemetery, Herkimer, NY
References: Louis N. Chapin. *A Brief History of the 34th Regiment New York State Volunteers.* New York City, NY, 1903. Pension File and Military Service File, National Archives. Obituary, *Utica Observer*, Jan. 12, 1906. Obituary, *Little Falls Journal and Courier*, Jan. 16, 1906.

Charles Beebe Stuart
Massachusetts MOLLUS Collection, USAMHI. Brady's National Photographic Portrait Gallery, 352 Pennsylvania Avenue, Washington, DC.

James Anthony Suiter
New York State Military Museum and Veterans Research Center.

James Anthony Suiter (postwar)
Courtesy of the author. C. C. Miller, Herkimer, NY.

James Anthony Suiter (postwar)
Courtesy of the author.

Timothy Sullivan

Colonel, 24 NY Infantry, May 16, 1861. Commanded 1 Bri-
    gade, 1 Division, 3 Army Corps, Army of Virginia, July 7,
    1862-July 27, 1862 and Aug. 28, 1862-Sept. 12, 1862.
    Discharged for disability, Jan. 14, 1863, due to bleeding
    hemorrhoids and scrotal hydrocele.

Born: May 1820 Ireland
Died: April 21, 1900 Oswego, NY
Occupation: Boot and shoe maker
Miscellaneous: Resided Oswego, NY
Buried: Riverside Cemetery, Oswego, NY (Section N, Lot 71)
References: Pension File and Military Service File, National
    Archives. Obituary, *Oswego Daily Palladium*, April 21,
    1900.

Timothy Sullivan
Massachusetts MOLLUS Collection, USAMHI. Published by E. Anthony, 501
Broadway, New York, from Photographic Negative in Brady's National Por-
trait Gallery.

Timothy Sullivan
New York State Military Museum and Veterans Research Center.

James Barrett Swain

2 Lieutenant, 1 US Cavalry, Nov. 1, 1861. 1 Lieutenant, 1 US
    Cavalry, Feb. 24, 1862. Colonel, 11 NY Cavalry, April 30,
    1862. Dismissed Feb. 12, 1864, for "making false mus-
    ters, neglect of duty, and repeated and perseverant disobe-
    dience of orders." Dismissal revoked, Feb. 24, 1866, and
    he was honorably discharged as of date of dismissal.

Born: July 30, 1820 New York City, NY
Died: May 27, 1895 Ossining, NY
Occupation: Newspaper publisher, editor and correspondent.
    Involved in several unsuccessful transit projects after war.
Miscellaneous: Resided Ossining, Westchester Co., NY
Buried: Sleepy Hollow Cemetery, Tarrytown, NY (Section 15,
    Plots 648-649)
References: *Dictionary of American Biography*. William C.
    Swain. *Swain and Allied Families*. Milwaukee, WI, 1896.
    Pension File, National Archives. Thomas W. Smith. *The
    Story of a Cavalry Regiment, "Scott's 900," 11th New York
    Cavalry, From the St. Lawrence River to the Gulf of
    Mexico*. Chicago, IL, 1897. Obituary, *Highland Democrat*,
    June 1, 1895. Obituary, *New York Times*, May 28, 1895.

Above Right: *Timothy Sullivan (left, with Adjutant Robert Oliver, Jr.)*
Patrick A. Schroeder Collection.
Right: *James Barrett Swain*
Massachusetts MOLLUS Collection, USAMHI.

James Barrett Swain
Massachusetts MOLLUS Collection, USAMHI. Brady's National Photographic Portrait Gallery, 352 Pennsylvania Avenue, Washington, DC.

James Barrett Swain (right, with his son, Adjutant Chellis D. Swain)
The Story of a Cavalry Regiment, "Scott's 900," 11th New York Cavalry, From the St. Lawrence River to the Gulf of Mexico.

Edward Payson Taft

Major, 138 NY Infantry, Aug. 24, 1862. Major, 9 NY Heavy
    Artillery, Dec. 19, 1862. Lieutenant Colonel, 9 NY Heavy
    Artillery, May 21, 1864. GSW left leg (amputated below
    knee), Monocacy, MD, July 9, 1864. Colonel, 9 NY Heavy
    Artillery, Sept. 15, 1864. Discharged for disability, Nov.
    28, 1864, due to the effects of his wound. Colonel, 9 NY
    Heavy Artillery, Jan. 5, 1865. Honorably mustered out,
    July 6, 1865.

Born: Sept. 10, 1832 Lyons, NY
Died: Jan. 20, 1867 Lyons, NY
Education: Graduated Williams College, Williamstown, MA,
    1855
Occupation: Engaged in iron foundry business with his father
Offices/Honors: US Commercial Agent, San Juan del Sur,
    Nicaragua, 1866-67
Miscellaneous: Resided Waterville, Oneida Co., NY; Elgin,
    Kane Co., IL; and Lyons, Wayne Co., NY
Buried: Rural Cemetery, Lyons, NY

Edward Payson Taft
Roger D. Hunt Collection, USAMHI. Hurlburt, Canal Street, Lyons, NY.

David Miller Talmage (postwar)
Brooklyn Daily Eagle, Sept. 10, 1900.

Alfred W. Taylor
Roger D. Hunt Collection, USAMHI. Fredricks, 585 & 587 Broadway, New York.

References: Alfred S. Roe. *The 9th New York Heavy Artillery.* Worcester, MA, 1899. Pension File and Military Service File, National Archives. *A Biographical Record of the Kappa Alpha Society in Williams College.* New York City, NY, 1881.

David Miller Talmage

Colonel, 56 NY National Guard, June 20, 1863. Succeeded by Colonel John Q. Adams.

Born: 1827 New York City, NY
Died: Sept. 9, 1900 Whitestone, Long Island, NY
Occupation: Cork merchant, horse railroad promoter and contractor
Offices/Honors: Special Envoy for the US in the settlement of claims against Venezuela
Miscellaneous: Resided Brooklyn, NY
Buried: Mount Peace Cemetery, Philadelphia, PA (Section D, Lot 748)
References: Obituary, *Brooklyn Daily Eagle,* Sept. 10, 1900. Arthur W. Talmadge. *Talmadge-Tallmadge and Talmage Genealogy.* New York City, NY, 1909. J. Gardner Bartlett. *Gregory Stone Genealogy.* Boston, MA, 1918.

Alfred W. Taylor

Captain, Co. A, 4 NY Infantry, April 24, 1861. Major, 4 NY Infantry, April 25, 1861. Colonel, 4 NY Infantry, May 15, 1861. Cashiered March 5, 1862, for "drunkenness on duty." Restored to command April 15, 1862, upon Presidential pardon. Resigned July 7, 1862, "having exerted everything in my power towards harmonizing matters in this regiment" and failing to obtain the required support from the officers. *Colonel,* Horatio Seymour Cavalry, May 29, 1863. Succeeded by Colonel Henry S. Gansevoort, June 1, 1863.

Born: 1813? NY
Died: Oct. 5, 1878 Memphis, TN
Other Wars: Mexican War (Captain, Co. B, 1 NY Volunteers)
Occupation: Auction and commission business
Offices/Honors: US Gauger of Internal Revenue
Miscellaneous: Resided New York City, NY; and Memphis, TN
Buried: Elmwood Cemetery, Memphis, TN (Turley Section, Lot 612, unmarked)

References: Pension File and Military Service File, National Archives. Death Notice, *Memphis Public Ledger*, Oct. 7, 1878. Thomas P. Lowry. *Tarnished Eagles: The Courts-Martial of Fifty Union Colonels and Lieutenant Colonels.* Mechanicsburg, PA, 1997.

Robert F. Taylor

Captain, Co. A, 13 NY Infantry, May 1, 1861. Colonel, 33 NY Infantry, May 22, 1861. Commanded 1 Brigade, 2 Division, 6 Army Corps, Army of the Potomac, Jan. 26, 1863-March 24, 1863. Honorably mustered out, June 2, 1863. Colonel, 1 NY Veteran Cavalry, July 20, 1863. Commanded 1 Brigade, 1 Cavalry Division, Army of West Virginia, June-July, 1864 and Aug. 29-Sept. 5, 1864. Commanded 2 Brigade, 1 Cavalry Division, Army of West Virginia, Aug. 15-22, 1864. Dismissed Nov. 17, 1864, for "failing to obey the written orders of the Major General Commanding, and showing disrespect thereto." Dismissal revoked, July 21, 1865, and he was honorably discharged as of date of dismissal.

Born: June 19, 1826 Erie, PA
Died: March 4, 1896 Chicago, IL
Other Wars: Mexican War (1 Sergeant, Co. D, 10 US Infantry)
Occupation: Engaged in merchant tailoring business. Postal Superintendent during President Harrison's administration.
Miscellaneous: Resided Rochester, Monroe Co., NY; Toronto, Ontario, Canada; and Chicago, IL
Buried: Rosehill Cemetery, Chicago, IL (Section 114, Lot 109)
References: David W. Judd. *The Story of the 33rd N. Y. S. Vols: or Two Years Campaigning in Virginia and Maryland.* Rochester, NY, 1864. Obituary, *Chicago Daily Tribune*, March 5, 1896. Pension File and Military Service File, National Archives.

Robert F. Taylor
Courtesy of Michael Albanese. R. W. Addis, Photographer, 308 Penna. Avenue, Washington, DC.

Robert F. Taylor
Roger D. Hunt Collection, USAMHI.

Robert F. Taylor
Roger D. Hunt Collection, USAMHI.

Robert F. Taylor
USAMHI. R. W. Addis, Photographer, 308 Penna. Avenue, Washington, DC.

Robert F. Taylor (postwar)
USAMHI. Greig & Co., Photographers, 14 State Street, Rochester, NY.

Daniel W. Teller

Colonel, 4 NY National Guard Heavy Artillery, June 20, 1863. Honorably mustered out, July 24, 1863.

Born: 1825? NY
Died: Dec. 26, 1873 New York City, NY
Occupation: Merchant
Miscellaneous: Resided New York City, NY. An earnest student of geographical science, he fitted out an expedition at his own expense to survey the ground for a canal through the Isthmus of Darien.
Buried: Green-Wood Cemetery, Brooklyn, NY (Section 86, Lot 17340, Grave 16, unmarked)
References: Obituary, *New York Herald*, Dec. 28, 1873.

Winslow M. Thomas

Captain, Co. D, 60 NY Infantry, Sept. 13, 1861. Major, 60 NY infantry, Dec. 30, 1862. GSW hand, Chancellorsville, VA, May 3, 1863. Lieutenant Colonel, 60 NY Infantry, July 18, 1863. GSW lower jaw and neck, Lookout Mountain,

TN, Nov. 24, 1863. Shell wound head, Resaca, GA, May 15, 1864. *Colonel*, 60 NY Infantry, Sept. 13, 1864. Discharged for disability, April 3, 1865, due to wound of lower jaw "which interferes with the process of mastication to such an extent as to render him unable to use anything but the softest articles of diet."

Born: Feb. 1832 Morristown, St. Lawrence Co., NY

Died: April 15, 1878 Auburn, NY

Occupation: Civil engineer before war. Prison keeper after war.

Miscellaneous: Resided Auburn, Cayuga Co., NY

Buried: Fort Hill Cemetery, Auburn, NY (Glen Alpine Section, Lot 13)

References: Pension File, National Archives. Obituary, *Auburn Daily Bulletin*, April 15, 1878. Letters Received, Commission Branch, Adjutant General's Office, File T551(CB)1865, National Archives. Richard Eddy. *History of the 60th Regiment New York State Volunteers*. Philadelphia, PA, 1864.

George Whitfield Thompson

1 Lieutenant, Adjutant, 34 NY Infantry, May 30, 1861. Lieutenant Colonel, 152 NY Infantry, Jan. 28, 1863. Colonel, 152 NY Infantry, Nov. 15, 1863. Shell wound right foot, Spotsylvania, VA, May 12, 1864. GSW Petersburg, VA, June 30, 1864. Honorably mustered out, June 24, 1865.

Born: Feb. 12, 1830 Dalton, MA

Died: Jan. 16, 1910 Brooklyn, NY

Occupation: Paper manufacturer

Miscellaneous: Resided Herkimer Co., NY; New York City, NY; and Brooklyn, NY

Buried: Original interment, Green-Wood Cemetery, Brooklyn, NY. Removed April 14, 1910, presumably to New Hampton, Orange Co., NY, where his widow Josephine was taken for burial after her death, Sept. 26, 1924.

References: Pension File and Military Service File, National Archives. Obituary, *New York Times*, Jan. 17, 1910. Obituary, *Berkshire County Eagle*, Jan. 19, 1910. Louis N. Chapin. *A Brief History of the 34th Regiment New York State Volunteers*. New York City, NY, 1903. Henry Roback. *The Veteran Volunteers of Herkimer and Otsego Counties in the War of the Rebellion, Being a History of the 152nd New York Volunteers*. Little Falls, NY, 1888.

Winslow M. Thomas
Collection of The New-York Historical Society. G. H. Sherman, Main Street, Canton, NY.

George Whitfield Thompson
A Brief History of the 34th Regiment New York State Volunteers.

George Whitfield Thompson (1903)
A Brief History of the 34th Regiment New York State Volunteers.

William Linn Tidball (postwar)
Courtesy of Dave Zullo.

William Linn Tidball

Colonel, 59 NY Infantry, Oct. 23, 1861. Commanded 3 Brigade, 2 Division, 2 Army Corps, Army of the Potomac, Aug. 5, 1862-Sept. 7, 1862. Discharged for disability, Jan. 8, 1863, due to sciatica and articular rheumatism affecting his left knee. *Colonel*, 59 NY Infantry, Aug. 1, 1863. Lieutenant Colonel, 59 NY Infantry, Oct. 25, 1863. Discharged for disability, Nov. 19, 1863, due to asthma and bronchitis. Captain, VRC, April 8, 1865. Honorably mustered out, Jan. 1, 1868.

Born: Dec. 15, 1820 Pittsburgh, PA
Died: Jan. 29, 1893 New York City, NY
Other Wars: Mexican War (2 Lieutenant, Co. A, 3 OH Infantry)
Occupation: Newspaper editor and lawyer
Miscellaneous: Resided New York City, NY. Brother-in-law of Bvt. Brig. Gen. Noah L. Jeffries.
Buried: Woodlawn Cemetery, New York City, NY (Section 30, Hillside Plot, Lot 7379)
References: Obituary, *New York Tribune*, Jan. 31, 1893. Pension File, National Archives.

Silas Titus

1 Lieutenant, Adjutant, 12 NY Infantry, May 13, 1861. ADC, Staff of Brig. Gen. John J. Peck, Aug. 1861-July 1862. Colonel, 122 NY Infantry, July 22, 1862. Commanded 1 Brigade, 3 Division, 6 Army Corps, Army of the Potomac, May-June 1863. Resigned and honorably discharged, Jan. 23, 1865, due to physical disability (chronic diarrhea) and reduced command.

Born: May 30, 1811 Wolcott, Wayne Co., NY
Died: Oct. 4, 1899 Brooklyn, NY
Occupation: Lumber merchant
Miscellaneous: Resided Syracuse, NY; and Brooklyn, NY
Buried: St. Agnes Cemetery, Syracuse, NY (Section 18, Lot 8)
References: Research Files of Leo J. Titus, Jr. Obituary, *Syracuse Post-Standard*, Oct. 5, 1899. Pension File and Military Service File, National Archives. Obituary, *Brooklyn Daily Eagle*, Oct. 5, 1899. David B. Swinfen. *Ruggles' Regiment: The 122nd New York Volunteers in the American Civil War.* Hanover, NH, 1982. Letters Received, Volunteer Service Branch, Adjutant General's Office, File N420(VS)1862, National Archives.

Silas Titus and Family (1858)
Courtesy of Leo J. Titus, Jr.

John Gordon Todd

Captain, Co. H, 35 NY Infantry, May 13, 1861. Major, 35 NY Infantry, Aug. 10, 1861. Lieutenant Colonel, 35 NY Infantry, Jan. 1, 1863. Colonel, 35 NY Infantry, Feb. 9, 1863. Honorably mustered out, June 5, 1863.

Born: Oct. 31, 1835 Cazenovia, NY
Died: Nov. 7, 1919 Bangor, MI
Occupation: Shoemaker before war
Offices/Honors: Sheriff of Van Buren Co., MI
Miscellaneous: Resided Lawton, Van Buren Co., MI; and Bangor, Van Buren Co., MI
Buried: Arlington Hill Cemetery, Bangor, MI
References: Obituary, *Bangor Advance*, Nov. 13, 1919. Pension File, Department of Veterans Affairs. Albert D. Shaw. *A Full Report of the First Reunion and Banquet of the 35th New York Volunteers*. Watertown, NY, 1888.

John Gordon Todd
Massachusetts MOLLUS Collection, USAMHI.

Silas Titus
Courtesy of Leo J. Titus, Jr. H. Lazier, No. 8 S. Salina Street, Syracuse, NY.

George Washington Brown Tompkins

Colonel, 2 NY State Militia, May 21, 1861. Colonel, 82 NY Infantry, Dec. 7, 1861. Suffering from inflammatory rheumatism, attended with fever and congestion of the brain and liver, he resigned May 26, 1862. *Colonel*, Tompkins Cavalry, Jan. 28, 1863. Incomplete regiment consolidated with 13 NY Cavalry, June 20, 1863.

Born: Jan. 19, 1824 New York City, NY
Died: May 19, 1864 Fordham, Westchester Co., NY
Occupation: Merchant
Miscellaneous: Resided New York City, NY; and Kensico, Westchester Co., NY
Buried: Rural Cemetery, White Plains, NY
References: Robert A. and Clare F. Tompkins. *Tomkins-Tompkins Genealogy*. Los Angeles, CA, 1942. Pension File and Military Service File, National Archives. Letters Received, Volunteer Service Branch, Adjutant General's Office, File T325(VS)1862, National Archives.

Henry Denison Townsend

Colonel, 17 NY Cavalry, June 30, 1863. Regiment failed to complete organization and was merged into 1 NY Veteran Cavalry. Lieutenant Colonel, 1 NY Veteran Cavalry, Sept. 17, 1863. Resigned Sept. 26, 1863.

Born: Dec. 4, 1825 New York City, NY
Died: May 13, 1887 Clifton, Staten Island, NY
Education: Graduated New York University, 1845. Attended Yale University Law School, New Haven, CT.
Occupation: Lawyer
Miscellaneous: Resided New York City, NY
Buried: Moravian Cemetery, New Dorp, Staten Island, NY (Section O, Lots 284-286)
References: *Biographical Catalogue of the Department of Arts and Science of the University of the City of New York*. New York City, NY, 1894. Death notice, *New York Tribune*, May 16, 1887.

Above Left: *George Washington Brown Tompkins*
Roger D. Hunt Collection, USAMHI. Published by E. Anthony, 501 Broadway, New York, from Photographic Negative from Brady's National Portrait Gallery.
Left: *George Washington Brown Tompkins*
Courtesy of the author. J. Gurney & Son, Photographists, 707 Broadway, New York.

Benjamin Lamb Trafford

Captain, Co. B, 71 NY State Militia, May 3, 1861. Honorably
mustered out, July 31, 1861. Captain, Co. E, 71 NY National Guard, May 28, 1862. Honorably mustered out, Sept.
2, 1862. Colonel, 71 NY National Guard, June 30, 1863.
Honorably mustered out, July 22, 1863.

Born: Aug. 5, 1835 New York City, NY
Died: Dec. 23, 1883 Little Silver, Monmouth Co., NJ
Occupation: Hardware merchant and journalist
Miscellaneous: Resided New York City, NY; and Red Bank,
Monmouth Co., NJ
Buried: Presbyterian Church Cemetery, Shrewsbury, NJ
References: Henry Whittemore. *History of the 71st Regiment
N.G.S.N.Y.* New York City, NY, 1886. Pension File, Na-
tional Archives. Obituary, *New York Times*, Dec. 24, 1883.
Augustus T. Francis. *History of the 71st Regiment, N.G.,
N.Y.* New York City, NY, 1919.

Benjamin Lamb Trafford
Roger D. Hunt Collection, USAMHI.

Benjamin Lamb Trafford
*Michael J. McAfee Collection. Charles D. Fredricks & Co., "Specialite," 587
Broadway, New York.*

George W. Travers

Captain, Co. A, 46 NY Infantry, July 29, 1861. Lieutenant
Colonel, 46 NY Infantry, Dec. 17, 1862. Colonel, 46 NY
Infantry, Nov. 8, 1863. Commanded 2 Brigade, 3 Divi-
sion, 9 Army Corps, Army of the Potomac, June 17-18,
1864. GSW right side, Petersburg, VA, June 18, 1864.
Honorably mustered out, Oct. 15, 1864. Bvt. Colonel, USV,
March 13, 1865, for gallant and meritorious services in
the siege of Petersburg, VA.

Born: July 24, 1827
Died: Jan. 27, 1905 Wiesbaden, Germany
Occupation: Merchant
Miscellaneous: Resided Hoboken, Hudson Co., NJ; New York
City, NY; and Wiesbaden, Germany
Buried: Wiesbaden, Germany?
References: Pension File, National Archives.

George W. Travers (center, with officers of the 46th NY Infantry)
New York State Military Museum and Veterans Research Center.

Charles Satterlee Turnbull

Colonel, 131 NY Infantry, Aug. 15, 1862. Resigned Jan. 15, 1863.

Born: Aug. 1819 NY
Died: June 3, 1866 New York City, NY
Occupation: Police captain
Miscellaneous: Resided New York City, NY
Buried: Green-Wood Cemetery, Brooklyn, NY (Section 169, Lot 15265, unmarked)
References: Pension File and Military Service File, National Archives. Death notice, *New York Herald*, June 5, 1866.

Rockwell J. Tyler

Captain, Co. L, 56 NY Infantry, Oct. 5, 1861. Major, 56 NY Infantry, Nov. 23, 1862. Lieutenant Colonel, 56 NY Infantry, Feb. 13, 1864. *Colonel*, 56 NY Infantry, Sept. 27, 1865. Honorably mustered out, March 5, 1866.

Born: 1827 PA
Died: May 27, 1893 White Sulphur Springs, NY
Occupation: Lumber merchant, hotelkeeper and grocer
Offices/Honors: Deputy Collector and Assessor of Internal Revenue. Postmaster of White Sulphur Springs, NY.

Miscellaneous: Resided Cochecton, Sullivan Co., NY; Liberty, Sullivan Co., NY; and White Sulphur Springs, Sullivan Co., NY
Buried: Liberty Cemetery, Liberty, NY
References: Pension File, National Archives. Obituary, *Liberty Register*, June 2, 1893. Joel C. Fisk and William H. D. Blake. *A Condensed History of the 56th Regiment New York Veteran Volunteer Infantry*. Newburgh, NY, 1906.

Henry P. Underhill

Captain, Co. B, 160 NY Infantry, Sept. 1, 1862. Lieutenant Colonel, 160 NY Infantry, Jan. 27, 1865. *Colonel*, 160 NY Infantry, May 30, 1865. Honorably mustered out, Nov. 1, 1865.

Born: Dec. 25, 1835 Macedon, NY
Died: Oct. 4, 1889 Baltimore, MD
Occupation: Merchant, agent for grain drill manufacturing company, and real estate agent
Offices/Honors: President of Annapolis (MD) Short-Line Railroad
Miscellaneous: Resided Macedon, Wayne Co., NY; and Baltimore, MD
Buried: Macedon Cemetery, Macedon, NY
References: Pension File, National Archives. Josephine C. Frost, editor. *Underhill Genealogy: Descendants of Capt. John Underhill*. N.p., 1932. Obituary, *Macedon News Gatherer*, Oct. 12, 1889. Obituary, *Baltimore Sun*, Oct. 5, 1889.

Robert Bruce Van Valkenburgh

Colonel, 85 NY Infantry, Feb. 8, 1862. Declined. Colonel, 107 NY Infantry, July 18, 1862. Resigned Oct. 9, 1862, in order to run for re-election to Congress.

Born: Sept. 4, 1821 Prattsburg, NY
Died: Aug. 1, 1888 Suwannee Springs, near Live Oak, FL
Occupation: Lawyer
Offices/Honors: NY State Assembly, 1852, 1857-58. US House of Representatives, 1861-65. US Minister to Japan, 1866-69. Associate Justice, FL Supreme Court, 1874-88.
Miscellaneous: Resided Bath, Steuben Co., NY; and Jacksonville, Duval Co., FL
Buried: St. Nicholas Cemetery, South Jacksonville, FL

Henry P. Underhill (postwar)
Civil War Library & Museum, Philadelphia, PA.

Robert Bruce Van Valkenburgh
Frederick H. Meserve. Historical Portraits. Courtesy of New York State Library.

Robert Bruce Van Valkenburgh
Donald K. Ryberg Collection. W. J. Moulton, Photographer, Elmira, NY.

Robert Bruce Van Valkenburgh
National Archives.

References: Obituary, *Florida Times-Union*, Aug. 2, 1888. Irwin W. Near. *A History of Steuben County and Its People.* Chicago, IL, 1911. Military Service File, National Archives. *Biographical Directory of the American Congress.*

Koert S. Van Voorhees

Lieutenant Colonel, 137 NY Infantry, Aug. 29, 1862. GSW Gettysburg, PA, July 2, 1863. GSW right side, Wauhatchie, TN, Oct. 29, 1863. Commanded 3 Brigade, 2 Division, 12 Army Corps, Army of the Cumberland, Jan. 27, 1864-Feb. 9, 1864. *Colonel*, 137 NY Infantry, Oct. 14, 1864. Honorably mustered out, June 9, 1865. Bvt. Colonel, USV, March 13, 1865, for gallant and meritorious services during the recent campaign in Georgia and the Carolinas.

Born: 1815 Dutchess Co., NY
Died: Dec. 30, 1888 Larned, KS?
Occupation: Master mason
Offices/Honors: County Treasurer, Tompkins Co., NY, 1875-77
Miscellaneous: Resided Ithaca, Tompkins Co., NY; and Larned, Pawnee Co., KS
Buried: Larned Cemetery, Larned, KS (Northeast Section, Lot 131)

Robert Bruce Van Valkenburgh
New York State Military Museum and Veterans Research Center. Brady's National Photographic Portrait Gallery, Broadway & Tenth Street, New York.

Koert S. Van Voorhees
Scott Hilts Collection, USAMHI.

Koert S. Van Voorhees
USAMHI. Tolles & Seely, Photographists, 38 & 40 Owego Street, Ithaca, NY.

Koert S. Van Voorhees
Charles L. English Collection, USAMHI.

References: Pension File and Military Service File, National Archives. Margaret B. Corbet. *Larned Cemetery*. Larned, KS, 1990.

Jacob Van Zandt

1 Lieutenant, Adjutant, 25 NY State Militia, May 4, 1861. Honorably mustered out, Aug. 4, 1861. Colonel, 91 NY Infantry, Dec. 16, 1861. Commanded 2 Brigade, 4 Division, 19 Army Corps, Department of the Gulf, Jan. 20, 1863-March 23, 1863. Dismissed Dec. 29, 1863, for "conduct unbecoming an officer and a gentleman, conduct to the prejudice of good order and military discipline, and disrespectful language towards his superior officers." Upon the recommendation of the court, the sentence was commuted to "suspension from rank, pay and emoluments for six months." An accusation of interfering with the discipline of the regiment before resuming command providing evidence that his punishment "has not resulted in an amendment of his habits and conduct," he was dismissed

Feb. 2, 1865, for "interfering with the discipline of the 91st New York Volunteers, by ordering enlisted men thereof who were undergoing punishment to be released, and advising a non-commissioned officer not to obey the orders of the Lieutenant Colonel commanding the regiment, pleading drunkenness as an excuse therefor."

Born: Oct. 10, 1831 NY
Died: ?
Occupation: Carpenter
Miscellaneous: Resided Albany, NY; and Amite City, Tangipahoa Co., LA
Buried: ?
References: Military Service File, National Archives. Samuel Burhans, Jr., compiler. *Burhans Genealogy*. New York City, NY, 1894. US Census, 1880, Amite City, Tangipahoa Co., LA. Letters Received, Volunteer Service Branch, Adjutant General's Office, File M48(VS)1865, National Archives. Thomas P. Lowry. *Tarnished Eagles: The Courts-Martial of Fifty Union Colonels and Lieutenant Colonels*. Mechanicsburg, PA, 1997.

Joshua Marsden Varian

Captain, Co. I, 8 NY State Militia, April 20, 1861. Honorably mustered out, Aug. 2, 1861. Colonel, 8 NY National Guard, May 29, 1862. Honorably mustered out, Sept. 10, 1862. Colonel, 8 NY National Guard, June 17, 1863. Honorably mustered out, July 23, 1863.

Born: Jan. 24, 1815 New York City, NY
Died: July 24, 1882 New York City, NY
Occupation: Butcher and provision dealer before war. Provision dealer and clothing merchant after war.
Offices/Honors: Superintendent of Markets, New York City, NY, 1877-80. Brig. Gen., NY National Guard, 1866-82.
Miscellaneous: Resided New York City, NY
Buried: Maple Grove Park Cemetery, Hackensack, NJ (Plot 90-A)
References: Samuel Briggs. *The Book of the Varian Family.* Cleveland, OH, 1881. John D. Rupp. "Joshua Varian, 8th New York Militia," *North South Trader's Civil War*, Vol. 26, No. 2. Obituary, *New York Daily Tribune*, July 25, 1882. Obituary, *New York Herald*, July 25, 1882.

Joshua Marsden Varian
Roger D. Hunt Collection, USAMHI. H. F. Winslow, Photographer, 227 Sixth Avenue, Cor. 15th Street, New York.

Joshua Marsden Varian
Roger D. Hunt Collection, USAMHI. R. A. Lewis, 160 Chatham Square, New York.

Joshua Marsden Varian (right, with Lt. George B. Smith, center, and another officer)
Michael J. McAfee Collection. H. F. Winslow, Photographer, 227 Sixth Avenue, Cor. 15th Street, New York.

Henry Knickerbocker Viele

Colonel, 94 NY Infantry, Jan. 6, 1862. Military Governor of Alexandria, VA, March 22, 1862. Resigned May 2, 1862.

Born: April 29, 1819 Waterford, NY
Died: Aug. 8, 1881 St. Paul, MN
Education: Attended Albany (NY) Academy
Occupation: Lawyer
Offices/Honors: Superintendent of Schools, Buffalo, NY, 1850
Miscellaneous: Resided Buffalo, NY, to 1869; Minneapolis, MN, 1869-70; St. Paul, MN, 1870-81. Brother of Brig. Gen. Egbert L. Viele. First cousin of Colonel John J. Viele.
Buried: Forest Lawn Cemetery, Buffalo, NY (Section K, Lot 4)
References: Kathlyne K. Viele. *Viele Records, 1613-1913.* New York City, NY, 1913. *American Ancestry.* Vol. 4. Albany, NY, 1889. Obituary, *St. Paul Pioneer Press*, Aug. 9, 1881. Military Service File, National Archives. Obituary, *Buffalo Daily Courier*, Aug. 10, 1881. Truman C. White, editor. *Our County and Its People: A Descriptive Work on Erie County, NY.* Boston, MA, 1898.

Henry Knickerbocker Viele
Roger D. Hunt Collection, USAMHI. C. S. Hart, Photographer, Arcade Gallery, Watertown, NY.

John Jay Viele

Colonel, 94 NY Infantry, Nov. 4, 1861. Succeeded by Colonel Henry K. Viele, Jan. 6, 1862.

Born: July 31, 1806 Hoosick Falls, NY
Died: Oct. 18, 1863 near Eagle Bridge, Rensselaer Co., NY
Occupation: Lawyer
Offices/Honors: NY State Assembly, 1836. Brigadier General, NY State Militia.
Miscellaneous: Resided Valley Falls, Rensselaer Co., NY; and Troy, NY. First cousin of Brig. Gen. Egbert L. Viele and also of Colonel Henry K. Viele.
Buried: Island Hill Cemetery, Buskirk, NY
References: Kathlyne K. Viele. *Viele Records, 1613-1913.* New York City, NY, 1913. Obituary, *Troy Daily Times*, Oct. 19, 1863.

Nathan H. Vincent

Private, Co. D, 86 NY Infantry, Sept. 5, 1861. Corporal, Co. D, 86 NY Infantry, April 1, 1862. GSW left leg, 2nd Bull Run, VA, Aug. 30, 1862. Sergeant, Co. D, 86 NY Infantry, Sept. 12, 1862. Sergeant Major, 86 NY Infantry, Jan. 12, 1863. 2 Lieutenant, Co. D, 86 NY Infantry, Feb. 15, 1863. GSW scalp and face, Chancellorsville, VA, May 3, 1863.

Captain, Co. D, 86 NY Infantry, May 3, 1863. GSW left arm and left thigh, Spotsylvania, VA, May 10, 1864. Lieutenant Colonel, 86 NY Infantry, Dec. 2, 1864. *Colonel*, 86 NY Infantry, Nov. 13, 1864. Honorably mustered out, June 27, 1865.

Nathan H. Vincent
USAMHI. W. L. Sutton, Photographer, Hornellsville, NY.

George Von Amsberg
Frederick H. Meserve. Historical Portraits. Courtesy of New York State Library.

George Von Amsberg
Everitt Bowles Collection.

Born: Dec. 5, 1839 Almond Twp., Allegany Co., NY
Died: Jan. 17, 1892 Big Rapids, MI (Killed by accidental discharge of his own rifle while traveling in a sleigh)
Occupation: Farmer
Offices/Honors: Sheriff of Mecosta Co., MI, 1876
Miscellaneous: Resided Almond, Allegany Co., NY; Hornell, Steuben Co., NY; and Big Rapids, Mecosta Co., MI
Buried: Highland View Cemetery, Big Rapids, MI
References: *Portrait and Biographical Album of Mecosta County, MI.* Chicago, IL, 1883. Pension File, National Archives.

George Von Amsberg

Major, 5 NY State Militia, May 1, 1861. Honorably mustered out, Aug. 7, 1861. Colonel, 45 NY Infantry, Oct. 7, 1861. Commanded 1 Brigade, 1 Division, 1 Army Corps, Army of Virginia, July-Aug. 1862. Commanded 1 Brigade, 1 Division, 11 Army Corps, Army of the Potomac, Jan. 12,

1863-Feb. 2, 1863. Commanded 1 Brigade, 3 Division, 11 Army Corps, March 5, 1863-April 2, 1863, May-June 1863, July 1, 1863, Aug.-Sept. 1863. Discharged for disability, Jan. 22, 1864, due to asthma, resulting from acute bronchitis, and complicated with gastritis.

Born: June 24, 1821 Hildesheim, Hanover, Germany
Died: Nov. 21, 1876 Hoboken, NJ
Other Wars: Hungarian War of Independence, 1848-49
Occupation: Riding master before war. Hotel proprietor after war.
Miscellaneous: Resided Hoboken, Hudson Co., NJ. His full christian name was George Karl Heinrich Wilhelm Von Amsberg.
Buried: Palisades Cemetery, North Bergen, NJ (Section B, Plot 73, Block 11, Grave 2)
References: *Dedication of the New York Auxiliary State Monument on the Battlefield of Gettysburg.* Albany, NY, 1926. Obituary, *New York Herald*, Nov. 22, 1876. Military Ser-

vice File, National Archives. Edmund J. Raus, Jr. *A Generation on the March: The Union Army at Gettysburg.* Gettysburg, PA, 1996. Edmund Vasvary. *Lincoln's Hungarian Heroes.* Washington, DC, 1939.

Gotthilf Von Bourry de Ivernois

Captain, Staff of Brig. Gen. Louis Blenker, Oct. 16, 1861. Colonel, 68 NY Infantry, Aug. 6, 1862. Commanded 1 Brigade, 3 Division, 11 Army Corps, Army of the Potomac, Jan. 19, 1863-Feb. 5, 1863. Commanded 1 Brigade, 1 Division, 11 Army Corps, May 25, 1863-June 5, 1863. Dismissed Oct. 25, 1863, on charges of drunkenness on duty, neglect of duty, and conduct prejudicial to good order and

military discipline. Disability resulting from dismissal removed, May 17, 1864.

Born: 1823?
Died: ?
Occupation: Austrian Army and Papal Army service
Buried: ?
References: Military Service File, National Archives. Wilhelm Kaufmann. *The Germans in the American Civil War.* Translated by Steven Rowan and edited by Don Heinrich Tolzmann with Werner D. Mueller and Robert E. Ward. Carlisle, PA, 1999. Joseph Tyler Butts, editor. *A Gallant Captain of the Civil War, Being the Record of the Extraordinary Adventures of Frederick Otto Baron von Fritsch.* New York City, NY, 1902.

George Von Amsberg
Collection of The New-York Historical Society.

Gotthilf Von Bourry de Ivernois
Massachusetts MOLLUS Collection, USAMHI.

Leopold Von Gilsa

Colonel, 41 NY Infantry, June 6, 1861. GSW right leg, Cross Keys, VA, June 8, 1862. Commanded 1 Brigade, 1 Division, 11 Army Corps, Army of the Potomac, Sept. 12, 1862-Jan. 12, 1863, Feb. 2, 1863-May 25, 1863, and June 5, 1863-July 17, 1863. Commanded 1 Brigade, South End of Folly Island (SC), Department of the South, Oct. 24-Nov. 28, 1863 and Jan 13-15, 1864. Commanded 1 Brigade, Folly Island (SC), Northern District, Department of the South, Jan. 15, 1864-June 10, 1864. Honorably mustered out, June 27, 1864. *Colonel*, 191 NY Infantry, Jan. 12, 1865. Regiment did not complete organization, only two companies being recruited.

Born: 1825 Prussia

Died: March 1, 1870 New York City, NY

Occupation: An officer in the Prussian army, he fought in 1848 with the patriots in Schleswig-Holstein against the Danes. School teacher and musician before war. Salesman in a piano establishment after war.

Miscellaneous: Resided New York City, NY

Buried: Green-Wood Cemetery, Brooklyn, NY (Section 153, Lot 19308)

References: *Dedication of the New York Auxiliary State Monument on the Battlefield of Gettysburg.* Albany, NY, 1926. Pension File, National Archives. Adolf E. Zucker, editor. *The Forty-Eighters: Political Refugees of the German Revolution of 1848.* New York City, NY, 1950. Death notice and funeral, *New York Herald*, March 2 and 4, 1870. Wilhelm Kaufmann. *The Germans in the American Civil War*. Translated by Steven Rowan and edited by Don Heinrich Tolzmann with Werner D. Mueller and Robert E. Ward. Carlisle, PA, 1999.

Leopold Von Gilsa
Michael J. McAfee Collection. Charles D. Fredricks & Co., "Specialite," 587 Broadway, New York.

Leopold Von Gilsa (postwar)
Massachusetts MOLLUS Collection, USAMHI.

Emil Ernest Von Schoening

Colonel, German Rangers, July 27, 1861. Mustered in Oct. 2, 1861. The German Rangers were consolidated with the Sigel Rifles to form the 52 NY Infantry, Oct. 29, 1861, but due to illness Colonel Von Schoening was not transferred to this regiment. By order of the Secretary of War, he was reinstated as Colonel, 52 NY Infantry, Dec. 4, 1861. Discharged Feb. 15, 1862, upon adverse report of a Board of Examination, which found that "his knowledge of tactics and the English language both so limited as to wholly unfit him for the command of a regiment."

Born: July 10, 1824 Buck, Posen, Prussia
Died: Feb. 7, 1885 New York City, NY
Occupation: Physician
Miscellaneous: Resided Brooklyn, NY

Leopold Von Gilsa
Michael J. McAfee Collection.

Buried: Evergreens Cemetery, Brooklyn, NY (Diehls Slope Section, Lot 100)
References: Pension File and Military Service File, National Archives. Letters Received, Volunteer Service Branch, Adjutant General's Office, File M288(VS)1861, National Archives. Obituary, *New York Herald*, Feb. 8, 1885. Thomas P. Lowry. *Tarnished Eagles: The Courts-Martial of Fifty Union Colonels and Lieutenant Colonels.* Mechanicsburg, PA, 1997.

Abram S. Vosburgh

Colonel, 71 NY State Militia, May 3, 1861

Born: Sept. 20, 1825 Kinderhook, NY
Died: May 20, 1861 Washington, DC (hemorrhages of the lungs following rupture of a blood vessel)
Occupation: Engaged in the storage business
Offices/Honors: Colonel, 71 NY State Militia, 1852-61
Miscellaneous: Resided New York City, NY
Buried: Green-Wood Cemetery, Brooklyn, NY (Section 123, Lot 13808)

Abram S. Vosburgh
Michael J. McAfee Collection. J. Gurney & Son, Photographic Artists, 707 Broadway, New York.

Gustave Friedrich Waagner
Roger D. Hunt Collection, USAMHI. E. Anthony, 501 Broadway, New York.

References: Henry Whittemore. *History of the 71st Regiment N. G. S. N. Y.* New York City, NY, 1886. Augustus T. Francis. *History of the 71st Regiment, N. G., N. Y.* New York City, NY, 1919. Obituary, *New York Herald*, May 21, 1861.

Gustave Friedrich Waagner

Colonel, Chief of Artillery, OH Volunteer Militia, May 27, 1861. Colonel, Chief of Ordnance, Staff of Major Gen. John C. Fremont, Sept. 20, 1861. Lieutenant Colonel, 2 NY Heavy Artillery, March 5, 1862. Colonel, 2 NY Heavy Artillery, March 14, 1862. Dismissed Aug. 26, 1862, for "habitual drunkenness."

Born: 1813? Dresden, Saxony
Died: Dec. 27, 1891 Hampton, VA
Other Wars: Hungarian War of Independence, 1848-49
Occupation: Civil engineer engaged in railroad and other construction projects
Miscellaneous: Resided New York City, NY; Pittsburgh, PA; and Hampton, VA
Buried: Hampton National Cemetery, Hampton, VA (Section F, Grave 6562)
References: Pension File, National Archives. Edmund Vasvary. *Lincoln's Hungarian Heroes.* Washington, DC, 1939. Letters Received, Volunteer Service Branch, Adjutant General's Office, File W729(VS)1862, National Archives.

Alfred Wagstaff, Jr.

Colonel, 16 NY National Guard, June 19, 1863. Regiment saw service in Brooklyn during New York Draft Riots, July 1863. Lieutenant Colonel, 15 NY National Guard, June 6, 1864. Honorably mustered out, July 7, 1864. 1 Lieutenant, Co. I, 91 NY Infantry, Nov. 5, 1864. Major, 91 NY Infantry, Feb. 2, 1865. Honorably mustered out, July 3, 1865.

Born: March 21, 1844 New York City, NY
Died: Oct. 2, 1921 Babylon, Long Island, NY
Education: Graduated Columbia University Law School, New York City, NY, 1866
Occupation: Lawyer
Offices/Honors: NY State Assembly, 1867-73. NY State Senate, 1876-79. Clerk of the Appellate Division of the NY Supreme Court, 1896-1921. President of the Society for the Prevention of Cruelty to Animals, 1906-21.
Miscellaneous: Resided New York City, NY; and Babylon, Long Island, NY

Alfred Wagstaff, Jr. (1867)
Collection of The New-York Historical Society. Haines & Wickes, Photographers, 478 Broadway, Albany, NY.

Buried: Poughkeepsie Rural Cemetery, Poughkeepsie, NY (Section 16, Lot 1)

References: Obituary, *New York Times*, Oct. 3, 1921. Pension File, National Archives.

Horace Hall Walpole

Captain, Co. E, 122 NY Infantry, Aug. 15, 1862. Captured Spotsylvania, VA, May 11, 1864. Confined at Macon, GA; Savannah, GA; Charleston, SC; and Columbia, SC. Escaped Nov. 1, 1864. Entered Union lines at Knoxville, TN, Dec. 26, 1864. Lieutenant Colonel, 122 NY Infantry, Jan. 27, 1865. Rejoined regiment March 24, 1865. *Colonel*, 122 NY Infantry, March 25, 1865. Honorably mustered out, June 23, 1865.

Born: 1837? Cayuga Co., NY

Died: June 3, 1903 Dayton, OH

Occupation: Lawyer before war. Insurance agent after war.

Miscellaneous: Resided Syracuse, Onondaga Co., NY

Buried: Dayton National Cemetery, Dayton, OH (Section N, Row 24, Grave 53)

References: Pension File, National Archives. David B. Swinfen. *Ruggles' Regiment: The 122nd New York Volunteers in the American Civil War*. Hanover, NH, 1982.

Ezra LeRoy Walrath

Colonel, 12 NY Infantry, May 7, 1861. Resigned Sept. 25, 1861, due to the reduced strength of the regiment, "feeling that his services may be of more consequence to the service in some other position." Captain, Co. I, 115 NY Infantry, Aug. 20, 1862. Major, 115 NY Infantry, June 27, 1863. Provost Marshal, Beaufort, SC, Aug.-Oct. 1863. Commanded 3 Brigade, 2 Division, 10 Army Corps, Army of the James, Aug. 16, 1864. Shell wound left side, Deep Bottom, VA; Aug. 16, 1864. Lieutenant Colonel, 115 NY Infantry, April 29, 1865. Honorably mustered out, June 17, 1865.

Born: April 30, 1827 Clockville, Madison Co., NY

Died: June 26, 1894 Syracuse, NY

Occupation: Manufacturer of jewelry and gold pens, canal collector, and US pension agent

Miscellaneous: Resided Syracuse, Onondaga Co., NY; and New York City, NY

Buried: Oakwood Cemetery, Syracuse, NY (Section 58, Lot 128)

References: Obituary, *Syracuse Standard*, June 27, 1894. James H. Clark. *The Iron Hearted Regiment, Being an Account of the Battles, Marches and Gallant Deeds Performed by the 115th Regiment New York Volunteers*. Albany, NY, 1865. Pension File, National Archives. Letters Received, Volunteer Service Branch, Adjutant General's Office, File J78(VS)1863, National Archives.

Ezra LeRoy Walrath
Massachusetts MOLLUS Collection, USAMHI.

Ezra LeRoy Walrath
New York State Military Museum and Veterans Research Center.

Ezra LeRoy Walrath
New York State Military Museum and Veterans Research Center. J. H. Abbott, No. 480 Broadway, Albany, NY.

William Greene Ward
Massachusetts MOLLUS Collection, USAMHI. Brady's National Photographic Portrait Gallery, 352 Pennsylvania Avenue, Washington, DC.

William Waltermire

Captain, Co. E, 167 NY Infantry, Oct. 14, 1862. Captain, Co. E, 159 NY Infantry, Oct. 28, 1862. Major, 159 NY Infantry, Jan. 10, 1864. Lieutenant Colonel, 159 NY Infantry, June 2, 1864. *Colonel*, 159 NY Infantry, Aug. 4, 1865. Honorably mustered out, Oct. 12, 1865. Bvt. Colonel, USV, March 13, 1865, for conspicuous gallantry at Winchester, VA, September 19, and at Cedar Creek, VA, October 19, 1864.

Born: Oct. 19, 1832 Ghent, Columbia Co., NY
Died: March 11, 1908 Honey Grove, TX
Occupation: Farmer before war. Cotton planter and sheep farmer after war.
Miscellaneous: Resided Ghent, Columbia Co., NY; Rome, Floyd Co., GA, 1865-73; Sherman, Grayson Co., TX, 1873-75; and Honey Grove, Fannin Co., TX, 1875-1908
Buried: Oakwood Cemetery, Honey Grove, TX (Section L)
References: Pension File, National Archives. William F. Tiemann. *The 159th Regiment Infantry, New York State Volunteers in the War of the Rebellion.* Brooklyn, NY, 1891.

William Greene Ward

Lieutenant Colonel, 12 NY State Militia, May 2, 1861. Honorably mustered out, Aug. 5, 1861. Colonel, 12 NY National Guard, May 31, 1862. Captured Harper's Ferry, WV, Sept. 14, 1862. Paroled Sept. 15, 1862. Honorably mustered out, Oct. 8, 1862. Colonel, 12 NY National Guard, June 19, 1863. Honorably mustered out, July 20, 1863.

Born: July 20, 1832 New York City, NY
Died: Jan. 16, 1901 New York City, NY
Education: Graduated Columbia University, New York City, NY, 1851
Occupation: Banker
Offices/Honors: Brigadier General, NY National Guard, 1866-86
Miscellaneous: Resided New York City, NY
Buried: Green-Wood Cemetery, Brooklyn, NY (Section 77, Lot 72, unmarked)
References: Obituary, *New York Times*, Jan. 17, 1901. *Report Annual Reunion and Dinner of the Old Guard Association, 12th Regiment, N. G. S. N. Y.* New York City, NY, 1894. Anita Kershaw Jacobsen. "The Ward Family Grymes Hill," *The Staten Island Historian*, Vol. 6, No. 2 (April-June 1943). Clarence W. Bowen. *The History of Woodstock, CT: Genealogies of Woodstock Families.* Norwood, MA, 1935.

David William Wardrop

Colonel, 3 MA Infantry, April 23, 1861. Honorably mustered out, July 22, 1861. Colonel, 99 NY Infantry, Aug. 21, 1861. Commanded Reserve Brigade, 7 Army Corps, Department of Virginia, April 24, 1863-May 13, 1863. Commanded Sub-District of the Albemarle, District of North Carolina, April 21, 1864-Dec. 10, 1864. Honorably discharged, Dec. 10, 1864, on account of the reduced strength of his command.

Born: May 18, 1824 Philadelphia, PA
Died: July 10, 1898 Dorchester, MA
Occupation: Merchant connected with the shipping and whaling interests of New Bedford, MA, before war. Inspector in the Boston Custom House after war.
Miscellaneous: Resided New Bedford, MA; and Dorchester, MA
Buried: Cedar Grove Cemetery, Dorchester, MA (Section 5, Dahlia Path, Lot 1021)

William Greene Ward
Roger D. Hunt Collection, USAMHI. Brady's National Photographic Portrait Gallery, 352 Pennsylvania Avenue, Washington, DC.

William Greene Ward
Report Annual Reunion and Dinner of the Old Guard Association, 12th Regiment, N. G. S. N. Y.

David William Wardrop
Massachusetts MOLLUS Collection, USAMHI. J. W. Black, 173 Washington Street, Boston, MA.

David William Wardrop
USAMHI.

Andrew Sylvester Warner, with first wife, Mary (prewar)
Courtesy of the author.

References: Pension File and Military Service File, National Archives. Philip Corell. *History of the Naval Brigade, 99th New York Volunteers, Union Coast Guard.* New York City, NY, 1905. Obituary, *Boston Evening Transcript*, July 11, 1898. John G. Gammons. *The 3rd Massachusetts Regiment Volunteer Militia in the War of the Rebellion.* Providence, RI, 1906.

Andrew Sylvester Warner

Colonel, 147 NY Infantry, Aug. 25, 1862. Resigned Feb. 4, 1863, due to his lack of military qualifications, having taken command of the regiment "at the request of citizens of my locality without presuming upon any military qualifications but for the purpose of speedily placing in the field an efficient regiment."

Andrew Sylvester Warner
Massachusetts MOLLUS Collection, USAMHI.

Born: Jan. 12, 1819 Vernon, Oneida Co., NY

Died: Dec. 26, 1887 Sandy Creek, NY

Occupation: Farmer

Offices/Honors: NY State Assembly, 1855-56. NY State Senate, 1860-61.

Miscellaneous: Resided Sandy Creek, Oswego Co., NY. Known in state political circles as "Farmer Warner."

Buried: Sandy Creek Cemetery, Sandy Creek, NY

References: Crisfield Johnson. *History of Oswego County, NY.* Philadelphia, PA, 1877. Pension File and Military Service File, National Archives. Lucien C. Warner and Josephine G. Nichols, compilers. *The Descendants of Andrew Warner.* New Haven, CT, 1919. Obituary, *Oswego Palladium,* Dec. 27, 1887. Obituary, *Pulaski Democrat,* Dec. 29, 1887.

Lewis D. Warner

Captain, Co. C, 154 NY Infantry, Aug. 18, 1862. Major, 154 NY Infantry, May 30, 1863. Lieutenant Colonel, 154 NY Infantry, Sept. 30, 1864. *Colonel,* 154 NY Infantry, Feb. 20, 1865. Honorably mustered out, June 11, 1865.

Andrew Sylvester Warner (postwar)
The Descendants of Andrew Warner.

Lewis D. Warner
William C. Welch Collection, USAMHI.

Lewis D. Warner
New York State Military Museum and Veterans Research Center. R. W. Addis, Photographer, 308 Penna. Avenue, Washington, DC.

Lewis D. Warner (postwar)
William C. Welch Collection, USAMHI.

Frederick Fuller Wead
Special Collections, Schaffer Library, Union College.

Born: May 1822 near Weston Mills, NY

Died: Nov. 18, 1898 Portville, NY

Occupation: Carpenter and joiner

Miscellaneous: Resided Portville, Cattaraugus Co., NY; and Little Valley, Cattaraugus Co., NY

Buried: Chestnut Hill Cemetery, Portville, NY

References: William Adams, editor. *Historical Gazetteer & Biographical Memorial of Cattaraugus County, NY.* Syracuse, NY, 1893. Pension File, National Archives. Obituary, *Olean Morning Times*, Nov. 18, 1898. Mark H. Dunkelman and Michael J. Winey. *The Hardtack Regiment: An Illustrated History of the 154th Regiment, New York State Infantry Volunteers.* Rutherford, NJ, 1981.

Frederick Fuller Wead

1 Lieutenant, Co. I, 16 NY Infantry, May 7, 1861. Acting ADC, Staff of Major Gen. Henry W. Slocum, Sept. 1861-Aug. 1862. Lieutenant Colonel, 98 NY Infantry, Aug. 9, 1862. Colonel, 98 NY Infantry, Feb. 25, 1863. GSW neck, Cold Harbor, VA, June 3, 1864.

Born: Jan. 26, 1835 Malone, NY

Died: June 3, 1864 KIA Cold Harbor, VA

Education: Graduated Union College, Schenectady, NY, 1856. Graduated Poughkeepsie (NY) Law School, 1860.

Occupation: Lawyer

Miscellaneous: Resided Malone, Franklin Co., NY

Buried: Morningside Cemetery, Malone, NY

References: Frederick J. Seaver. *Historical Sketches of Franklin County, NY.* Albany, NY, 1918. Duane H. Hurd. *History of Clinton and Franklin Counties, NY.* Philadelphia, PA, 1880. William Kreutzer. *Notes and Observations Made During Four Years of Service with the 98th New York Volunteers in the War of 1861.* Philadelphia, PA, 1878. Newton M. Curtis. *From Bull Run to Chancellorsville: The Story of the 16th New York Infantry.* New York and London, 1906. *Catalogue of the Sigma Phi.* N.p., 1915. *Encyclopedia of Contemporary Biography of New York.* Vol. 2. New York City, NY, 1882.

Henry Astor Weeks

Lieutenant Colonel, 12 NY State Militia, Oct. 1, 1861. Colonel, 12 NY Infantry, Jan. 24, 1862. GSW both thighs, 2nd Bull Run, VA, Aug. 30, 1862. Commanded 3 Brigade, 1 Division, 5 Army Corps, Army of the Potomac, Aug. 30, 1862 and Dec. 1862-Jan. 1863. Honorably mustered out, May 17, 1863.

Frederick Fuller Wead
Courtesy of Henry Deeks. Fredricks & Co., 179 Fifth Avenue, Madison Square, New York.

Frederick Fuller Wead
Massachusetts MOLLUS Collection, USAMHI.

Born: May 12, 1822 New York City, NY

Died: April 20, 1891 New York City, NY

Education: Graduated Yale University, New Haven, CT, 1843. Graduated College of Physicians and Surgeons, Columbia University, New York City, NY, 1848.

Occupation: Physician

Miscellaneous: Resided New York City, NY

Buried: Woodlawn Cemetery, New York City, NY (Section 13, Daisy Plot, Lot 10651)

References: *National Cyclopedia of American Biography.* Pension File, National Archives. Obituary Circular, Whole No. 346, New York MOLLUS. Obituary, *New York Herald*, April 21, 1891. *Report Annual Reunion and Dinner of the Old Guard Association, 12th Regiment, N. G. S. N. Y.* New York City, NY, 1894.

Henry Astor Weeks
Report Annual Reunion and Dinner of the Old Guard Association, 12th Regiment, N. G. S. N. Y.

Francis Weiss

Lieutenant Colonel, 20 NY Infantry, May 16, 1861. Colonel, 20 NY Infantry, April 28, 1862. Resigned July 4, 1862, "for reasons well known to the commanding general of the brigade." According to his *Reminiscences*, he resigned because he was "suffering from the results of a kick from a horse on my left foot" and also "the annoyance of chronic rheumatism."

Born: Feb. 20, 1821 Vienna, Austria
Died: April 25, 1915 Troy, NY
Other Wars: Hungarian War of Independence, 1848-49
Occupation: Soldier of fortune early in life. Served as Major in the Hungarian and British armies before entering the fire and life insurance business.
Miscellaneous: Resided New York City, NY; and Troy, Rensselaer Co., NY. His true christian name was Karl De Unter-Schill.
Buried: Oakwood Cemetery, Troy, NY (Section T, Lot 71)
References: Pension File, National Archives. *Reminiscences of Chevalier Karl De Unter-Schill, Later Known as Colonel Francis Weiss.* Troy, NY, 1903. Obituary, *Troy Times,* April 26, 1915.

Henry Astor Weeks (postwar)
Courtesy of Dave Zullo.

Edward Wehler

1 Lieutenant, Co. A, 103 NY Infantry, Jan. 12, 1862. 1 Lieutenant, Adjutant, 103 NY Infantry, April 7, 1862. Captain, Co. E, 103 NY Infantry, June 30, 1862. GSW left leg, Antietam, MD, Sept. 17, 1862. Discharged for disability, Sept. 29, 1862. *Colonel*, Burnside Rifles, Jan. 10, 1863. Colonel, 178 NY Infantry, June 20, 1863. Honorably discharged, Jan. 21, 1865, due to consolidation of the regiment into a battalion of five companies.

Born: 1816? Vienna, Austria
Died: May 15, 1888 Vienna, Austria
Other Wars: Mexican War (Musician, 7 NY Volunteers)
Occupation: Hotelkeeper and artist
Miscellaneous: Resided California; Evansville, Vanderburgh Co., IN; and Vienna, Austria
Buried: Vienna, Austria
References: Pension File and Military Service File, National Archives.

Francis Weiss
Massachusetts MOLLUS Collection, USAMHI. Brady's National Photographic Portrait Gallery, Broadway & Tenth Street, New York.

Francis Weiss (postwar)
Reminiscences of Chevalier Karl De Unter-Schill, Later Known as Colonel Francis Weiss.

Joseph Welling
Roger D. Hunt Collection, USAMHI. John Holyland, Metropolitan Gallery, 250 Pennsylvania Avenue, Washington, DC.

Joseph Welling

Colonel, 9 NY Heavy Artillery, Aug. 12, 1862. Commanded 3 Brigade, Defenses North of the Potomac, 22 Army Corps, Department of Washington, March 26, 1864-May 21, 1864. Discharged for disability, May 21, 1864, due to hemorrhoids which existed prior to entering service.

Born: March 22, 1822 Trenton, NJ
Died: March 18, 1897 Philadelphia, PA
Occupation: Lawyer
Miscellaneous: Resided Lyons, Wayne Co., NY; Rochester, Monroe Co., NY; Harrington, Kent Co., DE; and Philadelphia, PA
Buried: Rural Cemetery, Lyons, NY
References: Alfred S. Roe. *The 9th New York Heavy Artillery*. Worcester, MA, 1899. Pension File, National Archives. Obituary, *Wayne Democratic Press*, March 24, 1897. Obituary Circular, Whole No. 560, New York MOLLUS.

Charles H. Weygant

Captain, Co. A, 124 NY Infantry, Aug. 12, 1862. GSW scalp, Chancellorsville, VA, May 3, 1863. Major, 124 NY Infantry, July 2, 1863. Lieutenant Colonel, 124 NY Infantry, July 2, 1863. GSW leg, Spotsylvania, VA, May 12, 1864. *Colonel*, 124 NY Infantry, Sept. 19, 1864. GSW left side, Boydton Plank Road, VA, Oct. 27, 1864. Honorably mustered out, June 3, 1865. Bvt. Colonel, USV, March 25, 1865, for excellent services in the battle before Petersburg, VA.

Born: July 8, 1839 Cornwall, NY
Died: March 10, 1909 Newburgh, NY
Education: Attended Claverack (NY) Collegiate Institute
Occupation: Carriage manufacturer and real estate developer
Offices/Honors: Sheriff of Orange Co., NY, 1870-73. Mayor of Newburgh, NY, 1878-80.
Miscellaneous: Resided Newburgh, Orange Co., NY
Buried: Woodlawn Cemetery, New Windsor, NY (Section H, Lot 33)
References: Obituary, *Newburgh Daily Journal*, March 10, 1909. Esther W. Powell. *Weygandt-Frase-Bechtel Family Record*. Akron, OH, 1965. Charles H. Weygant. *History of the 124th Regiment New York State Volunteers*. Newburgh, NY, 1877. Charles H. Weygant. *The Sacketts of America*. Newburgh, NY, 1907. *Historical Society of Newburgh Bay and the Highlands*. Publication No. 14. Newburgh, NY, 1909. *Portrait and Biographical Record of Orange County, NY*. New York and Chicago, 1895.

Charles H. Weygant
Roger D. Hunt Collection, USAMHI. F. Forshew, Photographer, Hudson, NY.

Alvin White

Captain, Co. A, 117 NY Infantry, Aug. 8, 1862. Lieutenant
   Colonel, 117 NY Infantry, Aug. 16, 1862. Colonel, 117
   NY Infantry, Aug. 26, 1863. GSW left shoulder, Drewry's
   Bluff, VA, May 16, 1864. Discharged for disability, July
   18, 1864, due to wound of left shoulder.

Born: May 9, 1805 (or April 6, 1805) Utica, NY
Died: Jan. 17, 1877 Utica, NY (from injuries received when
   he fell down an elevator shaft)
Occupation: Hotelkeeper and freighter before war. Deputy
   sheriff, Assistant Assessor of Internal Revenue, and Stew-
   ard of Faxton Hospital after war.
Miscellaneous: Resided Utica, Oneida Co., NY.
Buried: Forest Hill Cemetery, Utica, NY (Section 21A, Lot
   539)
References: Obituary, *Utica Daily Observer*, Jan. 18, 1877.
   James A. Mowris. *History of the 117th Regiment New York
   Volunteers, Fourth Oneida*. Hartford, CT, 1866.

Alvin White
Roger D. Hunt Collection, USAMHI. W. C. North, Photographer, Devereux
Block, Utica, NY.

Alvin White
Roger D. Hunt Collection, USAMHI.

Alvin White
Frederick H. Meserve. Historical Portraits. Courtesy of New York State Library.

Amos Hall White

1 Lieutenant, Co. D, 5 NY Cavalry, Oct. 1, 1861. Captain, Co. D, 5 NY Cavalry, Dec. 9, 1861. GSW Front Royal, VA, May 23, 1862. Captured Front Royal, VA, May 23, 1862. Confined Salisbury, NC. Exchanged Sept. 21, 1862. Major, 5 NY Cavalry, Feb. 2, 1863. GSW right foot, Hanover, PA, June 30, 1863. GSW both hips and abdomen, Ashland, VA, June 1, 1864. Captured Ashland, VA, June 1, 1864. Confined Libby Prison, Richmond, VA. Paroled Sept. 1, 1864. Lieutenant Colonel, 5 NY Cavalry, Sept. 15, 1864. Colonel, 5 NY Cavalry, Nov. 14, 1864. Honorably mustered out, July 19, 1865.

Born: June 27, 1837 Ames, Montgomery Co., NY
Died: Dec. 22, 1897 Detroit, MI
Occupation: Clerk before war. Tea merchant after war.
Miscellaneous: Resided Canajoharie, Montgomery Co., NY; and Detroit, MI
Buried: Prospect Hill Cemetery, Canajoharie, NY
References: Obituary, *Detroit Free Press*, Dec. 23, 1897. Pension File, National Archives. Obituary Circular, Whole No. 183, Michigan MOLLUS. Obituary, *Canajoharie Courier*,

Amos Hall White
Historic Records of the 5th New York Cavalry, First Ira Harris Guard.

Amos Hall White (postwar)
Proceedings of the 5th New York Veteran Volunteer Cavalry Regimental Association, 1921.

Michael Wiedrich
New York State Military Museum and Veterans Research Center.

Michael Wiedrich
National Archives.

Dec. 28, 1897. Louis N. Boudrye. *Historic Records of the 5th New York Cavalry, First Ira Harris Guard.* Albany, NY, 1865. *Proceedings of the 5th New York Veteran Volunteer Cavalry Regimental Association.* Burlington, VT, 1921. William H. Powell, editor. *Officers of the Army and Navy (Volunteer) Who Served in the Civil War.* Philadelphia, PA, 1893.

Michael Wiedrich

Captain, Battery I, 1 NY Light Artillery, Aug. 30, 1861. Lieutenant Colonel, 15 NY Heavy Artillery, Jan. 30, 1864. GSW right shoulder, Weldon Railroad, VA, Aug. 18, 1864. GSW right arm, Five Forks, VA, April 1, 1865. *Colonel*, 15 NY Heavy Artillery, Aug. 12, 1865. Discharged for disability, June 2, 1865, due to wound of right arm. Bvt. Colonel, USV, March 13, 1865, for gallant and meritorious services in the battle on the Weldon Railroad, VA.

Born: Sept. 23, 1820 Hochorville, Alsace, France
Died: March 21, 1899 Buffalo, NY
Occupation: Shipping clerk before war. Fire insurance agent after war.
Offices/Honors: Collector of Internal Revenue
Miscellaneous: Resided Buffalo, NY
Buried: Forest Lawn Cemetery, Buffalo, NY (Section DD, Lot 17)

Michael Wiedrich (postwar)
A Record of Battery I, 1st New York Light Artillery Volunteers, Otherwise Known as Wiedrich's Battery, During the War of the Rebellion, 1861-65.

References: Pension File, National Archives. Obituary, *Buffalo Morning Express*, March 22, 1899. Truman C. White, editor. *Our County and Its People: A Descriptive Work on Erie County, NY.* Boston, MA, 1898. Edmund J. Raus, Jr. *A Generation on the March: The Union Army at Gettysburg.* Gettysburg, PA, 1996. Cyrus K. Remington, compiler. *A Record of Battery I, 1st New York Light Artillery Volunteers, Otherwise Known as Wiedrich's Battery, During the War of the Rebellion, 1861-65.* Buffalo, NY, 1891.

Samuel Henry Wilkeson

1 Lieutenant, Co. H, 21 NY Infantry, May 1, 1861. Honorably mustered out, Jan. 2, 1862. Captain, Co. C, 11 NY Cavalry, Feb. 22, 1862. Major, 11 NY Cavalry, June 24, 1862. Lieutenant Colonel, 11 NY Cavalry, Dec. 24, 1862. President, US Relief Commission, New Orleans, LA, July-Oct. 1864. Acting AIG, Staff of Brig. Gen. John W. Davidson, Nov.-Dec. 1864. *Colonel*, 11 NY Cavalry, March 15, 1865. Honorably mustered out, March 27, 1865.

Born: June 28, 1836 Buffalo, NY

Died: Jan. 12, 1915 Buffalo, NY

Education: Attended Union College, Schenectady, NY (Class of 1859)

Occupation: Government assayer of gold before war. Grain elevator business after war.

Miscellaneous: Resided Buffalo, NY; and Cheektowaga, Erie Co., NY

Buried: Forest Lawn Cemetery, Buffalo, NY (Section K, Lot 1)

References: Obituary, *Buffalo Morning Express*, Jan. 13, 1915. Pension File and Military Service File, National Archives. Thomas W. Smith. *The Story of a Cavalry Regiment, "Scott's 900," 11th New York Cavalry, From the St. Lawrence River to the Gulf of Mexico.* Chicago, IL, 1897. *Memorial and Family History of Erie County, NY.* New York and Buffalo, 1906-08.

Samuel Henry Wilkeson
New York State Military Museum and Veterans Research Center. J. T. Upson, Buffalo, NY.

Samuel Henry Wilkeson
Frederick H. Meserve. Historical Portraits. Courtesy of New York State Library.

George Lamb Willard
Massachusetts MOLLUS Collection, USAMHI. Published by E. & H. T. Anthony, 501 Broadway, New York, from Photographic Negative in Brady's National Portrait Gallery.

George Lamb Willard
Massachusetts MOLLUS Collection, USAMHI. Published by E. & H. T. Anthony, 501 Broadway, New York, from Photographic Negative in Brady's National Portrait Gallery.

George Lamb Willard

Colonel, 2 NY Infantry, April 24, 1861. Declined. Captain, 8 US Infantry, April 27, 1861. Major, 19 US Infantry, Feb. 19, 1862. Colonel, 125 NY Infantry, Aug. 15, 1862. Captured Harper's Ferry, WV, Sept. 15, 1862. Paroled Sept. 16, 1862. Commanded 3 Brigade, Abercrombie's Division, 22 Army Corps, Department of Washington, April 26, 1863-May 6, 1863. Commanded 3 Brigade, 3 Division, 2 Army Corps, Army of the Potomac, June 28, 1863-July 2, 1863. Shell wounds chin and shoulder, Gettysburg, PA, July 2, 1863.

Born: Aug. 15, 1827 New York City, NY
Died: July 2, 1863 KIA Gettysburg, PA
Other Wars: Mexican War (Sergeant, Co. B, 15 US Infantry)
Occupation: Regular Army (1 Lieutenant, 8 US Infantry)
Miscellaneous: Resided Troy, Rensselaer Co., NY
Buried: Oakwood Cemetery, Troy, NY (Section B-2, Lot 1)
References: Ezra D. Simons. *A Regimental History, The 125th New York State Volunteers.* New York City, NY, 1888. Charles H. Pope, editor. *Willard Genealogy.* Boston, MA, 1915.

James McClellan Willett

Major, 8 NY Heavy Artillery, Aug. 12, 1862. GSW right side, Cold Harbor, VA, June 3, 1864. Lieutenant Colonel, 8 NY Heavy Artillery, June 3, 1864. Colonel, 8 NY Heavy Artillery, July 1, 1864. Commanded 2 Brigade, 2 Division, 2 Army Corps, Army of the Potomac, Oct. 27, 1864-Nov. 3, 1864. Commanded 1 Brigade, 2 Division, 2 Army Corps, Nov. 15, 1864-Jan. 14, 1865. Resigned Jan. 14, 1865, on account of "pressing private reasons" and a "constitution ... much impaired from the effects of a wound."

James McClellan Willett
New York State Military Museum and Veterans Research Center. J. H. Young, Photographer, 231 Baltimore Street, Corner of Charles, Baltimore, MD.

Officers of the 8th New York Heavy Artillery (Major James M. Willett, left; Adjutant Edwin L. Blake, right; at Headquarters, Fort Federal Hill, Baltimore, MD, 1862)
Casualties by Battles and by Names in the 8th New York Heavy Artillery.

Born: Oct. 10, 1831 Argyle, Washington Co., NY

Died: June 6, 1877 Buffalo, NY

Education: Graduated Albany (NY) Law School, 1856

Occupation: Lawyer

Miscellaneous: Resided Batavia, Genesee Co., NY; New York City, NY; and Buffalo, NY, after 1870

Buried: Forest Lawn Cemetery, Buffalo, NY (Section D, Lot 102)

References: Obituary, *Buffalo Commercial Advertiser*, June 6, 1877. F. W. Beers, editor. *Gazetteer and Biographical Record of Genesee County, NY.* Syracuse, NY, 1890. *Appletons' Annual Cyclopedia and Register of Important Events of the Year 1877.* New York City, NY, 1886. Pension File, National Archives. H. Perry Smith, editor. *History of the City of Buffalo and Erie County.* Syracuse, NY, 1884. James M. Hudnut. *Casualties by Battles and by*

Names in the 8th New York Heavy Artillery, August 22, 1862-June 5, 1865, Together With a Review of the Service of the Regiment Fifty Years After Muster-in. New York City, NY, 1913.

John Williams

Colonel, 108 NY Infantry, July 10, 1862. Resigned July 28, 1862.

Born: Jan. 7, 1807 Utica, NY

Died: March 26, 1875 Rochester, NY

Occupation: Miller and flour manufacturer

Offices/Honors: Mayor of Rochester, NY, 1853-54. US House of Representatives, 1855-57. Major Gen., NY National Guard. City Treasurer of Rochester, NY, 1871-75.

Miscellaneous: Resided Rochester, Monroe Co., NY

Buried: Mount Hope Cemetery, Rochester, NY (Section G, Lot 137)

References: *Biographical Directory of the American Congress.* Obituary, *Rochester Union and Advertiser*, March 25-26, 1875. Blake McKelvey. "Rochester Mayors Before the Civil War," *Rochester History*, Vol. 26, No. 1 (Jan. 1964).

Benjamin Albertson Willis

Captain, Co. H, 119 NY Infantry, Aug. 22, 1862. Major, 119 NY Infantry, March 25, 1863. Resigned to accept promotion, March 9, 1864. *Colonel*, 12 NY Infantry, Jan. 23, 1864. Never joined regiment since reduced strength of regiment prevented his muster as colonel.

Born: March 24, 1840 Roslyn, Queens Co., NY

Died: Oct. 14, 1886 New York City, NY

Education: Attended Union College, Schenectady, NY (Class of 1861). Attended Poughkeepsie (NY) Law School.

Occupation: Lawyer and real estate agent

Offices/Honors: US House of Representatives, 1875-79

Miscellaneous: Resided New York City, NY

Buried: Woodlawn Cemetery, New York City, NY (Section 65, Poplar Plot, Lot 5162)

References: *Encyclopedia of Contemporary Biography of New York.* Vol. 2. New York City, NY, 1882. Obituary, *New York Daily Tribune,* Oct. 16, 1886. Obituary, *New York Herald,* Oct. 16, 1886. Obituary, *New York Times*, Oct. 16, 1886. Pension File, National Archives. *Biographical Directory of the American Congress.*

Benjamin Albertson Willis
Courtesy of Robert T. Lyon.

John Newhall Wilsey (postwar)
Hartford Times, June 3, 1909.

John Newhall Wilsey

Captain, Co. E, 22 NY National Guard, May 28, 1862. Honorably mustered out, Sept. 5, 1862. Captain, Co. E, 22 NY National Guard, June 18, 1863. Honorably mustered out, July 24, 1863. Colonel, 102 NY National Guard, Aug. 25, 1864. Honorably mustered out, Nov. 13, 1864.

Born: June 3, 1837 New York City, NY
Died: June 2, 1909 Dayton, OH
Occupation: Clerk in US Postal Service, being for many years chief clerk of the US envelope works
Miscellaneous: Resided New York City, NY, to 1874; Hartford, CT, 1874-1907; and Dayton, OH, 1907-09
Buried: Spring Grove Cemetery, Hartford, CT (Section F, Lot 18)
References: Pension File, National Archives. Obituary, *Hartford Times*, June 3, 1909.

John Wilson

Captain, Co. A, 43 NY Infantry, Aug. 6, 1861. Major, 43 NY Infantry, July 17, 1862. Lieutenant Colonel, 43 NY Infantry, Sept. 24, 1862. *Colonel*, 43 NY Infantry, Feb. 1, 1864. GSW right leg (amputated), Wilderness, VA, May 6, 1864.

Born: Dec. 29, 1838 Albany, NY
Died: May 7, 1864 DOW Wilderness, VA
Education: Attended Albany (NY) Academy
Occupation: Florist and nurseryman
Miscellaneous: Resided Albany, NY
Buried: Rural Cemetery, Albany, NY (Section 62, Lot 23)
References: Rufus W. Clark. *The Heroes of Albany*. Albany, NY, 1867. Funeral account, *Albany Evening Journal*, May 30, 1864.

John Wilson
Jeff Kowalis Collection.

John Wilson
New York State Military Museum and Veterans Research Center. J. H. & J. L.
Abbott, Photographers, 480 Broadway, Albany, NY.

Cleveland Winslow

Captain, Co. K, 5 NY Infantry, April 25, 1861. Captain, Co. E, 5 NY Infantry, Sept. 11, 1861. Major, 5 NY Infantry, Sept. 26, 1862. Colonel, 5 NY Infantry, Dec. 4, 1862. Honorably mustered out, May 14, 1863. *Colonel*, 5 NY Veteran Infantry, May 25, 1863. Lieutenant Colonel, 5 NY Veteran Infantry, Oct. 24, 1863. *Colonel*, 5 NY Veteran Infantry, June 1, 1864. GSW left shoulder, Bethesda Church, VA, June 2, 1864.

Born: May 26, 1836 Medford, MA
Died: July 7, 1864 DOW Alexandria, VA
Occupation: Merchant
Miscellaneous: Resided New York City, NY
Buried: Green-Wood Cemetery, Brooklyn, NY (Section 11, Lot 3909)
References: David P. Holton. *Winslow Memorial: Family Records of the Winslows and Their Descendants in America.* New York City, 1888. Alfred Davenport. *Camp and Field Life of the 5th New York Volunteer Infantry.* New York City, NY, 1879. Obituary, *New York Times*, July 12, 1864. Patrick A. Schroeder. *We Came to Fight: The History of the 5th New York Veteran Volunteer Infantry, Duryee's Zouaves (1863-1865).* Brookneal, VA, 1998.

John Wilson
Michael J. McAfee Collection. T. S. Wiles, Amateur, Albany, NY.

Cleveland Winslow
Massachusetts MOLLUS Collection, USAMHI.

Cleveland Winslow
Michael J. McAfee Collection. J. Gurney & Son, Photographic Artists, 707
Broadway, New York.

Cleveland Winslow
Civil War Library & Museum, Philadelphia, PA.

Cleveland Winslow
Massachusetts MOLLUS Collection, USAMHI.

Reuben Porter Wisner

Colonel, 58 NY National Guard, Sept. 2, 1864. Honorably
  mustered out, Dec. 2, 1864.

Born: March 1, 1810 Springport, Cayuga Co., NY
Died: Oct. 22, 1872 Mount Morris, NY
Occupation: Lawyer and railroad president
Offices/Honors: NY State Assembly, 1841
Miscellaneous: Resided Mount Morris, Livingston Co., NY
Buried: Mount Morris Cemetery, Mount Morris, NY
References: Levi Parsons and Samuel L. Rockfellow, compil-
  ers. *1794-1894. Centennial Celebration Mount Morris, NY.*
  Mount Morris, NY, 1894. Obituary, *Rochester Union and
  Advertiser*, Oct. 22, 1872.

Reuben Porter Wisner (postwar)
1794-1894. Centennial Celebration Mount Morris, NY.

Alfred M. Wood

Colonel, 14 NY State Militia, May 23, 1861. GSW right hip,
  1st Bull Run, VA, July 21, 1861. Captured 1st Bull Run,
  VA, July 21, 1861. Confined at Richmond, VA. Paroled
  Feb. 22, 1862. Colonel, 84 NY Infantry, Dec. 7, 1861.
  Discharged for disability, Oct. 18, 1862, due to wound of
  right hip.

Born: April 19, 1828 Hempstead, NY
Died: July 28, 1895 Queens, NY
Occupation: Dry goods merchant and US government clerk
Offices/Honors: Colonel, 14 NY State Militia, 1858-62. Col-
  lector of Internal Revenue, 1862-66. Mayor of Brooklyn,
  NY, 1864-66. US Consul, Castellamare, near Naples, Italy,
  1878-94.
Miscellaneous: Resided Brooklyn, NY; and Queens, NY
Buried: Greenfield Cemetery, Hempstead, NY (Section 10,
  Lot 94)
References: Henry R. Stiles. *History of Kings County, NY.* New
  York City, NY, 1884. Pension File, National Archives.
  Henry R. Stiles. *History of the City of Brooklyn.* Brook-
  lyn, NY, 1867. C. V. Tevis. *The History of the Fighting
  Fourteenth.* New York City, NY, 1911. Obituary, *Brook-
  lyn Daily Eagle*, July 29, 1895.

Alfred M. Wood
Roger D. Hunt Collection, USAMHI.

Above Right: *Alfred M. Wood*
Roger D. Hunt Collection, USAMHI. Charles D. Fredricks & Co., "Specialite,"
587 Broadway, New York.
Right: *Alfred M. Wood*
Roger D. Hunt Collection, USAMHI. Published by E. Anthony, 501 Broad-
way, New York, from Photographic Negative in Brady's National Portrait
Gallery.

Isaac Wood, Jr.

Colonel, 166 NY Infantry, Sept. 6, 1862. Regiment failed to complete organization and was merged into the 176 NY Infantry, Dec. 15, 1862.

Born: Dec. 4, 1823 Newburgh, NY
Died: Jan. 13, 1885 Newburgh, NY
Occupation: Dry goods merchant. Later engaged in the towing business on the Hudson River and operated an auction mart.
Offices/Honors: Chief Engineer of the Newburgh Fire Department, 1852. NY State Assembly, 1856.
Miscellaneous: Resided Newburgh, Orange Co., NY
Buried: St. George's Cemetery, Newburgh, NY (Row D, Lot 33, unmarked)
References: Albert G. Barratt. "The Ancient Newburgh Family of Cornelius Wood," *Historical Society of Newburgh Bay and the Highlands*, Historical Papers No. 10. Newburgh, NY, 1903. Obituary, *Newburgh Daily Journal*, Jan. 13, 1885.

John Blackburne Woodward
Roger D. Hunt Collection, USAMHI. Sherman & Co., 272 Fulton Street, Brooklyn, NY.

John Blackburne Woodward

2 Lieutenant, Co. G, 13 NY State Militia, May 14, 1861. Honorably mustered out, Aug. 6, 1861. Lieutenant Colonel, 13 NY National Guard, May 28, 1862. Honorably mustered out, Sept. 12, 1862. Colonel, 13 NY National Guard, June 20, 1863. Honorably mustered out, July 21, 1863.

Born: May 31, 1835 Brooklyn, NY
Died: March 7, 1896 Brooklyn, NY
Occupation: Engaged in the South American import/export business
Offices/Honors: Major Gen., NY National Guard, 1869-75. New York Inspector General, 1875-79. New York Adjutant General, 1879.
Buried: Green-Wood Cemetery, Brooklyn, NY (Section 72, Lot 10915)
References: Obituary, *Brooklyn Daily Eagle*, March 7, 1896. Elijah R. Kennedy. *John B. Woodward, A Biographical Memoir*. New York City, NY, 1897. Obituary Circular, Whole No. 505, New York MOLLUS. James De Mandeville. *History of the 13th Regiment, N. G., S. N. Y.* New York City, NY, 1894.

John Blackburne Woodward
Massachusetts MOLLUS Collection, USAMHI.

John Blackburne Woodward (right; with Lt. Col. William A. McKee, center; and Major Joseph B. Leggett, left)
History of the 13th Regiment, N. G., S. N. Y.

John Blackburne Woodward (postwar)
John B. Woodward, A Biographical Memoir.

Joseph Wright

Colonel, 21 NY National Guard, June 27, 1863. Honorably mustered out, Aug. 6, 1863.

Born: 1807? NY
Died: ?
Occupation: Merchant and farmer
Miscellaneous: Resided Poughkeepsie, Dutchess Co., NY
Buried: Poughkeepsie, NY?
References: Douglas W. Cruger, compiler. *A Genealogical Dictionary of Wright Families in the Lower Hudson Valley to 1800.* Baltimore, MD, 1987. James M. Caller and Mrs. M. A. Ober. *Genealogy of the Descendants of Lawrence and Cassandra Southwick.* Salem, MA, 1881. Military Service File, National Archives. Poughkeepsie Directory, 1864-65.

Anthony Francis Wutschel

Captain, Co. K, 8 NY Infantry, April 23, 1861. Major, 8 NY Infantry, Aug. 5, 1861. Lieutenant Colonel, 8 NY Infantry, Aug. 10, 1861. Colonel, 8 NY Infantry, Nov. 12, 1861. Dismissed Aug. 23, 1862, "for ordering his regiment into the battle of Cross Keys, June 8, 1862, contrary to an order of General Stahel, thereby bringing his command in danger of almost total destruction."

Born: 1822? Vienna, Austria
Died: May 20, 1871 New York City, NY (from injuries received in a fall from the roof of a shed during a period of mental instability)
Occupation: Insurance agent
Miscellaneous: Resided New York City, NY
Buried: Evergreens Cemetery, Brooklyn, NY (Hickory Knoll Section, Lot 138, unmarked)
References: Obituary, *New York Times*, May 23, 1871. Pension File and Military Service File, National Archives. Adolf E. Zucker, editor. *The Forty-Eighters: Political Refugees of the German Revolution of 1848.* New York City, NY, 1950. Letters Received, Volunteer Service Branch, Adjutant General's Office, File W620(VS)1862, National Archives.

Joseph Yeamans

1 Lieutenant, Co. E, 1 NY Infantry, April 23, 1861. Captain, Co. E, 1 NY Infantry, Aug. 7, 1861. Major, 1 NY Infantry, Oct. 14, 1862. Captured Chancellorsville, VA, May 3, 1863. Paroled May 23, 1863. Honorably mustered out, May 25, 1863. *Colonel,* 10 NY Infantry, Dec. 9, 1863. Commission revoked.

Born: 1820?
Died: May 8, 1891 New York City, NY
Occupation: Clerk
Miscellaneous: Resided New York City, NY
Buried: New York Bay Cemetery, Jersey City, NJ (Section M-South, Lot 311, unmarked)
References: Pension File and Military Service File, National Archives. Death notice, *New York Herald*, May 10, 1891.

Robert P. York

1 Lieutenant, Co. H, 114 NY Infantry, Aug. 14, 1862. Captain, Co. H, 114 NY Infantry, Aug. 19, 1863. Provost Marshal and Asst. Commissary of Musters, 3 Brigade, 1 Division, 19 Army Corps, Department of the Gulf, Aug. 23, 1863-Feb. 1864. Provost Marshal, 1 Division, 19 Army Corps, Feb. 20, 1864-July 1864. Commissary of Musters, 19 Army Corps, Army of the Shenandoah, July 3, 1864-Dec. 1864. GSW slight, Winchester, VA, Sept. 19, 1864. Lieutenant Colonel, 75 NY Infantry, Dec. 16, 1864. *Colonel,* 75 NY Infantry, Jan. 1, 1865. Provost Marshal, District of Savannah, Department of the South, Feb. 21, 1865-Aug. 1865. Honorably mustered out, Aug. 31, 1865.

Born: Sept. 6, 1835 Lincklaen, Chenango Co., NY
Died: Feb. 20, 1887 DeRuyter, NY
Occupation: Merchant and farmer before war. Auctioneer and dry goods merchant after war.
Miscellaneous: Resided Syracuse, Onondaga Co., NY, 1866-76; and DeRuyter, Madison Co., NY, 1876-87
Buried: DeRuyter Cemetery, DeRuyter, NY
References: Pension File and Military Service File, National Archives. Elias P. Pellet. *History of the 114th Regiment New York State Volunteers.* Norwich, NY, 1866. Harris H. Beecher. *Record of the 114th Regiment New York State Volunteers.* Norwich, NY, 1866. James H. Smith. *History of Chenango and Madison Counties, NY.* Syracuse, NY, 1880. Henry and James Hall. *Cayuga in the Field, A Record of the 19th New York Volunteers, All the Batteries of the 3rd New York Artillery, and 75th New York Volunteers.* Auburn, NY, 1873.

Robert P. York
New York State Military Museum and Veterans Research Center. Theo. Lilienthal's Photographic Gallery, 102 Poydras Street, New Orleans, LA.

William Henry Young
New York State Military Museum and Veterans Research Center.

William Henry Young

Lieutenant Colonel, 18 NY Infantry, May 13, 1861. Colonel, 18 NY Infantry, Nov. 11, 1861. Discharged for disability, Aug. 14, 1862, due to typhoid fever complicated with excessive nervous prostration.

Born: April 22, 1824 England

Died: Oct. 31, 1876 Albany, NY (from head injuries received when thrown from his horse in a political parade)

Occupation: Superintendent of the moulding department of Rathbone & Co.'s Stove Works

Miscellaneous: Resided Schenectady, NY; and Albany, NY.

Buried: Vale Cemetery, Schenectady, NY (Section G, Lot 17)

References: Homer Eaton. *Memorial of Colonel William H. Young*. Albany, NY, 1876. Obituary, *Schenectady Daily Union*, Nov. 1, 1876. Military Service File, National Archives.

Index

Abbott, Chauncey, 18, 24
Abbott, George, 19, 24
Abert, William S., 93, 143
Adams, Alexander Duncan, 15, 24, 25
Adams, Alonzo W., 11
Adams, John Quincy, 17, 25, 273
Adams, Julius Walker, 18, 25, 26
Ainsworth, Ira Washington, 23, 27
Alden, Alonzo, 22
Alford, Samuel M., 13, 27
Allen, Augustus Franklin, 20, 28
Allen, William H., 13, 21, 28, 29
Ames, Cheney, 20, 29, 30
Anderson, Robert, 260
Arnold, Lewis G., 112
Ashley, Ossian Doolittle, 16, 30
Aspinwall, Lloyd, 15, 30, 31
Austin, John S., 18, 32
Avery, Matthew H., 11, 12
Axtell, Nathan Gibbs, 23, 32, 33
Ayres, Romeyn B., 246

Bagley, James, 18, 34
Bailey, Benajah P., 19, 34, 35
Bailey, Guilford Dudley, 12, 35, 36
Baird, William Henderson, 21, 37
Baker, Benjamin F., 16
Baker, Henry Michael, 19, 38
Baker, Joel Brigham Goodell, 13, 14, 38, 39
Baker, Stephen, 13, 39
Banks, Nathaniel P., 72
Barlow, Francis C., 17
Barnes, William Benson, 13, 39, 40
Barney, Albert M., 21
Barney, Lewis T., 20, 23
Barnum, Henry A., 22
Bartlett, Joseph J., 15
Bartlett, Washington Allen, 19, 40
Barton, William B., 16
Bassford, Abraham, 11, 40
Bates, Willard W., 13, 41, 42
Beardsley, John, 11, 42, 43
Beardsley, Samuel Raymond, 15, 43
Beecher, Henry Ward, 219
Belknap, Jonathan S., 19, 43, 44
Bendix, John E., 14

Benedict, Lewis, 22, 134
Benjamin, William H., 11
Bennett, Michael, 15, 44
Bentley, Richard C., 17
Berens, William F., 23, 44
Betge, Robert J., 18, 44, 45
Biddle, George H., 19, 45, 46
Biddle, William F., 143
Bidwell, Daniel D., 16
Bingham, Daniel Galusha, 17, 46
Birney, David B., 113
Blaine, James G., 85
Blake, Edwin L., 228, 306
Blanchard, Justus W., 22
Blenker, Louis, 14, 288
Bokee, David Alexander, 15, 47
Bomford, James V., 114
Bouck, Gabriel, 97
Bouck, William C., 97
Boughton, Horace, 21
Boyer, Leonard, 22, 47
Bradley, Leman W., 17, 47
Brady, James Dennis, 17, 48
Brainerd, Wesley, 13, 48, 49
Braulik, Francis H., 22, 49, 90
Breckinridge, John C., 229
Brewster, William R., 18, 120
Britt, James W., 17
Broady, Knut Oscar, 17, 50
Brown, Edwin Franklin, 15, 51, 52
Brown, James Malcolm, 19, 53, 54
Brown, John Smith, 21, 53, 54
Brown, Philip P., Jr., 22
Brown, William Rufus, 15, 22, 54, 55
Browne, William Cresap, 16, 55
Browne, William H., 16
Bryan, Michael Kirk, 15, 23, 55, 56
Buckingham, George Andrew, 17, 23, 56, 57
Buel, Clarence, 22, 57
Bull, James M., 21, 58
Burger, Louis, 13, 58, 59
Burke, Denis Francis, 19, 59
Burke, James C., 14, 59
Burke, John, 17, 60
Burns, Michael William, 18, 60
Burnside, Ambrose E., 168

Burr, Allen Lysander, 23, 60
Burtis, Charles H., 14, 18, 61
Butler, John, 208
Butler, John Germond, 22, 61
Butterfield, Daniel, 14, 247
Byrne, James J., 12
Byrne, John, 22, 62
Byrnes, Richard, 48

Cameron, James, 18, 62, 63, 64
Cameron, Simon, 62
Camp, Walter Bicker, 19, 63
Cannon, Madison Mott, 16, 64, 65
Carmichael, James Campbell, 22, 66
Carpenter, Lewis E., 112
Carr, Joseph B., 13
Carroll, Howard, 20, 67
Cassidy, Ambrose S., 21
Catlin, Isaac S., 20
Caw, David J., 18, 67
Chamberlin, James Roswell, 23, 68
Chambers, William Richard Washington, 19, 68
Chapin, Edward P., 20
Chapin, Gurden, 12, 68
Chapman, Alford B., 17, 68, 69
Charles, Edmund Cobb, 16, 69, 70
Chatfield, Harvey Strong, 20, 71
Chester, George Foote, 19, 72
Chittenden, Henry C., 118
Christian, William H., 15
Chrysler, Morgan H., 12
Claassen, Peter J., 21, 72
Clark, Charles Henry, 17, 73
Clark, John S., 15
Clark, Robert Bruce, 14, 73, 74
Clarke, William W., 19, 74, 75
Cluseret, Gustave P., 129
Coan, William Bloomfield, 16, 75, 76
Cochrane, John, 17
Cocks, John Samuel, 16, 76, 77
Cogswell, Milton, 12, 16
Colburn, Albert V., 143
Cole, Matthias W., 17, 77
Colgate, Clinton Gilbert, 13, 77
Cone, Spencer Wallace, 17, 77
Confort, Felix, 23, 78

Conk, Anthony, 21, 78
Conkling, Frederick Augustus, 19, 78, 79
Conkling, Roscoe, 79
Conner, Freeman, 16, 79, 80
Conrad, Joseph Speed, 13, 81, 82
Cooke, Erastus, 22, 82, 83
Coonan, John, 23, 84
Coppinger, John Joseph, 11, 23, 84, 85
Corcoran, Michael, 18
Corning, Joseph Walker, 23, 85
Coster, Charles Robert, 21, 86, 87
Coster, John Henry, 23, 86
Couch, Darius N., 184, 230
Cowles, David Smith, 21, 87
Cram, George Clarence, 12, 88
Crandell, Levin, 21, 88, 89
Crane, Nirom M., 20
Crawford, Samuel W., 260
Creney, James, 19, 89
Crocker, John S., 19, 207
Croft, Marriott N., 22, 90
Crooks, Samuel J., 11, 12, 90
Cropsey, William J., 18, 90
Crosby, John Schuyler, 93
Cross, Nelson, 18, 26
Cullen, Edgar Montgomery, 19, 90, 91
Cummins, Francis Markoe, 21, 91, 92
Currie, Leonard Douglas Hay, 21, 92, 93, 94
Curtis, Newton M., 21
Curtiss, James E., 22
Cushing, William B., 123

d'Epineuil, Lionel Jobert, 17, 94, 95
d'Utassy, George Frederick, 16, 95, 96, 97, 98
Daggett, Rufus, 20
Dandy, George B., 19
Danforth, George Erskine, 21, 97
Davidson, John W., 304
Davies, Henry E., Jr., 11, 99
Davies, Jared Mansfield, 11, 99
Davies, Thomas A., 14, 99
Davis, Benjamin Franklin, 11, 99
Davis, Edwin P., 22
Davis, Jefferson C., 260
Davis, Uriah L., 19, 100, 127
Davis, William W. H., 167
Day, Nicholas W., 21
DeForest, Jacob J., 18, 100, 101
DeForest, Othneil, 11, 102
Degive, Peter, 15, 102, 129
DeLacy, William, 16, 22
DeMonteil, Antoine Joseph Vignier, 95
Depew, Chauncey Mitchell, 23, 102, 103
DeRussy, Gustavus A., 12
DeTrobriand, Philip R., 16, 17

Devin, Thomas C., 11
DeWitt, David P., 21
DeZeng, P. Mark, 26
di Cesnola, Louis Palma, 11, 103, 104
Dickel, Christian Friedrich, 11, 104
Dininny, John W., 21, 105
Diven, Alexander S., 20
Dix, John A., 263
Dobke, Adolphus, 16, 105
Dodge, Charles C., 12
Dodge, John Augustus, 18, 106
Dodge, Stephen Augustus, 19, 106
Donnelly, Dudley, 15, 107
Doubleday, Abner, 107, 178, 260
Doubleday, Thomas Donnelly, 12, 107, 108
Doubleday, Ulysses, 107
Drake, Jeremiah Clinton, 20, 28, 108
Drum, Richard C., 109
Drum, William Findlay, 13, 109
Durkee, Charles, 19, 109
Duryea, Hiram, 13
Duryea, Richard Cornell, 13, 110
Duryee, Abram, 13
Dutton, William, 19, 110
Dwight, Augustus Wade, 20, 111
Dwight, Charles Chauncey, 22, 112, 113
Dwight, James F., 112
Dwight, William, Jr., 18
Dyckman, Garret W., 13, 113

Eagan, Michael J., 195
Edson, John Henry, 13, 114
Egan, Thomas W., 16
Ellis, Augustus V.H., 21
Ellsworth, Ephraim Elmer, 14, 114, 115, 116, 117
Embick, Frederic Ely, 20, 115
Emerson, William, 22, 117, 261
Enright, Richard C., 17, 118
Evans, David Morris, 12, 118
Everdell, William, Jr., 15, 119

Fairchild, Harrison S., 19
Fairman, James, 18, 19, 120
Fardella, Enrico, 19
Farnham, Noah Lane, 14, 121
Farnsworth, Addison, 18
Farnum, J. Egbert, 18
Fenton, Reuben E., 182
Ferguson, Alonzo, 22, 122
Ferrero, Edward, 16
Fisk, Henry C., 17
Fisk, John, 12, 122
Fitzhugh, Charles L., 11, 12
Fitzsimons, Charles, 12
Flood, Hugh C., 22, 123
Floyd, Elbridge G., 13, 123

Floyd, Horace W., 123
Floyd-Jones, DeLancey, 21
Forbes, David S., 18, 123, 124
Foster, James Prentice, 21, 124
Foster, John A., 23
Foster, John G., 264
Fowler, Douglas, 125
Fowler, Edward B., 19
Fowler, Henry Thomas, 17, 125
Fox, Watson A., 18, 125, 126
Franchot, Richard, 20
Frank, Paul, 17, 23
Franklin, William B., 112
Fraser, James Leslie, 16, 126
Fremont, John C., 227, 251, 291
French, Winsor B., 18
Frisby, Edward, 15, 100, 127
Fuller, James M., 20, 127
Fullerton, William S., 12, 128
Funk, Augustus, 16, 128

Gansevoort, Henry S., 11, 273
Garrard, Kenner, 21
Gates, Theodore B., 18, 82
Gerhardt, Joseph, 16
Gibbs, Alfred, 12
Gibson, Robert P., 13, 129
Gifford, Haviland, 19, 129
Gillmore, Quincy A., 260
Gittermann, John, 15, 129
Gleason, John H., 17
Glenny, William, 17, 219
Godard, Abel, 17, 130
Goldie, William, 238
Goodrich, William Bingham, 17, 131
Gott, Benjamin Frank, 23, 131
Gould, Charles, 23, 131, 132
Graham, Charles K., 18
Graham, Samuel, 12
Grantsynn, William S., 21, 132
Gray, Charles Osborn, 19, 132, 133
Grayson, John B., 229
Green, Nelson Winch, 18, 133, 134
Greene, George S., 17
Gregg, William M., 23
Gregory, David Elmore, 21, 134
Grindlay, James G., 21
Griswold, John Augustus, 21, 135
Grower, William Thomas Campbell, 15, 135, 136
Grumbach, Nicholas, 22, 137
Guion, George Murray, 22, 137, 138
Guion, John M., 138
Gurney, William, 21

Hall, George B., 18, 139
Hall, Henry Hills, 12, 139, 140, 141
Hall, James F., 13
Hall, Thomas Spencer, 19, 141

Hall, William, 78
Hamblin, Joseph E., 17
Hamilton, Charles, 20, 141, 142
Hamilton, Theodore Burns, 17, 142
Hammell, John S., 17
Hammerstein, Herbert Von, 18, 20, 142, 143
Hammond, John, 11
Hancock, Winfield S., 81
Hardenbergh, Jacob B., 18
Harhaus, Otto, 11, 142, 143
Harrower, Gabriel Theodore, 22, 143, 144
Harrower, Henry George, 22, 143, 144
Hartmann, Louis F., 15, 144, 145
Hatheway, Samuel Gilbert, Jr., 21, 145
Hawkins, Rush C., 14
Hayman, Samuel B., 16
Hayt, William W., 23, 146
Hayward, William Brown, 17, 146
Heckman, Charles A., 233
Heine, William, 20
Heintzelman, Samuel P., 260
Hendrickson, John, 19
Higgins, Benjamin Lucius, 19, 147
Hoffman, Henry C., 15
Holley, John Calvin, 21, 147
Holt, Erastus Dutton, 16, 147
Holt, Thomas, 18
Hooker, Joseph, 232
Hopper, George Faulkner, 14, 148
Howard, William A., 13, 148, 149
Howland, Joseph, 14
Hoyt, Mark, 23, 131, 149
Hoyt, Thomas J., 247
Hudson, Edward McKeever, 13, 143, 150, 151
Hudson, Henry Wadsworth, 17, 19, 150
Hughston, Robert Savage, 21, 151
Hull, Harmon Daniel, 22, 151
Hull, Walter Clarke, 11, 151, 152
Hunt, Lewis C., 19
Husk, Lewis Webb, 20, 153
Huston, James Francis Xavier, 19, 153, 154
Hyde, Joseph, 21, 154

Innes, Charles Henry, 16, 154
Ireland, David, 21, 155
Irvine, William, 11

Jackson, Allan Hyre, 21, 155, 156, 157
Jackson, William Ayrault, 15, 158
Jacobs, Ferris, Jr., 12
James, Edward Christopher, 20, 158
Jeffries, Noah L., 277
Jenkins, David Tuttle, 21, 159
Jenkins, John P., 23, 102, 160

Jenney, Edwin Sherman, 23, 160, 161
Johnson, Charles A., 15
Johnson, Nathan J., 20, 161
Johnson, William, 22, 162
Jones, Frank, 15, 162
Jones, Patrick H., 22, 238
Jourdan, James, 22
Judd, Schuyler F., 20, 163
Judson, Roscius W., 21

Kapff, Edward Ernst Reinhold, 14, 163
Karples, Henry Morris, 17, 163
Kearny, Philip, 184
Keese, Oliver, Jr., 20, 164
Kelly, Patrick, 19, 165
Kennedy, John A., 166
Kennedy, William D., 16, 166
Kerrigan, James E., 15, 166
Ketcham, John H., 22
Kibbe, George C., 13, 166
Kiernan, James L., 213
Kilpatrick, Judson, 11
Kingsley, Hale, 22, 167
Kitching, J. Howard, 13
Kozlay, Eugene A., 17
Krettner, Jacob, 17, 167
Kreutzer, William, 19, 167, 168
Krzyzanowski, Wladimir, 17

Ladew, William, 16, 168
Laflin, Byron, 16
Lake, James, 15, 168, 169
Lane, James Crandall, 20, 169, 170
Lansing, Henry S., 14
Lansing, Jacob H., 19, 170
Lazelle, Henry Martyn, 12, 171
Ledlie, James H., 12
Leet, James M., 42, 228
Lefferts, Marshall, 14, 172, 173
LeGal, Eugene, 17, 174
LeGendre, Charles W., 16
Leggett, Joseph B., 313
Lemmon, John Cockey, 11, 174
Leoser, Charles McKnight, 14, 175, 176
Lewis, Charles, 23, 176
Lewis, George W., 11, 176, 177
Lewis, James, 21, 177, 178
Liebenau, Henry Frederick, 12, 178
Littlejohn, DeWitt C., 20, 29
Livingston, Charles Edward, 18, 178
Lockman, John T., 20
Logie, William Kenneth, 21, 179
Lopez, Narciso, 208
Lord, Newton Bosworth, 12, 16, 179, 180
Lord, William, 123
Love, George M., 20

Lowell, Charles R., 143
Ludwick, Ephraim A., 20, 180, 181, 182
Lynch, Thomas, 18, 181
Lynch, William A., 16, 182
Lyon, Nathaniel, 81
Lyons, George, 14, 182, 183

MacDougall, Clinton D., 20
MacGregor, John D., 13
MacIvor, James P., 22
Mackenzie, Ranald S., 257
Magruder, James Alexander, 13, 183
Maidhof, Joachim, 14, 184
Mallon, James Edward, 16, 184, 242
Markell, William Lester, 11, 184
Marshall, Elisha G., 13, 14
Martin, Henry Patchen, 18, 185, 186
Martin, Joel O., 15, 186
Martindale, John H., 225
Mason, Joel Whitney, 14, 187
Matheson, Roderick Nicol, 15, 187, 188
Mayer, William, 23, 188
McCaffrey, Edward, 195
McChesney, Waters W., 14, 188, 189
McClellan, Arthur, 143
McClellan, George B., 142, 143, 150
McConihe, John, 22
McConihe, Samuel, 19
McCunn, John H., 16, 189, 190
McDermott, Peter, 22, 190
McDonald, Andrew N., 20, 190
McDonald, Christopher R., 16, 191
McDougall, Archibald L., 21, 191, 192
McEvily, William, 22, 191, 192
McGuigan, Surgeon, 238
McKean, James Bedell, 18, 192, 193
McKee, William A., 313
McKibbin, Gilbert H., 16
McMahon, James Power, 22, 194, 195, 196
McMahon, John, 23, 68
McMahon, John Eugene, 22, 196
McMahon, Martin Thomas, 196
McMartin, Duncan, 22, 196, 200
McNary, William H., 22
McNett, Andrew J., 21
McQuade, James, 14
McReynolds, Andrew Thomas, 11, 196, 197, 198
Meagher, Thomas F., 194
Merritt, Robert Burnett, 18, 198, 199
Meserole, Jeremiah V., 16, 199
Miles, Nelson A., 17
Miller, Francis Charles, 22, 199, 200
Miller, Timothy Wadsworth, 22, 200
Milliken, Charles Austin, 16, 200

Mix, Simon Hosack, 11, 12, 201
Moesch, Joseph Anton, 19, 202
Moffitt, Stephen, 19
Molineux, Edward L., 22
Monroe, James, Jr., 15, 202, 203
Montgomery, Thomas, 195
Moore, Henry, 16, 202, 203, 204
Morgan, Edwin D., 113
Morgan, Joseph S., 19, 204, 205
Morris, Lewis, 205, 208
Morris, Lewis Gouverneur, 13, 204, 205
Morris, Lewis Owen, 13, 205, 206, 208
Morris, Orlando Harriman, 17, 206, 207
Morris, Thomas Ford, 19, 205, 207, 208
Morris, William H., 13, 204
Morrison, Andrew Jackson, 11, 208
Morrison, David, 18
Morrison, Joseph J., 13
Morton, Charles Beatty, 23, 209
Mott, Thaddeus Phelps, 11, 209, 210
Mulford, John E., 13
Murphy, John McLeod, 13, 211
Murphy, Mathew, 23, 211
Murphy, Michael C., 195
Murray, Edward, 12
Murray, John B., 22
Myers, George R., 15

Nelson, Homer Augustus, 22, 212
Nevin, David J., 17, 213
Newberry, Walter C., 12
Nichols, George F., 20
Nichols, George S., 11
Northedge, William, 17, 213
Nott, Charles Cooper, 23, 214
Nugent, Robert, 18

O'Brien, Henry F., 14, 59, 214
O'Mahony, John, 19, 215
O'Rorke, Patrick Henry, 21, 216
Olcott, Egbert, 20, 217
Oliver, Robert, Jr., 271
Olmsted, William A., 17
Olone, Hugh F., 195
Onderdonk, Benjamin F., 12, 217
Otis, Elwell S., 21
Owen, Joshua T., 154

Palmer, Innis N., 208
Palmer, Jeremiah, 12, 218
Palmer, Oliver H., 20
Park, Sidney W., 13
Parker, Thomas Jefferson, 17, 218, 219
Parmele, Theodore Weld, 23, 219
Paul, Gabriel R., 68

Pease, William R., 20
Peck, John J., 160, 201, 277
Peck, Lewis M., 23
Peirce, Oliver Beale, 18, 219, 220
Peissner, Elias, 20, 220, 221, 222
PerLee, Samuel R., 20
Perry, James H., 16, 223
Perry, Matthew C., 257
Pettes, William Henry, 13, 224
Phelps, Walter, Jr., 15
Pickell, John, 14, 225
Pierson, J. Fred, 13
Pinckney, Joseph C., 14, 17
Pinto, Francis E., 15
Piper, Alexander, 13, 225, 226, 227
Platner, John S., 12
Pope, Edmund M., 11
Porter, Burr Baldwin, 12, 227, 228
Porter, Peter Augustus, 13, 228, 229
Potter, Henry Langdon, 18, 229
Potter, James Neilson, 21, 230
Potter, Robert B., 16, 230
Powers, Charles J., 20
Pratt, Calvin E., 15
Pratt, George Watson, 15, 18, 230, 231
Preston, John B., 118
Prey, Gilbert Gibson, 20, 232
Price, Edward Livingston, 21, 232, 233
Price, Francis, Jr., 232
Pye, Edward, 19, 233

Quinby, Isaac F., 14

Randol, Alanson M., 11
Raulston, John B., 18, 233, 234, 235
Raulston, William C., 12, 233, 235, 236
Reed, Horatio Blake, 12, 237, 238
Repetti, Alexander, 98
Rice, Addison Gardiner, 22, 238
Rice, James C., 16
Richards, Samuel Thomas, 20, 239
Richardson, Israel B., 194
Richardson, Richard H., 15, 239
Richardson, Robert Mark, 11, 240
Riker, John Lafayette, 17, 240, 241
Riley, Edward Johns, 16, 184, 242
Ringold, Benjamin, 20, 243
Roberts, Samuel H., 21
Robertson, James M., 238
Robinson, Wardwell Greene, 23, 243
Rogers, James C., 21
Rogers, William F., 15
Roome, Charles, 16, 219
Root, Adrian R., 19
Rorbach, John, 20, 243
Rosa, Rudolph, 16, 244
Rose, Edwin, 18, 244, 245
Ryan, George, 21, 246

Ryder, Henry Wines, 13, 247, 248
Ryder, James, 15, 248

Sackett, William, 11
Sage, Augustus B., 14, 248, 249
Sage, Clinton Hezekiah, 20, 249
Salm, Felix Prince, 14, 18
Sammons, Simeon, 20, 250
Sanford, Jonah, 19, 250
Savage, James Woodruff, 11, 251
Schirmer, Louis, 13, 251
Schnepf, Engelbert, 15, 252
Schurz, Carl, 66, 129
Schwarzwaelder, Christian, 13, 252
Scott, George W., 17
Searing, William Marsh, 15, 252
Seaver, Joel J., 14
Segoine, Jesse, 20, 253, 254
Selkirk, George Holden, 16, 254
Serrell, Edward W., 13
Seward, William H., Jr., 13
Seymour, Truman, 260
Shaler, Alexander, 17
Sharpe, George H., 20
Sharpe, Jacob, 22
Shaurman, Nelson, 19
Shedd, John Wright, 20, 254
Shedd, Warren, 254
Sherburne, John Pitts, 11, 255
Sherrill, Eliakim, 21, 255
Sickles, Daniel E., 18, 32
Siebert, Louis Philipp, 12, 256
Skinner, Lewis C., 20, 257
Slidell, John, 257
Slidell, William Johnson, 21, 257, 258
Slocum, Henry W., 15, 297
Smith, Abel, 14, 258, 259
Smith, Abel, Jr., 258
Smith, Alfred B., 22
Smith, Elisha Brown, 20, 259
Smith, George B., 285
Smith, Hiram, 21, 259
Smith, James, 21
Smith, John Fellows, 20, 259, 260
Smith, William F., 92
Sniper, Gustavus, 23
Snyder, George W., 14, 260
Snyder, James William, 13, 260
Soest, Clemens, 15, 261
Spalding, Franklin, 22, 261
Spinola, Francis B., 22
Spofford, John P., 19
Springsteed, Edward A., 13, 262
Stafford, Spencer H., 134
Stahel, Julius, 14, 313
Steele, Frederick, 171
Sternberg, Chester W., 15, 262
Stevens, Ambrose, 21, 23, 263

Stevens, Isaac I., 18
Stevens, William Oliver, 18, 263
Stewart, Charles Hoffman, 12, 264
Stiles, John Wesley, 14, 19, 264, 265
Stoneman, George, 151
Strang, John Russell, 20, 265, 266
Strong, James C., 16
Stryker, Stephen Williamson, 16, 266, 267, 268
Stuart, Charles Beebe, 13, 268, 269
Stuyvesant, Peter, 129
Suiter, James Anthony, 16, 269, 270
Sullivan, Timothy, 15, 270, 271
Sumner, Edwin V., 184
Sumner, Edwin V., Jr., 12
Swain, Chellis D., 272
Swain, James Barrett, 11, 103, 271, 272
Sweitzer, Nelson B., 12
Sykes, George, 246

Taft, Edward Payson, 13, 272
Talmage, David Miller, 273
Tarbell, Jonathan, 19
Taylor, Alfred W., 13, 273
Taylor, Nelson, 18
Taylor, Robert F., 12, 15, 274, 275
Teller, Daniel W., 12, 275
Thomas, Winslow M., 17, 275, 276
Thompson, George Whitfield, 22, 276, 277
Thorp, Thomas J., 12
Tibbits, William B., 12
Tidball, John C., 12
Tidball, William Linn, 17, 277
Titus, Silas, 20, 277, 278
Todd, John Gordon, 16, 278
Tompkins, George Washington Brown, 13, 19, 279
Torbert, Alfred T. A., 175
Townsend, Frederick, 13, 158
Townsend, Henry Denison, 12, 279
Tracy, Benjamin F., 20
Trafford, Benjamin Lamb, 18, 280
Travers, George W., 16, 280, 281
Turnbull, Charles Satterlee, 21, 281
Tyler, Rockwell J., 17, 281

Ullmann, Daniel, 18
Underhill, Henry P., 22, 112, 281, 282
Upton, Emory, 20

Van Alen, James H., 11
Van Buren, Thomas B., 20
Van Petten, John B., 23
Van Valkenburgh, Robert Bruce, 19, 20, 282, 283
Van Voorhees, Koert S., 21, 283, 284
Van Wyck, Charles H., 17
Van Zandt, Jacob, 19, 284
Varian, Joshua Marsden, 14, 183, 285
Viele, Egbert L., 286
Viele, Henry Knickerbocker, 19, 286
Viele, John Jay, 19, 63, 286
Vincent, Nathan H., 19, 286
Vinton, Francis L., 16
Vogdes, Israel, 260
Von Amsberg, George, 16, 287, 288
Von Bourry De Ivernois, Gotthilf, 18, 288
Von Egloffstein, Frederick W., 20
Von Gilsa, Leopold, 16, 23, 289, 290
Von Radowitz, Paul, 143
Von Schack, George W., 14
Von Schoening, Emil Ernest, 17, 290
Von Steinwehr, Adolph, 15, 129
Von Vegesack, Ernest, 15
Vosburgh, Abram S., 18, 290

Waagner, Gustave, 12, 291
Wagstaff, Alfred, Jr., 14, 291
Wainwright, Charles S., 12
Wainwright, William P., 18
Walker, William, 139, 208
Walpole, Horace Hall, 20, 292
Walrath, Ezra LeRoy, 14, 292, 293
Waltermire, William, 22, 293
Ward, John H. H., 16, 32
Ward, William Greene, 14, 293, 294
Wardrop, David William, 19, 40, 294, 295
Warner, Andrew Sylvester, 22, 295, 296
Warner, George W., 248
Warner, Lewis D., 22, 296, 297

Warren, Gouverneur K., 13
Wead, Frederick Fuller, 19, 297, 298
Weber, Max, 15
Weeks, Henry Astor, 14, 297, 298, 299
Wehler, Edward, 23, 299
Weiss, Francis, 15, 299, 300
Weitzel, Godfrey, 199
Welling, Joseph, 13, 300
Wentworth, Obed F., 183
Weygant, Charles H., 21, 300, 301
Wheaton, Frank, 257
Wheelock, Charles, 19
Whipple, Amiel W., 255
Whistler, Joseph N. G., 12
White, Alvin, 20, 301, 302
White, Amos Hall, 11, 302
White, David B., 18
Wiedrich, Michael, 13, 303
Wilkeson, Samuel Henry, 11, 304
Willard, George Lamb, 13, 21, 305
Willett, James McClellan, 13, 305, 306
Williams, John, 20, 306
Willis, Benjamin Albertson, 14, 306, 307
Willson, Lester S., 17
Wilsey, John Newhall, 20, 307
Wilson, John, 16, 307, 308
Wilson, William, 14, 18
Winslow, Bradley, 23
Winslow, Cleveland, 13, 308, 309, 310
Winthrop, Frederick, 13
Wisner, Reuben Porter, 17, 310
Wood, Alfred M., 14, 19, 310, 311
Wood, Isaac, Jr., 22, 312
Wood, James, Jr., 21
Woodward, John Blackburne, 14, 312, 313
Wool, John E., 135
Wright, Edward H., 143
Wright, John G., 16
Wright, Joseph, 15, 313
Wutschel, Anthony Francis, 14, 313

Yeamans, Joseph, 14, 314
York, Robert P., 18, 314
Young, William Henry, 15, 315

Zook, Samuel K., 17